God, Science, and Humility

God, Science, and Humility

Ten Scientists Consider Humility Theology

EDITED BY ROBERT L. HERRMANN

Templeton Foundation Press
Philadelphia & London

Templeton Foundation Press
Five Radnor Corporate Center, Suite 120
100 Matsonford Road
Radnor, Pennsylvania 19087

Library of Congress Cataloging-in-Publication Data
God, science, and humility: ten scientists consider humility theology / edited by Robert L. Herrmann.
    p. cm.
  Includes bibliographical references.
  ISBN 1-890151-34-3 (pbk.:alk. paper)
  1. Religion and science. 2. Humility. I. Herrmann, Robert L., 1928-

  BL240.2 G64 2000
  215—dc21   00-041164
Designed and typeset by Nesbitt Graphics, Glenside, PA
Printed in the United States of America

  01 02 03 04 05 06   10 9 8 7 6 5 4 3 2

Contents

Foreword

JOHN MARKS TEMPLETON

In our day, the acceleration of learning through science has become breathtaking. More than half the discoveries in the natural sciences have been made during the twentieth century, and it is estimated that at present the amount of new information is doubling every two and one-half years. Not only is the rate of our learning accelerating, but along with it has come a new awareness of just how big and complex the universe is. Most scientists are now willing to admit that they will never reach the end of learning, and some are even talking about other sources of truth—philosophy and especially theology—as crucial components in the search for reality. A new kind of humility has begun to express itself as we recognize the vastness of God's creation and our very small place in the cosmic scheme of things.

Every person's concept of God is too small. Through humility we can begin to arrive at a true perspective of the infinite mind of God. It is also in humility that we learn from one another, for it makes us open to one another and ready to study things from the other's point of view and share ours with him or her freely. It is by humility that we avoid the sins of pride and intolerance and avoid religious strife. Humility opens the door to the realms of the spirit, and to research and progress in religion.

I have called this new kind of humility, this new awareness of the unlimited, all-pervasive, all-encompassing creative spirit, humility theology. Perhaps this guiding principle will help as we begin a new phase of evolution, a spiritual exploration using the tools of science that have been so productive in the study of the physical universe.

It might be helpful to view humility theology in terms of particular emphases.

Human Limitations

Humility theology recognizes that there are multiplying mysteries, that we may never comprehend more than a small part of reality, and that maybe we are not the only spiritual beings in the visible and invisible cosmos.

Questions we might ask ourselves in pondering this aspect include:

1. If we do not understand why matter or light or gravity exists, could that mean that reality is vastly more complex than humans yet comprehend, just as our ancestors did not comprehend television, germs, atoms, or galaxies?
2. Is the visible only a tiny temporary manifestation of reality?
3. Is it egotistical to think that humans can ever comprehend all of reality or of God or of his nature or of his methods or purposes?
4. Could the comprehension of God and his accelerating creativity and purposes by any species on one little planet be as limited as the comprehension of the ocean and its creativity by a clam or by a little ocean wave?

Progress in Obtaining New Spiritual Information Is Possible

Humility theology says that many wonderful concepts of God in various civilizations are yet only a tiny beginning of humankind's comprehension of God. Such comprehension may increase more than one hundredfold through the research of enthusiastic scientists.

Questions to ponder:

1. Can human concepts of God expand even more rapidly than our scientific knowledge of the universe?
2. Are there multiplying evidences of purpose and creativity in the universe?
3. How is the search for increasing comprehension of God helped by the New Testament statements "God is love and he who dwells in love dwells in God and God in him" and "With God were all things made and without him was not anything made that was made"?
4. If human information has multiplied more than one hundredfold in only two centuries, will that progress continue to accelerate, so that in the year 2000 information can be more than ten thousand times as great as in 1800?

A New Spirit of Inquiry

Humility theology means enthusiasm for new spiritual information and additional concepts. It signifies an eagerness to learn and a freedom of inquiry.

Questions to ponder:

1. Have human concepts of God always been too small? Too anthropomorphic?
2. Should we listen carefully, thoughtfully, and gratefully to everyone's concepts of God and God's purposes for humanity?
3. Were many major religions held back by an unconscious concept that God is somehow separate from reality, a sort of wise old king as in the ancient story of Adam and Eve?
4. What is the evidence that free and loving competition may be part of God's method for progress, productivity, and prosperity for his children?

The Value of Scientific Research

Humility theology applauds the opportunities for new spiritual information through scientific studies of both the physical and the spiritual spheres. It anticipates a great influx of new ideas and concepts to supplement the wonderful ancient scriptures. It also seeks through research of spiritual laws evidence concerning the benefits of thankfulness, forgiveness, love, etc.

Questions to ponder:

1. Can I be an expression or agent of God in love and creativity?
2. Are there some laws from the great religions that help produce a happy and fruitful life that can be tested by some scientific methods?
3. How can we learn to be helpers in achieving God's purpose?
4. Is it possible that research in genetics or other sciences can accelerate progress in human intelligence?

Worship

Humility theology is concerned with humility toward God. Past discoveries about the universe and about its Creator can lead to a sense of awe and an overwhelming feeling of thankfulness.

Questions to ponder:

1. Is trying to help God's creative processes a way to express our thankfulness?
2. What is the evidence that enthusiasm for worship can increase as we learn more of the timeless, limitless, omnipresent God?
3. Can prayer, worship, and service to others help each of us to discover more of the nature of God?
4. What evidence indicates that heaven can be the result of prayer, worship, service and giving, forgiving, thanksgiving, and unlimited love?

This has been an exciting time for the John Templeton Foundation. To aid in this new search for spiritual truth, we have expanded in scope with the formation of a research center dedicated to the acquisition of new spiritual information. The new center has been named the Humility Theology Information Center and has as two of its major goals the sponsoring of various research programs and the formation of an advisory board of respected scientists and theologians interested in progress in obtaining new spiritual information. The chapters that follow are contributions from ten of these advisers.

Introduction

This is a collection of the impressions of ten working scientists, leaders in their fields who have published extensively about their scientific work. Their uniqueness lies, however, in the fact that they have made time to think about the relevance of their science to theological questions.

It has been especially helpful to Sir John Templeton that they have agreed to advise him in his goal of a major expansion in knowledge about divinity, a goal he sees as attainable, as he says in the Foreword to this book, through humility theology, a humble approach to our truth seeking about God. The scientists contributing to this book come from a variety of scientific disciplines and bring a variety of religious experiences to the consideration of humility theology. Probably none of these scientists sees the world and understands God in just the way John Templeton does. But all have been impressed with his humble spirit and his eagerness to know, and we hope these chapters will not only honor the concept of humility theology but also demonstrate the power of a humble approach in the expansion of humanity's vision of God.

In chapter 1, physicist F. Russell Stannard provides an excellent overview of humility theology. In "Theology as a Science," he calls for a new conception of theology in which truth is approached in an experimental, hypothetical mode, as is done in the sciences. In fact, he demonstrates that the difference between this experimental approach in theology and scientific methodologies is not great. The hard-core sciences are also faced with much data of a historical, non-repeatable kind. And in the social sciences, we are faced with additional limitations in manipulating social groups or individual patients.

Stannard's agenda for humility theology would include experimental studies of God's involvement in creation, the significance of the anthropic principle, the reflection of God in nature, human beings' religious experience, and the spiritual laws of life.

In chapter 2, physicist and theologian Robert John Russell takes as his primary focus the interaction between cosmology and theology, pointing out that a great opportunity lies before us through the humble approach for mutual learning. Scientists are becoming aware of the limitations of scientific explanations—specifically in the formulation of and choice between cosmological theories—and are beginning to recognize that there are important clues coming from theological and philosophical arguments. On the other hand, theologians are reconsidering what Russell calls "a more nuanced view of creation" and "a robust theological framework" that can meet the rigorous demands of the discoveries and theorizing of the natural sciences.

In chapter 3, Charles L. Harper, Jr., writes with great enthusiasm of the opportunity for a flowering of planetary science through a joint partnership between science and religion. These two disciplines, he argues, need each other. Planetary science holds the potential of revealing many worlds, and religious faith plays an important role in guiding scientific development in directions that are noble and wise. Harper issues a cogent call for fairness in the way science and theology evaluate each other's contributions to the welfare of humanity.

Owen Gingerich, as a historian of science, looks at the other side of humility theology: the possibility that we may be so concerned with being egalitarian that we actually arrive at unreasonable expectations in this case, about the existence and nature of extraterrestrial intelligence. The uniqueness of *Homo sapiens* and our very special environment could mean that, as Gingerich says, "the evolution of intelligent, self-conscious life elsewhere is by no means assured or even probable."

In chapter 5, "The Limits of Knowledge and the Hope for Progress," Francisco J. Ayala begins with the surprising contrast between the very brief period of human evolution and its remarkable and utterly unique end product, *Homo sapiens*. Research in the biology of this human species has taken a strong turn in the direction of genetics, but Ayala feels the program for sequencing the entire human genome is receiving far too much emphasis and that it will provide only limited success in achieving the lofty goals set for it. In contrast, he believes that real hope of progress lies with research in two critical areas: ontogenetic decoding (the egg-to-adult transformation) and the mind-brain problem. Cancer and aging are both ontogenetic decoding problems. And understanding how the brain works and how the mind emerges from the brain will be true progress with the real prospect of understanding ourselves.

Psychologist David G. Myers points out in chapter 6 that intuition—immediately knowing something without reasoning or analysis—can be a powerful faculty, but that there are many limitations to this "inner knowing." Recent research demonstrates that our self-explanation of our behaviors and our reconstructions of past memories and attitudes are often untrustworthy. We should be humble about what we think we know. On the other hand, if some of us suffer from excessive humility (low self-esteem), the majority of us have a "good reputation of ourselves," a kind of "illusory optimism." At base is a self-serving bias, the cure for which is, in theology's words, "in humility count others better than yourselves."

In "The Case of Chemistry," Giuseppe Del Re gives us an interesting view of the history of the development of chemistry as a discipline. One salient aim of chemistry has been the transformation of matter, a process of great practical value and one that led to the ancients' interest in the mysticism of alchemy. Its emphasis on the total personal involvement of the practitioner remains relevant to the science of our day.

The chapter by Herbert Benson and Patricia Myers, "Mind/Body Medicine and Spirituality," describes an exciting area of research pioneered by Benson and his coworkers in the early 1970s and given national attention through his best-selling book *The Relaxation Response*. More recently, he has analyzed the components of mind/body medicine that relate to the rubric of self-care, which includes relaxation techniques, nutrition, exercise, stress management, and beliefs or faith. Benson and Myers go on to analyze the well-known placebo effect. Based on current knowledge of brain mechanisms, they are able to define the placebo effect in a surprising new way as "remembered wellness." When combined with the relaxation response, especially when religious faith is also involved, remembered wellness has been shown to improve health outcomes dramatically.

In chapter 9, David B. Larson and Susan S. Larson introduce readers to a new field of medical science that focuses on the impact of spiritual values on patients' health. The authors describe a new method for analysis of the medical literature called systematic review, which they have used to achieve a less biased evaluation of the medical literature. What they have discovered is a distinct resistance on the part of researchers and clinicians to consider religious values, and they call for a new humility on the part of the medical profession in light of the significant healing associated with such values.

In the concluding chapter, experimental psychologist Fraser Watts gives us a fascinating look at artificial intelligence (AI) research and a balanced view of its theological implications. AI's scientific value includes helping us to understand how human intelligence works, especially in light of the important technical advance, "parallel distributed processing," which appears to emulate to some extent a network of neurons in the human brain. The rather grandiose claims sometimes made for AI bring it into conflict with religion, but if, as Watts says, it is "pursued in a more humble spirit the sense of conflict disappears."

In the epilogue we consider some possible experimental approaches that might hold promise in contributing to Sir John Templeton's goal of a one hundredfold increase in spiritual information. Examples have been chosen from astronomy, the neurosciences, genetics, medicine, and the social sciences.

Contributors

Francisco J. Ayala is Donald Bren Professor of Biological Sciences and Professor of Philosophy at the University of California, Irvine. He is a member of the President's Committee of Advisors on Science and Technology and has been President and Chairman of the Board of the American Association for the Advancement of Science and of the Society for the Study of Evolution. His research focuses on population and evolutionary genetics, including the origin of species, genetic diversity of populations, and the molecular clock of evolution.

Herbert Benson is the Chief of the Division of Behavioral Medicine at Deaconess Beth Israel Medical Center, founding President of the Mind/Body Medical Institute and the Mind/Body Medical Institute Associate Professor of Medicine at the Harvard Medical School. Dr. Benson is the author of *The Relaxation Response, Beyond the Relaxation Response*, and with Marg Stark, *Timeless Healing: The Power and Biology of Belief.*

Giuseppe Del Re is Professor of Theoretical Chemistry at the University of Naples and a member of the International Academy for the Philosophy of Science and the European Academy for Environmental Problems. He has published more than 180 papers in scientific journals and has edited a book on the brain-mind problem. Papers in his honor are being published in the journal *Advances in Quantum Chemistry.*

Owen Gingerich is Professor of Astronomy and the History of Science at Harvard University and a Senior Astronomer at the Smithsonian Astrophysical Observatory. In 1992–93, he chaired Harvard's

History of Science Department. Professor Gingerich's research interests have ranged from the recomputation of an ancient Babylonian mathematical table to the interpretation of stellar spectra. He is a leading authority on Johannes Kepler and Nicholas Copernicus. Professor Gingerich has given the George Darwin Lecture and an Advent sermon at the National Cathedral in Washington, D.C. He has also witnessed eight solar eclipses.

Charles L. Harper Jr. is Executive Director and Senior Vice President of the John Templeton Foundation. He is trained as both a planetary scientist and as a theologian, having received his bachelor's degree in civil engineering at Princeton, a doctorate of philosophy in cosmology and planetary science at Oxford University (Balliol College), and a diploma of theology, also from Oxford. Before coming to the Foundation, he was a research scientist at Harvard University and a research fellow with the National Aeronautics and Space Administration in Houston. Dr. Harper has published extensively in scientific journals. He also holds a Certificate in Management and Administration from Harvard.

Robert L. Herrmann taught biochemistry to medical school students for twenty-two years. During that time, he developed a keen interest in interrelating science and religion. In 1981, he left medical education to become executive director of the American Scientific Affiliation, an organization of Christians in Science. There he met fellow member John Templeton, and they have since cooperated in writing several books, including *The God Who Would Be Known* and *Is God the Only Reality?* Dr. Herrmann is currently on the staff at Gordon College in Wenham, Massachusetts, where he directs several projects for the Templeton Foundation.

David B. Larson is a psychiatrist and former Senior Fellow at the National Institute for Mental Health (NIMH). He is currently President of the National Institute for Health Research. He has published numerous journal articles and a psychiatric training manual that demonstrates that spirituality and religious practice can benefit physical and mental health and healing.

Susan S. Larson is an independent science journalist and former newspaper staff writer. Her work has appeared in medical textbooks, professional journals, and magazines.

David G. Myers, social psychologist, is John Werkman Professor of Psychology at Hope College, Holland, Michigan. He is an award winning researcher and the author of psychology's most widely studied textbook. His research and digests of research have appeared in some fifty periodicals, from *Science* to *Scientific American*, and in twelve books. His latest book is *The American Paradox: Spiritual Hunger in an Age of Plenty* (Yale University Press, 2000)

Patricia Myers is Research Associate at the Mind/Body Medical Institute.

Robert John Russell is founder and Director of the Center for Technology and the Natural Sciences and Professor of Theology and Science in residence at the Graduate Theological Union in Berkeley, California. In 1968, he graduated from Stanford University with a major in physics and minors in music and religion. He then began concurrent studies in physics and theology, receiving an M.A. in theology from the Pacific School of Religion in Berkeley in 1972. He received his Ph.D. in experimental solid state physics from the University of California, Santa Cruz in 1978, on the same day that he was ordained in the United Church of Christ (Congregational). Dr. Russell has co-edited *Physics, Philosophy and Theology: A Common Quest for Understanding; Quantum Cosmology and the Laws of Nature: Scientific Perspective on Divine Action; and Chaos and Complexity: Scientific Perspectives on Divine Action.*

F. Russell Stannard is the former Vice President of the Institute of Physics and currently Emeritus Professor of Physics of the Open University in Milton Keynes, United Kingdom. He was educated at the University College, London, where he received his Ph.D. in cosmic ray physics in 1956. In 1983, he began studies of the relationship between science, religion, psychology, and philosophy. Dr. Stannard's recent books in science and religion include *The God Experiment*, based upon his 1998 Gifford lectures, and the best-selling *Uncle Albert Trilogy*, introducing young people to physics. In 1998, he was awarded the Order of the British Empire by Queen Elizabeth for services to science.

Sir John Marks Templeton is Chairman of the Templeton Foundations and President of the First Trust Bank, Nassau Bank, Nassau, Bahamas. Widely recognized as one of the world's most successful financial investors, he has devoted his time since 1990 to philanthropy and research in spiritual progress through the John Templeton Foundation. For twenty-five years he has funded the Templeton Prize for Progress in Religion, which recognizes individuals who have made contributions to the world's understanding of God.

Fraser Watts is Starbridge Lecturer in Theology and Natural Science at The University of Cambridge. An experimental psychologist, his latest books are an edited volume, *Science Meets Faith* (SPCK) and a chapter entitled "Towards a Theology of Consciousness," in J. Cornwell (ed.), *Consciousness and Human Identity* (Oxford University Press).

God, Science, and Humility

1

Theology as a Science

F. RUSSELL STANNARD

Can theology be regarded as a science?

Most would undoubtedly say no. In doing so, they might point out that science is fundamentally based on experiment and observation. Although the formulation of a theoretical hypothesis might be made in response to some guiding principle derived from notions of simplicity, economy, or symmetry, in the end the arbiter is not aesthetics but experiment. If the data are not in conformity with the theory, then the hypothesis has to be abandoned, or at least modified. Essentially, it is a humble approach. One's powers of philosophical reasoning concerning how the world "ought" to be—one's preference or "pet theory"—must always give way to the practical evidence.

This down-to-earth, pragmatic approach appears to stand in sharp contrast to that adopted toward religious questions. Where theology is concerned, the final arbiter is held to be the Bible (or some other set of holy writings). Holy scripture, as the very word of God, is to be venerated as the unchanging, ultimate authority on all matters.

If that is one's view of theology, then clearly it has little in common with science. Science recognizes no such authority rooted in the past. But it is not the only approach. There is another, one that resonates much more closely with the modern scientific outlook. It has come to be known as humility theology. It takes as its starting point not the Bible but our experiences of the world and of life—the same basis as that adopted by science. It asks whether these show evidence for the existence of God, and if so, what type of God. It asks: Does the totality of our experience make better sense in the light of the God hypothesis, or not? Like the pursuit of science, this type of theology is humble in the sense that it is prepared to adapt its understanding of God to whatever the evidence indicates. As the total fund of knowledge and experience grows, so one's conception of God is expected to develop and become ever more refined. Like science, humility theology is progressive.

Because there is no faster-expanding area of knowledge today than that afforded by the sciences, it is further to be expected that humility theology will forge especially close links to the sciences, examining each new finding with a view to seeing whether it has something to offer regarding an improved understanding of God in relation to his created world.

What I hope to do in this essay is draw parallels between humility theology, as I understand it, and science. In doing so, we shall examine the different types of evidence that could be thought of as coming within the scope of humility theology.

An Experiment into Prayer

When thinking of a scientific investigation, it is natural to have in mind a study conducted under carefully controlled laboratory conditions. A situation is devised in which, as far as possible, the particular effect under investigation is isolated and all other extraneous background effects are reduced to a minimum. That is indeed the aim of many scientific studies.

The best attempt to apply such a methodology to a religious question is to be found in a project often referred to as the prayer experiment. Belief in the power of prayer is widespread. If miraculous healings could be demonstrated, then this would seem on the face of it to be evidence for God—God directly intervening and having an effect in the world. In 1997, the John Templeton Foundation agreed to finance this study into the effectiveness of intercessory prayer. The project's chief investigator is Herbert Benson of the Mind/Body Medical Institute at Deaconess Beth Israel Medical Center in Boston, Massachusetts.

The main idea is that patients about to undergo coronary artery bypass graft surgery at five major U.S. hospitals are divided into groups. One group of six hundred is being prayed for by special teams of intercessors drawn from a variety of religious denominations. Each team is assigned a particular batch of patients drawn from the six hundred. In addition to these patients, another group of six hundred is *not* being prayed for. The latter acts as a control group. As patients present themselves to the hospitals, they are randomly assigned to these groups. They are told that they might, or they might not, be prayed for. But none of them knows to which group he or she has been assigned.

Over a period of two to three years, the patients' case histories are followed to see if there are any differences between the two groups. Indicators of recovery include measurements of the physical functioning of the heart, the frequency of death from all causes, length of stay in hospital, and whether patients discharged from the hospital return to their homes or enter a nursing home.

The medical staff tending the patients over this period have no access to information concerning which patients are being prayed for. Those doing the praying know only the first names of the people assigned to them, together with some details of their condition—nothing sufficient to reveal the identity of the individual. Only at the very end of the experiment will all the data be collated. The project has been designed as a rigorously controlled scientific experiment.

There is, however, a third group of six hundred patients. Like those in the first group, these are prayed for, but unlike the first, they *are* informed that they are to be the subject of prayer. The intention here is to examine whether there is any additional benefit to be gained (of a psychosomatic or placebo nature) from knowing that one is the subject of prayer. This part of the study will test hypotheses to do with "patient expectation."

What of the results? It is too early to say, but no matter. The reason for mentioning the experiment here is that it is instructive to consider the implications of the various possibilities for the outcome of this and of any other experiment of the scientifically controlled type.

As regards the first two groups of patients—those that are unsure whether they are being prayed for—should the project eventually yield a statistically significant positive correlation between prayer and good recovery from the operation, that would of course be fascinating. Doubtless such a discovery would trigger a series of follow-up experiments. In the first place, one would want to establish, beyond all reasonable doubt, that the positive correlation was no mere statistical freak. Different prayer techniques would be tried to see whether some were more effective than others. One would want to investigate whether other medical conditions yielded to this form of treatment—cancer, perhaps. Clearly, an important field of study would be opened up.

It must be noted, however, that none of this would amount to proof of God's existence. Both the investigators themselves and the funding agency have made it clear from the outset that the project is *not* to be thought of as an attempt to provide definitive proof of God's existence. Supporting evidence, maybe, but not proof. An alternative explanation of a positive correlation might involve, for example, some form of direct transference of thought between the mind of the person praying and that of the patient, presumably of a telepathic nature. There would accordingly be no need to invoke God as an "intermediary" in the process. The beneficial effect would pass directly from intercessor to patient.

As for the other possible result—namely, *no* measurable difference between the two groups—what might that mean?

Doubtless many would jump to the "obvious" conclusion: intercessory prayer does not work—perhaps because there is no God. But again one must be careful. In the same way that a positive result does not necessarily vindicate belief in God, so a negative result does not have to be damaging to belief. There are alternative explanations of a null result.

For instance, when it is said that one of the groups will not be prayed for, that simply means there will be no special prayer team at work on their behalf. That of course will not stop the patients praying for themselves, nor their loved ones and friends from praying. The investigators refer to this (somewhat tongue in cheek) as "unwanted background noise." All the experiment is trying to do is to measure whether there is any *additional* benefit coming from the prayers of the special team. It could well be that the efforts of these strangers will be swamped by the heartfelt prayers of those directly involved with the patients.

There is another concern: when scientists investigate the physical world, provided they ask the right questions and adopt sound scientific methodology, nature has no alternative but to yield up its secrets. But applying that methodology to God (or to anyone else with a will of their own) is *not* a guarantee of success. God might simply not cooperate. It could be argued that a loving God might indeed be reluctant to disadvantage patients merely because some strangers deliberately decide not to include them in their prayers.

Not only that, God might well appreciate better than we ourselves some of the drawbacks of allowing us to probe too deeply into his manner of working. By the very nature of the clear-cut way in which the experiment has been designed, the result will be a quantitative one. That means it becomes possible to put a price on whatever benefit might be gained from this type of prayer exercise. Do we *really* want some government official to use a positive result as an excuse to close down hospital wards—because ministers of religion can be hired to pray more cheaply? While we all are doubtless in favor of cost-effective medical care, it seems a far cry from what many would regard as the true nature of prayer: a natural expression of a loving, trusting, personal relationship with God. For this reason, it would not be altogether surprising if God, in his wisdom, were to decide to frustrate the best efforts of the investigators—for their own good. We would do well to recall that it does say in the Bible: "Thou shalt not put the Lord thy God to the test."

The Benson experiment has aroused enormous interest; it has been beautifully designed, and it deserves to be done. I for one await with great interest both the outcome itself and the heated discussions that are bound to ensue as to what interpretation should be put on the result—whatever that turns out to be.

The Need to Widen the Scope of the Investigation

In view of the ambiguities that will inevitably attend the result of this experiment, it may not be clear why I have chosen it as the starting point for our discussion of the evidence for God. The reason is that I wish to draw attention to the fact that even when we are able to set up conditions of our own choosing, in accordance with scientific constraints, it becomes surprisingly difficult to arrive at any firm, incontrovertible conclusion as to whether a supernatural intervention has taken place or not. If we cannot get knockdown proof when we are controlling everything, it is surely unreasonable to expect *any* single, decisive proof of God's existence, and of his influence in the world. Humility theology makes no such claim to certainty, and those insisting on such assurance are certain to be disappointed.

So does that mean the application of scientific thinking to the study of God is ill-conceived? Is humility theology doomed to failure from the outset? Not so. It is important to recognize that the kinds of difficulties encountered over the interpretation of the outcome of the prayer experiment are nothing unusual; they are to be found all the time—in hard-core physical science.

Take, for example, my own field of research: high-energy nuclear physics. This is the study of the behavior of subatomic particles. These particles are so small they cannot be seen directly (under a microscope, say). Instead, one has to observe their *effects* and from these draw inferences. The usual effect is that they leave a trail or track behind them marking where they have been. (The track might be in the form of a string of tiny bubbles in a transparent liquid, or a series of small sparks in a gas subject to a high electric voltage.) As the subatomic particles collide with one another, or as they spontaneously disintegrate, they leave behind characteristic patterns of tracks marking out the paths followed by the various particles involved.

The trouble is that for any given pattern of tracks, there might be a number of competing interpretations. If all one has is a single event, there might be very little that can be deduced from it. Many examples might have to be collected, perhaps using a variety of detection techniques; statistical analyses have to be carried out as to the likelihood of the various rival explanations. Only after a period of time might a consensus emerge as to which is the more likely interpretation. Throughout this process there will not be any well-defined point at which the interpretation is *proved* correct. Rather, the evidence progressively accumulates, the odds become stronger in favor of one particular explanation, the controversies die down, and the scientific community as a whole finds that it is no longer seriously questioning the conclusion.

Cosmology provides another example. It is now generally agreed that the universe began with a great explosion called the Big Bang. Why do we think that? For a start, we find that the universe is still expanding in the aftermath of that explosion. At least, that is the interpretation put on it. But there is another possibility. According to a rival theory, new matter is continually being created throughout space. As fast as matter moves away, the gaps left behind are filled by the newly created material. Thus, the overall picture remains essentially unchanged over time: in particular, there was *no* explosive beginning. This Steady State theory was to become a serious rival to the Big Bang theory. And that is how the situation would have remained, had not other indications come along.

The Big Bang theory holds that the initial conditions in the universe must have been very hot; the explosion would have been accompanied by a fireball. It is argued that the cooled-down remnants of that fireball ought still to be about in the universe today. Indeed, this radiation has now been discovered. At least, it has all the hallmarks expected of it. But of course there are many sources of radiation in the universe. It could well be argued that, just as the expansion of the universe on its own was not proof of the Big Bang hypothesis, neither is this form of radiation, on its own, clinching proof. Rather, it is to be seen as helping to strengthen the overall case.

The expected conditions of the Big Bang also allow one to calculate what kind of atomic particles were likely to emerge from it. The calculated abundances of the different kinds of atoms to be expected in outer space are found to be in good agreement with those found. This constitutes yet further confirmatory evidence.

Finally, we note that it takes time for light to reach us from the far depths of space. Examining distant objects through a telescope is like looking back in time. We are able to see directly how the universe was long ago—and it looked different than it does now. The density of matter throughout space appears greater then than it does now—in agreement with the Big Bang theory, and contrary to what would be expected on the basis of the Steady State theory. In saying that, it has to be recognized that there are difficulties involved in trying to estimate distances to far-off astronomical objects. Systematic errors can creep in, and if present, they distort one's estimates of density. For this reason, the evidence, once again, is not by itself conclusive.

What one discovers from a discussion like this is that acceptance of the Big Bang does not rest on any single decisive piece of evidence. Instead, the case has to be progressively built up by examining a range of indicators, all of which point in the same direction and are indicative of the same conclusion. The Big Bang hypothesis is an economical and elegant way of accounting for a wide variety of disparate phenomena. The evidence is cumulative; it is *persuasive* rather than clinching. Moreover, different scientists need different degrees of persuasion to be won over.

One lesson we can draw from this is that, rather than look for one decisive experiment to establish the reality of God, humility theology must broaden its horizons to take in a wide variety of phenomena. Only so can we judge whether, *taken as a whole*, this spectrum of indicators adds up to a compelling case.

Working with Data not under Our Control

Does that mean we now have to devise a range of experiments that, like the Benson experiment, are carried out under controlled conditions of our own choosing? Not necessarily. To appreciate why, we look once more to science. Although it is true that many branches of science are laboratory based and lend themselves to the type of investigation in which conditions are under the control of the experimenter, this is not invariably the case.

Take, for example, cosmology—the study of the universe on the largest scale. We have just been discussing the scientific evidence for the Big Bang. But, of course, there was never any question of our controlling the circumstances of the Big Bang. The cosmos cannot be contained in a laboratory. In fact, the whole subject of cosmology and astronomy is one in which we control virtually nothing. We are reduced to observing, in a purely passive manner, whatever radiation signals happen to come our way.

And yet, no one would deny that cosmology and astronomy are "sciences." They gain that status from (1) the systematic and scrupulously objective way the data are gathered and (2) the manner in which the theories are held to be but tentative working hypotheses, open to modification in the light of those empirical findings.

The same holds in certain branches of the biological sciences. Take for instance Darwin's theory of evolution by natural selection. It is widely accepted that humans, in common with the other animals, have descended from more primitive ancestors—stretching all the way back to the inanimate chemicals to be found on the surface of Earth soon after it formed some 4,600,000,000 years ago. But how has this assessment been made? The evolution of humans happened only once, and is not a repeatable process. There were no witnesses—obviously. Indeed, if the evolution of intelligent life-forms were to take place on other planets in the cosmos, it would be most unlikely to give rise to creatures looking like us. And yet evolutionary biology is most definitely a "science."

Again, the reasons are the same: the systematic collection of a wide range of different types of data (the fossil record, anatomical comparisons between species, genetic comparisons, etc.), together with a willingness to allow the weight of those empirical data to be the final arbiter on the success or otherwise of the theoretical hypotheses. Nor is it necessary for the data to be so overwhelming as to convince everyone. There are many professional biologists, let alone laypersons, still unhappy about various aspects of the conventionally accepted evolutionary theory.

Finally, we might mention the earth sciences. These have been transformed in recent times by the theory of plate tectonics—the manner in which various parts of the earth's crust move about the surface of the globe, causing earthquakes and the building of mountains. Once again, these processes are not under our control.

Thus, the ability to control the circumstances under which an experiment is conducted, together with the possibility of repeating the experiment under the same or different conditions, though desirable, is not a prerequisite for that field of study to be regarded as scientific. For that reason we speak of the social sciences—despite the strong limitations on the extent to which it is acceptable to manipulate social groupings; we might also speak of psychology as a science, even though there are strict ethical limits on the degree to which a therapist might seek to "experiment" on his or her clients.

The same kind of situation confronts us with respect to humility theology. God is not some object we can control. We cannot expect God to submit to repeated experimentation under conditions of our choosing. The prayer experiment, although clearly coming under the umbrella of humility theology, is unlikely to be typical of the type of investigation open to us. For this reason, as stated earlier, we must not expect a single, neat, unambiguous proof of God's existence and of his manner of working. Instead, we have to examine, as objectively as we can, a whole range of experience—a multitude of diverse indications, *whatever happens to be on offer*.

The remainder of this chapter is devoted to surveying the various types of indicators that might be considered as coming within the scope of humility theology.

God as Creator

We begin with a cluster of questions related to the subject of *creation*. One of the aims of humility theology is to expose the ever-present tendency toward anthropomorphism and expand our conception of God. The consideration of problems to do with the universe as a whole clearly has an important role to play in this respect.

Having already drawn attention to the manner in which the universe originated, are we to infer that God must have been the cause of the Big Bang? Humility theology cannot simply jump to that conclusion; it must explore the possibility of alternative interpretations. In particular, it must examine the claim that the universe might have spontaneously created itself—through a quantum fluctuation. What does that mean?

According to classical Newtonian physics, everything that happens has to have a cause. Cause is followed by effect. The effect in turn becomes the cause of the next effect down the causal chain. With the advent of quantum theory, all that changed. Thanks to Werner Heisenberg's uncertainty relation, we now know that from a given state of affairs, one can predict only the relative *probabilities* of a whole variety of possible later states. This element of uncertainty—unpredictability— affects everything happening in the world. It is not obvious in everyday life because the effects become noticeable only on the small scale. This generally means one has to be examining the behavior of individual atoms, or of subatomic particles. Its applicability to the Big Bang derives from the fact that the universe began small—perhaps infinitesimally small. Under those conditions the effects of quantum uncertainty are expected to be dominant.

That being so, some physicists have proposed that the universe might have come into being by way of a violent quantum fluctuation. Accordingly, from an initial state of nothing, there could have been a small but finite chance that this would be succeeded by a state consisting of a universe. One has only to wait around for this quantum fluctuation to occur. Having begun as a minute-sized quantum event, the cosmos then promptly underwent violent expansion to become the universe we know today.

The suggestion, at first sight at least, appears quite plausible. But it is not without its difficulties. For example, it is all very well talking of a quantum fluctuation, but what exactly is fluctuating if there really is nothing there to begin with? Not only that, but quantum theory was devised to account for the behavior of the component parts of the universe. It does not by any means follow that one is justified in applying it to the universe as a whole. Besides, the theory is intended to provide a way for an observer to order his or her measurements on that component part of the universe. So, who in the present context is supposed to be the "observer"—an observer external to that which is being observed? Is this not by implication God once more? A further difficulty is that if there is a finite probability of this universe popping into existence at some point in time, why not other universes at other points in time? Is one not led to the conclusion of there being universes without number? That seems a rather extravagant claim—a costly way of getting rid of a Creator God. It is one of the characteristics of scientific investigation that one goes for the simpler, the more economical, of two rival hypotheses.

But setting aside for the moment these various objections, suppose for the sake of argument we were to concede that the world had its beginning in a quantum fluctuation, would that in fact undermine the idea of a Creator God?

No. It is all very well putting the Big Bang down to a quantum fluctuation, but why a *quantum* fluctuation? Why was it quantum physics that was in charge of the process rather than some other type of physics? After all, we can all dream up imaginary worlds run according to laws of nature different from our own. Science fiction writers do it all the time. Where is quantum physics supposed to have come from? Would it not have taken a God to have set up the laws of physics in the first place—a God who chose the laws for bringing this world (and perhaps others) into existence?

This would put God at one step removed from the origin of the universe. Instead of initiating the world by direct intervention, he created the law—the natural outworking of that law then being the agency for bringing the world into existence. Thus, ultimate responsibility for the existence of the world would remain invested in God— the creator of the law.

Such argumentation stems from the general observation that we live in a world that is lawlike: it is intelligible. It presumably did not have to be that way. It is easy enough to imagine a world that was entirely chaotic in its operation. That being so, ought we not to be inquiring as to the source of that intelligibility? Is not the intelligibility of the laws *in itself* evidence for God?

In describing the Big Bang, I have probably given the impression that it was an explosion much like any other explosion—bigger, yes, but essentially the same. By that I mean that it takes place at a particular location in space, and after detonation fills up the rest of the surrounding space. But this is not how it was with the Big Bang. Not only was all of matter concentrated initially at a point, but also all of space. There was no surrounding space outside the Big Bang. In fact, we now think that the Big Bang marked the origins not only of the contents of the universe but also of space itself.

That in itself is a remarkable thought. But an even more extraordinary conclusion is in store. According to Einstein's theory of relativity, space and time are more alike than one would guess from the very different ways we perceive and measure them. We measure spatial distances with rulers, and intervals of time with a watch or clock. Yet despite these different approaches, there is an exceedingly close link between the two, to the extent that we speak today of time as the fourth dimension. We are all familiar with the three spatial dimensions; for example, we can designate them as up-down, backward-forward, and left-right. Time has now to be added as the fourth dimension. Time is as indissolubly welded to space as the three spatial dimensions are to themselves. One cannot have space without time, nor time without space.

The reason this assumes importance in the context of cosmology is the fact that if the Big Bang saw the origins of space, it must also have marked the beginning of time. There was no time before the Big Bang. Indeed, the very phrase *"before* the Big Bang" has no meaning. The word *before* necessarily implies a preexistent time—but where the Big Bang was concerned, there was none.

For those who seek a *cause* of the Big Bang—whether a Creator God or some impersonal agency—there is a problem here. We have already spoken of the causal chain: cause followed by effect. Note the word *followed.* It refers to a sequence of events *in* time: first the cause, then the effect. But in the present context we are regarding the Big Bang as the effect. For there to have been a cause of the Big Bang, it would have had to have existed prior to the Big Bang. But this we now think of as an impossibility. "What place then for a creator?" as Stephen Hawking asked in his book *A Brief History of Time.*

The absence of time before the Big Bang gets rid of the kind of Creator God that most people probably have in mind: a God who at first exists alone. Then at some point in time God decides to create a world. The blue touch paper is lit, there is a Big Bang, and we are on our way. God becomes the cause of the Big Bang. But as we have seen, without time before the Big Bang, there could not have been a cause in the usual sense of that word.

So, where have we got to? Have these considerations dispensed with a Creator God? Before jumping to that conclusion, we need to remind ourselves of the need to draw a distinction between the words origins and creation. Whereas in normal everyday conversation we might use them interchangeably, in theology they acquire their own distinctive meanings.

For example, if one has in mind a question along the lines, "How did the world get started?" that is a question of origins. As such, it is a matter for scientists to decide, their current ideas pointing to the Big Bang description.

The creation question, on the other hand, is quite different. It is not particularly concerned with what happened at the beginning.

Rather it is to do with the question, "Why is there something rather than nothing?" It is as much concerned with the present instant of time as any other. "Why are *we* here? To whom or to what do we owe our existence? What is keeping us in existence?" It is an entirely different type of question, one concerned not with the mechanics of the origin of the cosmos but with the underlying ground of all being.

It is for this reason one finds that whenever theologians talk about God the Creator, they usually couple it with the idea of God the Sustainer. God's creativity is not especially invested in that first instant of time (if there was one); it is to be found distributed throughout all time. We exist not because of some instantaneous action of God that happened long ago: an action that set in train all the events that have happened subsequently—an inexorable sequence requiring no further attention by God. We do not deal with a God who lights the fuse on the fireworks and then retires. God is involved at first hand in *everything* that goes on.

An atheistic response to this would be to dismiss the "creation question" as meaningless. Why not simply accept the existence of the world as a brute fact? What is to be gained by saying that God created the world? That only raises in its turn the question of who created God.

This is to misunderstand how we are using the word *God*. God is not an existent object. One cannot say that God exists in the same way that an apple exists. If that were the case, then postulating one more existent thing—God—would not be any real advance in understanding. The important point is that God is the *source* of all existence. *God* is the name we give to whatever is responsible for the existence of things—including you and me.

So, strictly speaking, the question posed by humility theology ought not to be "Does God exist?" but rather "What, if anything, can we meaningfully say about God, the source of all existence?" In particular, can we think of that source as being in any way personal or conscious? Does it have an interest in us, or is it rather some mindless, inanimate "force" (for want of a better word)?

One reason many believers resist the idea of there being no God before the Big Bang is the thought that this seems to imply that God too must have come into being at that instant. How could God have made himself?

The trouble with this is that again the conception of God is too small. Not only are we once more mixing up existent things with the source of existence, but here we are compounding the mistake by regarding God as an object confined within the limits of space and time;

it assumes that God can exist only *in* time. But again that is not how we have to view God. Certainly God is to be found in time; we are interacting with God in time whenever we pray. But he is also *beyond* time—God *transcends* time.

How God manages this we simply do not know. Nor should this limitation on our understanding be regarded as a source of embarrassment. One of the reasons for the designation *humility* in the type of theology we are considering is that it reminds us that God is all we are and much more besides. Although our descriptions of God inevitably draw upon analogies taken from human life, these are but starting points; the analogies always break down when pressed too far. We must constantly be on our guard against conceptions of God that are too small—a God made in our own image.

These then are just some of the types of questions that humility theology seeks to clarify concerning God's relationship to creation. In the process, we are led to an enriched understanding of what it means to regard God as the Creator.

The Cosmos in Relation to Life

Humility theology, if it has any aspirations to be regarded as a science, must take on board not only evidence in favor of its current working hypotheses but also any counterindications. According to Steven Weinberg, one has only to look at the type of universe we find ourselves in to see that it could never have been intended as a home for life. Toward the end of his popular introduction to Big Bang cosmology, *The First Three Minutes,* he concludes: "The more the Universe seems comprehensible, the more it also seems pointless." A little earlier, he dismisses human life as "a more-or-less farcical outcome of a chain of accidents."

It is not difficult to understand how Weinberg arrives at such a gloomy assessment. Consider the size of the universe. Traveling at 300,000 kilometers per second, it takes light 12 billion years to reach us from the farthest depths of space. Are we really expected to believe that God designed such a vast universe specifically as a home for living creatures? There are 100 billion stars in our Milky Way Galaxy. There are 100 billion such galaxies. Each star is a sun, a significant proportion of them being accompanied by planets. Can one seriously regard humans living on one of those planets as being of any significance?

Most places in the universe are hostile to life. The depths of space are incredibly cold; that is why most planets are freezing. To be warm a planet needs to be close to a star. But get too close—like Mercury and Venus—and they become too hot. And of course the most prominent objects in the sky, the sun and the other stars, are in themselves balls of fire and hence not suitable places to find life. Planets either have no atmospheres, or if they do have one, it is not likely to be the right sort for sustaining life.

For much of the history of the universe there was no intelligent life. Looking to the future, we expect after a further 5,000 million years our sun will swell up to become a star of a type known as a *red giant*. Although it is unlikely that its fiery surface will reach out far enough to engulf the earth, our planet will become unbearably hot—to the extent that all life will be burned up. Indeed, life might already have been eliminated long before then through the violent impact of a meteorite.

And what of the long-term future of the universe and of life elsewhere? We have spoken much about the *origins* of the universe in the Big Bang, but what of its *end*?

We have seen how the universe is expanding. The distant galaxies of stars are still receding in the aftermath of the Big Bang. But as they rush off into the distance, they are slowing down. This is due to gravity, each galaxy being subject to an attraction exerted by every other one. Either gravity will eventually bring the expansion to a halt and thereafter pull everything back together in a Big Crunch, or alternatively the expansion will go on forever. In the latter case, all the stars will at some stage have burned up their fuel and become cold, making life on accompanying planets impossible—the so-called heat death of the universe. Either way, the future is bleak for life. As I said, it is easy to see how Weinberg was led to the conclusion that the universe seems pointless, and life but an accidental by-product of no significance.

This is not something humility theology can ignore. We must squarely face the question: Is the type of universe revealed to us by modern astronomy as inappropriate as a "home for life" as it would appear?

It is at this point we must draw attention to the fact that if a universe came into being with laws of nature chosen purely at random, the chances of its being capable of supporting life anywhere within itself would be virtually zero. A whole set of seemingly disparate conditions had to be satisfied. This goes under the name of the anthropic principle.

There is not space here to go into details. Suffice it to note, for instance, that the violence of the Big Bang could have been neither much greater nor much less than it actually was. In one case, the gases coming out of the Big Bang would have dispersed without the formation of stars; in the latter, the universe would have collapsed back on itself before life had had a chance to develop. Then the strength of the force of gravity must be neither weaker nor stronger than it actually is. In the first case, there would be no stars, whereas in the latter, the stars would burn faster and die out too quickly. Then there are problems associated with the manufacture and distribution of the materials for making living bodies. These have to be synthesized through nuclear processes occurring in stars and then ejected in supernova explosions. And so the list of conditions could be extended.

All in all, an extraordinary set of circumstances had to prevail in order for life to develop within our universe. It is impossible to put a hard figure on the likelihood of this happening had the physical laws been thrown together at random—laws incorporating arbitrary values for the various physical constants. In talking, for example, about the strength of gravity having to lie within a narrow range, it is impossible to be more quantitative unless there is some way of specifying a permissible range of values that the strength could conceivably take on. If it could have been *any value whatsoever,* then the finite range compatible with the production of life would be divided by infinity—and the chances would be virtually zero. Whatever the true odds are, they certainly defy the imagination.

Although we are presented with a universe that appears at first sight to be overwhelmingly hostile to life, on closer examination it is found to be exceptionally fine-tuned for the development of life. What might be the explanation of the mysterious appropriateness of the universe? There are essentially three alternatives.

The first is to pin one's faith on science and assert that in the end a natural explanation for it all will be forthcoming. From that vantage point we shall be able to realize that there was no mystery —no need to invoke coincidences.

The second is to assert that our universe is not alone. There are a great many universes—perhaps an infinite number of them—and they all run on different lines with their own laws of nature. The vast majority of them have no life in them because one or other of the conditions were not met. In a few—perhaps in ours alone—all the conditions happen by chance to be satisfied and here life is able to get a hold.

The probability of a universe being of this type is small, but with there being so many attempts, it is no longer surprising that it should have happened. As a form of life, we must, of course, find ourselves in one of these freak universes.

This is a suggestion that has been put forward by some scientists, but note that it goes against the conventional way scientific reasoning develops. Scientists are in the business of trying to explain things as economically as possible. Postulating the existence of an infinite number of universes, all run according to their own laws of nature, is to go as far in the opposite direction as is imaginable.

The third alternative is simply to accept that the universe is a put-up job: it was designed for life, and the designer is God.

When it comes to arguments about God based on design, we need to be cautious. The original argument from design held that everything about our bodies, and those of other animals, is so beautifully fitted to fulfill its function that it must have been designed that way—the designer being God—and therefore one must believe in God. The rug was pulled from under that argument by Darwin's theory of evolution by natural selection—at least in terms of it being a knockdown proof of God's existence—one aimed at convincing the skeptic.

Bearing that in mind, it would be foolhardy to attempt to treat the anthropic principle as a knockdown proof of God's existence. Rather, one should adopt the humility theology approach whereby one might regard this argument as providing persuasive confirmatory evidence for the God hypothesis—but that is all. As such, it is evidence to be assessed in conjunction with the other indications we are in the process of discussing.

The Cosmos as a Reflection of God's Nature

Accepting God as the creator of the world opens up the possibility of learning more about him from the study of that world. After all, if we look at human creations (for instance, a disturbing painting by Francis Bacon of a screaming pope with his face horribly distorted compared to the serenity of a saint painted by Fra Angelico), we can hardly escape the conclusion that the paintings reveal something of the artists as well as their subjects. Or, to use another analogy, one that takes note of the feminine attributes of God, we might think of the world as being born from the womb of God. Again, we would be looking for similarities between the originator and that which is produced. Thus humility theology leads us to expect a cosmos containing clues to God's own nature.

For instance, take the size of the cosmos. Although one's first reaction might be to think of one's own insignificance in the face of such vastness, perhaps it would be more appropriate to think of it as reflecting the unimaginable glory and the sheer power of God. In which case, with such a powerful God taking a personal interest in each and every one of us, that can only enhance our own significance.

Then there are the vast eons of time over which God has worked, through evolution, to bring us into being. Surely this bears testimony to longsightedness and patience. It puts a different perspective on our own petty annoyances at things not being sorted out immediately to our liking. One of the difficulties of life is always that of keeping things in perspective—God's perspective.

We see in nature the way God is prepared to employ an element of randomness. We see how God allows chance to give rise to planets with the right conditions for supporting life, as well as the chance occurrences involved in the processes of evolution by natural selection by which intelligent life forms arose. There is an openness to creation; God is the kind of god who allows the universe to be itself, knowing that in broad terms at least, his will for the world will be accomplished.

There is an orderliness to the way the world runs—it is not chaotic. It is beautiful: there is a lovely use of symmetry; there is breathtaking simplicity and economy in the basic building blocks of matter and the interactions between them—and yet these are able in ingenious ways to give rise to unlimited richness and variety. Humility theology seeks to uncover what this might be implying about the way the mind of God works.

The Religious Experience

The physical world is not the only place where one might search for evidence of God. Indeed, many would say that the main focus of any quest for God ought to be mental rather than physical—the God within, rather than the God outside ourselves. After all, one asks, "Is there a God?" not merely to satisfy some disinterested academic curiosity, but as a prelude to entering into a personal relationship with that God, a relationship founded on love. The most convincing evidence for God, therefore, is likely to be found in the exercise of that relationship. Religion is nothing except outward show and ritual if it *is* not accompanied by a deeply felt inner religious experience. This being psychological in character, humility theology needs to examine the life of the mind, and in particular, the nature of prayer.

Earlier we noted an experiment investigating the effectiveness of prayers for the sick. But there is much more to prayer than intercessions. Prayer in its totality is multifaceted, consisting as it does of worship, thanksgiving, contrition, self-dedication, contemplation, meditation, and so on. Intercession is but one component. These different forms of prayer are various aspects of the relationship with God. It is in these acts that we are confronted with the sense of the numinous—a great power that is other than ourselves. We become exposed to a wisdom that is not our own, a wisdom that can take us by surprise. These experiences have an "otherness" about them: in them, we are encountering another mind.

Or are we? Is the perceived otherness of this experience genuine evidence of God's having a direct impact on the human mind? Perhaps we should be seeking some other explanation. For example, might not the sense of otherness derive from the unconscious mind impacting on consciousness in a way that mimics an input from a supposed God?

Ideally, of course, we would like some scientific means of deciding the issue. But from the outset, the prospects do not look hopeful. The contents of an individual's mind are not open to direct public scrutiny, in the way a biological specimen, say, can be jointly examined, and experimented upon, by a group of scientists. Sigmund Freud, the founder of modern psychology, did in fact, however, regard his work as a science. In his defense, it can be argued that open access to the data is unnecessary, provided the description given by the individual faithfully and truly relays to others the nature of the psychological experience he or she has had. Again, when it comes to the repeatable nature of scientific investigations, there is no problem; the psychological experiences reported by many individuals can be collected and compared, these leading to the identification of reproducible, repeated patterns of common experience. Of course, one does on occasion come across aberrant experiences—perhaps of individuals convinced that they are Napoleon or God. Rogue results are to be expected in any scientific study. But these are easily sifted out, leaving a reproducible set of psychological experiences common to large sections of the population and hence requiring some universally applicable, overarching explanation.

As with many other scientific investigations, it is the interpretation of the raw data that can prove problematic. Freud was of the view that religious belief arose from wish fulfillment. This is a process whereby the unconscious takes something that is devoutly wished for and causes the conscious mind to believe that the wish has indeed been fulfilled. Freud claimed that as one grows up, one becomes anxious and fearful of losing the fatherly protection one has enjoyed in childhood. One wishes that it would continue into adult life. So the unconscious invents a heavenly father figure to take the place of the earthly father. Thus, the idea of there being a God out there is just a projection arising out of this unacknowledged infantile fear. According to Freud, belief in God is an illusion. It is immature and mentally unhealthy.

Carl Jung took a diametrically opposed view. He pointed out that we all inherit certain mind-sets that help to shape our subsequent experiences. He called them archetypes. Some, at least, of these can be regarded as the psychological equivalents of what evolutionary biologists call genetically influenced behavior. Among the archetypes is an especially important one, named "the self," associated with the religious idea of the God image within us. A tendency to be religious seems to lie at the very core of what it is to be human. According to Jung, a well-sorted-out religion is an integral part of psychological maturity; it is something one should actively seek to cultivate.

The psychology of religion is, I believe, a potentially rich source of study for humility theology. Special attention might be devoted to exploring potential links between, on the one hand, the religious archetype with its accompanying moral sense and, on the other, genetically influenced behavior fashioned through evolution by natural selection, including in particular those traits having a bearing on altruism.

Laws of Life

Religion is concerned with promoting the truly fulfilled life. Strange to say, the achievement of this goal appears to have little to do with what one might at first think was relevant: fame, power, riches, influence. Rather it is to be attained in unexpected ways: through giving rather than receiving, through forgiveness rather than revenge, through loving one's enemies rather than fighting them, to name but a few examples. This "wisdom," if such it is, strikes us as so counterintuitive that it appears to point to some source other than human common sense—perhaps a spiritual source. Collectively these aphorisms have come to be known as the laws of life. If they can be demonstrated to be valid, then they could be counted as important indicators having a bearing on the existence and nature of God. One of the preoccupations of humility theology has therefore to be the testing of these laws.

Does Our Conception of God Make Sense?

The conception of God that emerges from the preceding considerations can perhaps be summed up by saying that there is just one God; the creator of the universe and of ourselves: all-powerful, all-loving, all-good, all-knowing.

That being so, what are we to make of evidence that seems to go against such a conclusion? How can such a view be reconciled with the evil and suffering we find in the world, to say nothing of death? For many people, the existence of evil and suffering poses an insuperable problem to belief in a benign God.

If humility theology is to aspire to being a science in its own right, it cannot simply be aimed at finding evidence *in favor* of God's existence. It must take on board *all* the evidence—whether or not it appears to be in favor of, or contradictory to, one's chosen hypothesis. In contending, as I do, that humility theology needs to address the problems of evil and suffering, it is not that I expect it to come up with a complete answer to this perennial difficulty. But at least it should provide pointers as to where partial answers might lie. These need to be sufficient to satisfy us that belief in God does not have to be blind and irrational.

Such pointers are to be found through the recognition that, if God's all-important characteristic is *love*, and his purpose in making us is that we might enter into a loving relationship with him, then certain consequences follow: We must be granted free will, a freedom that can be abused. We must operate in a predictable, dependable environment—one in which we risk running afoul of that law-governed behavior. There must be occasions of need that can be the focus of loving acts on the part of others. Proof of love comes only through voluntarily undertaken sacrifice and suffering. Sometimes great good comes from suffering. God does not abandon us to our suffering, but through his Son, shares in it. These are but some of the components of an approach that might demonstrate that the presence of evil and suffering in the world might not be as damaging to the loving God hypothesis as it might seem at first sight. It is certainly a field of study humility theology needs to address.

Progress in Theology

Although humility theology is based on an open exploratory approach rather than one that takes as its starting point the authority of the Bible, that does not mean it has to ignore what is to be found in scripture. No one is expected to discover everything for themselves. Each of us benefits from the experience of past generations. The Bible is a storehouse of insights gleaned by the great spiritual figures of the past. It would be foolishness to ignore them. After all, the scientific approach fully accepts that today's scientists stand on the shoulders of those who have gone before. Today's experiments build upon the achievements of the past. Science is a cumulative study. So it should be with theology.

At the very least, the Bible is a record of the changing perception of God over the ages. On placing the writings in the chronological order in which they were written (as best this can be done), we see a remarkable pattern of development:

- From the god who was tied to his mountain retreat—to the creator of the whole world;
- From one god among many gods—to the one and only God;
- From the tribal god of the Israelites who cared nothing for Egyptians and Canaanites—to the one who is God of all people equally;
- From a warlike god of wrath and vengeance—to the God of love and mercy;
- From a god who would strike people dead if they dared approach too closely—to the God who dwells in our hearts;
- From the lofty God of the heavens—to the one who comes to earth and suffers alongside us.

Theology, just like science, is revealed as a progressive subject. This is in marked contrast to the common perception of it being static—fixed in stone, rooted for all time in the Bible. The Bible itself demonstrates that this is not so.

It is probably true to say that the understanding of God has undergone changes and development as radical as any that have taken place, through science, in our understanding of the world. One would no more wish to revert to past conceptions of God than one would wish to go back to earlier notions of science.

Nor is this progress in theology to be regarded as something that took place solely in the dim and distant past. Take, for example, the way we in our own time have begun to recognize and take an interest in the feminine side of God; we are now able to enrich our conception of God by exploring female analogies as well as male ones. We have already noted the ways in which modern astronomy, cosmology, and evolutionary theory have enriched our understanding of God, and how God interacts with creation.

In the philosophy of science, it has become customary to speak of critical realism. This term acknowledges that we can never expect at any stage to be absolutely certain that our scientific theories are correct and will never need further amendment. But at least we are convinced that there is a real world out there (we are not making it up) and that our current descriptions of it are superior to those they have superseded.

I reckon the term critical realism can be applied as appropriately to humility theology. This approach to religious questions is undogmatic in that it never claims to provide the last word on the ultimate truth about God. Our understanding of God is fallible; it is ongoing; it is open to correction and refinement in the light of greater experience—and that is how it will always be. The fact that humility theology, like science, is constantly in a state of flux is not to be taken as a sign of weakness and indecision; it is its strength. It is this very open-mindedness that fits it for the inexhaustible challenges that lie ahead.

Finally, what of that opening question: Can theology be regarded as a science? If nothing more, I hope the foregoing discussion has demonstrated that theology and science need not be as different from each other as most people suppose. At least, that appears to be the case for humility theology.

2

God and Contemporary Cosmology

Continuing the Creative Interaction

ROBERT JOHN RUSSELL

The theme of this collection of essays is humility theology, a term Sir John Marks Templeton has developed to express an attitude of openness to the discoveries of the sciences, particularly on the part of religious scholars interested in what nature can teach us about faith in God. As Sir John indicates in his foreword, contemporary science can and should be an ally in our spiritual journey. Science discloses the enormity and complexity of the universe in an unending process of continual discovery. Through an attitude of humility we can be more fully open to what these discoveries imply about the infinity of God the Creator, and in the process we can more fully come to appreciate the spiritual insights and perspectives of others. Humility theology stresses the limits to all human knowledge whose reach will never encompass all that is to be known. At the same time, it urges us not to remain complacent, content with prior understanding, but instead to seek to expand our knowledge of "the God who would be known."[1] Moreover, progress in spiritual knowledge can be found through the discoveries of scientific research since, as Sir John suggests, knowledge about the universe is ultimately knowledge as well about its Creator, the God "πάντα δι᾽ αὐτοῦ ἐγένετο" (John 1:3: "through whom all things were made"). Finally, like any spiritual practice, humility theology should be judged by its fruits, and these, in Sir John's view, are a profound sense of awe and thankfulness.

As a physicist and a Christian theologian, I welcome Sir John's insights and the direction in which they points us. The Greek word for humility, ταπεινοφροσυνης, (tapeinophrosune), in the context of the

New Testament, means having a modest opinion of oneself, a humbleness about one's accomplishments. I believe such humility is grounded theologically in our recognition that God is incomprehensible and limitless. Such an attitude is essential, I believe, not only to the journey of spirit but also to the practice of science, whether or not one is explicitly religious.[2] Such practice can lead us to recognize, through the growing discoveries of science, the underlying mystery of existence and the unfathomable depths of the universe. Surely such mystery and depth are indications that nature is, after all, the creation of God who, even in being known, remains ultimate mystery. Similarly, theological reflection in the Western monotheistic religions—Judaism, Christianity, and Islam—has for centuries underscored the mystery of God known through scripture, tradition, reason, and experience. Religion and science should work creatively together, then, to illuminate our knowledge of God while recognizing the ultimate ineffability and fallibility of such knowledge.[3]

What is particularly encouraging, as we enter a new millennium, is that more and more persons who combine these fields in their own lives and research are pointing to the stunning importance of science to their spiritual journey and of spirituality to their scientific research.[4] I am extremely excited about the number of internationally distinguished scientists who are beginning to lecture publicly about the fruits of their research, and to engage in common scientific research projects based on their spiritual journeys, through the CTNS program, Science and the Spiritual Quest (SSQ), funded by the John Templeton Foundation. The importance and promise of humility theology lie in its ability to foster and inspire this kind of research as one of a variety of key approaches to the creative interdisciplinary field of science and religion. As a world-renowned biochemist at Oxford University, Pauline Rudd is a wonderful example of the approach taken by many participants in the SSQ project. In lecturing at a recent international public SSQ conference on the University of California-Berkeley campus, Dr. Rudd said eloquently that "in approaching God, we come clothed in humility, aware of our limited vision. . . . Nonetheless, even a single cell responds to its environment . . . it is by being in the environment of God that we gain some small insight into the mind of God."

In this short essay, I'd like to touch on three issues whose broader context is this kind of interdisciplinary research. First, I'd like to reflect back on what has now been two decades of intense scholarly research on the relation between contemporary scientific cosmology and creation theology, touching on the highlights and offering new questions for the future. Second, I'd like to consider recent discussions of the meaning of life in the universe, particularly what we might learn if and when we discover intelligent extraterrestrial life. Finally, I'd like to underscore the challenge to Christian faith posed by the cosmological scenarios of the far future. Rather than do this in a strictly academic mode, though, I'd like to introduce the material through personal experiences that illustrate, as perhaps only a narrative can, what I at least find to be some of the intimate connections between science and spirituality.

Cosmology and Creation

When I was a kid growing up in Los Angeles in the 1950s, I loved to spend time in the Griffith Park Observatory. The monthly shows in the planetarium were great, and observing planets, nebulae, and globular clusters through the rooftop telescope was always an adventure. But my favorite was tucked inconspicuously away, far down a long corridor on the ground floor of the building. There, almost hidden by an unassuming simplicity, was a backlit black-and-white photo that I returned to again and again. At first it always looked like the usual star fields of the Milky Way, stars perhaps several thousand light-years away. Yet if you looked closely you could see that those fuzzy points of light weren't stars but galaxies—it was actually a field of galaxies hidden deep in the immense folds of space, the light of each galaxy emitted hundreds of millions of years ago by hundreds of billions of stars!

The feeling it brought to me was always one of astonishment and joy: what a glorious and staggering universe surrounds us! At the same time, in a muted but ever present way, I could feel the recognition and, with it, the dread boil up within me that all this need not exist. But it does. Why? Why does the universe exist? Why is there anything at all, and not nameless, beingless, inconceivable nothing?

In reflecting back over the years, I have come to understand just how special that experience was, how fortunate I was to have it, and what a lasting impact it had on my life, both in terms of the scientific research I later undertook and, more recently, in my wrestling with science and religion. As I now realize, standing quietly and staring fixedly at that field of galaxies, until the photographic plate seemed to vanish and I moved within their midst, was not only a genuinely scientific experience of asking and learning about them but also a truly *religious* experience of encounter, of coming into relation with them, and of being grasped by the enormity of the question of contingency when it is posed at the level of the universe itself.

Certainly each of us is aware at some level of the questions posed to us by the contingency of our own personal existence: why was I born? How should I live? Why must I die? Will I live again after death? But these questions, though ultimate for us as individuals, still fall short of the radical contingency encountered when we think not just of our own lives but of the existence of the universe as a whole. For no matter how compelling life and death are for each of us, they are routinely and unconsciously circumscribed by the way we take for granted the enduring world around us—the soil and the seas, the mountains and the sky, the stars fixed in the night sky. Even though we are mortal, we take for granted that the world, at least, goes on relatively undisturbed by our presence or absence. Our "whyness," the "iffyness," of our life are relativist, and the anguish of death is in some ways blunted by the constancy of the world around us.

But that givenness, that thereness, of the world is an outmoded assumption. Instead, because of three centuries of science, we now know that the mountains and oceans are transient, that countless species of life have thrived and gone extinct, and that humanity itself, and not just our own individual life, may one day be gone. Gone forever are the static heavens of crystalline spheres that pervaded Western thought from ancient Greece to Copernicus. Gone, too, is the infinite, eternal, absolute, and unchanging cosmos of Newton. Instead, we are heirs of modern geology, Darwinian biology, and Einsteinian cosmology. The discoveries of science lead me to a profound sense that the universe as such need not even exist, and that its continuing existence, moment by moment, is not self-explanatory. Although it is not identical to the theological contingency of existence, the radically temporal, historical character of the universe underscores how impermanent and dependent all that is, is on something that is not impermanent, on whose permanent existence all impermanence can depend. Why should the universe, whose fundamental particles flicker into and out of existence and whose global history is constantly changing, be real and present and continuously in existence? What power sustains all that is, even in its multilayered state of impermanence and change? What gives existence to that which cannot give it to itself—to you and me, to the particles of our bodies and the universe as a whole?

It is ironic that the discoveries of science have vastly augmented this fundamental sense of contingency even while an answer to the question of existence lies forever beyond the grasp of science. Science both increases our perception of the question of contingency and exposes ever more clearly its inability to answer this question. For everything science discovers only compounds the question of what it in turn depends upon, and thus why there should be anything at all.

Looking back on those early days at the observatory, I remember how, in asking this question—a question of fundamental existence or nonexistence—the response that welled up inside of me was "God." Indeed, central to Judaism, Christianity, and Islam is the recognition that God stands for that without which there would be nothing. Not just endless empty space, not just totally chaotic matter ungoverned by the laws of nature; just pure nothing, what the Greeks called *ouk on,* absolute nonbeing. I was soon to learn that this insight is precisely what drives the "cosmological argument for God": that if all I know about need not exist, something beyond all that I know must necessarily exist, and out of that existence must come all else. When we look out at the universe with an open mind and heart, the question that wells up within us is, "Why is there anything at all, rather than sheer nothing?" The answer is "God."

Recent pictures from the Hubble Space Telescope have given us even more dramatic views of deep space and those ever-receding fields of galaxies. And cosmology has matured tremendously since the 1950s, too. Now there's inflation, and beyond this there may be the infinite and endless topology of Andrej Linde's "eternal inflation" or the boundary less superspace geometry of Stephen Hawking's timeless cosmology. Still, it seems to me that the mere fact (actually the staggering fact) that the universe exists—however it is structured, however infinite it might be —is the best "evidence" for God, at least within philosophical theology. Whatever else I say here, I want to underscore this insight. It is not, of course, a "proof" of God, for one can always choose to view the universe as necessarily existing and stop at that. Similarly, there is always the pantheistic option of elevating nature into divinity such as Baruch Spinoza proposed in the seventeenth century. More recently, and with less philosophical sophistication (but arguably more appeal), Carl Sagan seemed to take this approach in the opening sentence of his *Cosmos* series: "The cosmos is all that is or ever was or ever will be."[5] Both sides, then, appeal to the same data, but draw very different conclusions, and this is as it should be, since faith in—or against—God is, at its core, a deeply personal experience nurtured, for those who believe, by an ongoing relationship to sacred text, worship, tradition, and contemporary experience. Like all other claims about God, the "cosmological argument" is more like a "character witness" to what the religions of the West have called God, but not an "eyewitness." After all, who can "do the experiment" and "subtract" God from the universe to see whether, without God, the universe will continue to exist?

Enough said. The fact of the universe, together with the incredible discoveries by science of its historical, interdependent, and unrepeatable character, underscores the cosmological argument in ways that were never fully anticipated in the prescientific West. The task of this chapter, then, is to turn our focus to some very specific debates surrounding the details of cosmology in relation to theology. The fundamental cosmological question (why?) leads me to a reasoned response formed by theological reflection on the resources of Christianity made present in weekly worship and proclamation and critically reformulated in light of the discoveries of science. This move transforms the conversation from personal, religious language into philosophical, systematic, and theological discourse as it engages with science. It is to this that we now turn.

Is It Important Theologically?

Let's start with the standard (noninflationary) Big Bang. There has been a voluminous outpouring of writing that takes the Big Bang as the starting point for theological discussions. For now I can only briefly review some of the positions taken. The discussions have primarily focused on two areas: the "beginning of time" ($t = 0$) and the anthropic principle.

First, $t = 0$. If the Big Bang model of the universe is characterized by an essential singularity, as we know it is according to the Hawking and Penrose theorems, how is that fact relevant to our understanding of God as the Creator?

Responses to this question are legion, but I'll boil them down to four positions, following roughly the ways Ian G. Barbour suggests we relate science and religion.[6] The first position sees $t = 0$ as directly relevant and endorse it as "proof" of God. This includes Pope Pius XII in a famous statement made in 1951, Robert Jastrow in his *God and the Astronomers* (1978), and "Reasons to Believe," the ongoing project of Hugh Ross. Advocates of the second position—"direct conflict"—see t = 0 as directly relevant to religion and want to get rid of it. The clearest example is Fred Hoyle, who constructed an alternative model, the "Steady State" universe, in the late 1940s. According to this model, the universe is infinitely old and lacks a beginning of time at t = 0. It has been expanding eternally, and it will continue to expand forever. Hoyle's model competed successfully with Big Bang for more than two decades until its demise with the discovery, among other things, of the microwave background radiation. More recently, Stephen Hawking proposed a strategy that might overcome the t = 0 problem in Big Bang through his work in quantum gravity. Carl Sagan wrote in the introduction to Hawking's *A Brief History of Time* that with t = 0 gone, there was nothing left for God to do.

What is interesting in both groups is the total focus on a putative direct connection between t = 0 and theology to the complete neglect of the cosmological argument, based on the contingency of nature, and underlying the relation between theology and cosmology whether or not there is a beginning of time. In effect, the cosmological argument seems to fade off into oblivion, leaving all the weight on a specific cosmology. The problem, then, is that when the cosmology changes, the direct and model-specific connection is severed and we are left without a clue as to how to proceed. This applies not only to those using t = 0 to support Christian theology, but also to the atheists who seek to undermine theology by ridding cosmology of the singularity. Again Hoyle is a particularly interesting example. His model undercut what was seen as clear evidence of divine creation, namely, t = 0. But, ironically, while getting rid of t = 0, Hoyle's model introduced a new feature: since Hoyle's universe expands constantly, in order to keep a constant density he had to posit the continuous creation of matter in time. What, then, is the cause of such continuous creation? In effect, Hoyle wound up postulating a feature of the universe, the continuous creation of matter, which, arguably, could be used as direct evidence for God's ongoing creation of the universe as t = 0 could be used for God's creation of the universe in an original event.

The third group takes a "two world" approach: since they believe science and religion are totally separate fields, there can't be anything of relevance theologically about some specific result like t = 0. Georges Lemaître, a Catholic priest and key contributor to the formation of Big Bang cosmology, took this position. It has been suggested that Lemaître eventually succeeded in convincing Pope Pius XII to refrain from further mention of the putative theological significance of t = 0.[7] This is also the approach adopted by members of the National Academy of Sciences. If conflict is the only alternative, it may be a welcome relief, but eventually by cutting off the conversation it precludes the possibility of creative dialogue.

The fourth group sees the relevancy as indirect. I like to call this group's approach the "interaction" model. On the one hand, no attempt is being made to "prove" or "disprove" theology, as the first two approaches do. On the other hand, it doesn't isolate theology from what can be a vigorous and creative interaction with science, as the third approach does. Instead, this approach allows for and encourages a rich exchange between science and theology, and it recognizes the important role of philosophy in the process. Moreover, the approach depends on openness and mutual respect on the part of both scientists and theologians. Neither party should speak authoritatively beyond the limits of their competency. The criterion by which we can assess the value of this approach is simple: both sides should find the interaction productive according to their own professional criteria of research progress.

Within this broad approach, I have found it increasingly helpful to distinguish between two different processes. One involves a movement from the world to God as typified by the cosmological argument. Recall that the cosmological argument starts with the sheer existence of the universe and points inferentially toward God. It normally does not entail a detailed discussion between theology and a specific scientific cosmology, since the cosmological argument holds no matter what scientific theory we are working with. This seems reasonable, since it is often argued that science per se cannot explain why the universe exists; it can only explain how the present state of the universe arose from its previous state by causal processes. Incidently, this is why the issue of "t = 0" in Big Bang cosmology is so controversial to scientists: how can science point to an "uncaused event"? (The answer is that it can't, and therefore the theory in which it arises, Einstein's general relativity, should be modified, as in inflationary theory, or replaced, perhaps in terms of quantum gravity.)

The other process begins with a theology of creation and moves from there to a philosophical conception of the world as contingent, rational, and purposive.[8] God is seen as creating the world not as an emanation of the divine being but ex nihilo, "out of nothing;" its mode of existence is contingent upon God as its source of being. God is also understood as creating the world through the word of God, the Λογος (Logos), thus giving the contingent world its rational character. Finally, God creates the world for a purpose, the bringing to be of creatures capable of communion with God and each other. The world is therefore intelligible and dependable, orderly and laced with novelty, and temporally moving toward the evolution of creatures capable of self-consciousness of moral agency. As historians have pointed out, the conception of nature as creation, particularly as contingent and rational, played a pivotal role in the rise of modern, empirical science.[9] Scientific method is built indirectly upon the presupposition that nature is the creation of God by treating every event in nature as contingent on previous events and by expressing this contingency through the rationality of mathematics.[10] Things need not be the way they are, and science explains them in terms of cause-and-effect processes guided by the laws of nature. Even the laws of nature are contingent: with each revolution in physics we come to a new set of laws, and we discover natural explanations for things that seemed intractable in previous theories. A totally uncaused event, or an event that entirely broke with the laws of nature, would fall outside the jurisdiction of science because of its methodological presuppositions and their philosophical roots in monotheism.

Moving on from philosophy, this approach then makes contact with the specific theories of empirical science such as Big Bang cosmology or Darwinian evolution. Moreover, it does so in a particularly creative way. By separating out the permanent philosophical assumptions underlying science (such as contingency and rationality) from the actual scientific theories, it allows these theories to be open to revision and eventually to replacement as science undergoes both normal development and occasionally a paradigm shift. In this way it encourages a discussion of specific features of a given cosmological model while remaining aware of their vulnerability to change. So where once we used the Ptolemaic system to deploy a Christian narrative of the world, as depicted so grandly by Dante in *The Divine Comedy*, or the Newtonian cosmology to view the universe as the divine sensorium, now we are called to give our account of God's relation to the universe in terms of twentieth-century cosmology, moving from standard Big Bang to inflationary Big Bang and then perhaps to eternal inflation or some other model. Conversely, there have been and will continue to be tremendous changes in Christian theology as the living religion it reflects upon continues to grow and move in response to God's Spirit in the world. This approach allows for such changes by building change into the conversation.

Let us then reflect on t = 0 in this way, keeping in mind its context, namely, standard Big Bang cosmology. Clearly, t = 0 is one way to speak about the contingent existence of the universe as a whole: not only need it not exist, it has in fact existed for only a finite amount of time. Here the universe reflects the contingency we each feel in our own lives, but in a much more profound way, since, unlike our short lives amidst the ongoing world, there is no "permanent environment" within which the universe comes and goes. Thus, if the universe has a "beginning" as Big Bang depicts, it brings together not only the sheer question of why there is a universe (a question even an eternal universe such as Hoyle's would raise) but why the universe should have "come about" in the first place. Thus, t = 0 elicits the cosmological argument and points to God as the ultimate cause of the sheer existence as well as the source of the beginning of the universe. Conversely, if we start with a theology of creation in which the universe is the ex nihilo creation of God, we can move from theology into the language of philosophy by claiming that such a universe will be contingent and rational, and thus amenable to scientific analysis. From here we move into the domain of science in which the equations of Einstein's general relativity and the assumption of a homogeneous and isotropic universe[11] give us the space-time picture of an expanding universe with an essential singularity, t = 0. Moreover, starting with the observations of Edwin Hubble in the 1920s and continuing through the victory of Big Bang over Hoyle's Steady State in the 1960s and the very recent results of the COBE satellite, the empirical results of astrophysics confirm the expansion of the universe and support the theoretical claim that this expansion can be traced back to the initial singularity, t = 0.

Now what's important here is that the discovery of t = 0 serves in turn as a kind of indirect confirmation of our theological belief in God as creator. This is particularly true since, though theology has traditionally conceived of the universe as having a beginning (what Augustine called "creation of time" and not "creation in time"), it is only with the specific development of general relativity and the empirical discoveries of astrophysics that a physical beginning, t = 0, has been embraced within a scientific model. In this sense, t = 0 constitutes what philosophers of science would call a "novel fact": something about nature that was not known until general relativity and astrophysics pointed to it. It not only confirms general relativity, but in a very *indirect* sense, it confirms the theology of creation. To recap: according to this second process in their interaction, theology leads through the path of philosophy to the domain of science in which an empirical result then confirms not only the scientific theory directly but also, indirectly, the underlying philosophical and theological framework.

From Big Bang to Inflation and Quantum Cosmology: What Happens to the t = 0 Argument for Creation?

Now let's turn to the problem of change in science: what happens to this kind of indirect confirmation when we move from standard Big Bang to inflationary Big Bang cosmology, and then to quantum cosmology and such proposals as Andrej Linde's "eternal inflation"?[12] This question takes us to the frontiers of research in theology and science, in which this question is currently being debated.[13] I can suggest the following directions for further reflection, and leave the interested reader to work through the relevant technical literature.

(1) Inflationary Big Bang raises the possibility that we may never be able to decide whether the universe had a beginning or not. As John Barrow puts it, the question of the finite past of the universe may well be an in principle "unanswerable"or an "undecideable" scientific question.[14] (2) In such quantum cosmology scenarios as Linde's eternal inflation, the present universe arises as one of an uncountable infinity of previous universes, and it will in turn give rise to future infinities of universes. In both cases, the cosmological argument is unchallenged. If we denote the absolute totality of all universes that might exist by capital *U*, then the claim would be that, regardless of the "size" of the infinity of universes, the totality, or the Universe, need not exist.

But what about the indirect theological confirmation achieved by t = 0 in standard Big Bang? Perhaps the most productive response is to recognize that regardless of what happened at the beginning of *our* universe, it is still succinctly described by Big Bang theory: an expanding universe with a history of unrepeatable epochs (such as first and second generation stars), and one with either an infinite (open) or finite (closed) future—something we'll return to when we consider eschatology in a later section. So *our* universe at least is finite, historical, and thus what a theology of creation would expect. Perhaps, then, it doesn't fundamentally matter whether it also has a beginning event, t = 0.

I am increasingly convinced that the finitude and historicity of our universe is much more significant theologically than the additional claim that it had an absolute beginning. What this means is that we should refocus our attention on the unique character of its history and the question posed by the evolution of life to the meaning and purpose of the universe. It is in this direction that we shall turn shortly. But first, the anthropic principle deserves our attention, since it addresses these questions in terms of the universe as a whole.

The Anthropic Principle

Another issue raised by standard Big Bang cosmology is the anthropic principle. Christian theologians claim not only that God creates the universe out of nothing and holds it in existence at every moment, but that God does so for a purpose: in order that creatures capable of self-conscious intentionality and moral agency can come into communion with God. Does anything within science correlate to the universe being the purposive creation of God?[15]

Design arguments flourished in the century before Darwin. Since the mid-nineteenth century, though, the scientific explanation of biological complexity was rendered in terms of variation and natural selection. We no longer explain scientifically the adaptation of organs and organisms to their environment in terms of God's previsioned design and special interventionist creation of each species. Instead, we view species as adapting to their environments according to the competitive reproductive fitness of their progeny: varying phenotypic traits yield relative fitness within the context of a changing environment of scarce resources. In the early twentieth century, the rediscovery of Mendelian genetics was incorporated into Darwin's theory; it served to explain what Darwin left simply as the phenomenon of variation. With the discovery of the molecular structure of DNA in 1956 by James Watson and Francis Crick, the biological explanation of adaption in terms of genetic variation and selection, and not in terms of the direct, interventionist design by God, was complete.

This fact renders all the more stunning that, over the past few decades, a number of scientists have pointed to an apparent "design" argument pertaining to the universe as a whole. By now the argument is well known: one first points out that if the laws and constants of nature were slightly different, the evolution of life anywhere in the universe would have been impossible. The argument can be rendered with incredible precision: if the values of constants such as the speed of light were other than they are by one part per million—or even one part per billion—then life such as we know it on earth could never have evolved. This leads many to conclude that the universe is "fine-tuned" for the evolution of life, and this underscores the theological claim that God creates the universe for the purpose of producing intelligent, morally capable life.

But does it succeed as an argument from design, starting with "fine-tuning" as a given feature of the world and seeking to conclude from it a purposeful God? Probably not. For one thing, it runs into the same objection raised by Enlightenment philosophers such as David Hume: what kind of God would design a universe with this much pain and suffering? For another, it raises the question whether reason can ever reach to the God revealed in the history of Israel and the life of Jesus Christ. Most of all, though, it runs up against competing ways of explaining the apparent fine-tuning of the universe via inflation and quantum cosmology.

How Do Inflation and Quantum Cosmology Affect the Anthropic Principle?

Models such as inflation or quantum cosmology offer a natural explanation of the anthropic principle without appealing to God's handiwork in designing our universe: instead, many universes exist, each with a different value of the constants of nature. Inflation suggests that there are countless domains of a single megauniverse, one of which is ours. In quantum cosmology, there may be an endless creation of "daughter" universes such as ours. In either case, the "fine-tuning" of the constants of our universe seems like it gets "explained away": we simply live in that one particular universe that is consistent with the requirements for biological life. But does this thoroughly overturn the anthropic principle?

As usual, "the devil is in the details"! For upon closer inspection we see that there are many "layers" to the argument.[16] Suppose there are countless universes, each of which is marked by a different value for the constants and initial conditions. We can still find an aspect that is "designed": if we move to the next "layer" of the argument, we recognize that all these universes, whose constants and initial conditions vary, nevertheless obey the same laws of physics. So why are the laws the way they are? Is this evidence of God's design at the level of the laws? Or can we speculate further: perhaps there are many variations on the laws, and again many universes instantiating each one. Even so, we can move up another "layer" and ask about the kind of logic underlying all these diverse laws. Why is it "two-valued"? Did God design logic this way? Once again, we can seek to move up the layering still further; on the other hand, we may well be moving away from any

sensible discussion into pure speculative abstraction. What is important to note for our purposes, however, is the intricate intermingling
between the specific meaning of divine design and the scientific discussion of such possible design features as the values of the constants
of nature, the laws of nature, and so on. Clearly, if we want to engage
in a design argument in the context of science, the science both shapes
the theological meaning of design while raising the possibility of design. This fact speaks well for the necessity of the "theology and science
dialogue." It is also important to note how model dependent the form
of the question is: we must be particularly clear about our scientific and
theological assumptions as we enter into dialogue.

Life in the Universe

As I suggested in talking about t = 0, there is still another way to relate cosmology and creation theology, namely in terms of the universe
as we now observe it. Surely we would commit the "genetic fallacy" if
we assumed that the most important clue to the universe is found in
its ancient origins, or that what it has produced over the past fifteen
billion years is irrelevant to its meaning.

Ours is indeed an astonishing universe. Its unrepeatable history of
distinct epochs form a luminous string of stories that stretches from the
incredibly early period of extraordinarily rapid inflation, when symmetry between the fundamental forces was broken, to the relatively recent
evolution of intelligent life on, at least, our planet. These epochs include
the decoupling of light from matter 800,000 years after inflation, the
production of first-generation stars that fused hydrogen first into helium, then lithium, and, if they were large enough, continued the
process until exploding violently (in what astronomers call a "supernova") and strewing all the heavy elements into the local intragalactic
region. There second-generation stars like our sun formed, surrounded
by planets composed of all the elements needed for the potential evolution of life. Needed too were the right conditions, and certainly on
earth these prevailed. As a Christian, I take all this to be the result of the
ongoing, continuing creation of the living God acting in, with, under,
and through the processes of nature as described scientifically in terms
of the laws of nature. The result, at least in the case of humanity, is the
coming to be of living creatures capable of conscious, intentional
covenantal relationship with, and invited into it by, their Creator.

Let us turn, then, to more specific questions. (1) Life could be ubiquitous or rare in the universe. Does that matter theologically? (2) What can we hope to learn theologically from the possible encounter with, or at least communication with, other intelligent life in the universe? Let's start with the question of the ubiquity of life. It is possible that intelligent life has evolved voluminously throughout the universe, as Carl Sagan believed. If life is abundant, it seems to underscore the view that God creates the universe for a purpose, even if it takes fifteen billion years and many planets like ours! On the other hand, life may be very rare in the universe, as others argue. This might reduce life to a meaningless surd, but in my view even if life is extremely scarce, it only renders it all the more precious. If I were lost and thirsty in the trackless wastes of a desert and I happened to see a palm tree on the horizon, I wouldn't say, "Oh well, since there's only one of them, it can't be important." Instead, I would rejoice in the fact that even one tree exists, since it might mark an oasis and water.

What are the scientific prospects for deciding whether life is ubiquitous or rare? Some scientists are focusing on the search for evidence of primitive life in our own solar system—and here the emphasis is on *primitive*. Only two years ago, scientists at NASA thought they had found evidence of early forms of life on Mars, taken from meteors that had been knocked off the Red Planet and eventually trapped by Earth's gravity to land in the arctic wastelands. We all saw the photos of those wormlike fossils, more like pasta than plasma. There's much less enthusiasm now for the Martian sample; indeed, many scientists have given up on it entirely. But primitive life may still exist elsewhere in the solar system. European and American space agencies are considering an unmanned landing on the surface of Europa, that icy moon of Jupiter. Beneath its vast oceans, whose surface is permanently frozen, there could be just the right conditions for life to evolve.

Other scientists are seeking ways to answer the question directly about intelligent life in the universe. Perhaps advanced life has already evolved on the planets of nearby stars—and we almost daily discover evidence of those planets, at least. The mission of the SETI project (the Search for Extraterrestrial Intelligence) is to detect signals from space. Suppose we one day discover a signal whose transmitted information somehow makes it possible for us to meet the creatures who sent it. What could we hope to learn from the encounter?

First of all, we will learn whether intelligent life throughout the universe reasons the way we do, say, by writing down the same laws of physics. It is possible that the way we reason is tied up with the specific evolutionary history of our species, and extraterrestrials will think in ways we can't even recognize. For example, even if we recognize their signals could not be a natural phenomena, it is possible that we won't be able to actually understand what the signals are about. So decoding, and not just receiving, "artificial" signals will be a tremendous answer to a key question about humanity.

Next, with the evolution of the capacity for rational thought, will intelligent life also evolve the capability for moral reflection? Some scholars, such as Michael Ruse, believe that our morality (i.e., the specific content of our moral systems such as altruism) is bequeathed us by evolution. We may believe we make free moral choices, but to a large extent our decisions are at least predisposed, perhaps predetermined, by our genes. Others, such as Francisco Ayala and Camilo Cela-Conde, disagree: moral capacity may have evolved, but the particular values we hold, either as individuals, as families, or as societies and cultures, are "free variables" among which we can genuinely choose. What about extraterrestrial life? Perhaps by learning how it makes moral choices (again, assuming that such choices are "recognizable" to us) we may gain insight on just how short the "genetic leash" is on both reason and morality.

Let's go one step further: suppose ET is a moral creature. Will its actions be entirely virtuous, the "angelic" ETs that Carl Sagan apparently thought we'd find one day? Or will it, like us, be conflicted with profound moral dilemmas, its choices ambiguous and ambivalent, reflecting vices similar to those that beset us? Augustine believed that all humans "sin"; we will never find people on Earth leading an entirely blessed life. What about extraterrestrials? Is our pension for wickedness, again as Sagan thought, just the result of something that went tragically wrong on Earth as life and intelligence evolved? Or is it built into the very fabric of life, something that no intelligent creature can avoid? In my view, moral failure is an emergent phenomenon like self-consciousness and rationality: something that emerged and became fully manifest in humankind, but which emerged out of predispositions formed in the trail of predation, disease, suffering, death, and extinction that marks the long, arduous evolutionary journey to mind and values.

Since we've gone this far in our thought experiment, let's go a final step. Suppose ET is not that different from us after all: grasping for the good, the true, the beautiful, yet thwarted by "clay feet," throttled in the quagmires of moral ambiguity. Will God provide a pathway of healing, a means of "saving grace" for ET as God has done for us on Earth? This is, of course, the horizon-breaking image of the "cosmic Christ," as Pierre Teilhard de Chardin called it.

With this discussion in mind, I'm willing to go out on a limb and make what I consider to be a genuinely empirical theological prediction. Surely this move is a rarity for theologians! Hollywood offers two stark alternatives of ET: the insipidly angelic *E.T.* variety and the unmitigatedly demonic alien that *Independence Day* and *Alien* portray. I predict that when we finally make contact with intelligent life in the universe, it will be neither of these extremes. Instead, I predict that it will be a lot like us: seeking the good, beset by failures, and open to the grace of forgiveness and new life that God always offers all God's creatures, regardless of their "planet of origin." In short, I predict that the discovery of extraterrestrial life will "hold a mirror up" to us and we will see someone, from the point of view of rationality and moral capacity, not really unlike ourselves—filled with questions like ours and beckoning to us in hopes of discovering the answers, too. And I predict that, against those voices who say life in the universe is meaningless, or that human life is absurd, we will be able to recognize the common journey of life everywhere, and we will finally be able to understand our place and the place of all life in the universe. We may come, then, to a point where we at last feel truly at home in the cosmos. What a wondrous event that would be!

Eschatology and Cosmology: Will the Cosmos Become the "New Creation"?

Tahiti. Floating near the shore at twilight, I'm looking up at a glowing mauve sky turning slightly bluer near the zenith. The water is incredibly warm and soft below me, buoying me up on gently rocking waves. Below, schools of tropical fish swirl in hundred-yard-long ribbons, moving between staghorn coral whose delicate tendrils extend to strain the flowing water of tiny nutrients. Day life is preparing for darkness and the safety of a cove, while night creatures begin to move out of the depths to feed and forage. My mind drifts easily in the growing quiet of darkening twilight, aware on the edges of consciousness of the lush dinner and the enticing anticipation of the exotic night ahead. My eyes fix on a ruby red point of light just above the curves of a palm tree on the edge of the white sandy beach. Is it an incoming interisland plane, lazily floating toward me in search of the landing strip and its hangar? Or perhaps an ember drifting up from the fiery coals that are cooking roast boar for tonight's dinner. Oh, no, of course: it's a star, the first one I've seen tonight. How beautiful it is, glowing red against the purpling sky, now even casting a faint wiggle of light on the water below. And I recognize what it is: the red star Antares, nested right in the middle of the Scorpion, which, because we're far south of the equator, now floats calmly far above the horizon. I can see the entire constellation, from its head to its stinging tail. It's part of the ecliptic, marking the path of the sun in its annual movement across the sky.

Then suddenly I recognize it for what it really is, and my stomach lurches with vertigo as if I were peering over the cliff of a hundred-mile-deep canyon. Gone is the friendly spherical sky that beguiles us with the domesticated appearance of Earth centeredness. Instead, I'm actually looking out from Earth across the sheer vastness of 520 light-years, and I'm looking at the swollen fiery mass of a red giant star. Its ten-billion-year stint as a main sequence star, during which it fused hydrogen into helium and maintained a roughly constant size, is over. Now Antares has blown off the outer layers of its stellar atmosphere, and this expanding shell of plasma is roughly equivalent to Earth's orbit. What a catastrophe to mark the death of that star! And were there planets circling like Earth in close orbit, allowing for the possibility of life to evolve there, too? Could there have been a civilization of intelligent creatures born on that far-off planet? Did they possess the technological capacity to escape before their planet was vaporized by the star that had nourished it for so long? And did they leave behind all the other species, all the fragile environments, to perish in the stellar ordeal? And if they escaped, where did they go? And for what purpose? what future? We know that the universe as a whole faces one of two future scenarios: "freeze" or "fry." In the first scenario, the universe expands forever, and this now seems likely according to the evidence. As it expands, it will continue to cool asymptotically to absolute zero. Worse yet, all its stars will eventually wink out, decay into white dwarfs, neutron stars, or black holes, and these eventually will decay further, ending up as an endlessly expanding sea of elementary particles. Obviously, such a scenario is incompatible with life as we know it—at least biological life. In the second scenario, the expansion of the universe will slow down until the universe finally reaches a maximum size in a couple hundred billion years, and then the universe will start to contract upon itself, falling back until it eventually moves to infinite temperature and density in a singularity something like t = 0—the "Big Crunch." Again, however, such a universe will eventually become incompatible with life: the same scenario applies about stars decaying and eventually resulting in a sea of elementary particles long before the final episode. So we're back to the question, Where would life go to escape the certain demise of its planets when parent stars expand into enormous "red giants" like Antares, or supernova?

Fortunately, we have a lot of time to consider the options. Our star is a main-sequence star, too, but it's only about halfway through its process and won't turn into a red giant for another five billion years or so. This is no reason, however, for simply ignoring the issue since it's an in principle issue, and not merely one of immediacy. It's like the problem of death: though we die only once, we daily face the question of death, the fact of mortality that conditions, in some ways, all we do. Our death as such poses a profound existential question to us, and beckons toward a theological response. Now astrophysics poses a profound challenge to Christian eschatology beyond the question of individual human death, for the earth itself faces inevitable extinction, and with it whatever ecosystem and whatever species then thrive within it. For one day the Antares scenario will come to pass for our planet when the Sun swells to red giant size. Will *our* distant descendants take flight in stunning starships? What about what they leave behind? What will happen to the distant descendants of the coral reef below me and *its* myriad moving creatures, who know nothing of what lies beyond the watery surface of their coral home?

Perhaps life is ultimately meaningless, a brute fact, nothing more, perishing forever when its environment collapses. In our ecological consciousness we are coming to recognize that terrestrial species by the millions are threatened and by the thousands destroyed annually because of human greed. To quote a well-known environmentalist call to action, for our planet's species, "Extinction means forever—endangered means there's still time." But what about the extinction of not just an ecosystem but a whole planet, and one caused not by human willfulness but by law-abiding, natural processes? Are we really "at home" in the universe, a clue to its meaning and purpose, a universe created and providentially cared for by God and guided to its ultimate purposes through God's redemptive love, if, as we now know, planetary extinction, and beyond this, the extinction of all life in the universe, is almost certainly what the far future promises?

The inevitable doom of life on Earth may pose an insurmountable challenge to theology. Bertrand Russell wrote about this a century ago: that we are not purposefully made, but formed by sheer accident; that nothing we can do can give us life beyond death. Of course this was not entirely new, but what was stunning was Russell's recognition of the cosmic scope of this fatalistic drama: "all the labours of the ages, all the devotion, all the inspiration, all the noonday brightness of human genius, are destined to extinction in the vast death of the solar system." All our achievements will be buried in the debris of a "universe in ruins." In light of this, Russell closed by calling for a philosophy built on the "firm foundations of unyielding despair."[17] His sentiments have been echoed, though only in a pale light, by Steven Weinberg's now classic remark: "The more the universe seems comprehensible, the more it also seems pointless."[18]

Is there any way, then, to make sense of religious hope for the future that can take seriously these cosmic scenarios? This is perhaps the greatest and as yet almost entirely unresolved challenge posed by science to Christian faith. I will offer a possibility that is admittedly only very nascent in my mind, but one which I am slowly, but increasingly, believing may have real promise. Suppose we could construct a testable scientific cosmology that took on board everything we now know about the universe, as Big Bang cosmology does, but which operated out a different set as assumptions about the universe. The approach to relating theology and science that I have taken here is that of mutual creative interaction, and I have already suggested that the doctrine of creation provided key elements in the conception of the world as creation which served as presuppositions for science: contingency and rationality, in particular. But there's more to the story, since other key assumptions were excluded from the scientific conception. Perhaps the most important is that from a theological perspective, what God creates is "heaven and earth," or what I call a "differentiated unity." But science took on board a simpler conception. With Copernicus, Galileo, and especially Newton, it extended the laws of the terrestrial sphere to the celestial sphere: the laws of gravity that apply on Earth, Newton argued, should apply to the moon in its orbit around the earth. In his universal theory of gravity, Newton extended his $1/r^2$ law to apply to every mass in the universe. In the process, the classical distinction between the realms of the moon, sun, and planets on the one hand, and the earth on the other, was obliterated. The universe, from Newton through Einstein, was to be a single whole, governed by a universal set of laws that applied equally everywhere: what I call an "undifferentiated unity."[19]

Now I am certainly not suggesting that any crude notion of different realms in the universe or different law of nature should be reconsidered here. We have obviously learned from the stunning success of science that such things are out of the question. But what I am suggesting is that we at least flag for further careful attention the fact that we no longer build into our presuppositions about the universe or the laws of nature any set of categories which would allow for a more nuanced view of creation which would make possible a scientifically intelligible interpretation of "heaven and earth." Neither do we allow for a way in which God's will might be both hidden in, with, under, and through the processes of nature as we normally take it to be, but might also be more explicit in and through these processes, without at the same time in any way intervening in them, violating or suspending them, or acting without these processes as necessary instruments to mediate God's will. Instead, what would it mean to start with a differentiated unity and a more subtle notion of divine and natural causality reflected in a more nuanced view of the laws of nature and divine action, and from this premise to construct a scientific cosmology in the full light of current empirical evidence? Lest such a proposal be dismissed out of hand as a sort of "high-brow creationist argument," we should recall that Fred Hoyle and his colleagues constructed the Steady State cosmology based on what they considered an atheistic view of the universe: they sought a cosmology that, while being consistent with all the known data of the time, nevertheless was free of the problem of t = 0 and, instead, depicted the universe as eternally old and expanding forever in time. Their achievement withstood two decades of the most rigorous testing and was considered a genuine competitor to Einstein's cosmology until the late 1960s, when the discovery of the microwave background and arguments from the relative abundances of hydrogen and helium convinced most scientists that Big Bang cosmology was preferable to Steady State. Could we do something like this today, but based not so much on worries about t = 0 as about the far cosmological future?

Actually, this suggestion may not be quite as unusual as it can first seem. It has certainly become commonplace now to recognize that nonscientific factors including religious and philosophical views about space, time, matter, causality, and ultimately about nature and God play a role in both (1) the formation of new theories (i.e., what philosophers call the context of discovery), and (2) the reasons for choosing between them (i.e., the criteria of theory choice).[20] I've just suggested how nonscientific factors influenced Hoyle's formation of Steady State cosmology. A more detailed and extensive example that supports both these claims can be found in the early history of quantum mechanics, circa 1900–1930. Einstein's views had roots in Spinoza, Erwin Schrödinger's in Hinduism, Max Planck's in Protestantism, Niels Bohr's in Kierkegaard (he even chose the yin-yang symbol for his family crest), and so on. Their work can be seen both as the construction of competing scientific approaches to atomic data and as competing philosophies of nature reflecting, in turn, differing theological views of God and nature, but framed in the language of mathematics and held accountable to the unforgiving restrictions of empirical evidence.

Of course the usual argument is that the extrascientific roots are routinely set aside and the theories get tested by public data, that is, the context of justification. Obviously, one needn't subscribe explicitly to the philosophical, let alone the religious, roots of the views of scientists when using their theories. But it is not at all clear that these roots do not remain implicit within these theories, even as one of them comes to predominance, or several are unified into an all-encompassing approach such as relativistic quantum mechanics.

As for the criteria of theory choice, scholars have increasingly shown that many of the arguments raised by scientists in favor of one or another competing theory are remarkably similar to arguments raised by theologians concerning competing views of God's relation to creation. A nice example comes from a comparison of two possible directions for a quantum cosmology. In Roger Penrose's approach, the universe arises through a fluctuation in a quantum field in superspace. According to Stephen Hawking, however, the universe arises from the dovetailing of three geometries in a quantum superspace leading to the formation of the four-dimensional space-time manifold. How do we decide between them? Actually, a number of scientists have pointed out that the Penrose approach runs into trouble by its arbitrariness: why should one point in an infinite superspace be the seed for the universe and not others, possibly even every one? Hawking's model avoids this problem and is thus seen as preferable. What is interesting here is that these scientists, including Paul Davies, Chris Isham, and Hawking have noticed the similarity in reasoning with that of Augustine, who argued for the creation of time against those who had argued for creation in time.[21] In Augustine's opinion, for God to wait, as it were, for a long time and then suddenly create the universe would undercut the unchangeable character of God. Like the criticism of Penrose's model, it would introduce an entirely arbitrary feature into the notion of creation. It would be fascinating to see if other decisions by the scientific community on competing models in quantum cosmology reflect, at least in part, a common feature within the theological community as it, too, wrestles with the meaning of divine creation.

What I am proposing, then, is that if extrascientific factors play a key role in both theory formation and theory choice, it is not a violation of science to suggest that Christians seek to construct a scientifically viable cosmology that at least moves us one step forward in addressing the distinction between the conception of nature and the laws of nature that underlie Big Bang cosmology and a conception of creation as a differentiated unity and a more subtle view of the relation between divine action and the laws of nature. Perhaps then we will be in a better position to raise the question of the meaning and purpose of life in the universe and the eschatological meaning of the cosmic far future, and through this, the foundational notion of God as both creator and redeemer of all that is. If we hold ourselves accountable not only to a robust theological framework but also to the uncompromising demands of empirical science and testable conclusions, I believe we will have achieved a form of progress in religion that reflects the "humble approach" of being tirelessly willing to subject our ideas to radical openness to the discoveries and vision of the universe given us by the natural sciences.

Notes

1. John M. Templeton and Robert L. Herrmann, *The God Who Would Be Known: Revelation of the Divine in Contemporary Science* (Philadelphia: Templeton Foundation Press, 1999).
2. The reason for this is that epistemic humility is built into scientific method: to count as scientific, we must formulate our convictions about nature in terms of theories that are explicitly falsifiable in terms of empirical data, the "tribunal of evidence," i.e., theories that can be publicly tested by anyone with the proper technical expertise regardless of their religious of philosophical convictions. The religious belief that the universe is the creation

of God provides *a* basis for such epistemic humility, since the recognition of the limitless Creator and the limitations of all creation, including our own theories, can justify holding these theories as inherently falsifiable. Indeed, to do otherwise would border on idolatry, the confusion of an icon (which in this case would be the scientific theory as a partial and tentative representation of absolute truth) with divinity itself (i.e., absolute truth). Obviously not all scientists reflect an attitude of humility even if they accept a formal methodology based on epistemic humility. Moreover, there may well be other, nontheistic bases, for epistemic humility, of course. The entailment claimed here is from religious to epistemic humility, and not the converse.

3. In a recent essay, I sought to show how recent discoveries in the mathematics of infinity can enhance the theological conception of God as absolute infinity, emphasizing both how God is revealed and at the same time hidden in "transfinite" characteristics of the created world. See Robert J. Russell, "The God Who Infinitely Transcends Infinity," in *How Large Is God? Voices of Scientists and Theologians,* ed. John Marks Templeton (Philadelphia: Templeton Foundation Press, 1997).

4. Organizations that foster this kind of work include the European Society for the Study of Science and Theology, the center of Theological Inquiry, the Chicago Center for Religion and Science, the American Scientific Association, and the Center for Theology and the Natural Sciences (CTNS). Programs include the decade-long research collaboration between CTNS and the Vatican Observatory and research dimensions of the CTNS Science and Religion Course Program (funded by the John Templeton Foundatin).

5. Carl Sagan, *Cosmos* (New York: Random House, 1980).

6. Ian G. Barbour, *Religion in an Age of Science: The Gifford Lectures, 1989–91,* vol. 1 (San Francisco: Harper & Row, 1990).

7. See comments in Ernan McMullin, "How Should Cosmology Relate to Theology?" in *The Sciences and Theology in the Twentieth Century,* ed. A. R. Peacocke (Notre Dame, Ind.: University of Notre Dame Press, 1891).

8. R. J. Russell, "Finite Creation without a Beginning: The Doctrine of Creation in Relation to Big Bang and Quantum Cosmologies," in *Quantum Cosmology and the Laws of Science: Scientific Perspectives on Divine Action,* ed. Robert John Russell, Nancey Murphy, and C. J. Isham (Vatican City State: Vatican Observatory Publications, and

Berkeley: Center for Theology and the Natural Sciences, 1993, 1996). See also Robert John Russell, "Theological Lessons from Cosmology," in *Cross Currents: Religion and Intellectual Life* 41.3 (Fall 1991) and "Cosmology: Evidence for God or Partner for Theology?" in *Evidence of Purpose: Scientists Discover the Creator,* ed. John Marks Templeton (New York: Continuum, 1994).

9. The notion of purpose was eclipsed by the rise of Darwinian science, but we shall see later in this chapter that it, too, has resurfaced in terms of cosmology.

10. This argument is related to my previous claim that theology provides a possible basis for the epistemic humility in science, since both arise from the contingency of the world—here the ontological contingency of causal connections, previously the epistemic contingency of scientific theories.

11. Technically, the universe must also obey the following condition on its density ρ momentum p: $\rho + 3p/c > 0$, where c is the speed of light.

12. In passing, we should recall that in both Big Bang and its potential replacement, Hoyle's Steady State, there are features that suggest or illustrate the theological view of nature as creation. This suggests the following generalization: there will be some feature in every scientific cosmology that confirms the specific claims of the theology of creation along with the generic claim that the existence of the universe triggers the cosmological argument. It would be interesting to pursue this suggestion in future research.

13. Russell, *Finite Creation without a Beginning.*

14. In some inflationary models, the condition $\rho + 3p/c > 0$ is not met and we simply cannot determine whether or not there was an initial singularity, $t = 0$, and thus whether or not the universe has a finite past. For details, see John D. Barrow, *Impossibility: The Limits of Science and the Science of Limits* (Oxford: Oxford University Press, 1998). For additional technical details, see Edward W. Kolb and Michael S. Turner, *The Early Universe* (Reading, Mass.: Addison-Wesley, 1990).

15. Robert John Russell, "Cosmology, Creation, and Contingency," in *Cosmos as Creation: Theology and Science in Consonance,* ed. Ted Peters (Nashville, Tenn.: Abingdon Press, 1989).

16. Russell, "Cosmology, Creation, and Contingency."

17. Bertrand Russell, "A Free Man's Worship" (1903), in *Mysticism and Logic, and Other Essays* (London: Allen & Unwin, 1963), 41.

18. Steven Weinberg, *The First Three Minutes: A Modern View of the Origin of the Universe* (New York: Basic Books, 1977).

19. Robert John Russell, "Philosophy, Theology and Cosmology: A Fresh Look at Their Interaction," in *Scienza, Filosofia e Teologia di Fronte alla Nascita dell'Universo*, ed. Padre Eligio, Giulio Giorello, Giachino Rigamonti, and Elio Sidoni (Como: Edizioni New Press, 1997), 215–43.

20. For extensive discussion and helpful references, see Ian G. Barbour, *Myths, Models, and Paradigms: A Comparative Study in Science and Religion* (New York: Harper & Row, 1974).

21. Paul Davies, *God and the New Physics* (New York: Simon and Schuster, 1983), 38; C. J. Isham, "Creation of the Universe as a Quantum Process," in *Physics, Philosophy and Theology: A Common Quest for Understanding*, eds. Robert John Russell, William R. Stoeger, S.J., and George V. Coyne, S.J. (Vatican City State: Vatican Obervatory, 1988) 375–408, esp. 387; Stephen W. Hawking, *A Brief History of Time: From the Big Bang to Black Holes* (Toronto: Bantam Books, 1988). For an important critique, see Willem B. Drees, *Beyond the Big Bang: Quantum Cosmology and God* (LaSalle, Ill.: Open Court, 1990), 55–56; for my response to Drees, see Russell et al. (eds.), *Quantum Cosmology and the Laws of Nature*, 316, footnote 77.

3

Beginning to Explore an Infinite Cosmos of Living Worlds

The Amazing Future of the New "Planetary Cosmology"—A Mutual Adventure of Science and the Spiritual Quest

CHARLES L. HARPER, JR.

The greatest obstacle to discovery is not ignorance,
but the illusion of knowledge.

—DANIEL J. BOORSTIN[1]

A little knowledge separates us from God,
Much knowledge brings us back.
One should never be afraid to go too far,
For the truth is beyond.

—MARCEL PROUST[2]

Vision and Overview

Wolfgang Pauli gave a lecture at Columbia in 1958 in which he proposed a somewhat flamboyantly speculative conceptual scheme in particle theory he had been developing with Werner Heisenberg. Pauli's presentation aroused the intellectual ire of the redoubtable pioneer of quantum mechanics, Niels Bohr. The story has it that at the conclusion of the lecture Bohr rose in disapproval. Striding forth, he faced Pauli across the table on which the lectern had been placed, glowering. Pauli glowered back, noting defensively that the idea surely had merit precisely because it seemed so radical. Best of all, Pauli remarked, it was "crazy." "Not crazy enough!" responded Bohr. The two great physicists began to circle each other round the table, Pauli repeating, "Crazy!" Bohr responding, "Not crazy enough!" [3]

To many intelligent, well-educated people, the scientific search for "other life-bearing worlds" may seem to be an odd fascination. In everyday experience, such issues are left mostly to the domain of popular Hollywood fantasy; to take the quest for extraterrestrial life and intelligence seriously does seem a bit crazy. To take it seriously in terms of the future development of religious thought seems truly wacky. However, if we are stretched by science and its futuristic frontiers in directions that seem peculiar, perhaps it is only because the boldness of our imagination fails us—because we as scientists simply are "not crazy enough."

In this chapter, I provide an overview of an area in which the future horizons of scientific discovery are likely to be so astonishing that the "spiritual imagination" may be of assistance. Indeed, planetary science in the twenty-first century may begin to discover aspects of reality first developed in the imaginative vision of the Renaissance philosopher-theologian Giordano Bruno (1548–1600) more than four centuries ago. Neither the science nor the theology of sixteenth-century Europe welcomed Bruno's idea of an "infinite cosmos of living worlds."[4] The new extrasolar planetary science, however, may provide an opportunity over this next century to renew this possibility. It may also hold considerable potential for expanding the horizons of religious thinking onto an infinite cosmic stage of "other worlds." To be successful, however, "planetary cosmology" may require a depth of public enthusiasm and support to justify very large-scale research investment in developing and deploying high-technology space telescope interferometers. Perhaps only a broad popular appreciation of an exploration of wonder, or a "spiritual quest," can provide this depth of sustained support. In this sense, and with the encouragement of extraordinary mutual respect and carefulness, it may be possible for planetary science and religion to work together for common benefit in an ambitious way.

Concerns and Caveats

One should take care to be clear that planetary science and matters of the spirit do not mix easily, naturally, or comfortably. Some people I have met in passing seem to think that planetary science *is* a spiritual quest. In one case, having identified myself as a planetary scientist, a seat neighbor on an airline flight offered what I presumed were intended to be scientifically collegial "insights." These notions were about interplanetary prophecies obtained through "channeling" by a spiritual medium. My "colleague" was enthusiastic about the reception of telepathic communications from higher civilizations on other planets. Wasn't I as well?[5]

Most scientists find such situations awkward. Typically, no amount of conversation is likely to bridge an untraversable gap between a scientific view of the world and a spiritual disposition of gullibility toward fantastical claims. Habits of scientific empiricism can mix well with a sense of wonder and an appreciation of the spiritual dimension of life. However, they do not mix well with a headstrong irrationality toward embracing spiritual exoticism. This tendency is quite common among some spiritually inclined people, especially those of "New Age" sensibilities. In such cases, there really are "two cultures" that cannot meet. Scientists have an important ethical obligation to skepticism. They cannot leap into belief, as do so many people who are not so constrained by a skeptical scientific cast of mind.

Perhaps ironically, in view of the above discussion, I do suspect that the long-term future of planetary science could put us in contact with living beings and possibly even higher civilizations on other planets. If so, undoubtedly this will have considerable theological significance. But I expect that scientists will lead this exploration, not telepathic spirit mediums. What is needed to bridge the gap is to develop a well-informed and nuanced relationship between science and the spiritual quest, in which the interaction works in a constructive manner, respecting the seriousness and depths of the cultures of science and of serious theology, respectively. Mutually informative dialog and high standards of careful and disciplined rationality will be required. Without such care, any appeal to develop a kind of "symbiotic" relationship between science and religion is not likely to be fruitful.

Basic misunderstandings of the relationship between the widely distinct cultures of the sciences and religions are widespread. The discussion also is infused with rich accretions of myth. Only the development of serious, detailed, rigorous, multifaceted, and personally invested dialog can dispel the present deeply ingrained habits of thought that encourage so many highly intelligent people to see science and religion as fundamental enemies. Efforts to promote a constructive, practical, and workable symbiosis should not in any sense distract from the intense rationality, intellectual rigor, and well-demonstrated empiricist methodology of science. It should provide support to defend it—and, if possible, to extend it.

The Cosmic Horizon: Science and Religion

One of the deep lessons of science is that reality is profound, that it can be profoundly surprising, and that one should expect profound surprise as science expands the horizons of our knowledge. Reality may sometimes richly reward great leaps of human imagination, especially if reality is—as physicist Freeman Dyson so felicitously described it—"infinite in all directions."[6] However, reality may not be infinite in all directions; maybe scientific endeavor will end in a nice, neat, closed box—in the "end of science," as some critics have suggested. Nevertheless, the rich experience of scientific progress provides a hope-inspiring hint suggesting that reality may be an "infinite sea of wonder." This concept is also a prejudice of scientific optimists who envision science more as a portal into wonder than as a quest for human cerebral conquest, brought about by reducing the world to a set of mathematical T-shirt formulae.

Perhaps the prospects turn on what we are. Are we humans nothing but a lonely, chance effervescence of oddity within a mindless universe of meaningless matter and energy in motion? Or does our arising in the process of biological evolution on planet Earth reflect, however dimly, the outflow of the creative purposes of a divine mind undergirding the evolving cosmic reality of which we are but a small part? Is the universe "constructed" in such a way that life will arise in a natural process in many places and contexts, given certain suitable circumstances? Could life therefore correspond in some way to an underlying purpose? Are we, as Stuart Kauffman, Christian de Duve, and Paul Davies have suggested, "at home" in the universe?[7] Or is that wishful thinking? Is the stark truth that we are nothing but a freak accident? Do we exist unplanned and alone in an immensity of otherwise lifeless vastness?

Science in time may provide significant constraints on these and similar questions. However, by itself, science may not provide definitive guidance on which view of the universe—mindless/meaningless or mind-derived/meaningful—is more likely to be closer to the truth. Ultimately, the issue may be a formally undecidable metaquestion. However, it should be clear, at least, that if the latter view is plausible for real consideration, then science categorically should be open to considering aspects of reality that are not seeable as parts of the world, but instead constitute what theologians have referred to as the "ground of being." The idea that a divine Mind upholds the cosmos is scientifically an open question. Such a perspective clearly involves the boundaries and limits of science. This therefore offers an important challenge to science, one that science clearly sometimes finds difficult and uncomfortable to face. But it would be unwise not to address the issue. Many people expect that science and matters of the spirit exist necessarily in a seesaw relationship: If one goes up, the other must go down. I believe this view to be incorrect and hope to persuade readers that searching for points of constructive contact *can* be a win-win opportunity.

For science to engage in serious dialog with the possibility of a spiritual view of the world would be an element of scientific progress in ontology, but of course only if such a view corresponded with reality. Yet, on the practical side, it also would provide much-needed support for science in an age in which science is viewed with increasing public distrust and cynicism. Anti-science cynicism is not only part of the perennial complaint of the so-called disenchantment of the world, but it also applies to the common perception that the culture of science is dystopic, or that it lacks sufficient moral vision to provide cultural leadership in areas in which its contribution can be decisively transformative. Such areas would include improving human health and prosperity in developing countries or engaging with the interaction between civilization and nature—dealing with the loss of biodiversity, anthropogenic atmospheric change, disruption of oceanic ecosystems, and so forth. The key is to explore whether it would be possible to inspire large segments of the population to become excited about the potential of science to support a vision of the world that encourages a deep sense of meaning and purpose in life, as well as constructive action to attend to persistent large-scale problems. An appropriately nuanced spiritual vision might also be helpful in addressing problems of human limitation and mortality in the context of increasingly technologically advanced medical science. Finally, such a vision would provide a welcome replacement to the somewhat tired philosophy of Stoical cosmic nihilism, which many intelligent people during the twentieth century came to believe that science supports.

Science as an endeavor supporting a philosophy of cosmic nihilism was perhaps best described by Bertrand Russell. Its pessimism reflects the terrible loss of faith in goodness and progress generated by the devastating and morally horrifying death toll of World War I:

> Such, in outline, but even more purposeless, more void of meaning, is the world which Science presents to our belief. Amid such a world, if anywhere, our ideals henceforth must find a home. That man is the product of causes which have no prevision of the end they were achieving; that his origin, his growth, his hopes and fears, his loves and his beliefs, are but the outcome of accidental collocations of

atoms; that no fire, no heroism, no intensity of thought and feeling, can preserve an individual life beyond the grave; that all the labours of the ages, all devotion, all the inspirations, all the noonday brightness of human genius, are destined to extinction in the vast death of the solar system, and the whole temple of Man's achievement must inevitably be buried beneath the debris of a universe in ruins—all these things, if not quite beyond dispute, are yet so nearly certain, that no philosophy which rejects them can hope to stand. Only within the scaffolding of these truths, only on the firm foundation of unyielding despair, can the soul's habitation be safely built. Brief and powerless is Man's life, on him and all his race the slow, sure doom falls pitiless and dark. . . .[8]

Exactly where the "scaffolding of these truths" might be located in the world of science remains unclear. It seems more to be based on the idea that a spiritual view of the world is generically outmoded by scientific empiricism. This may be the case when such views are primitively anthropocentric. (Consider the notion of God that Soviet propaganda intended to deflate when cosmonauts reported not seeing God in space.) Folk concepts of God may indeed be exploded by the advance of science. Yet a subtler, healthier view will obtain when science can be seen as providing stimuli toward expanding concepts of God. This vision is classically stated in a book by John Bertram Phillips:

> We can never have too big a conception of God, and the more scientific
> knowledge (in whatever field) advances, the greater
> becomes our idea of His vast and complicated wisdom.[9]

Indeed, one of the deep lessons of modern experience is that the adventure of science continually expands the human conceptual horizon, as metaphorically depicted in Figure 1. Science helps us to see new aspects of reality. It encourages us to discard outdated notions. It sharpens, informs, and empowers human thinking. In subtle ways, it can challenge us to expand our sense of place in the universe and therefore impact our spiritual concepts. The planetary science of the twenty-first century clearly will offer a variety of uncomfortable challenges to religions. It may tend to make local traditions *seem* trivial. But by taking the horizon-expanding futuristic challenges seriously, and by addressing them proactively rather than reactively, religions should be able to benefit by engaging with the expanding vista of the scientific view of the world.

FIGURE 1. Woodcut by 19th-century French astronomer Camille Flammarion: *"Un missionnaire du moyen âge raconte qu'il avait trouvé le point où le ciel et la Terre se touchent . . ."* ("A Medieval missionary recounts that he had found the point where the sky and the Earth touch . . .").[10]

The Vista of "Reality": An Expanding Scale of Knowledge

Scientific discoveries in the twentieth century have greatly expanded the scale of human understanding of the situatedness of planet Earth within the astrophysical cosmos. The massive discovery of what Edwin Hubble termed the "realm of the nebulae" placed the Milky Way galaxy within an apparently infinite ocean of other galaxies. Recent counts suggest that the visible universe alone may contain roughly 100 billion galaxies, and each of these, like our Milky Way, may contain roughly similar vast populations of individual stars (mostly like our sun). An approximate sum for the visible universe yields 10^{22} stars. This is a lot of solar worlds!

Scientifically, modern observational cosmology has provided a context for the new cosmic vista, describing an expanding universe that emerged from a "Big Bang" about 15 billion years ago. The total extent of the universe, however, remains unconstrained because it is not limited to the extent of our vision. Much more may exist beyond the limits of transmitted light. Very rough theoretical calculations based on inflation theory suggest that the extent of the total universe might well be greater than 10^{20} times the radius of the visible universe—and, possibly, its extent is infinite. Beyond this, theoretical cosmology has even further radicalized this vista of possibility by adding yet another horizon of possible infinity. Although the theoretical notions involved are highly speculative, they have raised the possibility that our universe is but one among an infinite ensemble of other universes, each arising out of a primordial process of creativity called "eternal inflation." The grandeur of the set of possibilities that cosmology has unveiled is awe inspiring at whatever degree of vastness reality might actually have realized itself.

The progressive discovery of the vastness of the cosmos is one of the greatest accomplishments of physical science. The advance of the human imagination in this direction has a distinguished history. Today it continues vibrantly in the radical cosmological theorizing of Andrei Linde and others.[11] The trend seems to be that the cosmos progressively discloses itself as being far vaster than it previously was considered to be. How far and in what new ways this trend will continue is, of course, unknown.

Modern cosmology has expanded concepts of reality because of the vastness and effectively infinite plurality of galactic worlds it has unveiled. Similarly, modern biology has expanded concepts of the nature of life in the direction of appreciating the indeterministic openness, randomness, and diversity-generating aspects of the rise of life in an evolutionary context. Twenty-first-century planetary science likely will explore both tendencies in some very interesting ways. Planetary science already is beginning to make visible the close reaches of what may be an effectively infinite tableaux of planetary worlds. A major prospect is that science may begin to "see" that at least a few of these are *living* worlds. If so, prospective theoretical advances may begin to comprehend some form of a generalized understanding of how life arises and evolves. This may extend to an effort to comprehend the circumstances under which intelligent life arises in order to determine whether it is frequent or rare and even how its development might extend beyond the current stage of human existence.

If and when such possibilities are realized, science might then have begun to sketch out a new vision of the cosmos as a vast ocean of life-generating, intelligence-bearing, creativity-generating worlds.

Determining whether this is or is not the case will be a challenging scientific task. Also, science may have to develop new conceptual schemes very much in the spirit of Bohr's challenge to Pauli that it is "not crazy enough."

In spiritual terms, the vista of a life-intelligence, creativity-generating universe would provide a wonder-inspiring perspective. Such a vista would challenge religions to comprehend senses of ultimate reality and of meaning sufficient to encompass the whole of the cosmos in all of its vastness and variability. Religions would have to consider ways to "bind together" an understanding and appreciation of this radical cosmic diversity, if and when it becomes known through the lens of science.

This is not an inappropriate task with which to challenge religions. The word "religion" itself is derived from the Latin root *religare,* which means "to weave or bind together" (literally, to "bind back"). Historically, religions have typically functioned as powerful binding agents that have drawn unrelated people together into groups sharing a common set of values and a sense of meaning and spiritual purpose. They have played especially large-scale socially transformative roles by catalyzing transitions from tribal to supratribal social groupings—binding together smaller groups of kin-linked peoples into national and supranational scales by creating common cultural superidentities that transcended smaller ethnic boundaries. A major problem has been that the very success of this binding process has been to create particularly sharp and large-scale boundaries of difference between one religious/cultural system and another.

As the development of cosmology begins to generate widespread public understanding of the cosmos as an infinite diversity of living worlds, an important task for religions will be to interpret and communicate the meaning of this prospective "new" cosmos in constructive ways. Generally one can hope that such interpretations will develop many facets of a common vision that will value and embrace the virtues of openness, humility, and wonder in recognition of the lavish infinity of divine creativity. Such virtues seem appropriate to a progressive "unveiling" of the created order in what might well be an endless cascade of surprises.

The challenge to science, as well as to religion and theology, is to help to create a large-scale regard for the vastness of reality and the limitedness of our concepts. This essentially represents a recognition of a proper sense of epistemological humility, which this book explores as a basis for mutual adventure in science and theology. An appreciation of epistemological humility is theologically vital. It recognizes that God is likely to be far more complex than the conceptual models and analogies we are familiar with and that are suited to our limited frame of reference. Epistemological humility also goes hand-in-hand with the sense of wonder and open adventure that science at its best draws on and cultivates.

The Future of Planetary Science

The future of planetary science may offer much to stimulate the senses of humility and wonder. The horizon of exploration for the field in the long term may encompass a vast universe of life in an infinity of forms, an intrinsically humbling prospect. For example, it is not unreasonable to expect that at least some of these forms of life might have far deeper insight into the meaning and significance of reality than we humans do. To such beings, our intellectual abilities might seem like those of an insect.

Sir Isaac Newton (1642–1727) was the first scientist to provide humanity with a way of thinking about the night sky that correctly explained the motion of the moon and the planets. He also explained the ebb and flow of tides. His scientific work illuminated the fundamental principles of motion, inertia, and the force of gravity. It showed why and how apples fell from trees using an identical method that predicted accurately the return of comets. Newton towers as perhaps the greatest scientific pioneer in human history; many across the ages have been awed by his accomplishments. Yet, as an old man reflecting back on his life, this prince of scientists made a memorable remark of great humility:

> I do not know what I may appear to the world; but to myself I seem to have been only like a boy, playing on the sea-shore, and diverting myself, in now and then finding a smoother pebble or a prettier shell than ordinary, whilst the great ocean of truth lay all undiscovered before me.[12]

The story of wonder that science continues to unveil has expanded tremendously since Newton. Indeed, planetary science is now perhaps the preeminent sector in the scientific enterprise for which Newton's "great ocean of truth" looms before us most strikingly in terms of what remains to be explored. What we have observed and studied thus far in any degree of detail is only one solar system existing among an infinity of others. About these worlds we know next to nothing—the great ocean of truth looms undiscovered before planetary scientists in a very real way!

How far might that ocean extend? What dimensions of reality might it include? It is useful to cultivate a creative tension between the proper empirical skepticism of science and an openness to a radical sense of expectant wonder. Carl Sagan—certainly a popular, well-known skeptic—provided a noteworthy, moving, and extreme example of this expectant sense of wondering in his popular book *Cosmos*:

> There is an idea—strange, haunting, evocative—one of the most exquisite conjectures in science or religion. It is entirely undemonstrated; it may never be proved. But it stirs the blood. There is, we are told, an infinite hierarchy of universes, so that an elementary particle, such as an electron, in our universe would, if penetrated, reveal itself to be an entirely closed universe. Within it, organized into the local equivalent of galaxies and smaller structures, are an immense number of other, much tinier elementary particles, which are themselves universes at the next level, and so on forever—an infinite downward regression, universes within universes, endlessly. And upward as well. Our familiar universe of galaxies and stars, planets and people, would be a single elementary particle in the next universe up, the first step of another infinite regress. This is the only religious idea I know that surpasses the endless number of infinitely old cycling universes in Hindu cosmology. What would those other universes be like?[13]

The Backdrop of the Visible Cosmos

Scientific cosmology has pioneered a vast expansion of understanding of the scale of the cosmos over the course of the twentieth century. This largely has been through its ability to image galaxies. Wherever telescopes look, they have mapped out what appears to be an infinite ocean of these vast gravitational agglomerations of stars. The galactic field observed telescopically "sees" back along the so-called light cone, which corresponds to the view backward in time along the tracks of photons emitted in the past. What is "seen" at greater and greater distances corresponds to a record of the distant cosmos at times increasingly longer and longer ago: a progressively unfolded history of cosmic evolution across a transmission distance of 12–15 billion light-years (LY) since the Big Bang. Recent observations have begun to image galaxies even out to very high red-shift distances probing the early epoch of galaxy formation in excess of 90 percent of the age of the universe.

The oldest and most distant image is that of the primordial cosmic fireball, the so-called *Face of God* map of the temperature variation structure of the 2.7-degree cosmic microwave background (CMB) radiation obtained by the differential microwave radiometer (DMR) of the National Aeronautics and Space Administration's (NASA) Cosmic Background Explorer (COBE) satellite. These images, shown in Figures 2a and 2b, represent the last scattering surface when the universe became transparent to light and cool enough for neutral (nonionized) hydrogen atoms to form about 300,000 years after the Big Bang. With this farthest possible image, the science of astronomy now has brought essentially the entire visible universe into view. This feat is an outstanding accomplishment—one of the most magnificent of twentieth-century science.

Visible Stars, Invisible Planets

By contrast with the massive success of galactic cosmology, efforts to envision the cosmos of planetary systems remain in their earliest infancy. We are only now beginning to detect the existence of exoplanets orbiting nearby stars, as discussed in the next section. The domain of successful exploration to date is located within a relatively minuscule sphere of view less than 200 LY in radius. (Note that our Milky Way galaxy is itself roughly 5×10^4 LY in radius, whereas the visible universe has a radius of approximately 15×10^9 LY.)

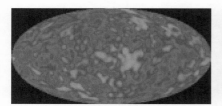

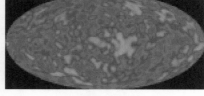

FIGURE 2A   FIGURE 2B

FIGURES 2A AND 2B. Full sky maps exhibiting variation on a parts-in-10^5 scale in temperature of the CMB radiation. The initial report of the CMB anisotropy based on data collected during the first two years of operation can be seen in Figure 2a. Figure 2b shows the CMB variation structure containing the superior set of a full four years' worth of data. *References: Figure 2a—NASA COBE Slide Set, Slide 28; Figure 2b—NASA Goddard Space Flight Center and the COBE Science Working Group.*[14]

Planets, of course, are not luminous objects like stars. They reflect light only from their central star and glow faintly by thermal emission. Thus, the luminosity of planets is extremely small compared with that of their parent star, even at the most favorable wavelengths. Also, the requirements for resolving the dim planetary source with respect to the vastly more luminous parent star are exceedingly demanding. Even the most dreamily ambitious prospects for futuristic space interferometry (discussed below) do not conceive of the possibility of imaging Earth-like planets (say, with not less than four pixels) at distances in excess of about 500 LY. This represents only a very small part of our galactic neighborhood, as shown in Figure 3.

The number of stars in a sphere of radius 500 LY centered in our solar system is roughly 3 million. This represents a sampling of only about 30 out of each million stars within the $\sim 10^{11}$ stellar population of the Milky Way galaxy. Although this is a very small fraction, in absolute numbers it represents quite a substantial sampling of stars. Therefore, with the foreseeable technology, a substantial sampling of planetary worlds could be studied by imaging techniques in our solar neighborhood. Very substantial resources will be required to open up this vista by creating extremely powerful interferometric space observatories.

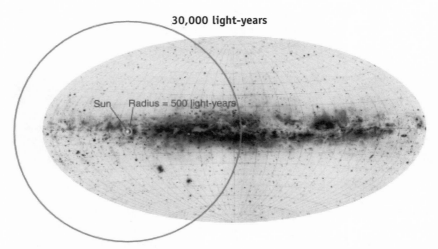

FIGURE 3. A 500 LY (0.15 kiloparsec [kpc]) radius sphere sized against a map of the Milky Way Galaxy, with the sun located at a galactocentric radius of 8.5 kpc. The number of stars within a sphere of radius 500 LY surrounding the sun is roughly 3 million. *Conceptual image courtesy of the European Space Agency's (ESA) GAIA project.*[15]

The Beginning: Detecting Invisible Exoplanets by Their Gravitational Effects and Light-Obscuring Transits

Research in planetary science in the twenty-first century should be magnificent based on recent advances in the discovery of extrasolar planetary systems by indirect methods. Astrometric evidence for a very-short-period (4.23 days) exoplanet orbiting a nearby star, 51 Pegasi B, was first made public by two Swiss astronomers, Michel Mayor and Didier Queloz, in October 1995. The initial evidence for this historic discovery is shown in Figure 4a. Within days of this announcement, two San Francisco-based astronomers, Geoff Marcy and Paul Butler at the Lick Observatory, combined the velocity variations for many orbits of 51 Pegasi into a single orbital period, as shown in Figure 4b. The saga of this exciting initial discovery in planetary astronomy has inspired several recent book-length popular accounts of the early evolution of the field.[16]

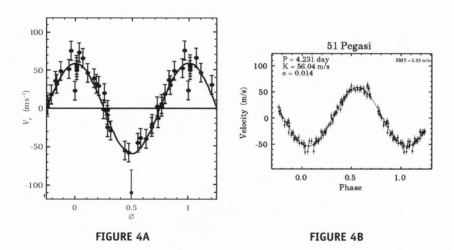

FIGURE 4A   FIGURE 4B

FIGURES 4A AND 4B.   Figure 4a shows the discovery data (radial velocity curve) for the first exoplanet inferred to be in orbit around the sun-like star 51 Pegasi by Michel Mayor and Didier Queloz. The solid line fit to the periodic Doppler velocity shifts in the star implies that it is orbited by a planet at least half as massive as Jupiter. *Reprinted with permission from Michel Mayor and* Nature *(Copyright 1995 by Macmillan Magazines Limited).* Figure 4b shows confirmation of the velocity variation of 51 Pegasi from Geoff Marcy and Paul Butler at the Lick Observatory obtained within days of the discovery announcement. This graph shows the velocity variations for many orbits combined into a single orbital period. *Reprinted with permission from Geoffrey W. Marcy and R. Paul Butler.*[17]

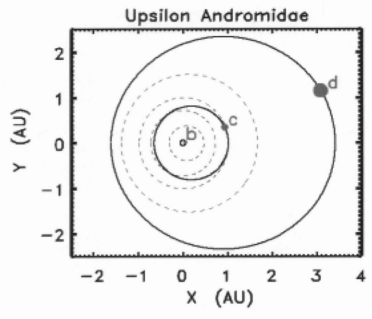

FIGURE 5. The first discovery of a system of three detected planets orbiting a sun-like star, Upsilon Andromidae. *Reprinted with permission from Geoffrey W. Marcy and R. Paul Butler.*[18]

At the time that the main portions of this chapter were being written in April 1999, the tally stood at 21 confirmed exoplanet detections, all obtained by indirect astrometric methods that measure periodic stellar Doppler variations due to motion of the star around an off-center center of mass. This includes the first-ever discovery of a system of three detected planets orbiting a sun-like star, Upsilon Andromidae, as shown in Figure 5.

At the time of initial editing of this chapter in November 1999, the first semidirect detection had just been reported, as shown in Figure 6. The method of detection involved observing repeated periodic dimming in the luminosity of a star, HD 209458, caused by orbital occultations across its disk by the planet.[19] Also, claims are being debated over a possible first direct detection of a planet's reflected light—of a Jovian-type planet orbiting the star τ (Tau) Boötis.[20] Planet detections also are now being reported by an observational team using the method of detecting light-curve deviations in gravitational microlensing events.[21] The pace of detections is accelerating rapidly, while a wide range of new theoretical insights also are being developed. The field of extrasolar planetary science clearly will be a boom industry in research in the twenty-first century.[22] By December 1999, another semidirect detection was reported based on an apparent signature of Doppler-separated reflected light originating from a giant planet orbiting τ Boötis.[23] At the time of final editing of this chapter in April 2000, at least 35 exoplanets had been detected.[24] New technologies are being rapidly developed for detecting exosolar planets by observing their influences on the light emitted from the stars they orbit. For example, the European Space Agency's (ESA) GAIA project is expected to detect in excess of 10,000 exoplanets out to 500 LY (see Figure 3).

The explosion of discoveries of exoplanets since 1995 has begun a scientific process that is beginning to confirm the theologically inspired prediction of multiple worlds made more than four centuries ago by Giordano Bruno (see the discussion below and also Note 4). It may take additional centuries for science to examine Bruno's further prediction that these other planetary systems would be inhabited by intelligent beings. However, for now, science seems to be on track with the general trend of Bruno's idea that the cosmos should contain a dispersed infinity of worlds rather than simply one central world as understood in the Ptolomeic cosmology.

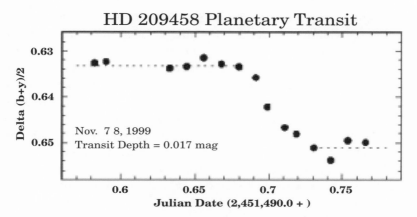

FIGURE 6. The first semidirect detection was reported in November 1999. The photometry data show ingress of the planet orbiting HD 209458 across the stellar disk of its parent star, decreasing its luminosity. *Reference: NASA Science News, Marshall Space Flight Center.*[25]

Science sometimes plods where the human imagination leaps. And, of course, imagination is a vital part of science itself. Albert Einstein once said, "I am enough of an artist to draw freely upon my imagination. Imagination is more important than knowledge. Knowledge is limited. Imagination encircles the world."[26] Perhaps only our descendants will have the privilege of knowing whether a fraction of the "other" planetary worlds in our galactic neighborhood are life bearing. At present, we can only imagine that they exist. However, the accelerating pace of technological innovation in astronomy provides a basis for optimism that such astonishing potential discoveries might appear on a timescale of decades rather than centuries. In large part, this may depend on the willingness of the tax-paying public to support innovative frontier planetary science research in an aggressive way.[27]

The Future: Imaging Exoplanets with Interferometric Hypertelescopes

The future of the development of planetary science into planetary cosmology will depend on how quickly major initiations are put in place to develop the technology of ultra-high-resolution interferometric telescopes and apply this technology very ambitiously in space. Interferometry is necessary to move from detection to imaging. Only imaging can open up the new world vista of exoplanets to our study. The process of advancing the field will be very challenging and very expensive.

Several such projects are under way. Antoine Labeyrie of the Collège de France and Observatoire de Haute-Provence (OHP) has been a primary proponent of the prospect that arrays of very large telescopes might become integrated to operate interferometrically.[28] In 1995, the year that Mayor and Queloz discovered 51 Pegasi B at OHP, Labeyrie introduced the idea of the "hyperinterferometer," or "densified-pupil diluted telescope." He had found a way to circumvent the widely accepted "golden rule" that an imaging interferometer had to have an exit pupil identical to the entrance aperture. Similar to a telescope with a multihole mask on top (a Fizeau interferometer), such a system is thought to be useless when highly diluted because of the presence of a wide diffractive halo in the image. Although these obstacles appeared to rule out the possibility of producing direct images with giant diluted arrays, large optical arrays limited to a few apertures *are* usable with beam-splitter systems that combine the beams. Labeyrie realized that

the flaw in the rule had been to assume that non-Fizeau-beam com-
biners could not provide direct images if they included many apertures.
Images, however, can be generated if the pattern of subpupil centers
does not vary from the entrance to the exit of the optical train. Consequently, large space-based hyperinterferometers should make it possible to produce very-high-resolution images of exoplanets.

Projects that Labeyrie is involved with include both ground- and
space-based hypertelescopes. A ground-based system of intermediate
size, the Grand Interféromètre à deux Télescopes (GI2T), was built by
Labeyrie and his colleagues at Calern in the Southern Alps over the last
few decades. Recently upgraded, the GI2T now collects visible and infrared (IR) data. Of interest now is the extension toward more apertures for obtaining high-resolution images of increasing quality. The
first use for such images will be to monitor stellar surfaces and their
variable activity caused by accretion disks and polar jets.

The CARLINA (named after an alpine flower) ground-based
interferometer, shown in Figure 7, is a possible precursor for space-
based hypertelescopes of 200-1,000 m. Optical interferometers as large
as a few hundred thousand kilometers (km) also will be possible in the

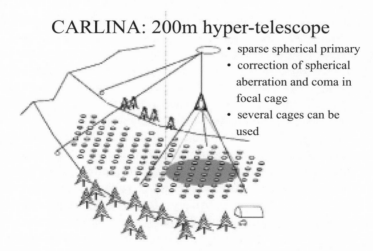

CARLINA: 200m hyper-telescope

- sparse spherical primary
- correction of spherical aberration and coma in focal cage
- several cages can be used

FIGURE 7. The CARLINA ground-based hypertelescope is a precursor for possible large 200-1,000 m space-based hypertelescopes. *Reprinted with permission
from Antoine Labeyrie, OHP.*[29]

FIGURE 8. The larger 1-10 km ground-based OVLA uses dozens of mobile 1.5 m telescopes. *Reprinted with permission from Antoine Labeyrie and Olivier Lardière, OHP.* [30]

future. Such size offers resolution in the nano-arcsecond range, which is enough to resolve detail at the surface of a 20 km neutron star within hundreds of parsecs (pc). Telescopes having a spherical primary mirror and a corrector for spherical aberration also can have a wide field. In space, this can be achieved in the form of the "Moth Eye Hypertelescope." As calculated for CARLINA, two-mirror correctors of spherical aberration and coma can be as small as one percent of the mirror size if the primary focal ratio is larger than F/1.8. Thus, a diluted bubble mirror can be used with a number of focal stations, each containing a corrector and a pupil-densifier. The cost-effectiveness increases with the number of stations because each segment of the primary mirror serves simultaneously for several independent observations on different objects. Also, in space the segments would not have to move and thus would require no ion thrusters, only cool devices such as small solar sails providing enough thrust for station keeping.

The 1-10 km ground-based Optical Very Large Array (OVLA) is another OHP project. It uses dozens of mobile 1.5 m telescopes. Figure 8 shows a prototypical telescope of 1.52 m for the OVLA.

In addition, a major ground-based interferometry project, currently in the planning phase, is the "Atacama Large Millimeter Array" (ALMA). The ALMA is a six-mile-diameter, 64-dish, millimeter (mm)-wavelength array proposed for installation in the Chilean Andes sometime after 2006. The ALMA will have the capability to image structure in planet-forming disks around nascent stars.[31]

Another advanced project is a very-high-resolution ground-based telescope—the OverWhelmingly Large Telescope (OWL), shown in the conceptual image in Figure 9. The OWL would have a 100-meter (m) mirror array with 10 times the collecting area of all existing professional telescopes put together. It is currently under study at the European Southern Observatory (ESO). If constructed, it will dwarf all existing telescopes in collecting power, including the ESO's ground-based Very Large Telescope (VLT), now under construction in Chile (a similar VLT is being built in Hawaii to augment the Keck system).[32]

European initiatives in futuristic concept planning for large space-based interferometers include the 100 m Exo-Earth Discoverer space

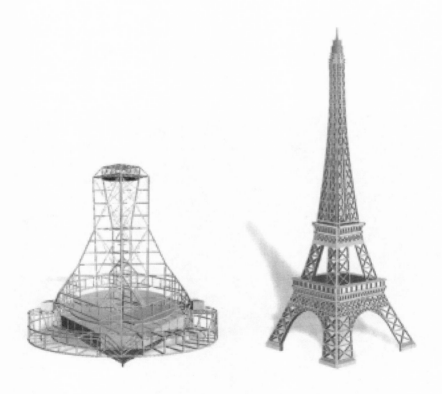

FIGURE 9.　The OWL's support structure would rival the Eiffel Tower in size. *Reproduced by permission. ©1999,* Astronomy *magazine, Elisabeth Rowan and ESO.*[33]

interferometer, shown in Figure 10, being designed by Labeyrie and colleagues. The expected advantages of hypertelescopes are demonstrated when the number of apertures is large enough (at least nine). With 36 elements, for example, and a fully densified exit pupil, the hypertelescope can be equipped with a coronagraph to remove light from a star's image and search associated planets. This is of particular interest at 10-IR wavelengths where the planet/star contrast improves about 1,000 times. The image obtained allows an efficient separation of the zodiacal light contamination.

A futuristic 150 km version of the Exo-Earth Discoverer, the Exo-Earth Imager, is based on the same technologies, but is expected to provide high-resolution images of nearby exoplanets to the degree that features such as green spots of vegetation would be detectable, as shown in Figures 11a and 11b. This new class of interferometer will have a sparse array of many mirrors forming a directly usable image. The principle is applicable to the 150 km array size required for obtaining a 30 × 30-pixel portrait of an Earth-like exoplanet at 10 LY (3 pc).

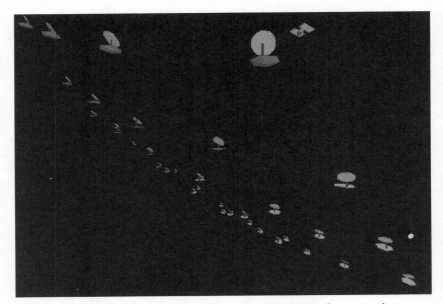

FIGURE 10.   The 100 m Exo-Earth Discoverer space interferometer has coronagraphic capabilities for observing exoplanets. *Reprinted with permission from Antoine Labeyrie, OHP.*[34]

The Vital Role of NASA

The most hopeful possibilities for realizing such hyperambitious (and hypercostly) space interferometry projects are through the direct support and international leadership of NASA. However, strategic reform of NASA's mission to embrace such technologically adventurous opportunities may require an expression of popular will in the United States. This is where a serious constructive rapprochement between the worldviews of science and religion in America really could make a vital difference. Religiously sensitive people should be *excited* about the expanding vision of the cosmos offered by planetary cosmology.

The space agency is fortunate in having a world-class visionary in its top leadership position. Dan Goldin is an articulate, passionate, and tireless advocate for solar system astrobiology and for aggressive technological innovation toward building the kinds of huge, space-based interferometric telescope arrays necessary to image exoplanets, discussed in the next section. At present, however, the strategic future of the space agency in pursuing this vision remains unclear.

Organizationally, NASA suffers from being bound within the world of the civil service such that its direction is most powerfully tied to the

 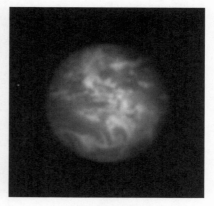

FIGURE 11A   FIGURE 11B

FIGURES 11A AND 11B. Earth (left) and simulated image of Earth (right) as it would be seen from a distance of 10 LY (3 pc) with the futuristic 150 km Exo-Earth Imager space hypertelescope. The simulation assumes 150 mirrors (each 3 m in diameter) arrayed in three concentric rings with a total diameter of 150 km and a single exposure lasting 30 minutes to freeze the 24-hour rotation of the planet. *Reprinted with permission from Antoine Labeyrie, OHP.* [35]

servicing of politically useful tasks. Consequently, it does not appear to be able to extricate itself from a future heavily mortgaged to spend well over half of its annual budgets on the Space Shuttle and Space Station projects. Both of these projects are scientifically uninteresting when considered on a cost-effectiveness basis.[36] Despite its visionary leadership, NASA's future may remain in the control of political interests motivated principally by the political benefits of sustaining large, stable cash flows to contractor beneficiaries. So it is not clear whether NASA will be able to plan and execute a major series of space interferometry projects at a financial scale sufficient to allow imaging of Earth-like planets to a distance of 500 LY (see Figure 3) within the next few decades.

NASA Plans for Imaging Exosolar Planets by Interferometry

NASA's Origins Program contains a ramped series of increasingly technologically sophisticated and astronomically powerful space telescope missions to develop the frontier of interferometry. These are divided chronologically into four groups, depicted in Figures 12 through 16 and discussed by category below:[37]

1. Space-based precursor missions include the Hubble Space Telescope (HST), shown in Figure 12, deployed by a NASA Space Shuttle in 1990. A subsequent Shuttle mission in 1993 serviced HST and recovered its full capability; a second successful servicing mission took place in 1997. Subsequent servicing missions through 2002 will add additional capabilities to HST, which observes the universe at ultraviolet, visual, and near-IR wavelengths. Other new and scheduled NASA space observatories include the Chandra X-ray Observatory (CXO), named in honor of the late Indian-American Nobel laureate Subrahmanyan Chandrasekhar and operated for NASA at the Harvard-Smithsonian Center for Astrophysics. Chandra was deployed from a Shuttle and boosted into a high-Earth orbit in July 1999. This observatory will observe such objects as black holes, quasars, and high-temperature gases throughout the x-ray portion of the electromagnetic spectrum. Finally, the Space InfraRed Telescope Facility (SIRTF) is scheduled to be launched in late 2001 to fill in an important gap in wavelength coverage—the thermal IR—not available from the ground.[38]

FIGURE 12. The Hubble Space Telescope. *Reference: NASA Origins Program.*[39]

2. First-generation missions serve as technological pathfinders to the second generation and will require new technologies currently under development. These developments include optics much larger but much lighter than those in HST and a variety of technologies for stabilizing interferometric arrays and integrating their signals. The two planned missions include the Space Interferometry Mission (SIM) shown in concept in Figure 13, expected to launch somewhere around 2005. (Note that before SIM, a precursor mission called Space Technology 3 [ST3] will be launched to demonstrate interferometry in space; ST3 was first named New Millennium Interferometer and then Deep Space 3.) Although not an interferometer, the Next Generation Space Telescope (NGST), shown in concept in Figure 14, will be a part of this effort.

FIGURE 13. Conceptual image of the Space Interferometry Mission (SIM). *Reference: NASA Origins Program.*[40]

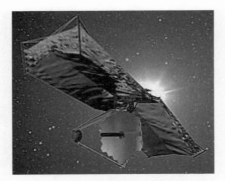

FIGURE 14.   Conceptual image of the Next Generation Space Telescope. *Courtesy of TRW Space & Electronic Systems Group and the Goddard Space Flight Center.*[41]

3. Second-generation missions at present consist of only one plan, for the Terrestrial Planet Finder (TPF), shown in the concept schematic in Figure 15. The ESA has plans for a similar mission, called *Darwin*. Both are still at the planning stage, and may eventually be merged. ESA has just completed an industrial study of *Darwin*, and NASA's Jet Propulsion Laboratory recently announced that several different design (industrial and academic) teams will begin to plan TPF, which is expected to launch somewhere around 2012.[42]

4. The prospective, super-high-technology third-generation missions at present consist of only a vision for bringing the results learned from earlier-stage efforts into a new set of highly ambitious efforts.

FIGURE 15.   Conceptual image of the Terrestrial Planet Finder. *Courtesy of TRW Space & Electronic Systems Group and the Jet Propulsion Laboratory.*[43]

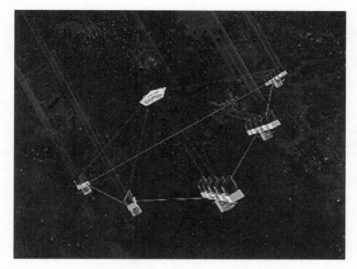

FIGURE 16. Conceptual image of the Planet Imager. *Reference: NASA Origins Program.*[44]

The only such mission currently in rough concept stage is the Planet Imager (PI), shown in Figure 16.

Are Other "Earth-Like" Worlds Likely?

Will it be possible to constrain the question of how frequently conditions in other solar systems resemble ours in terms of various specific steps of likeness? These might include general features such as being "Earth-like" in the sense of (1) having liquid oceans and a protective atmosphere over at least a billion years, (2) being life bearing, and (3) being intelligent life bearing.

Consider the first factor, which has the advantage that it can in principle be determined by large-scale space-based interferometry. How unusual are planets with liquid oceans and protective atmospheres around stars older than a billion years? If this factor is smaller than 10^{-2}, the available sample of ~3 million stars may be sufficiently robust to provide a useful broad distribution of Earth-like planetary worlds existing in the cosmos. This, of course, would not provide insights into exceedingly rare and interesting worlds, but it might be able to satisfy some basic questions about the ubiquity or nonubiquity of life similar to ours throughout the cosmos in planetary contexts.

Beyond such considerations, it remains to be shown that the locus of the solar system in the Milky Way galaxy is not highly selective. This assumption, however, seems reasonable based on what we know about the typical galactic environment. Thus, it may not be overly unrealistic to expect a reasonable probability that a survey of the solar neighborhood will be representative of common sites in most galaxies throughout the cosmos.

One way to consider the possible adequacy of the potential sampling domain is to consider the question in terms of a dilemma comparing the Copernican Principle and the Anthropic Principle. The Copernican Principle represents a working assumption that our particular astrophysical location is likely to be average rather than special. Applied in the present context as a working hypothesis, this would suggest that the conditions of our solar system may be typical rather than rare and therefore that a survey of our stellar neighborhood might observe solar systems broadly similar to ours. In this view, Earthlike planets would be expected to be common.

While it is clear that our sun is a typical star, the question of whether our planetary system is also typical remains very much an open one. Most of the observations of exoplanets thus far indicate conditions very much different from those in our solar system. (But it is clear that strong observational selection is biasing the sample.) It may be that the type of solar system we inhabit is quite rare, especially if the conditions in our solar system were especially conducive to the evolution of life. Clear possibilities in this vein could include an absence of giant gas planets near the area of the "habitability zone" (where water is found primarily in liquid form). Another might have to do with a lesser average impact rate on planets due to efficient scattering of icy planetessimals early in the formation era of the solar system. (This took place in our solar system with the formation of the gas-rich giant planets Jupiter, Saturn, Uranus, and Neptune in the outer region of the system.[45])

Such considerations as these and the second factor, whether an exoplanet is life bearing, demonstrate that much depends on what specifically is meant by the term "Earth-like." To the degree that this refers to issues such as the existence of life, or of intelligent life, or of technologically intelligent life, then the Copernican Principle generically is likely to be challenged by Anthropic selectivity constraints. The Anthropic Principle states that the condition of being an intelligent technological observer of the universe (and asking questions about the universe) is intrinsically highly selective. It may incorporate conditions of very low generic probability, both in consideration of circumstances within the universe and also possibly in terms of specific general aspects of the universe as a whole (for example, the exact values of particle masses and interaction couplings, nuclear reactions such as the triple alpha combination to form carbon, cosmological states such as closeness to the critical density at the early scale of density fluctuations leading to galaxy formation, chemical features such as the existence of RNA and DNA, properties of water, and so forth).[46]

In the context of the present discussion, we are concerned with the former issue—specifically, the case of Earth and the conditions associated with the evolution of life on it. It is clear that generically these conditions are highly peculiar. The issue of how Earth has sustained its broad climatic stability or habitability over 4,500-million years is not yet a solved problem. Over the history of the Earth, the solar luminosity has risen by more than 25 percent, whereas the average climate has remained relatively constant. The rough stability of Earth's climate over geological time is known as the "Goldilocks Problem." Research in this area represents complicated interdisciplinary efforts. Eventually, it should illuminate the general question of the degree of rarity of Earth-like situations. At present, initial indications seem to suggest that very long-lived Earth-like habitability conditions may be quite unusual.[47]

In regard to the third factor of an exoplanet being Earth-like and intelligent life bearing, other conditions indicate the possibly extreme unusualness of Earth-like conditions. It has been pointed out by Stanley Jaki that the highly peculiar and improbable conditions of the formation of the Earth-moon system (by giant impact) are related to the stability of the Chandler wobble of the Earth's pole of rotation and could be interpreted to modify the Drake equation by a factor possibly as small as one in a million. (The Drake equation provides a formalism for estimating the likelihood of the existence of other scientifically and technologically advanced civilizations in the galaxy.) Jaki also has emphasized the possibility that the development of science itself has very highly contingent aspects, which he interprets as an improbability factor to be added into the Drake equation.[48]

One also may consider other highly contingent aspects of the geological history of the planet that clearly were important for evolution of life as we know it. A particularly good example is the KT boundary impact event at Chixulub, Yucatan, which caused the demise of the age of giant reptiles and opened niches for the evolution of the mammals.

Another very recently developed perspective involving highly contingent geological events is the implication of "snowball Earth" cycles, one of which appears to be closely related to the Cambrian explosion of life about 540 million years ago.[49] Another geological event (possibly related to human evolution) is the initiation of the current on-off Ice Age climate cycle initiated about 2 million years ago. This likely was related to the tectonic closure of the Isthmus of Panama, as well as to a trend of carbon dioxide drawdown from the atmosphere from increased global rock weathering, mostly caused by upthrust of the Himalayan mountain belt.[50]

When one considers the way that highly contingent events affect the outcome of evolution, it is easy to see why the existence of humans cannot be seen as the result of a specific teleological plan or design. One prominent evolutionary biologist, John Maynard Smith, has suggested that the history of life would have been radically altered if only one trilobite had been moved on the seabed by one foot. Note that this is the evolutionary equivalent of the butterfly effect in the chaotic theory of weather. However, it is well known that the chaotic unpredictability of weather does not imply that climate (the long-term average of the weather) cannot be predicted. The phenomenon of randomness at one level of behavior or description does not imply an absence of regular specific or probabilistic predictability at another. This is the case with planetary fluid dynamics and may apply to evolutionary history as well.

This question is a very vibrant one in the current debate as to whether the evolutionary process can be described in terms of the word "progress." Advocates on the positive side of the question have cited such phenomena as ecological niche diversification in species count trends, morphological co-evolution in tectonically isolated domains, and "arms race" encephalization trends indicating the generic value of intelligence in adaptation.[51] These issues have to do with the trajectory of a biosphere once it comes into being. More generally, advocates of the ubiquity of life's arising in the first place, given certain broad conditions, can point to the appearance of life at the earliest recognizable epoch in Earth history. This epoch is studied from the earliest known, 3,800-million-year-old sedimentary deposits preserved at Isua in southwestern Greenland. Isotopic studies of reduced carbon grains in these metasediments imply that these were deposited biogenically.[52]

In the context of considering the commonness or uncommonness of Earth-like planetary conditions around stars, the radical contingency or improbability of the Earth's specific path history may not provide a strong limiting factor on the likelihood of (very) broadly analogous conditions existing elsewhere under quite different circumstances. In summary, we really do not have a good understanding of the degree to which aspects of highly specific peculiarity in the history of terrestrial evolution constrain the generic improbability of life (or of intelligent life). One element of a highly contingent, highly improbable path within a very large set of diverse alternative possible paths that sum together to form a set (the "set of life" or of "intelligent life") may in itself be either probable or improbable. We will not know about the extent of living worlds in our universe until we engage seriously in the great scientific adventure of learning through empirical research. But the degree to which this research is supported will depend in large part on whether the public is enthusiastic or not. In the remainder of this essay, I will argue that science and religion can and should work together to build the broad public enthusiasm that the future of planetary cosmology deserves.

Can Science and Religion Work Together to Advance the New Planetary Cosmology?

Twenty-first century space science represents the greatest, most profound scientific adventure ever. It has the potential to open up a magnificent new window on the cosmos. If the necessary technological advances are developed ambitiously, in many readers' lifetimes we may begin to be able to see the closer reaches of an infinite sea of planetary worlds, many of which may be life bearing. The potential to generate broad-based and long-lived public interest and enthusiasm in this adventure will require that people be persuaded that it means something to them.

Science by itself has difficulty in providing such a context. The typical person is confused and uninspired by the pessimistic and desacralized matrix of meaning provided by some scientific popularizers, who may function as severe critics of the great religious/spiritual traditions that have supplied purpose and vision to people over many centuries. However, fundamental conflict between science and religion is unnecessary. While no means simple, a constructive transformation of the cultural and intellectual parameters of the science-religion relationship is possible. Progress in this area offers great potential for mutual benefit to both the sciences and religious traditions. This effort can be misunderstood easily, so clarity is required. In terms of the adventure of space science, the impartial objective is to find ways for people to find excitement and inspiration, which would include aspects of both a scientific and a spiritual quest, without in any way mixing together the roles of either science or religion in inappropriate ways. The key is to explore constructive interaction, mutuality, complementarity, and symbiosis, rather than fusion in any sense.

This potentially is very good news. It opens up the possibility of drawing on strong and wide-ranging motivational support for the future of space science as a profound movement in the history of human experience and exploration. For the scientific community, the challenge of learning how to embrace the interpretive spiritual task to link science with an extended context of meaning is well worthwhile. Such a venture, of course, could be pursued only with a very carefully nuanced approach. Working cautiously and in concert, science and religion together might be able to explore commonality sufficient to elevate the human spirit. This would represent a major accomplishment for both planetary science and for theology. However, to be successful, a perennial trap must be overcome.

The Trap of "Whiggish" Dialectic

In a very important book on the history of discourse over the "flat Earth," Jeffrey Burton Russell has documented the harm done by persistent myths of conflict that have infused the perception of religion within the culture of science:

> . . . fallacies or "myths" . . . take on a life of their own, creating a dialectic with each other and eventually making a "cycle of myths" reinforcing one another. For example, it has been shown that . . . the flat earth fallacy . . . is part of the "cycle" that includes the Dark Ages, the Black Legend, the opposition of Christianity to science, and so on. The cycle becomes so embedded in our thought that it helps to form our worldview in ways that are impervious to evidence.[53]

Many contemporary scientists who hold a strong aversion to religion can be seen to understand themselves within the context of a "Whig" interpretation of science that is intrinsically antithetical to religion. The Whiggish identity *prima facie* is very attractive to scientists. It lionizes the scientific role on a stage where the story of progress is enacted. On this stage of the imagination, the drama of history is a dialectic between good and evil in which the forces of light and reason (science) do battle against the forces of darkness and irrationality (religion) in order to save the world from itself and establish a reign of empiricism. The heroic narrative is framed as the progressive advance of the light of secular scientific reason out of the darkness of religious superstition. As the story goes, the forces of light and reason have won. Yet constant vigilance is required lest irrationality reverse the hard-won liberating accomplishments of rational scientific progress. Reactionaries prowl dangerously in the darkness.

According to the Whiggish myths, science and religion exist fundamentally as enemies in relation to each other. By the rules of the dialectic, science is modern, perfectible, rational; religion is antiquated, flawed, irrational. Science represents progress; religion, reaction. Science grows and unifies; religion shrinks and fragments. Science has a future; religion must perish. Religion is disjointed, incapable of merging its cacophony of claims expressed in myriad traditions and the vast and divergent literature of its inconsistent theologies.

The Whig perspective consigns religion to the dustbin of history, desiring, as the famous phrase puts it, "the last of the kings [to] be strangled with the guts of the last priest."[54] As American controversy over the public role of religion retains its eighteenth-century matrix, such anachronistic sensibilities still remain strong in cultural perceptions, even for highly educated citizens. Can intelligent people even pause to consider a possible joint future for science and religion? The Whiggish frame of reference simply does not allow such a notion to be considered.

In America, the Whiggish perspective provides the perfect symmetric companion to the light-versus-darkness mentality of religious fundamentalism. Because it fulfills the dialectic, the Whiggish view of religion by antireligious American scientists represents a kind of "photographic negative fundamentalism (PNF)," in which science takes the place of fundamentalist religion as a worldview. This viewpoint is surprisingly common among American scientists. In league with the cultural role of religious fundamentalism, PNF perpetuates the self-realizing tendency of the science-religion dialectic. Many very intelligent people *believe* in it, despite the fact that it is deeply naïve, philosophically and historically.

Giordano Bruno as Theological Hero, Not Scientific Martyr

No passion-evoking mythology can be complete without martyrs. In the hagiography of PNF, the most famous and widely cited are Giordano Bruno and Galileo Galilei. Both are widely misunderstood as martyrs *of* science *by* religion. Recent scholarly literature over the case of Galileo is extremely illuminating on the issue of Whiggish mythologizing, but I will not discuss it here.[55] Instead, I will focus entirely on the case of Bruno (see Note 4).

This year (2000) marks the 400th anniversary of the death of Giordano Bruno, whose statue is depicted in Figure 17. Bruno was burned at the stake for heresy, by order of the Inquisition, in the Campo de' Fiori, Rome on February 17, 1600. He was one of the earliest thinkers in the West to expand radically on the Copernican heliocentric theory

FIGURE 17. Giordano Bruno was born in 1548 and burned at the stake by order of the Inquisition on February 17, 1600. He is often (incorrectly) revered as a martyr of science. Bruno was a theological thinker who recognized that the stars were distant suns and therefore inferred that Earth might be only one of an infinite number of worlds. *Reprinted with permission, Bettmann/Corbis.*[56]

of 1543. Through his theological vision, he made a profound and imaginative leap. Planetary science is still trying to catch up with him. Bruno postulated, correctly, that the stars were objects like the sun and that the night sky revealed an infinite plenum of worlds.

Bruno was an angular, brilliant, controversial character. Trained as a Dominican monk, he later abandoned the order, becoming a Hermetic magus. In this process, he made a full break with Christianity (for example, he denied the divinity of Christ). He was involved in numerous intrigues, possibly including anti-Catholic espionage in Protestant England. Although none of the court papers survive, his demise at the hand of the Roman Inquisition was likely related primarily to theological and political matters rather than to his cosmological views. While one should never exculpate religious authorities for executing people on doctrinal issues, it is nevertheless historically incorrect to interpret Bruno as a martyr of science by religion. To do so represents a Whiggish error of intellectual anachronism in two senses.

First, in describing the sixteenth-century Roman Inquisition in its historical context, one could as easily describe it as a matter of politics as much as a matter of religion. At that exceedingly tumultuous time in European history, a form of what we would now call ideological barbarism reigned through various forms of terror in politics. The role of the Catholic Church had not been decoupled yet from the structure of political authority—although the titanic struggles that eventually led to this decoupling were then in process. The Papacy of the time had the primary features of a political regime. To relate such a situation either to Christianity or to religion in the context of the current usage of these terms is extremely anachronistic. Indeed, the very political sensitivity of the situation in Rome in the later sixteenth century was due in large part to a vast and turbulent movement of schism and fundamental reform within both Christianity and politics. This reform sought to restore faith to its (proper) nonpolitical role. Many of the aspects of liberty we now enjoy—such as rights of private religious conscience, religious and academic freedom, and the politics of classical liberalism—were forged in the brutal theologicopolitical dialectics of that rough-and-tumble era. To describe Bruno the magus-theologian as a scientist and victim of religion is therefore to smuggle in an ahistorical secularist animus.

Second, to describe Bruno as a martyr for science is bizarre because he was not even remotely a scientist. Bruno was uninterested in astronomy. He wrote *against* the use of geometry and mathematics. His main motivation for interest in the Copernican theory lay in the degree to which it provided ammunition against Aristotle's philosophical "hierarchy of substances" in favor of his predilection for a unitary view of the cosmos. Similarly, in Bruno's astronomically related thought, he principally was a devotee of magical thinking; he believed the stars and planets were living beings and admired the Copernican model because it comported with sun worship. Thus, Bruno really cannot properly be considered a scientific martyr, as he often has been eulogized in Whig histories of the triumph of the forward-thinking "enlightenment" of science and reason against the primitive "darkness" of religion and superstition. Far more accurate would be to describe him as a philosopher-theologian-magician who, encouraged by the science of Copernicus, exercised his theological imagination in a direction that serendipitously has proved to have been scientifically prescient. If Bruno is to be considered a martyr for anything, it should be for the private right of belief and freedom of theological scholarship. More properly, he is a theological hero for science in that he demonstrated that the unfettered theological imagination sometimes can lead in profoundly insightful directions where science may take centuries to follow.

Bruno's thinking was influenced by the many-worlds cosmology developed by the Greek atomists of the fourth century BCE.[57] It also built on the systems of earlier European theological thinkers who either favored, or left open, the possibility of an infinity of worlds in opposition to the Aristotelian view. Many highly prominent theologians considered that the principle of the infinity of divine power resonated with the possibility of a multiplicity of worlds. Such thinkers included: *in the thirteenth century*—Etienne Tempier, Bishop of Paris; the Parisian theologians Godfrey of Fontaine, Henry of Ghent, and Richard of Middleton; in Oxford, the theologians William of Ware, Jean of Bassols, and Thomas of Strasbourg; *in the fourteenth century*—both Jean Buridan (*c.* 1295–1358), rector of the University of Paris, and William of Ockham (*c.* 1280–1347) of Oxford; and *in the fifteenth century*—the famous theologian-philosopher and cardinal Nicholas of Cusa (1401–1464). Nicholas advocated an infinite universe of worlds without a center and merits special note as the first European Christian thinker to advocate life on other worlds.[58] His influence on Bruno was profound.

In very broad terms, Bruno pursued a logic that supposed that the activity of God as creator was infinite, and therefore that there were likely to be an infinity of other worlds beyond the (finite) terrestrial one. He promoted certain metaphysical-theological ideas, such as the unity of nature (posed against the Aristotelian cosmology), the infinity of divine power and creativity, and a corresponding principle of cosmic plentitude.

As a cosmological thinker, Bruno's thought expanded the Copernican dethronement of the Earth's centrality in a bold and imaginative step. In his book *De l'Infinito Universo et Mundi* of 1584, Bruno argued for an infinite cosmos of many worlds. Of particular significance is that he identified the stars as other worlds similar to the sun and the Earth and the other planets in the solar system. (Note that he did distinguish between bodies that gave primary and reflected light as compared with the planets.) The Earth (and the living beings it hosted) was therefore simply one among an infinitude of other broadly similar living worlds. Until Bruno, it had never been postulated that the sun and the stars were equivalent types of objects.[59]

Within a decade of Bruno's death, Galileo's observations had confirmed that the planets and the Earth were similar types of objects, as the Copernican system implied. In 1610, Galileo wrote in his book *The Starry Messenger:*

> I have observed the nature and material of the Milky Way. With the aid of the telescope this has been scrutinized so directly and with such regular certainty that all the aspects which have vexed philosophers through so many ages have been resolved, and we are at last freed from wordy debates about it. The galaxy is, in fact, nothing but a congeries of innumerable stars grouped together in clusters.

The more radical idea is then to look out on the night sky and see in the distribution of stars a vast plurality of other solar worlds similar in type to the sun-centered system that Copernicus had unveiled. Giordano Bruno was the first to do this. It was a gigantic step for the scientific understanding of humanity's place in the cosmos. For such a momentous cosmological breakthrough, it has been discussed remarkably little. The perspective of looking at the night sky and seeing an infinite panorama of other worlds did not become fully established for about a century. The concept is not discussed seriously until Descartes' *Principia Philosophiae* of 1644. Thereafter it occurs in the work of Descartes' follower Fontanelle in a 1686 publication on the plurality of worlds, *Entretriens sur la Pluralité des Mondes (A Plurality of Worlds)*. It also is developed at length in Huygens's treatise of 1698 on the plurality of inhabited worlds, *Kosmotheoros, Sive, de Terris Coelestibus Earumque Ornatu Conjecturae (The Celestial Worlds Discover'd: or, Conjectures Concerning the Inhabitants, Plants and Productions of the Worlds in the Planets).*[60]

It is worth noting that another philosopher, Immanuel Kant, was the source of the next major breakthrough in conceiving the vastness of the cosmos. In an early work published in 1755, *Allgemeine Naturgeschichte und Theorie des Himmels (Universal Natural History and Theory of the Heavens),* Kant postulated the idea that some of the fuzzy diffuse nebulae dimly observed in the telescopes of his day were in fact distant systems of stars similar in type to the Milky Way. Kant's bold idea blew the lid off of the cosmos. This vast insight was not confirmed scientifically until Henrietta Swan Leavitt's (1868–1921) work on Cepheid variables in the Small Magellanic Cloud (SMC) in 1912.[61] Leavitt's observations established the SMC as a mini-galaxy external to the Milky Way. This led to sustained controversy over the nebulae leading up to the so-called great debate of April 1920 at the Smithsonian Institution, pitting Herbert D. Curtis, arguing that the spiral nebulae were external galaxies, against Leavitt's observatory director at Harvard, Harlow Shapley, who thought the nebulae were local structures within the Milky Way. The debate continued for more than two decades. Clear and decisive observation put it to rest in October 1923, when J. C. Duncan and Edwin Hubble confirmed that the spiral nebulae were external galaxies of stars similar to the Milky Way. Using the 100-inch telescope on Mt. Wilson, they determined distances in excess of one million LY to Cepheid variable stars in the Triangulum and Andromeda nebulae. In February 1924, Hubble wrote to Shapley describing his discovery of a Cepheid variable in the Andromeda Nebula (M31). (When Shapley received the letter, he reportedly held it out and sighed, remarking, "This is the letter that destroyed my universe.")

The work of Henrietta Leavitt and of Edwin Hubble and his colleagues established a new perspective, which Hubble coined "the realm of the nebulae." On New Year's Day 1925, the full convincing details were presented at a meeting of the American Association for the Advancement of Science (AAAS) in Washington, D.C. The new telescopic eyes of science proved the much older theological/philosophical eyes of Bruno and Kant to have been quite farseeing indeed. Cosmology has never looked back.

Gazing into the night sky, humanity is only beginning to explore the vastness and touch on the significance of the infinite cosmos of worlds as first hypothesized by Giordano Bruno more than 400 years ago. Bruno's theologically motivated conjecture began a tradition of looking at Earth's place within the cosmos as perhaps one among an infinity of cases. It exemplifies the way that spiritual imagination *can* be a fertile source of concepts that have great scientific significance. Bruno deserves high honor as a prescient pioneer of the cosmological imagination. The great imaginative leap that he made at the end of the sixteenth century remains very much with us today at the beginning of the twenty-first. Still, it presents a worthy challenge to the human spirit, scientifically as well as spiritually. Bruno's fate as a theological heretic also reminds us that the creative mind will do well to let imagination range adventurously on both scientific and theological notions—and to beware of settled points of view, be they scientific or religious.

The "Humble Approach" and the Possible Complementarity of Science and Theology

In what sense can the scientific exploration of the cosmos be a theologically significant enterprise? The present volume presents views by scientists exploring what has been described as a "humble approach."[62] This enterprise is tentative and exploratory. It represents an effort to explore ways in which science can engage substantively with theological questions and issues.

The humble approach is not meant to marginalize other more traditional approaches in theology. Nor does it attempt to make a religion out of science. It recognizes that science generates profound insights into the nature of reality and that some of these insights may have theological significance. Such recognition is natural for any thinker who has caught the thrill of experiencing science as a window into wonder. This is not to say that one should ignore important critiques of the modernistic "enlightenment project" and suppose that knowledge is somehow compressible into a universally rational, decontextualized enterprise modeled after the empirical sciences. Not at all! The humble approach simply encourages hope that the scientific exploration of reality and the spiritual quest for deep understanding might be explored fruitfully in a spirit of complementarity. Such a hope can assist us in avoiding the perception of an unbridgeable chasm between the study of the world and the task of living within it wholesomely and meaningfully—thus also avoiding the unpleasantness of facing a shrunken either/or choice between nihilistic postmodernism and scientism. Religion, in fact, can be a friend of the scientific and humane truth-seeking traditions of enlightenment while also intrinsically appreciating the rich context of the situatedness of human culture, as well as the consequent limitations on knowledge. An integrative task within intellectual life is itself one of the more worthy reasons why the field of science and religion is so interesting.[63]

"Nonoverlapping Magisteria"?

Recently, the president of AAAS, distinguished essayist and Harvard evolutionary biologist Stephen Jay Gould, has argued at book length that science and religion are separate but equal domains that represent "nonoverlapping magisteria" (NOMA).[64] Gould's argument partitions the world into neat domains of objective fact and humane values. This naturally leaves religion in the unenviable position of presiding over a fact-free domain. It also represents the classic "separate domains" option in the famous fourfold typology outlined by Ian Barbour in his landmark 1966 study on the relationship between science and religion (which Gould does not cite).[65] In a contemporary context, this argument may be interpreted as an effort to provide a political resolution to the ongoing conflict between science and religion in the vein of the stolid New England prudence cited by Robert Frost in his poem "Mending Wall": "good fences make good neighbors." Yet, the poem continues:

> *Something there is that doesn't love a wall*
> *That sends the frozen groundswell under it*
> *Spilling boulders in the sun*
> *So that two can pass abreast as one . . .*

Something there is in the human spirit that ultimately cannot be content with walled-off solutions to longstanding and deep problems of conflict and misunderstanding. Far better to do the job right than to pretend pragmatically to uphold separate domains. Gould's own work itself rather clearly shows that science and issues of meaning, significance, and values are not so easy to partition into separate domains. For example, Gould's high standing as a noted public intellectual presumes that aspects of the empirical record in evolution have interpretive implications that carry significance in the domain of values. His work vibrantly engages discussions on such value-laden topics as whether evolution is progressive or to what degree randomness controls outcomes.[66] In itself, this is hardly an example of the separate but equal solution Gould commends.

The humble approach is focused on exploring and interpreting the natural world, or in theological language, the creation, according to the well-developed "two books" epistemology the (old tradition of "God's two books"—Nature and Revelation) advocated by Francis Bacon and cited by Darwin opposite the title page of *On the Origin of Species*.[67] The idea that the two books provide separate stories but yield deep and complementary and ultimately theological insights can be a source of valuation of the depth and moral seriousness of the scientific enterprise. It is clear that this was true during the formation phase of the development of modern science. For example, a particularly concise summary of the theological significance of the pioneering phase of the modern scientific enterprise is offered by John Langdon-Davies:

> The whole history of science has been a direct search for God, deliberate and conscious, until well into the eighteenth century . . . Copernicus, Kepler, Galileo, Newton, Leibnitz and the rest did not merely believe in God in an orthodox sort of way: they believed that their work told humanity more about God than had been known before. Their incentive in working at all was a desire to know God; and they regarded their discoveries as not only proving his existence, but as revealing more and more of his nature . . .[68]

The Challenge of Progress

It is clear, however, that the sciences develop in a relatively clear direction of progress. For example, we can expect with near certainty that within a decade solid-state physics, cell biology, astronomy, neuroscience, computer science, particle physics, oncology, evolutionary biology, pharmacology, astrophysics, genetics, cosmology, geology, protein chemistry, climatology, oceanography, planetary science, and so forth will be far better informed than at present. This progress will be a globally generated enterprise. It will integrate the activity of myriad scientists representing many cultures and various religious backgrounds. Basic information grows and flourishes in science and creates cross-cultural agreement. This general feature of the scientific enterprise may not hold up in all particulars. Some philosophers, sociologists, and other culture theorists will not want to agree. But most scientists will. The evidence for universal scientific progress in a wide variety of fields is far too great to ignore.

In contrast, the experience of theology is, of course, vastly different. Theology is not at all a common transcultural enterprise. The plural term "theologies" actually is more appropriate as a description of the field considered globally and cross-culturally. In the academic context, a cross-cultural, agreed-on content of theology has never really been established, nor is it expected to be possible. Even a number of universalizing efforts have been inspired by science. However, they have not on the whole lived up to expectations. The role of contingent, cultural, historical, communal, and generically contextual aspects of particular human experience are now generally appreciated to be essential rather than accidental. The trend of emerging thought is clearly toward nonfoundationalist, context-dependent perspectives that celebrate rather than seek to overlook the deep situatedness of religious points of view within cultural matrices.

To theologians and philosophers, processes of critical refinement, winnowing, nuancing, considering cultural polyphony, recognizing elements of "social construction," and so forth may seem normal. From the perspective of scientists, however, it *feels* to some degree intrinsically problematic. A scientist interested in theology as a discipline intrinsically wishes to know whether the field has any potential to yield bedrock knowledge, or at least some form of constraints that might be recognizable as being solid in the scientific sense.

Most of the world's great religions have in varying degrees a central identity related to the historical formation of a canon of authoritative sacred texts. Devotion is typically focused on forms of religious teaching and practice, which to varying degrees are authorized by the canon or by commentary on the canon, or by liturgies that enshrine and ritually enact the teachings of the canon. Focusing on a common core of revealed sacred truth lies at the heart of the power of religion to inspire deep and widespread community commitment. By filtering out what is sacred from what is not, and by upholding a (more or less) compact set of central sacred teachings, religions unlock a power of unification that can motivate groups of devotees in potent common cause within the sacred community. Spiritual practices that are interpreted as revelatory commonly are tested against the core tradition. The canonical repository is afforded a higher status than any perspectives or teachings arising out of individual experience. A consequence is that the great religions typically have a sense of spiritual truth that is in an important sense closed rather than open because of the vital function of the canon in defining the core of common belief. Religions often change by a process of fission, sometimes involving conflict and expulsion. New sources of sacred experience are developed in the form of new communities, and new canons are defined distinct from the parent. Thus, for example, Buddhism emerged from Vedic Hinduism, Bahaism emerged from Islam, Islam emerged from Christianity, Christianity emerged from Judaism, Protestantism emerged from Catholicism, and Mormonism and Swedenborgianism emerged from Protestantism. The tendency is away from unification rather than toward it.

The experience of modern science differs drastically from this picture. Essentially, science has no canons considered in the religious sense of the term. Scientists may revere in various ways the great scientific texts of the past, such as Copernicus' *De Revolutionibus*, Galileo's *Discorsi*, Newton's *Principia*, Darwin's *On the Origin of Species*, Hutton's *Theory of the Earth*, Lyell's *Principles*, Mendeleyev's *Principles*, or Maxwell's *Treatise*. For the most part, however, such pioneering works are often of very little daily importance to working scientists.

The central enterprise of science is that of active pioneering research directed toward discovery. Once a scientist has progressed beyond basic training, recognition is no longer given for mastery of the core ideas of what is known. What is given recognition and respect is the uncovering of new insightful information by research. Therefore, what matters is the leading edge in any specialty, new perspectives bringing information from the darkness of the unknown into the light of the known. At the creative frontier, the key places to be are at specialty scientific meetings, where the most exciting discoveries are introduced. The ethos of scientific research is highly competitive. It feeds an innate eagerness to learn. A field feels dead if it does not generate new insights regularly. It feels alive if many research groups are making exciting new discoveries regularly. Such discoveries often unseat and transcend older perspectives. If a persuasive new perspective outmodes an older conceptual frame of reference, this is usually considered to be a positive step. Such transitions are very common in scientific experience. Mostly, they are considered to be normal, however personally traumatic they might be to the developers of the old points of view.

Thus, the spirit of research science is to focus on gaining new information. This posture is quite distinct from aspects of religious practice that focus on tradition. The humble approach celebrates the vibrancy of the scientific explanation of the world and seeks to promote opportunities to develop and interpret new scientific developments that have spiritual significance. It is clear that the long-term future of planetary science offers two areas of implication in which the growth of scientific information likely will have very broad theological significance: purpose and spirituality. We consider each in turn in following sections.

Evolution, Astrobiology, and SETI: Windows into Cosmic Purpose?

Letting our imagination wander among the stars,
we too may hear whispers of immortality.

—FREEMAN DYSON[69]

The logic of the new field of astrobiology and the search for extraterrestrial intelligence (SETI) is motivated by an expectation that life arises naturally wherever appropriate conditions exist in the universe. This presumption will be empirically testable by searching for traces of life in the few environments in which conditions amenable to life may exist (e.g., Europa[70]), or where such conditions may have existed in the past such that remnants of a previous ecosystem may be surviving at depth in the lithosphere (e.g., in the case of Mars).

A second, more futuristic question is whether, given various aspects of Earth-like conditions, biological evolution develops according to broad trajectories of increased complexity. Thus, we can ask whether exospecies would develop biochemical features and physical forms and functions broadly recognizable to us based on our terrestrial zoology.

The future of astrobiology may make it possible to develop generalized perspectives on the evolutionary trajectories of life-bearing worlds over very long timescales in different types of planetary circumstances. Human beings have thus far experienced only one living world. Yet we live in a vast cosmos likely to contain an infinity of planetary worlds, many of which may be life bearing. Technologically, it is foreseeable that humans may be able to develop the ability to image many such worlds in our nearby galactic neighborhood. Thus, planetary science offers us the possibility of being able to gain perspective on what the potential for life is on timescales consistent with stellar lifetimes. Beyond this hope, were SETI to be successful, the consequences would be staggering.[71]

The future of astrobiological science has spiritual significance because it can begin to answer by empirical means a major metaphysical question that is widely discussed and debated in contemporary evolutionary theory: whether the evolutionary process is or is not consistent with an overall cosmic purpose. Is it reasonable to view evolution as a vehicle for serving a divine purpose, which, for example, might include human destiny within it? A number of prominent critics have suggested that evolution cannot be consistent with notions of divine purpose precisely because it is "blind."[72] This blindness can be construed in two senses. First, the outcomes of evolution are generically indeterminate as a consequence of the role of random events. Second, the process of evolution clearly seems morally cruel, and it does not correspond *prima facie* to what would be expected from a compassionate divine being. Both of these issues are very serious ones. Both may be illuminated by the long-term future of planetary science.

In regard to the first sense of blindness, we may note that a common misunderstanding in considering the concept of purpose in relation to evolution is to consider a process subject to chance as being inconsistent with serving a purpose. To see the generic fallacy of this logic, consider that gambling entrepreneurs design and use random processes *specifically for the purpose* of making money. Similarly, economists know that *for the purpose* of enhancing an economy's productivity, it is helpful to avoid purpose-directed central planning control on prices and the distribution of goods and services. Open, random processes of economic action are more productive in the cumulate.[73] Therefore, randomness, contingency, and purpose are not antithetical.

Where the debate becomes more substantial requires a finer point of analysis. Can a class of self-conscious creatures like us who have religious concerns and ask theological questions be said to be generically predictable outcomes of a large set of independent evolutionary processes active in a large set of independent planetary worlds? If *Homo sapiens* is a "freakish" outcome of the evolutionary process, then it may be unreasonable to continue to assert a theological claim that our existence is related to a cosmic purpose. Gould, for example, has argued that the evolutionary process is radically contingent: "Replay the tape a million times from a Burgess beginning and I doubt anything like *Homo sapiens* would ever evolve again."[74] Gould's thinking is targeted against the concept of progress conceived in the sense of seeing *Homo sapiens* as a kind of high point in the evolution of life on Earth.[75] Yet, teleological endpoint concepts of evolutionary progress do not need to identify *Homo sapiens* as the final *telos*. They only posit a tendency toward a secular increase in the populating of new domains of increased complexity. We are then left with the question of whether broad trends in the evolution of planetary biospheres are empirically discernible. Of particular interest would be trends toward increasing intelligence that eventually might be expected to generate culture-generating life aspects as in our own species. These would include language; advanced intellectual, artistic, political, and religious pursuits; scientific and technological evolution; and various forms of altruistic emotions and behaviors that can transcend kin relationships.

What evolution generates beyond the capacities of *Homo sapiens* on timescales of millions to tens of millions to hundreds of millions of years is, of course, unknown to us. However, it is an exceedingly interesting question. The nature of biological evolution clearly must change dramatically both in terms of tendencies and rates of change once it enters a technologically directed "Lamarckian" phase.[76]

Such questions should be tractable by studying exoplanetary worlds. In the meantime, the general question of progress in evolution is partly addressable by studying the history of terrestrial evolution in tectonically isolated domains. At present, the empirical evidence seems clearly contrary to Gould's assertion that no progressive tendency exists. The phenomena of morphological co-evolution and intelligence "arms races" both suggest that creatures like us, while clearly contingent, are not radically so. For example, the concept of the possibility of the development of marsupial primates seems quite reasonable in the same way that the (genetically unrelated) marsupial flying squirrels (sugar gliders) and nonmarsupial flying squirrels co-evolved into similar ecological niches and exhibit nearly identical morphology. Therefore, might something like a marsupial *Homo*-type line of creatures have arisen among such a hypothetical line of marsupial primates? The question, of course, cannot be answered scientifically. However, the possibility seems realistic based on what is known about morphological co-evolution among the Australasian marsupials. Similarly, the development of relatively advanced intelligence in the octopus suggests that the evolution of an intelligent, self-conscious creature is conceivable in a totally different line.[77]

These considerations provide intriguing clues that, in principle, the long-term project of extrasolar planetary science has the capability to provide substantial scientific insight into the metaphysical/spiritual question of purpose. Such topics already can be deliberated very interestingly on the basis of evolutionary findings in our *N = 1 world* of planet Earth. Certainly, far better illumination would be possible with a data set of $N = many\ worlds$. Whether other living worlds are "out there" in our nearby galactic neighborhood sufficient to realize this possibility remains to be seen. We can only wait for the necessary technology to be developed.

Are Religions Widespread in the Universe?

> *The planet is the cradle of intelligence, but it is impossible*
> *to live forever in the cradle.*
>
> —Konstantin Eduardovich Tsiolkovsky[78]

> *O' be prepared, my soul!*
> *To read the inconceivable, to scan*
> *The million forms of God those stars unroll*
>
> —Alice Meynell[79]

It is interesting to note that portrayals of "alien religions" are typically absent in Hollywood's envisioning of extraterrestrial life. This is somewhat curious. Religion is an anthropological universal for our species. Traces of religion appear at the earliest point in the archeological record with the species itself. Religions differ widely from group to group. Yet, with only very few (typically modern) exceptions, religion is always and everywhere to be found in human culture. It is developed in tremendous detail and complexity in both rituals and beliefs. Wherever people have developed cultures, they have developed religions. Any aspect of culture that is so clearly universal may be expected, not unreasonably, to have some degree of biological rootedness. Projections of various aspects of humanness onto aliens therefore should, in principle, include the imaginative creation of a wide variety of alien religions. It seems unavoidable that if aliens like us are out there, then they necessarily must have alien languages. Why not religions as well?

The idea that religiousness would be absent in superintelligent beings has no serious grounding within science itself. Indeed, much within the advancement of science—especially physics—seems to support the case for the involvement of a grand mind in the deep workings of the cosmos. Who can examine the current magnificent adventure in an area such as superstring theory and not be impressed by the degree to which reality is sufficiently deep to challenge the most creative and brilliant scientific and mathematical minds in our contemporary world? For several centuries, reality has been yielding up marvelous, immensely brilliant mathematical clues to its hidden inner workings. It has provided a magnificently exciting intellectual adventure for many of the most brilliantly skilled and creative minds humanity has produced. Can it be realistic to ascribe all of this astonishing *depth* to a mindless, purposeless, meaningless fluke?

My own expectation is the opposite of the "reality-is-ultimately-a-meaningless-accident" presumption that secularity is intelligence. Consequently, the rejection of the religious sense and its manifestations seems to me to be misguided. Advanced civilizations might be highly religious (although, of course, likely in very different ways than on our planet). Such an expectation follows naturally from considering religion, in the very broadest sense, to flow from a proper response of individuals and communities reverently and respectfully expressing humility and gratitude toward an ultimate reality to which we owe the great and precious gift of life. This seems to be both an ethically and an intellectually honest response to the most significant interpretive correlates of our scientific view of the world. Moreover, the secularist view of life seems like the "planet without laughter," described in a memorable short story by the logician Raymond Smullyan: "The inhabitants were extremely serious, conscientious, sincere, hard-working, studious, well wishing and moral. But of humor they knew nothing."[80] Like humor, spirituality is part of the fullness of life. There is more to life than muscle and brain. Modernity has shown that people quite easily can dispense with religion. But a dimension that makes life rich and deep and inspiring is lost when it is absent. Perhaps the most profound reflection on religion in a cosmic context was written by the science fiction writer Olaf Stapledon in a deeply moving book:

> Sometimes we inclined to conceive it as sheer Power, and symbolized it to ourselves by means of all the myriad power-deities of our many worlds. Sometimes we felt assured that it was pure Reason, and that the cosmos was but an exercise of the divine mathematician. Sometimes Love seemed to us its essential character, and we imagined it with the forms of all the Christs of all the worlds, the human Christs, the Echinoderm and Nautiloid Christs, the dual Christ of the Symbiotics, the swarming Christ of the Insectoids. But equally it appeared to us as unreasoning Creativity, at once blind and subtle, tender and cruel, caring only to spawn and spawn the infinite variety of beings, conceiving here and there among a thousand inanities a fragile love-

liness. This it might for a while foster with maternal solicitude, till in a sudden jealousy of the excellence of its own creature, it would destroy what it had made.

But we knew well that all these fictions were very false. The felt presence of the Star Maker remained unintelligible, even though it increasingly illuminated the cosmos, like the splendour of the unseen sun at dawn.[81]

Alyosha's Tears: Concluding Reflections

. . . Alyosha stood, gazed, and suddenly threw himself down flat upon the earth.

He did not know why he was embracing it. He could not have explained to himself why he longed so irresistibly to kiss it, to kiss it all, but he kissed it weeping, sobbing and drenched it with his tears, and vowed frenziedly to love it, to love it for ever and ever. "Water the earth with the tears of your gladness and love those tears," it rang in his soul. What was he weeping over? Oh, he was weeping in his rapture even over those stars which were shining for him from the abyss of space and "he was not ashamed of that ecstasy." It was as though the threads from all those innumerable worlds of God met all at once in his soul, and it was trembling all over "as it came in contact with other worlds."

—FYODOR DOSTOYEVSKY[82]

In Dostoyevsky's great novel *The Brothers Karamazov*, Alyosha's tears are funereal tears. Mourning death, they have been transformed into a miracle of love that embraces all worlds. The brutality of death shows that the future of the species is not the future of our individual selves. Yet if the wonder of the cosmos is indeed very deep, then perhaps a power exists that resolves our own hoped-for significance within the greater frame of cosmic history. It is humble to hope that in our littleness and feebleness, love is vast and strong. It is an old and crazy idea. Maybe—just maybe—it is crazy enough.

Stars are distant fire, but the infinite space they inhabit is cold and inhospitable. We human beings live in homes. We enjoy being close to a warm fire. We enjoy the close companionship of others. The vast and wondrous panorama of the night sky can be inspiring. Yet it can be terrifying in its "otherness." Therefore, we are not physically and emotionally at home in that universe. We are at home here on Earth and in the communities and relationships we are woven into. Ultimately, the closeness of love is more important to us than the vastness of the cosmos.

In his *Pensées sur la Religion et sur Quelques Autres Sujets (Thoughts on Religion and on Other Subjects)*, the French physicist-theologian Blaise Pascal (1623–1662) wrote of the night sky that *"le silence eternel de ces espaces m'effraie"* ("the eternal silence of these infinite spaces frightens me"). He also made a famous distinction between the rational analysis of God—what he called "God of the philosophers"—and the God that mattered to him. Like the stars, the "God of the philosophers" is remote. The God Pascal had experienced was closer to home. When he died, a small scrap of paper dated November 23, 1654, was found sewn into his coat. It described an experience of profound personal revelation: *"FEU. Dieu d'Abraham, Dieu d'Isaac, Dieu de Jacob, non des philosophes et savants. Certitude. Certitude. Sentiment. Joie. Paix."* ("FIRE. God of Abraham, God of Isaac, God of Jacob, not of the philosophers and scholars. Certainty. Certainty. Feeling. Joy. Peace.")[83]

Science cannot provide such forms of personal experience. At best, it suggests only rumors. For example, it provides hints that a grand mind may undergird existence. Such a recognition can haunt the rational mind. It suggests that the heart of reality may not be a thing to be understood like the equations science uncovers, but rather a being who breathes fire into them. But science cannot measure or observe this presence. What science apprehends is only the distant fire. The inner reality is different, hidden. It comes to people only in extraordinary personal moments, recorded within. Such records are not scientific knowledge. They are private memories sewn into coats. Yet such thoughts can be a cloak, a comfort to us seekers in the dark, cold night when, through science, we, listening, hear only silence; and we, looking, see only cold, infinite space.

If God holds all things together, then there is a connectedness to all things in God's purpose. The prospect of this overarching unity can bring us comfort and hope when gazing into the vastness of the night sky. The mystic Julian of Norwich (*c.* 1343–1416) once described such comfort in a vision of the divine unity of all things:

> Our Lord showed me a spiritual sight of his familiar love. I saw that he is to us everything which is good and comforting for our help. He is our clothing, for he is that love, which is so tender that he may never desert us. And so in this sight I saw truly that he is everything

which is good, as I understand. And in this he showed me something small, no bigger than a hazelnut, lying in the palm of my hand, and I perceived that it was as round as any ball. I looked at it and thought: What can this be? And I was given this general answer: It is everything that is made. I was amazed that it could last, for I thought that it was so little that it could suddenly fall into nothing. And I was answered in my understanding: It lasts and always will, because God loves it; and thus everything has being through the love of God.[84]

Julian's vision is a beautiful one. However, in the twentieth century, serious reflection on the problem of evil increasingly has challenged the idea of divine love. Theologians and critics alike have focused on two major issues. The first has been the deep recognition of the challenge to a theism of love in view of the profound human evil that exists in the world. Particular focus has been given to the scale and brutality of evil demonstrated in the acts of the Nazis against innocent civilians. How could a God of love allow such unimaginable horrors to exist? Elie Wiesel described his recollection of "the silent blue sky" while, as a 13-year-old boy arriving at Auschwitz, he looked on in horror as children were thrown into burning pits:

> Never shall I forget that night, the first night in camp, which has turned my life into one long night, seven times cursed and seven times sealed. Never shall I forget that smoke. Never shall I forget the little faces of the children, whose bodies I saw turned into wreaths of smoke beneath a silent blue sky.
>
> Never shall I forget those flames which consumed my faith forever.
>
> Never shall I forget that nocturnal silence which deprived me, for all eternity, of the desire to live. Never shall I forget those moments which murdered my God and my soul and turned my dreams to dust. Never shall I forget these things, even if I am condemned to live as long as God Himself. Never.[85]

Twentieth-century theology has been deeply reflected by meditations on such views. They forever have challenged concepts of God such that classical theism to many sensitive thinkers seems no longer viable.

A parallel issue has been recognition of the natural evil that exists in the nonhuman world and that can be seen as part and parcel of the evolutionary process. Voltaire raised the question of natural evil in the eighteenth century in his book *Candide* and in the *Poem on the Lisbon Earthquake of 1755*. However, since Darwin's discoveries in the mid-nineteenth century, the repugnance and senselessness of aspects of suffering in the evolutionary process has been reflected on with great seriousness. For Christian theists who seek to affirm a God of love, the double challenge has been a profound one.

On a philosophical plane, the classic response has been to advocate the so-called freedom defense. It has been argued that evil is a necessary correlate to an intrinsically contingent, free and open world and that only in such a world is real love possible. Theologians in the latter half of the twentieth century have found this rationale to be only partly adequate. Those that have made contributions have not done so by purely rational persuasion, but rather by emphasizing the way the presence of God in the world is "emptied" to be dependent on our active human response. Such perspectives that have had the strategy of understanding God by including aspects of freedom, limitation, risk, and suffering correspond precisely to those aspects of human and natural tragic experience from which the theological problem of evil arises.[86]

Attempts to grapple with such issues also typically affirm that there cannot be a purely intellectual resolution to the mystery of existence, that the answer may be gained only in the action of an embrace of life rather than in any grasp of rational perception.[87] Consequently there has been recognition of the possibility of a profound role for human action. Therefore, there also has been recognition of the importance of considering the perspective of the future. Reflecting on the problem of theodicy, the distinguished literary critic George Steiner wrote:

> From the unreasoned, unanalyzable, often ruinous all-power of love stems the thought—is it, once more, a puerility?—that "God" is not yet. That He will come into being or, more precisely, into manifest reach of human perception, only when there is immense excess of love over hatred. Each and every cruelty, each and every injustice inflicted on man or beast justifies the findings of atheism insofar as it prevents God from what would indeed be a first coming. But I am unable, even at the worst hours, to abdicate from the belief that the two validating wonders of mortal existence are love and the invention of the future tense. Their conjunction, if it will ever come to pass, is the Messianic.[88]

This perspective of the future presents a final reason the future of planetary science is so important and exciting. In the great and ongoing debate over the meaning of evolution and the question of whether there is purpose to the cosmos, most of the potential answers will come in due course from unveiling the vast unseen universe of other worlds—

the cosmos of planets—hidden in the darkness of space. That darkness also serves as an image of the long-term future of life. When we speak of our history, typically we consider centuries. But the concept of history applied to the future of the cosmos is measured properly in units of millions of centuries. That future vista should include many new discoveries, insights, and surprises.

The engineer and space futurist Robert Zubrin has written a wonderfully visionary book in which he challenges us in practical and detailed ways to begin to look beyond our planetary home and take up a vision of the great adventure of space. He argues a "north-out-of-Africa" thesis that the destiny of human evolution from the start has been that of risky, technology-supported adventure into inhospitable regions:

> Today the stars beckon again, but this time not to new continents, but new solar systems. Multitudes of the new worlds yet unknown await, filled with menaces to be faced, challenges to be overcome, wonders to be discovered, and history to be made. The first chapter of the human saga has been written, but vast volumes lying out among the stars are still blank, ready for the pens of new peoples with new thoughts, new tongues, astonishing and beautiful creations, and epic deeds.[89]

As theology speculates about the long-term future of the biological destiny of life on Earth, it unhesitatingly raises one great question of the nature of the human adventure: Is the future ultimately an exploration of love—and therefore of God? Mystics have pointed the way. Scientists may do so as well. The study of the evolution of life is beginning to provide hints and clues that the great drama of life may be more than a meaningless fluke. Is life ultimately a drama of good versus evil in which reality groans as in childbirth, waiting in hope for the triumph of love? And, if so, what might the future bring? An answer, perhaps, is that we shall never know unless we create that world. In a future to be created, ignorance is a given. Perhaps such a vista of ignorance also can provide at least a humble recognition that, as a form of life, we may be really quite primitive. Perhaps we do not yet have a very good sense of what the universe is really like. A great ocean of possibility spreads out before us in all directions—unknown, untouched, unseen, dark but illuminated faintly by the distant fires of an infinity of stars—while, like a weak, flickering candle, the spirit of adventure and the possibility of love burn close within each of us.

Notes

1. I have not been able to locate the exact source for this quotation. A close analogy is found in Boorstin's essay "The Age of Negative Discovery," in *Cleopatra's Nose: Essays on the Unexpected* (New York: Random House, 1994): "The history of Western science confirms the aphorism that the great menace to progress is not ignorance but the illusion of knowledge." Note another Boorstin gem from the same essay: "Perhaps we are no longer merely *Homo sapiens* but rather *Homo ludens*—at play in the fields of the stars. Perhaps we have learned to luxuriate—as Stephen Hawking's little book suggests—in the expanding universe of expanding questions. Perhaps the modern realm of discovery is no longer a realm of answers but only of questions, which we are beginning to feel at home in and enjoy. Perhaps our modern discoverer is not a discoverer at all but rather a quester, in an age of negative discovery, where achievements are measured not in the finality of answers, but in the fertility of questions. So let us enjoy the quest together. As Claude Bernard (1813–1878), the great French physiologist, observed, 'Art is I; Science is We.'"

2. Anecdotally, it is reported that this quotation was written in the personal journal of English writer Malcolm Muggeridge as recorded in his biography. See: http://www.sanctuary-church.net/index.html.

3. This story may be apocryphal. A slightly different version draws from John Archibald Wheeler's telling of Bohr stories to his advanced physics class at Princeton in November 1962 on the news of Bohr's death (Joel Primack, private communication). Freeman Dyson confirms the version of the story used here based on his recollection of being at the lecture (note to the author). Abraham Pais has documented the event; however, he reported it as involving only private remarks between Bohr and Pauli following the lecture. Cf. *Niels Bohr's Times: In Physics, Philosophy, and Polity* (Oxford: Clarendon Press, 1991), 29 (footnote).

4. Charles L. Harper, Jr., "The View Towards Infinity: Four Centuries Ago, an Italian 'Heretic' Imagined an Infinite Cosmos. Increasingly, It Appears He Was Right." (Belief, Inc.: Beliefnet, http://www.beliefnet.com/story/11/story_1174_l.html, 2000).

5. The lady with whom the conversation took place made a perceptive comment. As I crossed my arms, she noted (correctly), "Your body language is showing evidence of hostility to this topic," adding (again

correctly) that it is typical of scientists to be "threatened by information which they do not have the capacity to understand or control."

6. Freeman J. Dyson, *Infinite in All Directions: Gifford Lectures Given at Aberdeen, Scotland, April–November 1985* (New York: Harper & Row, 1988).

7. Stuart Kauffman, *At Home in the Universe: The Search for Laws of Self-Organization and Complexity* (Oxford University Press, 1996); Christian De Duve, *Vital Dust: Life as a Cosmic Imperative* (New York: Basic Books, 1996); Paul C.W. Davies, *Are We Alone? Philosophical Implications of the Discovery of Extraterrestrial Life* (New York: BasicBooks, 1995).

8. Bertrand Russell, *A Free Man's Worship* (Portland, Maine: T. B. Mosher, 1923).

9. John Bertram Phillips, *Your God Is Too Small* (New York: Macmillan, 1953).

10. See Bruno Weber, *"Ubi caelum terrae se conjungit: Ein alterthmlicher Aufrisz des Weltgebaudes von Camille Flammarion,"* *Gutenberg Jahrbuch* (1973): 381–408, for a discussion of this woodcut by 19th-century French astronomer Camille Flammarion (1842–1925), which first appeared in *L'Atmosphere: Météorologie Populaire* (Paris, 1888): 163. For extensive information on the woodcut's history, see http://www. hypernote.com/med_thght.html and http://www. aei.ca/~anbou/ flammarion.html and http://www.iap.fr/saf/flammarion.htm.

11. Andrei Linde, "The Self-Reproducing Inflationary Universe," *Scientific American— Special Issue: The Magnificent Cosmos* (February 1998). This article updates a version that appeared in *Scientific American* in November 1994. A detailed description of inflationary theory is given in his book *Particle Physics and Inflationary Cosmology (Contemporary Concepts in Physics, Vol. 5)* (Newark, N.J.: Harwood Academic/Gordon and Breach Publishers, 1990). For an overview, see Alan H. Guth, *The Inflationary Universe: The Quest for a New Theory of Cosmic Origins* (New York: Addison Wesley, 1997).

12. Sir David Brewster, *Memoirs of the Life, Writings and Discoveries of Sir Isaac Newton*, 2 vols. (Edinburgh: Thomas Constable & Co., 1855; New York: Johnson Reprint Corp., 1965) 2:27.

13. Carl Sagan, *Cosmos* (New York: Random House, 1980).

14. From the COBE Science Working Group at NASA's Goddard Space Flight Center and the National Space Science Data Center (NSSDC). See http://space.gsfc.nasa.gov/astro/cobe/dmr_image. html, http://space.gsfc.nasa.gov/astro/cobe/slide_captions.html,

and http://nssdca.gsfc.nasa.gov/anon_dir/cobe/images/dmr/cmb_
fluctuations_big.gif.

15. See http://astro.estec.esa.nl/GAIA. Many thanks to Michael A. C.
Perryman, Ph.D. for his generous help with this conceptual image.
The GAIA project is projected to detect 10,000 to 30,000 planets
out to about 500 LY.

16. Alan Boss, *Looking for Earths: The Race to Find New Solar Systems*
(New York: John Wiley & Sons, 1998); Ken Croswell, *Planet Quest:
The Epic Discovery of Alien Solar Systems* (New York: Free Press,
1997); Donald Goldsmith, *Worlds Unnumbered: The Search for Extra-
solar Planets* (Sausalito, Calif.: University Science Books, 1997);
Michael D. Lemonick, *Other Worlds: The Search for Life in the Universe*
(New York: Simon & Schuster, 1998); John S. Lewis, *Worlds With-
out End: The Exploration of Planets and Unknown* (Reading, Mass.:
Perseus Books, 1998). For a more technical overview, see Stuart
Clark, *Extrasolar Planets: The Search for New Worlds* (New York: John
Wiley & Sons; Chichester: Praxis Publishing Ltd., 1998). See also
Geoffrey W. Marcy and R. Paul Butler, "Detection of Extrasolar
Giant Planets," *Annual Reviews of Astronomy and Astrophysics* (1998):
36:57–97.

17. See Michel Mayor and Didier Queloz, "A Jupiter-mass Companion
to a Solar-type Star," *Nature* (1995) 378:357 and http://www.
obs-hp.fr/www/nouvelles/51-peg.html.for the discovery data; see
http://cannon.sfsu.edu/~gmarcy/planetsearch/51Peg/51Peg.html
for the confirmation data.

18. See http://www.physics.sfsu.edu/~gmarcy/planetsearch/upsand.
html and http://astron.berkeley.edu/~gmarcy/planetsearch/upsand/
upsand.html. Also see Jack J. Lissauer, "Three Planets for Upsilon An-
dromedae," *Nature* (1999) 398:659–60.

19. Gregory W. Henry, Geoffrey W. Marcy, R. Paul Butler, and Steven
S. Vogt, "Transiting '51 Peg-Like' Planet," The Astrophysical Jour-
nal Letters (2000 January 20) 529:L41–44, and David Charbonneau,
Timothy M. Brown, David W. Latham, and Michel Mayor, "Detec-
tion of Planetary Transits Across a Sun-like Star," *The Astrophysical
Journal Letters* (2000 January 20) 529:L45-48, Also see T. Castellano,
J. Jenkins, D. E. Trilling, L. Doyle, and D. Koch, "Detection of Plan-
etary Transits of the Star HD 209458 in the Hipparcos Data Set," *The
Astrophysical Journal Letters* (2000 March 20) 532:L51-53, and Tsevi
Mazeh, Dominique Naef, Guillermo Torres, David W. Latham, et al.,
"The Spectroscopic Orbit of the Planetary Companion Transiting HD

209458," *The Astrophysical Journal Letters* (2000 March 20) 532:L55-58. Note that an extensive expansion of planet searching using this technique is proposed within NASA as the "Kepler Mission"—see http://www.kepler.arc.nasa.gov.

20. Mark Sincell, "Shadow and Shine Offer Glimpses of Otherworldly Jupiters," *Science* (1999) 286:1822–23.

21. D. P. Bennett et al., "Discovery of a Planet Orbiting a Binary Star System from Gravitational Microlensing," *Nature* (1999) 402: 57–59.

22. For an overview, see Elizabeth Culotta and Linda Rowan, "Planetary Systems Proliferate," *Science* (1999) 286:65-84; and Jack J. Lissauer, "How Common Are Habitable Planets?" *Nature* (1999) 402 supplement, "Impacts of Foreseeable Science": C11–14.

23. Andrew C. Cameron et al., "Probable Detection of Starlight Reflected from the Giant Planet Orbiting τ Boötis," *Nature* (1999) 402:751–55.

24. Geoffrey W. Marcy and R. Paul Butler, "Hunting Planets Beyond," *Astronomy* (2000 March): 43–47 (http://www2.astronomy.com/astro/); David J. Stevenson, "Planetary Science: A Space Odyssey," *Science* (2000) 287:997–1005; Kathy A. Svitil, "Field Guide to New Plants: Amazing Worlds Beyond Our Own Solar System," *Discover* (2000: 49–55); and Ron Cowan, "Less Massive Than Saturn: Astronomers Pass a Milestone in the Search for New Worlds," *Science News* (2000) 157:220–22. For updates on planet discoveries, visit *Astronomy*'s Web site at http://www:astronomy.com and *The Extrasolar Planets Encyclopaedia* at http://cfa-www.harvard.edu/planets/, http://cfa-www.harvard.edu/planets/sites.html, or http://www.obspm.fr/encycl/encycl.html. To learn the latest from the planet search team of Marcy and Butler, visit http://www.physics.sfsu.edu/~gmarcy/planetsearch/plane search. html and http://cannon.sfsu.edu/~gmarcy/planetsearch/planetsearch.html. Also see William Speed Weed, "Geoffrey Marcy: He Finds New Worlds" (San Francisco: *Salon Magazine*, http:/www.salon.com, 1999): 27–30.

25. See http://science.nasa.gov/newhome/headlines/ast14nov99_1.htm. Quoting from IAU Circular #7307 (11-12-99): "G. W. Henry, Tennessee State University, G. Marcy, U. C. Berkeley, R. P. Butler, Dept. of Terrestrial Magnetism, and S. S. Vogt, UCO Lick Observatory report that HD 209458 (G0V) exhibits sinusoidal velocity variations with semi-amplitude of 81 m/s, indicating presence of a

companion with Msini = 0.63 Jupiter masses and an orbital period of 3.523 d. Photometry reveals a transit ingress at JD 2451490.70 with depth of 0.017 mag, consistent with the transit time predicted from the velocities. Further measurements of transits and velocities would be valuable. The next three predicted times of ingress occur at UT times: 15 Nov 6:19, 18 Nov 18:53, 22 Nov 7:28, all times uncertain by 1 hour. If correct, the inferred mass is 0.63 Mjup and radius is 1.6 Rjup, implying a density of 0.21 g/cc."

26. "What Life Means to Einstein: An Interview by George Sylvester Viereck," *The Saturday Evening Post* (October 26, 1929).

27. For information on these programs, see http://www.hq.nasa.gov/office/oss/missions/index.htm. Also see Robert Naeye, "Looking for Life: Space Observatories of the Future Will Be Capable of Spotting Life-Bearing Planets in the Glare of Nearby Stars," *Astronomy* (1999) 27:45–47. This issue of *Astronomy* also contains a number of articles about these programs in a special section called "Forging the Future," including "Dan Goldin's Vision." An archive of Goldin's speeches is available at http://www.nasa.gov/bios/goldin_speeches.html.

28. See http://www.obs-hp.fr/%7Elabeyrie/index.html.

29. See http://obshpx.obs-hp.fr/~labeyrie/index.html.

30. See http://www.obs-hp.fr/~lardiere/these/news.htm.

31. For other details on ambitious future plans for other ground-based observatory projects, see Michael D. Lemonick, "From Here to Eternity: Get Ready for a New Generation of Telescopes That Can See Forever," *Discover* (1999): 48–55; Govert Schilling, "Giant Eyes on the Sky," *Astronomy* (1999) 27:48–59.

32. See http://www.eso.org/projects/vlti/ and http://www.eso.org/outreach/epr/slides/.

33. See http://www2.astronomy.com/astro/ and http://www.eso.org/projects/owl/.

34. See http://obshpx.obs-hp.fr/~labeyrie/index.html.

35. See http://obshpx.obs-hp.fr/~labeyrie/index.html and http://obshpx.obs-hp.fr/~labeyrie/danaweb/danaeei.html. Also see Antoine Labeyrie, "Snapshots of Alien Worlds—The Future of Interferometry," *Science* (1999) 285:1864–65.

36. For critical views on NASA programs, see Timothy Ferris, "A Space Station? Big Deal!" *New York Times* (November 28, 1999): 124–28 [Op-Ed Article]; Martin Rees, "A European Perspective on Space," *Science*, 284:1121 [Editorial]; Andrew Lawler, "Making a Deal with

the Devil," *Science* (1999) 284:1106–107 [News Focus]; Robert G. Oler, Richard Kolker, and Mark Whittington, "Thirty Years of Ineptitude: Time to Rescue Space Exploration from NASA," *Weekly Standard* (July 26, 1999): 27–29; and "Double, Double, Hubble Trouble," *The Economist* (1999 December): 83–84; http://www.economist.com/tfs/aarchive_tframeset.html).

37. See http://origins.jpl.nasa.gov/, http://origins.jpl.nasa.gov/missions/sbobs.html, http://origins.jpl.nasa.gov/education/images, and http://origins.jpl.nasa.gov/index.html.

38. See "NASA's Great Observatories" at http://sirtf.jpl.nasa.gov/Mission/Family/greatobs.html.

39. See http://origins.jpl.nasa.gov/missions/hst.html.

40. See http://origins.jpl.nasa.gov/education/ipff/ipff14.html.

41. For further information, contact Brooks McKinney, Manager, Public Relations, TRW Space & Electronic Systems Group, brooks.mckinney@trw.com, 310.814.8177, or see the Goddard Space Flight Center site, http://ngst.gsfc.nasa.gov/Hardware/designs.html. Also see *Astronomy* (1999) 27:46.

42. For further information, see http://www.jpl.nasa.gov/releases/2000/tpfcontracts.html or contact Media Relations Office, Jet Propulsion Laboratory, California Institute of Technology, National Aeronautics and Space Administration, Pasadena, CA 91109; (818) 354-5011. Also see http://www.economist.co.uk/editorial/freeforall/current/index_st8928.html, "A Roadmap for Planet Hunting," *The Economist* (2000 April 8–14) [Science and Technology].

43. For further information, contact Brooks McKinney, Manager, Public Relations, TRW Space & Electronic Systems Group, brooks.mckinney@trw.com, 310.814.8177, or see the Jet Propulsion Laboratory site http://www.jpl.nasa.gov/pictures/astro/tpf/. Also see *Astronomy* (1999) 27:46.

44. See http://origins.jpl.nasa.gov/education/ipff/ipff17.html.

45. G. W. Wetherill, "How Special Is Jupiter?" *Nature* (1995) 373:470 and "Occurrence of Earth-like Bodies in Planetary Systems," *Icarus* (1996) 119:219–38.

46. A common misunderstanding is that the Anthropic Principle implies cosmic anthropocentrism. While it is true that the use of *anthro* derives from certain species-solipsistic speculations linking human observership in quantum mechanics with the observed features of the cosmos (see, for example, Brandon Carter, "Large Number Coincidences and the Anthropic Principle in Cosmology"

in *Confrontation of Cosmological Theories with Observational Data*, ed.
M. Longair [Dordrecht: Reidel, 1974]: 291–98), in a wider view
the term "biocentric" is perhaps more accurate today. This term
was used by one of the first scientists to study cosmic "fine-tuning," the Harvard chemist Lawrence J. Henderson. In a lecture de-
livered at the Lowell Institute (see *The Fitness of the Environment:
An Inquiry into the Biological Significance of the Properties of Matter*
[New York: The Macmillan Company, 1913]), Henderson argued
that: "The properties of matter and the course of cosmic evolution
are now seen to be intimately related to the structure of the living
being and to its activities; they become, therefore, far more important in biology than has been previously suspected. For the
whole evolutionary process, both cosmic and organic, is one, and
the biologist may now rightly regard the universe in its very
essence as biocentric." For further information, see John D. Barrow and Frank J. Tipler, *The Anthropic Cosmological Principle* (Oxford University Press, 1986).

47. Michael R. Rampino and Ken Caldeira, "The Goldilocks Problem:
Climatic Evolution and Long-Term Habitability of Terrestrial Planets," *Annual Review of Astronomy and Astrophysics* (1994) 32:83–114
and David J. Stevenson, "Life-Sustaining Planets in Interstellar
Space?" *Nature* (1999) 400:32 [Scientific Correspondence]. Of recent importance is an understanding of recovery from an ice catastrophe by carbon dioxide buildup; see P. F. Hoffman, A. J. Kaufman, G. P. Halverson, D. P. Schrag et al., "A Neoproterozoic
Snowball Earth," *Science* (1998) 281:1342–46 and Paul F. Hoffman
and Daniel P. Schrag, "Snowball Earth," *Scientific American* (2000)
282:68–75. Important papers by James F. Kasting on this topic include: "How Climate Evolved on the Terrestrial Planets," *Scientific
American* (1988) 256:90–97; "Habitable Zones around Main Sequence Stars" (with Daniel P. Whitmire and Ray T. Reynolds),
Icarus (1993) 101:108–28; "Earth's Early Atmosphere," *Science*
(1993) 259:920; "Habitable Zones and the Search for Extraterrestrial Life," *Origins of Life* (1997) 27:291; "Planetary Atmosphere
Evolution: Do Other Habitable Planets Exist and Can We Detect
Them?" *Astrophysics and Space Science* (1996) 241:3–24; "Ultraviolet Radiation from F and K Stars and Implications for Planetary
Habitability" (with Douglas C. B. Whittet and William R. Shel-
don), *Origins of Life and Evolution of the Biosphere* (1997)
27:413–20); "Habitable Planets with High Obliquities" (with Dar-

ren M. Williams), *Icarus* (1997) 129:254–67; "Habitable Moons around Extrasolar Giant Planets" (with Darren M. Williams and Richard A. Wade), *Nature* (1997) 385:234–36 [Letters]; and "Long-term Stability of Earth's Climate" [in press]. Also see J. Laskar, F. Joutel, and P. Robutel, "Stabilization of the Earth's Obliquity by the Moon," *Nature* (1993) 361:615–17. For an overview favoring the view that Earth-like conditions are exceedingly rare, see *Rare Earth: Why Complex Life Is Uncommon in the Universe* by Peter D. Ward and Donald Brownlee (New York: Copernicus/Springer-Verlag, 2000). These authors argue that simple, single-celled life is abundant, but that complex life cannot be abundant because of problems such as radical climatic instability due to chaotic obliquity fluctuations.

48. Stanley L. Jaki, "Alone?" *Means to Message: A Treatise on Truth* (Grand Rapids, Mich.: William B. Eerdmans, 1999), 213–23; Frank D. Drake and Dava Sobel, *Is Anyone Out There? The Scientific Search for Extraterrestrial Intelligence* (New York: Delacorte Press, 1992).

49. Richard Kerr, "Early Life Thrived Despite Earthly Travails," *Science* (1999) 284:2111–13; Gabrielle Walker, "Snowball Earth," *New Scientist* (1999): 29–33; J. Kirschvink, "Snowball Earth," in *The Proterozoic Biosphere: A Multidisciplinary Study*, ed. J. William Schopf and Cornelis Klein (New York: Cambridge University Press, 1992); see P. F. Hoffman, A. J. Kaufman, G. P. Halverson, D. P. Schrag et al., "A Neoproterozoic Snowball Earth," *Science* (1998) 281:1342–46; and Paul F. Hoffman and Daniel P. Schrag, "Snowball Earth," *Scientific American* (2000) 282:68–75.

50. Steven M. Stanley, *Children of the Ice Age: How a Global Catastrophe Allowed Humans to Evolve* (New York: Harmony, 1996).

51. For details on this debate, see: Stephen J. Gould. *Wonderful Life: The Burgess Shale and the Nature of History* (New York: W. W. Norton, 1989); *Full House: The Spread of Excellence from Plato to Darwin* (New York: Harmony, 1996); Michael Ruse, *Monad to Man: The Concept of Progress in Evolutionary Biology* (Cambridge, Mass.: Harvard University Press, 1996); Simon Conway Morris, *Crucible of Creation: Burgess Shale & the Rise of Animals* (New York: Oxford University Press, 1998); Holmes Rolston III, *Genes, Genesis and God: Values and Their Origins in Natural and Human History: The Gifford Lectures, University of Edinburgh, 1997–1998* (New York: Cambridge University Press, 1999); and Robert Wright, *Nonzero: The Logic of Human Destiny* (New York: Pantheon, 2000).

52. S. J. Mojzsis et al., "Evidence for Life on Earth Before 3,800 Million Years Ago," *Nature* (1996) 384:55–59; Minik T. Rosing, "^{13}C Depleted Carbon Microparticles in the >3700-Ma Sea-Floor Sedimentary Rocks from West Greenland," *Science* (1999) 283:674–76. For an overview of additional arguments, see Paul C. Davies, *The Fifth Miracle: The Search for the Origin and Meaning of Life* (New York: Simon and Schuster, 1999).

53. Jeffrey Burton Russell, *Inventing the Flat Earth: Columbus and Modern Historians* (Westport, Conn.: Praeger, 1991).

54. Le Cur ϑ Jean Meslier (*c.* 1664–1733), *Testament* (ed. R. Charles, 1864), vol. I. ch. 2. This famous quotation is: *"Je voudrais . . . que le dernier des rois fϕt ϑtrangl ϑ avec les boyaux du dernier prΛtre"* ("I should like . . . the last of the kings to be strangled with the guts of the last priest"). However, Meslier is quoted by Diderot as having said he wished *"Et des boyaux du dernier prΛtre / Serrons le cou du dernia roi"* ("And [with] the guts of the last priest / Let's shake the neck of the last king"). See *The Oxford Dictionary of Quotations*, 4th. ed., rev. (New York: Oxford University Press, 1996), 458.

55. For detailed discussion and analysis of the science-religion interaction in the case of Galileo, see John Hedley Brooke, *Science and Religion* (Cambridge University Press, 1992) and John Hedley Brooke and Geoffrey Cantor, *Reconstructing Nature: The Engagement of Science and Religion* (Edinburgh: T & T Clark, 1998). Brooke is past president of the British Association for the History of Science. He recently was appointed to a newly endowed chair in theology and science at Oxford University.

56. See Constance Holden, "Burned by History," *Science* (2000) 287:1743 [Random Samples].

57. For example, Epicurus wrote in a letter to Herodotus (Cyril Bailey, ed. and trans., *Epicurus: The Extant Remains* [New York: Oxford University Press, 1926], 25): "There are infinite worlds both like and unlike this world of ours. For the atoms being infinite in number, as was already proved, are borne on far out into space. For those atoms which are of such nature that a world could be created by them or made by them, have not been used up either on one world or a limited number of worlds. . . . So that there nowhere exists an obstacle to the infinite number of worlds." Metrodoros wrote: "To consider the Earth the only populated world in infinite space is as absurd as to assert that in an entire field sown in millet, only one grain will grow." See http://www.britannica.com/bcom/eb/article/3/ 0,5716,109623+4,00.

html or http://www.2think.org/ aliens.html [personal communication from Douglas A. Vakoch, Ph.D.,SETI Institute].

58. In this regard, Pierre Duhem notes that, "the first time in Western Christianity that one heard someone speak about the plurality of inhabited worlds, it was proposed by a theologian who had spoken before the ecumenical council a few years before. The person who sought to reflect upon the characteristics of the inhabitants of the sun and moon in a book that became well known had the confidence of popes; the highest ecclesiastical honors were bestowed upon him. There can be no greater proof of the extreme liberality of the Catholic church toward the meditations of the philosopher and the experiments of the physicists" (Pierre Maurice Marie Duhem, *Medieval Cosmology: Theories of Infinity, Place, Time, Void, and the Plurality of Worlds,* ed. and trans. Roger Ariew [Chicago: University of Chicago Press, 1985]).

Nicholas' advocacy for these ideas was based broadly on notions of the infinity of God and a form of cosmological pantheism, which can be seen in the following quotation: "Rather than think that so many stars and parts of the heavens are uninhabited and that this earth of ours alone is peopled—and that with beings perhaps of an inferior type—we will suppose that in every region there are inhabitants differing in nature by rank and all owing their origin to God, who is the center and circumference of all stellar regions" (Nicholas of Cusa, *Of Learned Ignorance,* trans. Germain Heron, intro. by D. J. B. Hawkins [New Haven, Conn.: Yale University Press, 1954], 114–15).

59. Stephen Dick, *Plurality of Worlds: The Origins of the Extraterrestrial Life Debate from Democritus to Kant* (New York: Cambridge University Press, 1982).

60. The story of how the Milky Way was established as a vast disk-shaped stellar system has been told by Stanley L. Jaki in his book *The Milky Way: An Elusive Road for Science* (New York: Science History Publications, 1972). Newton made rough estimates of distances to the nearest stars by an ingenious method of comparison between the reflected brightness of Saturn and the direct brightness of stars. However, these astonishing distance estimates were not confirmed quantitatively until precise stellar parallax measurements were first made in the late 1830s by Thomas Henderson, Friedrich Wilhelm Bessel, and Friedrich von Struve.

61. Kitty Ferguson, *Measuring the Universe: The Historical Quest to Quantify Space* (London: Headline, 1999); Richard Panek, *Seeing and Be-*

lieving: How the Telescope Opened Our Eyes and Minds to the Heavens (New York: Viking, 1998).

62. Sir John Templeton, *Possibilities for Over One Hundredfold More Spiritual Information: The Humble Approach in Theology and Science* (Philadelphia: Templeton Foundation Press, 2000). Previously published as John Marks Templeton, *The Humble Approach: Scientists Discover God* (Philadelphia: Templeton Foundation Press, 1998; formerly published by Continuum, 1995).

63. For consideration of the enterprise of science and religion in the context of critical issues in postmodernism, see Jacobus Wentzel Vrede van Huyssteen, *The Shaping of Rationality: Toward Interdisciplinarity in Theology and Science* (Grand Rapids, Mich.: W. B. Eerdmans, 1999) and *Duet or Duel? Theology and Science in a Postmodern World* (Harrisburg, Pa.: Trinity Press International, 1999); also see Niels Henrik Gregersen and Jacobus Wentzel Vrede van Huyssteen, eds., *Rethinking Theology and Science: Six Models for the Current Dialogue* (Grand Rapids, Mich.: Eerdmans, 1998). For a clear statement in favor of an epistemology of critical realism shared at the interface, see John C. Polkinghorne's Terry Lectures: *Belief in God in an Age of Science* (New Haven, Conn.: Yale University Press, 1998).

64. Stephen Jay Gould, *Rocks of Ages: Science and Religion in the Fullness of Life* (New York: Ballantine, 1999).

65. Ian Barbour, *Issues in Science and Religion* (Englewood Cliffs, N.J.: Prentice-Hall, 1966); and *Religion in an Age of Science: The Gifford Lectures, 1989–1991*, vol. 1 (New York: HarperCollins, 1991).

66. Stephen J. Gould, *Full House: The Spread of Excellence from Plato to Darwin* (New York: Harmony, 1996).

67. Bacon's words reflected the old tradition of "God's two books"—Nature and Revelation: "Let no man think or maintain that a man can search too far or be too well studied in the book of God's word or in the book of God's works; but rather let men endeavour an endless progress or proficience in both." Charles Darwin, *On the Origin of Species* (London: John Murray, 1859), ii.

68. John Langdon-Davies, *Man and His Universe* (New York, London: Harper & Brothers, 1930). Also see Alister Hardy, *The Biology of God: A Scientist's Study of Man the Religious Animal* (London: Jonathan Cape, 1975).

69. Freeman J. Dyson, *Infinite in All Directions: Gifford Lectures Given at Aberdeen, Scotland, April–November 1985* (New York: Harper & Row, 1988).

70. See Robert T. Pappalardo, James W. Head, and Ronald Greeley, "The Hidden Ocean of Europa," *Scientific American* (October 1999): 54–63.

71. However, if advanced civilizations are common in the universe, they still could be very uncommon in individual galaxies. There really is no good sense yet on how to input realistic parameter estimates into the Drake equation (the method of estimating the likelihood of the existence of other scientifically and technologically advanced civilizations in the galaxy mentioned in the text). It is quite possible, of course, that the probability of advanced civilizations is very low, say one percent, per typical galaxy. Thus, if SETI is not successful, the prospects for extrasolar astrobiology would be subject to limits intrinsic to low-resolution interferometric visualization of planets. For an entertaining overview on SETI, see Joel Achenbach, *Captured by Aliens: The Search for Life and Truth in a Very Large Universe* (New York: Simon & Schuster, 1999). Also, from an active advocate, see Seth Shostak, *Sharing the Universe: Perspectives on Extraterrestrial Life* (Berkeley Ca.: Berkeley Hills Books, 1998). Some philosophical and theological issues are addressed in: Paul C. Davies, *Are We Alone?* (New York: Basic Books, 1995). An impressive detailed history is provided by Stephen J. Dick in his book *The Biological Universe: The Twentieth-Century Extraterrestrial Life Debate and the Limits of Science* (New York: Cambridge University Press, 1996).

72. Richard Dawkins, *The Blind Watchmaker* (New York: Norton, 1986); George C. Williams, *The Pony Fish's Glow and Other Clues to Plan and Purpose in Nature* (New York: Basic Books, 1997).

73. A wealth-creating economy spontaneously optimizes its gross productivity through the undirected freedom of action of the myriad purpose-directed agents that constitute it. Specific purposes identified in the minds of overseers may be best served by developing rules that sustain a level playing field as well as support and protect other interests that are external to the economic "game."

74. Stephen J. Gould, *Wonderful Life: The Burgess Shale and the Nature of History* (New York: W. W. Norton, 1989).

75. For background and critique, see Robert Wright, "The Accidental Creationist: Why Stephen Jay Gould is Bad for Evolution," *The New Yorker* (December 13, 1999): 56–65.

76. Use of the term "Lamarckian" applied to evolution following the development of innovative culture can be traced back at least to Sir

Peter Medawar in his Reith Lectures, presented in his book *The Future of Man* (London: Methuen, 1960): 98.

77. For further detailed discussions on the issue of evolution, complexity, progress, and purpose, see Stephen J. Gould, *Wonderful Life: The Burgess Shale and the Nature of History* (New York: W. W. Norton, 1989) and *Full House: The Spread of Excellence from Plato to Darwin* (New York: Harmony, 1996); Simon Conway Morris, *The Crucible of Creation: The Burgess Shale and the Rise of Animals* (New York: Oxford University Press, 1998); Michael Ruse, *Monad to Man: The Concept of Progress in Evolutionary Biology* (Cambridge, Mass.: Harvard University Press, 1996); Christian De Duve, *Vital Dust: Life as a Cosmic Imperative* (New York: Basic Books, 1996); Holmes Ralston, III, *Genes, Genesis and God: Values and Their Origins in Natural and Human History* (New York: Cambridge University Press, 1998); Kenneth Miller, *Finding Darwin's God: A Scientist's Search for Common Ground Between God and Evolution* (New York: Cliff Street Books, A Division of HarperCollins, 1999); John Haught, *God after Darwin: A Theology of Evolution* (Boulder, Colo.: Westview Press, 1999); and Robert Wright, *Nonzero: The Logic of Human Destiny* (New York: Pantheon, 2000).

78. *"Planeta yest' kolybel' rasuma, no nel'zia vechno zhit' v kolybeli."* Konstantin Eduardovich Tsiolkovsky, "The Investigation of Space by Means of Reactive Devices" (in Russian). In *Sobranie Sochineii K.E. Tsiolkovskogo*, vol. 2 (Moscow: Academy of Science of the U.S.S.R., 1954).

79. Alice C. Meynell, "Christ in the Universe," *The Poems of Alice Meynell* (New York: Scribner, 1923).

80. Raymond M. Smullyan, "Planet Without Laughter," in *This Book Needs No Title: A Budget of Living Paradoxes* (New York: Simon & Schuster, 1986).

81. Olaf Stapledon, *Star Maker* (New York: Dover Publications, Inc., 1937). Also note that Stapledon wrote one of the great classics in science fiction that powerfully influenced such writers as Arthur C. Clarke and Doris Lessing: *Last and First Men: A Story of the Near and Far Future,* foreword by Gregory Benford, afterword by Doris Lessing (Los Angeles: J. P. Tarcher; New York: distributed by St. Martin's Press, 1988, *c.* 1930).

82. Fyodor Dostoyevsky, *The Brothers Karamazov, A Novel in Four Parts and an Epilogue*, trans. Constance Garnett (New York: Macmillan, 1912).

83. Blaise Pascal, *The Oxford Dictionary of Quotations*, 4th. ed., rev. (New York: Oxford University Press, 1996), 508.

84. Julian of Norwich, *The Wisdom of Julian of Norwich,* Monica Furlong, ed. (Grand Rapids, Mich.: W. B. Eerdmans, 1996).

85. Elie Wiesel, "Nuit" (Paris: Les Editions de Minuit, 1958); English trans., "Night," by Francois Mauriac, in *The Night Trilogy* (New York: Hill and Wang, 1987), 43.

86. A particularly noteworthy example is William H. Vanstone, *Love's Endeavour, Love's Expense: The Response of Being to the Love of God* (London: Darnton, Longman and Todd, 1977). For a helpful discussion of some relevant issues in the context of the interdisciplinary interaction of science and religion, see the final chapter of Nancy Murphy and George F. R. Ellis, *On the Moral Nature of the Universe: Theology, Cosmology & Ethics* (Minneapolis, Minn.: Fortress Press, 1996). Also see John F. Haught, *God after Darwin: A Theology of Evolution* (Boulder, Colo.: Westview Press, 2000). For a relevant view by two biological scientists, see Harold J. Morowitz, *Cosmic Joy and Local Pain: Musings of a Mystic Scientist* (New York: Charles Scribner's Sons, 1987); and Kenneth R. Miller, *Finding Darwin's God: A Scientist's Search for Common Ground Between God and Evolution* (New York: Cliff Street Books, A Division of HarperCollins, 1999).

87. See especially Hans Urs von Balthasar, *Love Alone: The Way of Revelation* (London: Sheed & Ward, 1968).

88. George Steiner, *Errata: An Examined Life* (New Haven, Conn.: Yale University Press, 1997).

89. Robert Zubrin, *Entering Space: Creating a Spacefaring Civilization* (New York: Jeremy Tarcher/Putnam, 1999).

4

The Arrogance
of Mediocrity

OWEN GINGERICH

Towering above the apple orchards in bucolic Harvard, Massachusetts, stands a great antenna, a fully steerable eighty-five-foot aluminum dish that cocks its giant ear upward day and night, listening for signals from space. An alien object in the landscape, it is an essential piece in a visionary project to capture evidence for the existence of intelligent aliens far beyond our solar system. In the control room below, a megachannel receiver scans the frequencies around 1.4–1.7 GHz, corresponding to a particularly transparent wavelength region in interstellar space, the so-called water hole. As the earth spins on its axis, the stars silently march across the sky, and the antenna sweeps out a new half-degree swath of the sky each day.

False alarms trigger the circuitry from time to time, but so far no convincing extra–solar system intelligence has been found. Some years ago NASA had in place a standing committee of scientists, philosophers, and theologians to advise on how to break the news to the public when unmistakable signals were finally recorded. The excitement and anticipation were palpable. The breakthrough could take place at any moment, and its imminent arrival was awaited as keenly as Christ's second coming had been expected by the early apostles of the first century.

There is no question but that in certain ways the time is finally ripe for such a discovery. In humankind's long journey from the taming of fire to modern technological prowess, we have not only achieved the ability to radically alter the earth or its atmosphere, we have reached an understanding of the nature and place of distant stars plus knowledge of how to send or receive signals across vast distances. A century ago this would have been quite impossible. Today such communication is well within our ken, and the search for extraterrestial intelligence (SETI) goes on.

With the very first inkling that other celestial worlds resembled our own, imaginative writers began to populate these worlds with other creatures. The seventeenth-century German astronomer Johannes Kepler wrote a pioneering science fiction dream in which he described the inhabitants of the moon, though admittedly it was a form of Copernican propaganda to show his public how celestial movements would appear from a moving body different from the earth.[1] His younger contemporary, the chaplain John Wilkins (later bishop of Chester), wrote in vernacular English about a voyage to the moon.[2] A century later the Dutch polymath-astronomer Christiaan Huygens described why the inhabitants of Saturn would have hemp: "If their Globe is divided like ours, between Sea and Land, as it's evident it is, we have great reason to allow them the Art of Navigation, and not proudly ingross so great, so useful a thing to our selves. And what a troop of other things follow from this allowance? If they have Ships, they must have Sails and Anchors, Ropes, Pullies, and Rudders."[3]

As a new millennium dawns, we have learned of many more far-flung celestial worlds that are potential homes for extraterrestrial life. We know as well that there are about 200 billion stars in our Milky Way galaxy (more than thirty apiece for every man, woman, and child on our planet), and we know that there are more than 100 billion galaxies beyond the Milky Way system. There is every reason to believe that planets circle many of these distant stars even though they are generally too faint to be seen, and given the wealth of possibilities, there must be countless habitable environments scattered throughout these starry realms. Conservative speculators concede that on some there may be life. Enthusiasts argue that there *must* be life, and some of it will inevitably be intelligent life, including intelligence far beyond our own.

Theologically the way has been open to consider extraterrestrial life ever since 1277, when the bishop of Paris declared that it was heretical to limit God's power to create life only on Earth.[4] This edict placed the church in an awkward position, since the ethos of its teachings was that mankind occupied a central pinnacle of creation, and surely the Genesis story marked a crescendo with the creation of Adam and Eve. Whether or not God would have chosen to create additional intelligent life was another question, and most churchmen thought not. Today, at least, we have the possibility of putting that question to the test. And within the framework of humility theology, whose cardinal tenet is that there is far more to be learned about God than is already known, it makes good sense to hold open any question concerning the full range of God's creativity. Humility theology reminds us that our world may well just be a little corner of God's vast creative accomplishments. The search for extraterrestrial intelligence also works on a very similar premise, namely, that our intelligence may be frequently matched or superseded throughout the vastness of the cosmos. Within the scientific arena the rationale for this premise generally rests on what I shall call the principle of mediocrity. But in assuming that on a transgalactic scale we are average or mediocre, we can all too easily envision that those we might contact are equally average or mediocre, much as we pay lip service to a contrary view. Thus, in our zeal to avoid anthropocentricity, we can unwittingly fall into a trap of anthropocentrism. These are the themes I wish to explore in this essay.

Perhaps a short anecdotal digression will serve as a fable for this exploration. Some months ago a researcher for an interactive lobby exhibit for a major American planetarium came to me with a problem. She wanted to build a computer program that illustrated the lore associated with various constellations, but she did not want to restrict herself to the mythology and pictorial representations from the culture of Western Europe. Try as she would, she had not been able to find authentic pictures to represent Chinese or African or American Indian legends. It gradually dawned on me that she had backed herself into a marvelous catch-22 dilemma. "In your effort to avoid Western European chauvinism," I explained, "you are unconsciously superimposing all of your Western artistic sensibilities onto these other cultures. In effect, you are asking them to depict sky lore by the same artistic conventions that were developed over the centuries in Western civilization." Of course, that simply wasn't the way the Indians, Africans, or Chinese were prepared to think about the stars. Likewise, when we speculate that we are not alone in the cosmos, despite our recognition that alien life could be vastly more intelligent or in a very unfamiliar guise, we all too easily mentally clone ourselves, with our own understanding and limitations, as substitute extraterrestrials.

A central figure in the scientific quest to understand our place in the cosmos was the sixteenth-century astronomer Nicolaus Copernicus. A churchman affiliated with the Frauenburg Cathedral in the northernmost diocese of Poland, Copernicus dreamed of a "theory pleasing to the mind" and worked out the idea of a heliocentric cosmology. If the sun, rather than the earth, was at the center of the universe, the apparent complex motions of the planets could be explained more simply. Despite Copernicus's proposal, the time-honored and seemingly sensible conception of an Earth-centered universe did not die quickly. Nevertheless, the new heliocentric scheme gradually took root as an actual, physical description of the world.

In retrospect, we can see that the Copernican cosmology transformed the earth from being considered a central, unique locale in the cosmos to being just one of a number of planets, in some sense just an ordinary sort of place. In the steps that followed a century later, the sun, now recognized as a star, became only one of many. In the twentieth century it has become increasingly popular to refer to a "Copernican principle," the idea that we cannot flaunt any notions of unique or special identity. We should not be on a special planet circling round a special star in a special (central?) place in a special galaxy. With respect to the cosmos we should not be special creatures, even though we clearly are with respect to life on Earth. In full dress, this is the principle of mediocrity, and Copernicus would have been shocked to learn his name was to be associated with it.

Does the so-called Copernican principle gain us any leverage scientifically? I can think of at least two historical occasions when it might have contributed to significant advances in science. A long-perpetuated error involved the scale of the planetary system. Both Ptolemy and Copernicus accepted a value twenty times too small. This meant that after the telescope was invented, when it was possible to measure the angular diameters of the planets, the planetary sizes deduced from the apparent diameters and assumed distances were on average suspiciously small. If anyone had been bold enough to assume that the earth was an average size, he could have argued that the solar system had to be many times larger than was commonly accepted, and the distant planets proportionately larger. But of course the earth *could* have been a giant, and deductions from averages can be treacherous. In the actual event, this argument from an average earth was never persuasively made.

Another astronomical situation arose in the middle of the twentieth century when it seemed that our Milky Way was the largest galaxy in the universe. Again, had anyone said, "Well, by the principle of mediocrity, this cannot be," and proceeded to argue that the universe itself had to be larger than common consent agreed, she might have made a major breakthrough. I remember that Harlow Shapley, then one of the best-known astronomers in America, assigned a graduate student to the conundrum that the globular clusters surrounding the nearby Andromeda Galaxy appeared only half the size of those in our own giant Milky Way Galaxy. Neither Shapley nor the student guessed that if the scale of the universe was twice as great, both the anomalous size of the Milky Way and the diminished size of the Andromeda Galaxy's globular clusters would be resolved. The principle of mediocrity had not come to the rescue.

In neither case did the Copernican principle lead to a scientific advance, and it is not clear that it currently gives us any actual perspicacity with respect to the universe. Instead, it seems to be a strong philosophical principle, ardently believed, but not necessarily insightful. At first blush it might seem to mesh seamlessly with humility theology. Does it not seem arrogant to claim that we're at the top of the heap cosmically? Isn't it much more humble to accept that we're likely to be middling, literally mediocre? This is a point that requires a more subtle investigation.

The principle of mediocrity (alias the Copernican principle) is closely related to the principle of the uniformity of nature. Aristotle's chief error was the supposition that the earth was fundamentally different from the heavens, that the earth was made of four terrestrial elements—earth, air, fire, and water—whereas the incorruptible heavens were made of an ether and were governed by totally different physical laws. After Newton demonstrated that gravity attracted both apples and the moon, and the same physical laws applied both on Earth and in the planetary realm, natural philosophers began to assume that the same physical laws applied throughout the cosmos. The chemistry of distant stars would resemble the sun's, and the same gravitational constant would control distant binary systems as well as the earth and moon. Cepheid variable stars in the Milky Way system would pulsate with the same periods as their counterparts in the Virgo cluster of galaxies. Stars a thousand light-years away would at least sometimes have planetary systems like our own, albeit unseen, and some of these would offer habitable environments.

Science would scarcely function without assuming the uniformity of nature. To envision a universe with *habitable* planets seems well within the range of this assumption, but to demand that the uniformity of nature requires *inhabited* planets is undoubtedly a stretch of the principle. Hence the rhetorical flourish from those who make the claim: it is the *Copernican principle* that is popularly cited as an argument by the proponents of a universe teeming with alien intelligent life.

Not long ago one of the architects of the proposal of how to search for extraterrestrial intelligence, Philip Morrison, visited my class to explain how radio communication offered the best hope for getting in touch, because the distances were so vast that interstellar travel was hardly the method of choice. He pointed out that the optimum frequency for searching would be the wavelength region near the interstellar absorption lines of neutral hydrogen (H) and the hydroxyl radical (OH), the so-called water hole H_2O, where interstellar space was the most transparent.[5] I noticed in the shadows in the back of the hall another physics professor who had dropped by. A few days later I encountered the professorial eavesdropper, who remarked, "I find it curious that we are so convinced that everyone out there will gather at the water hole to communicate. Actually, they will do it with neutrinos."

His tongue-in-cheek comment underlined the fact that we have understood the rudiments of interstellar radio communication for only a relatively few decades. What we have now so recently understood we have already swiftly generalized into "the best way to confirm the existence of extraterrestrial intelligence." In accepting the principle of mediocrity, the "e pluribus unum" approach, we have had the arrogance to make everyone else sufficiently mediocre and uniform to communicate our way, but if there is actually a great range of intelligence out there, our way might be pretty primitive by cosmic standards. This is not to criticize the present search strategy—after all, we must start somewhere if we want any chance at all to test the hypothesis—but we should be ready to recognize our unwitting anthropocentrisms.

But anthropocentrism is not necessarily bad or even wrong. It is good to remember that the human brain is by far the most complex physical object known to us in the entire cosmos. (Only God, "the Old One," the "ground of being," can claim to surpass this complexity.) Of the roughly 75,000 genes coded by the DNA in the human genome, half are expressed in the brain. There are about 100 billion neurons in the brain, nerve cells many with long, intricately interconnected dendritic extensions. Each neuron connects with about 10,000 other neurons. While the number of estimated stars in all the galaxies in the universe vastly exceeds the grains of sand on all the beaches of the world, the number of synaptic interconnections in a single human brain vastly exceeds the number of stars in our Milky Way: 10^{15} synapses versus 2×10^{11} stars.

For a human at rest, roughly half the body's energy supply fuels the brain. Oxygen (required for slowly "burning" the organic fuel) is carried to the brain by the red blood cells. In these cells the oxygen is loosely bonded to the iron atoms in the middle of the heme complex in the blood's hemoglobin. The oxygen is transferred into the blood through the intricately branched and foliate lung system, where the solubility of oxygen in water and the diameter of the capillaries are finely tuned for an efficient rate of transfer of the oxygen to the heme. Of all the possible metallic complexes, iron has just the right bonding strength to allow the capture and subsequent easy release of the oxygen.

Fortunately for us, our atmosphere contains a reasonable supply of oxygen—about 20 percent by number of atoms. This percentage is high enough to sustain fire, but not so high as to allow cataclysmic combustion. In fact, the acceptable oxygen limits for life more complex than single cells are fairly narrow, and the Earth's atmosphere, like the little bear's porridge, seems just right. Early in the century, the chemist L. J. Henderson drew attention to this fact in his remarkable book, *The Fitness of the Environment*, and Michael Denton has recently updated and detailed even more of these extraordinary circumstances in his book, *Nature's Destiny*.

As the human brain develops from infancy, a substantial part is devoted to the control of the organs of speech. No other aspect of human powers differs so significantly from those of the other animals as our ability to communicate by spoken language. It can well be argued that the ability to speak was the first essential step toward becoming human, as Ian Tattersal has done quite eloquently in his book of the same name, *Becoming Human*. Harvard anthropologist David Pilbeam has remarked that if we could have observed Neanderthal for the 200,000 years beginning that long ago, we could hardly have extrapolated to the complex human civilization that eventually arose on the earth. The Neanderthals made the same kinds of tools at the beginning that they did at the end of their existence, with no dramatic advance in technology. Perhaps, as Tattersal has argued, this was owing to their lack of language. Watching the Neanderthals' lack of progress gives us some pause about the inevitability of the evolution of intelligence.

The evidence at hand is hardly conducive to modesty. *Homo sapiens* clearly represents the pinnacle of life on Earth, far outdistancing any rivals, and to say otherwise is to engage in a sort of scholastic fantasy. "What is man that thou are mindful of him?" asks the Psalmist. "For thou hast made him a little lower than the angels and hast crowned him with glory and honor." Yet part of the glory of human creativity and self-consciousness is the ability to ask questions beyond ourselves, about whether the human brain is really the most complex object in the universe or about whether we are alone in the universe—alone in either sense, whether God exists or whether extraterrestrial intelligence exists.

Let us pursue this inquiry further, noting first that the foregoing few paragraphs have outlined in only the most rudimentary fashion two remarkable conclusions. Each would require an entire book to be adequately defended. The first conclusion is that human beings are astonishingly well constructed within the framework of possibilities and that the cosmic environment in general and the earth's environment in particular are themselves wonderfully congenial for intelligent, self-conscious life. The second conclusion, less well delineated here, is that intelligent, self-conscious life was not necessarily inevitable in our planetary system, and by extension, is not necessarily inevitable elsewhere.

Historically, until the work of Charles Darwin, the first conclusion was explained by the designing hand of a beneficent Creator. *On the Origin of Species* (1859) offered a naturalistic alternative: the mysterious arrival of variations followed by natural selection of the fittest varieties gradually left the world with creatures singularly adapted to their environments. Darwin's evolutionary scheme offered a reasonable explanation of the variations in both time and place of organisms, and in its key reliance on common descent, helped biologists understand the relationships of plants and animals and especially the curious "imperfect" adaptations such as the webfooted boobies that nest in trees in the Galapagos. With increased understanding of genetics and then of molecular genetics, the idea of common descent and organismic relationships has become even more firmly emplaced.

The evolutionary picture is one of a curious zigzag, opportunistic process. Irven DeVore has remarked that if the ancient lungfish, crawling onto the shore, had turned left instead of right, the course of evolution of land vertebrates would no longer match our present fauna. Stephen Jay Gould, in recounting the strange life-forms that lived in the Middle Cambrian ocean as evidenced by the famous Burgess Shale fossils, has emphasized the role of contingency and accident; if the tape of life were rewound and played out again, he has declared, the results would have been unpredictably different. Life would "cascade down another pathway," and the chance that the rerun "will contain anything remotely like a human being must be effectively nil."[6] David Pilbeam, in criticizing the implications of the film *Planet of the Apes*, in which chimpanzees take over as the intelligent masters after a nuclear disaster has eliminated *Homo sapiens*, says, "If we wipe ourselves out through a nuclear catastrophe, don't expect that evolution will ever again replace humankind with anything like us."

These Darwinist scenarios reinforce the conclusion that the evolution of intelligent, self-conscious life elsewhere is by no means assured or even probable. The dean of international evolutionists, Ernst Mayr, feels so strongly about the absurdity of extraterrestrial intelligence that he has declined to come to my class even to debate the issue, but he did provide an essay in which he, while agreeing that it is quite conceivable that life could originate elsewhere in the universe, argues that such a process would "presumably result in living entities that are drastically different from life on earth."[7]

The Darwinian viewpoint has interesting implications for the principle of mediocrity. While insinuating that we are the unplanned outcome of a naturalistic, mechanistic process, essentially a glorious accident, it also leaves open the prospect that we are in fact at the top of the heap, or at the very least, we are on a pinnacle so different from the others that there would be little hope of communication. Advocates of the Copernican principle may well be victims of unwitting anthropocentrism when they assume mediocrity not only for humankind but for other life as well. Is it not a wonderful hubris to demand enough mediocrity for alien life in the universe so that we would actually be able to communicate with it?

"Why are there nevertheless still proponents of the SETI project?" Mayr goes on to ask. "When one looks at their qualifications one finds that they are almost exclusively astronomers, physicists, and engineers. They are simply unaware of the fact that the success of the SETI project is not a matter of physical laws and engineering capabilities but a matter of biological and sociological factors."

What, we may well ask, do the chemists, physicists, and astronomers know that the biologists don't? Or rather, what hidden assumptions have the physicists tacitly made that the biologists reject? One of my colleagues is fond of pointing out that physicists make their livings by simplifying physical problems to their bare essentials so they can cope with problem solving, whereas biologists thrive in a world of intricate and fascinating complexity. Physicists love the principles of uniformity and mediocrity—these principles help them get on with their business. If friction renders the study of motion too difficult, then consider an idealized world without friction—in a first approximation our planetary system provides such a case. Isaac Newton made brilliant progress by assuming that celestial motions are the frictionless counterparts of terrestrial motion—essentially an application of the principle of uniformity.

A physicist or chemist, seeing the beautiful efficiency and optimal design of a particular protein (such as the examples described in Denton's *Nature's Destiny*), will not assume that the atoms have fallen into place randomly, despite his commitment to uniformity. Even if he does not remember the absurdly low probabilities calculated for this five decades ago by LeComte du Nouy in his book *Human Destiny*, he will realize at once that random shakings are not the way to make a protein. Rather, he will assume that there are catalytic processes and natural pathways for the nonrandom building of such a complex molecule, and that the existence of such mechanisms does not violate the principle of uniformity. The physicist, more readily than the biologist, and probably rather unwittingly, is nonetheless making room for design.

Design should not necessarily be taken to mean the detailed working out of a preordained pattern. Can there be "design without a designer"? Yes and no. A combination of contingency and natural selection can logically produce organisms exquisitely attuned to their environment, astonishing marvels that stagger our imaginations. This is design without a designer. But contingency and natural selection do not create the extraordinary physical and chemical conditions—the solubilities, the diffusion coefficients, the bonding strengths, and so on—that permit the existence of such marvels. It's like a giant and very complex Lego set supplied without a blueprint. There may be no architect, but there is the designer of the set of little interlocking parts. And something about the set cries out for a construction.

The astronomers and physicists who assume that ETI is inevitable and ubiquitous are essentially saying that the set is rigged, that in some way it is designed not just to allow for intelligent life but to make it likely. Paul Davies gets straight to the bottom line:

> This viewpoint [that mind is in some sense predestined to arise in the universe], though prevalent, again conceals a huge assumption about the nature of the universe. It means accepting, in effect, that the laws of nature are rigged not only in favor of complexity, or just in favor of life, but also in favor of mind. To put it dramatically, it implies that mind is written into the laws of nature in a fundamental way.[8]

He goes on to describe the search for life elsewhere in the universe as "the testing ground for two diametrically opposed world-views."

The one view, that intelligent life emerges at best very rarely through extraordinary and improbable contingencies, encapsulates a strict Darwinian understanding: humankind is a glorious accident. The other view, that the universe is abundantly inhabited with intelligent creatures, carries the hidden assumption of design and purposes, in other words, of teleology.

For at least a century and a half scientists have dismissed a role for teleology—final or goal-directed causes—in science. As Ernst Mayr has written (as a strict Darwinian), "Cosmic teleology must be rejected by science. . . . I do not think there is a modern scientist left who still believes in it."[9] Yet, in their endorsement of the Copernican principle, the enthusiasts for ETI have opened a fascinating back door for a goal-directed cosmos. By assuming that there is other accessible alien intelligent life, they accept the existence of design principles that make life much like us a natural feature of the cosmos. In fact, they apply uniformity to the aliens as well as to ourselves to make them similar enough for possible interaction. They are, in effect, making an arrogant claim for our mediocrity: they use the principle to set a sufficiently similar standard for other intelligence in the universe so that we could actually hope to communicate with it.

Atheists and theists alike may be disconcerted and challenged by these conclusions. I am personally persuaded that a superintelligence exists beyond and within the cosmos, and that a rich fabric of congeniality toward the existence of self-conscious life shown by our universe is part of its design and purpose. Yet, like many Christians steeped in a conservative ethos that human beings are central to God's plan, my gut reaction is to disparage the existence of extraterrestrial intelligence. But, I remind myself, beware! Such a view is not only inconsistent with the notion that the universe has been deliberately established as a potential home for self-conscious contemplation, it also gives human limits to God's creativity.

Furthermore, the claim that human beings are the unique focus of God's creation goes against the central affirmation of humility theology, that God infinitely exceeds anything anyone has ever said of God and that God's creativity is beyond human comprehension. Nevertheless, as beings created in the image of God, we can hope at least in a limited way to share with God's understanding of the world in our science and theology. And as we look at the remarkable course of events that has brought *Homo sapiens* to our current level of understanding, we notice the astonishing commingling of contingency with the underlying rightness of physical and chemical design that has made our existence possible. To underscore the role of unpredicted contingencies I need only mention the asteroid impact that brought extinction to the dinosaurs and liberation for the mammals.

As I have explained elsewhere, our contemporary physical understanding shows a universe at its most fundamental level open to physically unpredictable events, occurrences that must be literally considered supernatural inputs.[10] This means that a strict Darwinist convinced of the extraordinarily poor odds of intelligent life ever emerging on Earth or in any other place cannot be sure such scenarios would not happen frequently in our galaxy.

M. B. Foster and later E. L. Mascall have argued that a belief in contingency played a critical role in motivating the scientific revolution of the seventeenth century.[11] The Judeo-Christian philosophical tradition provided a backdrop wherein God in his infinite wisdom had choices, that the world therefore had contingencies, and it behooved natural philosophers not just to theorize how God may have constructed the world, but to make experiments to find out in fact what the world was like.

Today, from a theological framework, the uncertainties of God-given contingencies drive us to both a humble approach and an inquisitive investigativeness, to find out what is in the greater universe. Whether atheist or theist, we can only stand in awe of the way the universe seems designed as a home for humankind. In the words of an eminent living cosmologist, "Humility in the face of the persistent great unknowns is the true philosophy that modern physics has to offer."[12] As for humility theology, which is deeply committed to the search for spiritual truths in the universe, we can hope that our increased scientific understanding will eventually reveal more to us about God the Creator and Sustainer of the cosmos.

Notes

1. Edward Rosen, translator and commentator, *Kepler's Somnium* (Madison: University of Wisconsin Press, 1967).
2. John Wilkins, *A Discourse Concerning a new World and Another Planet . . . another Habitable World in the Moone* (London, 1638). See Marjorie Hope Nicolson, *Voyages to the Moon* (New York: Macmillan, 1948).

3. Christiaan Huygens, *The Celestial Worlds Discover'd; or, Conjectures Concerning the Inhabitants, Plants and Productions of the Worlds in the Planets* (London, 1698), 83; see also 92.

4. See Stephen J. Dick, *Plurality of Worlds: The Origins of the Extraterrestrial Life Debate from Democritus to Kant* (Cambridge: Cambridge Univesity Press, 1982), esp. 28ff.

5. Giuseppe Cocconi and Philip Morrison first proposed this idea in *Nature* 184 (1959): 844–46, reprinted in Kenneth R. Lang and Owen Gingerich, *A Source Book in Astronomy and Astrophysics, 1900–1975* (Cambridge: Harvard University Press, 1979), 37–38.

6. The quotations from Stephen Jay Gould's *Life's Grandeur* (London, 1996), 175, 214, and 216 are cited by Paul Davies in *The Fifth Miracle* (New York: Simon & Schuster, 1999), 272; Gould makes essentially the same statement in *Wonderful Life* (New York: W. W. Norton, 1989), 289 and 320.

7. Ernst Mayr, privately communicated English translation of his article "Lohnt sich die Suche nach extraterrestrischer Intelligenz," *Naturwissenschaftliche Rundschau* 7 (1992): 264–66.

8. Davies, *The Fifth Miracle,* 271.

9. Ernst Mayr, "The Ideological Resistance to Darwin's Theory of Natural Selection," *Proceedings of the American Philosopical Society* 135 (1991): 131.

10. Owen Gingerich, "The Universe as Theater for God's Action," *Theology Today* 55 (1998): 305–16.

11. E. L. Mascall, *Christian Theology and Natural Science* (Hamden, Conn.: Archon Books, 1965), 94ff.

12. Sir Martin Rees, quoting with approval the words of Joseph Silk, in *Before the Beginning* (Reading, Mass.: Addison-Wesley, 1997), 6.

5

The Limits of Knowledge and the Hope for Progress

FRANCISCO J. AYALA

Man is but a reed, the weakest in nature, but he is a thinking reed.

BLAISE PASCAL, *Pensées*[1]

Present Humility, Future Heights

An evolutionist finds many grounds for humility. Life originated on Earth more than 3.5 billion years ago, shortly after our planet started to cool. There live now on Earth 10–30 million species, of which biologists have described about 1.5 million. Our species, *Homo sapiens,* represents, therefore, less than one ten-millionth of the biological diversity of the planet. Most species that lived in the past, more than 99 percent, became extinct without issue. Humans, then, amount to less than one billionth of the biodiversity produced on Earth by the stupendous process of evolution.

There are in the universe about one hundred billion galaxies, each with about one hundred billion stars. Our sun, thus, is but one of the ten thousand million million million stars in the universe. The earth is but just one tiny speck in the universe and humans are just a tiny speck on the earth.

Modern *Homo sapiens* came into existence in Africa 100–150 thousand years ago. That is less than one twenty-thousandth of the time since life started on Earth. We can think on a scale that we are better able to handle, by transforming the duration of life on Earth into a one-year scale. Life starts on January 1, modern humans appear on December 31, at 11:45 P.M. We have been in existence for just fifteen minutes on this one-year scale.

131

So, we are "but a reed," as Pascal put it. Less famously but more explicitly, he wrote elsewhere in his *Pensées*, "What is man in nature? Nothing in relation to the infinite, everything in relation to nothing, a middle between nothing and everything."[2] We are a middle, rather than nearly nothing, because, as he puts it in his other *pensée*, a human, although the weakest reed in nature, is a "thinking" reed.

Sir John Templeton has asked, "Is science research, which has flourished for only the latest 1% of 1% of human history, still in its infancy?" Elsewhere, he states that human information has multiplied more than one hundredfold in two centuries, and asks whether one would expect, if progress accelerates, that "in the year 2200 information can be more than ten thousand times as great as in 1800." In a similar vein, the greatest American inventor, Thomas Edison, wrote, "We don't know a millionth of one percent about anything."[3]

Science, in the modern sense, came to be in the sixteenth century. On the one-year time scale, that is December 31, at 11:59:57 P.M., just three seconds ago. One need not be sanguine to see that as the three seconds expand into minutes, or into hours, knowledge will reach (so long as we don't commit species suicide) heights that are now literally inconceivable. If scientific knowledge has increased one hundredfold in the past two hundred years, it is safe to estimate that only 10 percent, or tenfold, of the expansion happened in the first one hundred years; the other ninetyfold in the second one hundred years. The *rate* at which knowledge expands is increasing, and not just knowledge itself. One might expect, then, as the *rate* accelerates tenfold each century over the rate of the previous century, that knowledge will increase ten thousandfold by the year 2100 and ten millionfold by the year 2200, compared with the knowledge available in the year 1800.

I am, indeed, sanguine about humankind's knowledge potentialities. The potentialities come from the distinctive attributes of our species, Pascal's "thinking reed," an outcome of the evolutionary process. Let's pause now and look at what makes the reed a *thinking* reed.

A Cursory View of Human Evolution

Humankind is a biological species that has evolved from other species that were not human. In order to understand human nature, we must know our biological makeup and whence we come, the story of our humbler beginnings.

Our closest biological relatives are the great apes and, among them, the chimpanzees, who are more related to us than they are to the gorillas, and much more than they are related to other apes and monkeys. The hominid lineage diverged from the chimpanzee lineage 5–7 million years ago (Mya) and it evolved exclusively in the African continent until the emergence of *Homo erectus*, somewhat before 1.8 Mya. The first known hominid, *Ardipithecus ramidus*, lived 4.4 Mya, but it is not certain that it was bipedal or in the direct line of descent to modern humans, *Homo sapiens*. The recently described *Australopithecus anamensis*, dated 3.9–4.2 Mya, was bipedal and has been placed in the line of descent to *Australopithecus afarensis*, *Homo habilis*, *H. erectus*, and *H. sapiens*. Other hominids, not in the direct line of descent to modern humans, are *Australopithecus africanus*, *Paranthropus aethiopicus*, *P. boisei*, and *P. robustus*, who lived in Africa at various times between 3 and 1 Mya, a period when three or four hominid species lived contemporaneously in the African continent.

Shortly after its emergence in tropical or subtropical Africa, *H. erectus* spread to other continents. Fossil remains of *H. erectus* are known from Africa, Indonesia (Java), China, the Middle East, and Europe. *H. erectus* fossils from Java have been dated 1.81 ± 0.04 and 1.66 ± 0.04 Mya, and from Georgia between 1.6 and 1.8 Mya. Anatomically distinctive *H. erectus* fossils have been found in Spain, deposited before 780,000 years ago, the oldest in southern Europe.

The transition from *H. erectus* to *H. sapiens* occurred around 400,000 years ago, although this date is not well determined owing to uncertainty as to whether some fossils are *erectus* or "archaic" forms of *sapiens*. *H. erectus* persisted for some time in Asia, until 250,000 years ago in China, and perhaps until 100,000 years ago in Java, and thus was coetaneous with early members of its descendant species, *H. sapiens*. Fossil remains of Neanderthal hominids (*Homo neanderthalensis*) appeared in Europe around 200,000 years ago and persisted until 30,000 or 40,000 years ago. The Neanderthals had, like *H. sapiens*, large brains. Until recently, they were thought to be ancestral to anatomically modern humans, but now we know that modern humans appeared at least 100,000 years ago, much before the disappearance of the Neanderthals. Moreover, in caves in the Middle East, fossils of modern humans have been found dated 100,000–120,000 years ago, as well as Neanderthals dated at 60,000 and 70,000 years ago, followed again by modern humans dated at 40,000 years ago. It is unclear whether the *sapiens* and the Neanderthals repeatedly replaced one another by migration from other regions, or whether they temporarily coexisted in some areas. Recent genetic evidence indicates that interbreeding between *sapiens* and *neanderthalensis* never occurred.

There is controversy about the origin of modern humans. Some anthropologists argue that the transition from *H. erectus* to archaic *H. sapiens* and later to anatomically modern humans occurred consonantly in various parts of the Old World. Proponents of this "multiregional model" emphasize fossil evidence that shows regional continuity in the transition from *H. erectus* to archaic and then modern *H. sapiens*. In order to account for the transition from one to another species (something that cannot happen independently in several places), they postulate that genetic exchange occurred from time to time between populations, so that the species evolved as a single gene pool, even though geographic differentiation occurred and persisted, just as geographically differentiated populations exist in other animal species, as well as in living humans. This explanation depends on the occurrence of persistent migrations and interbreeding between populations from different continents, of which no direct evidence exists. Moreover, it is difficult to reconcile the multiregional model with the contemporary existence of different species or forms in different regions, such as the persistence of *H. erectus* in China and Java for more than 100,000 years after the emergence of *H. sapiens*.

Other scientists argue instead that modern humans first arose in Africa or in the Middle East, somewhat prior to 100,000 years ago, and from there spread throughout the world, replacing elsewhere the preexisting populations of *H. erectus* or archaic *H. sapiens*. This is the view currently favored by many anthropologists and geneticists.

Human Uniqueness

The most distinctive human anatomical traits are erect posture and large brain. We are the only vertebrate species with a bipedal gait and erect posture; birds are bipedal, but their backbone stands horizontal rather than vertical. Brain size is generally proportional to body size; relative to body mass, humans have the largest (and most complex) brain. The chimpanzee's brain weighs less than a pound; a gorilla's slightly more. The human male adult brain is 1,400 cubic centimeters (cc), about three pounds in weight.

Evolutionists decades ago raised the question whether bipedal gait or large brain came first, or whether they evolved consonantly. The issue is now resolved. Our *Australopithecus* ancestors had, since 4 Mya, a bipedal gait, but a small brain, about 450 cc, a pound in weight. Brain size starts to increase notably with our *Homo habilis* ancestors, about 2.5 Mya, who had a brain about 650 cc and also were prolific tool-makers (hence the name *habilis*). Nearly 2 Mya, there appeared *Homo erectus*, who persisted for about 1.5 million years, and had adult brains up to 1,200 cc. Our species, *Homo sapiens*, has a brain about three times as large as that of *Australopithecus*, 1,300–1,400 cc, or some three pounds of gray matter. Our brain is not only much larger than that of chimpanzees or gorillas, but also much more complex. The cerebral cortex, where the higher cognitive functions are processed, is in humans disproportionally much greater than the rest of the brain, when compared to apes.

Erect posture and large brain are not the only anatomical traits that distinguish us from nonhuman primates, even if they may be the most obvious. A list of distinctive anatomical features includes the following (of which the last five are not detectable in fossils):

- Erect posture and bipedal gait (entail changes of the backbone, hipbone, and feet)
- Opposing thumbs and arm and hand changes (make possible precise manipulation)
- Large brain
- Reduction of jaw and remodeling of face
- Changes in skin and skin glands
- Reduction in body hair
- Cryptic ovulation (and extended female sexual receptivity)
- Slow development
- Modification of vocal tract and larynx
- Reorganization of the brain

Humans are notably different from other animals, not only in anatomy, but also and no less importantly in their behavior, both as individuals and socially. A list of distinctive human behavioral traits includes the following:

- Subtle expression of emotions
- Intelligence: abstract thinking, categorizing, and reasoning
- Symbolic (creative) language
- Self-awareness and death awareness
- Toolmaking and technology

- Science, literature, and art
- Ethics and religion
- Social organization and cooperation (division of labor)
- Legal codes and political institutions

Humans live in groups that are socially organized, and so do other primates. But primate societies do not approach the complexity of human social organization. A distinctive human social trait is culture, a subject to which I shall return later. First, we can have another look at human biology.

Frontiers of Human Biology

Biological heredity is based on the transmission of genetic information from parents to offspring, in humans very much the same as in other animals. The genetic information is encoded in the linear sequence of the DNA's four nucleotide components (the "letters" of the genetic alphabet, represented by A, C, G, T) in a similar fashion as semantic information is encoded in the sequence of letters of a written text. The DNA is compactly packaged in the chromosomes inside the nucleus of each cell. Humans have two sets of twenty-three chromosomes, one set from each parent. The total number of DNA letters in each set of chromosomes is about three billion. The purpose of the Human Genome Project, which was undertaken in 1989, is to decipher the sequence of the three thousand million letters in a human genome (one set of chromosomes).

I estimate that the King James Bible contains one million letters, punctuation marks, and spaces. Writing down the DNA sequence of one human genome demands three thousand volumes of the size of the Bible. Surely, of course, the information will be stored in electronic form, in computers where fragments of information coming from different investigators can be reshuffled until obtaining their proper sequential arrangement, and for other purposes. But if a printout is wanted, three thousand volumes will be needed just for one human genome.

The complete information for just one individual will demand six thousand volumes, three thousand for each of the two chromosome sets. Surely, again, there are more economic ways of presenting the information in the second set than listing the complete letter sequence;

for example, by indicating the position of each variant letter in the second set relative to the first set. The number of variant letters between one individual's two sets is likely to be about ten million, about one in three hundred. The two sets of each individual are different from one another, and from the sets of any other human being (with the trivial exception of identical twins, who share the same two sets, since identical twins develop from one single fertilized human egg).

The Human Genome Project of the United States was initiated in 1989, funded through two agencies, the National Institutes of Health (NIH) and the Department of Energy (DOE). The goal set was to obtain the complete sequence of one human genome in fifteen years at an approximate cost of three billion dollars, coincidentally about one dollar per DNA letter.

Proponents of the project have used inflated rhetoric to extol its anticipated achievements. The project has been called the "Holy Grail" of biology, which will meet the ancient injunction "Know thyself." The Nobelist Walter Gilbert has said of a computer disk that will have an individual's DNA sequence information, "This is you."[4] The Nobelist and first director of the project, James Watson, has asserted that "our fate is in our genes."[5] Daniel Koshland, the editor of *Science,* has proclaimed that "when we can accurately predict future behavior, we may be able to prevent the damage" caused by violent behavior.[6] Will the Human Genome Project accomplish any of these lofty objectives?

Human biology faces two great research frontiers: ontogenetic decoding and the brain-mind puzzle.[7] By ontogenetic decoding I refer to the problem of how the unidimensional genetic information encoded in the DNA of a single cell becomes transformed into a four-dimensional human being, a creature heterogeneous in time and space, the individual that grows, matures, and dies. Cancer, disease, and aging are epiphenomena of ontogenetic decoding. By the brain-mind puzzle I refer to the interdependent questions of (1) how the physicochemical signals that reach our sense organs become transformed into perceptions, feelings, ideas, critical arguments, aesthetic emotions, and ethical values; and (2) how, out of this diversity of experiences, there emerges a unitary reality, the mind or self. Free will and language, social and political institutions, technology and art are all epiphenomena of the human mind.

The two issues may also be dubbed the egg-to-adult transformation and the physical-mental transformation. The egg-to-adult transformation is essentially similar, and similarly mysterious, in humans and other mammals. The physical-mental transformation, as I have defined it, is distinctively human; it defines the *humanum*, that which makes us specifically human. No other issue is of greater consequence for understanding ourselves and our place in nature.

Scientists have proposed that resources be committed for a coordinated and deliberate plan to determine the complete nucleotide sequence of the human genome. Without question, knowing the DNA sequence of one or several human beings would be of great use as a database to biologists and health scientists. I doubt, however, that such knowledge about the human genome will contribute much to the solution of either of the two conundrums I have identified here, or to the solution of any other fundamental biological problem.[8]

Ontogenetic Decoding

The instructions that guide the ontogenetic process, or the egg-to-adult transformation, are carried in the hereditary material. The theory of biological heredity was formulated by the Augustinian monk Gregor Mendel in 1866, but it became generally known by biologists only in 1900: genetic information is contained in discrete factors, or genes, which exist in pairs, one received from each parent. The next step toward understanding the nature of genes was completed during the first quarter of the twentieth century. It was established that genes are parts of the chromosomes, filamentous bodies present in the nucleus of the cell, and that they are linearly arranged along the chromosomes. It took another quarter century to determine the chemical composition of genes—deoxyribonucleic acid (DNA), which in turn consists of four chemical groups (nucleotides) organized in long, double-helical structures. The genetic information is contained in the linear sequence of the four nucleotides, very much in the same way as the semantic information of an English sentence is conveyed by the particular sequence of the twenty-six letters of the alphabet.

The first important step toward understanding how the genetic information is decoded came in 1941, when George W. Beadle and Edward L. Tatum demonstrated that genes determine the synthesis of enzymes, the catalysts that control all chemical reactions in living beings. It became known later that a series of three consecutive nucleotides in a gene codes for one amino acid (amino acids are the components that make up enzymes and other proteins). This relationship accounts for the precise linear correspondence between a particular sequence of coding nucleotides and the sequence of the amino acids that make up the encoded enzyme.

But chemical reactions in organisms must occur in an orderly manner; organisms must have ways of switching any gene on and off. The first control system was discovered in 1961 by François Jacob and Jacques Monod for a gene that determines the synthesis of an enzyme that digests sugar in the bacterium *Escherichia coli*. The gene is turned on and off by a system of several switches consisting of short DNA sequences adjacent to the coding part of the gene. The switches are activated by feedback loops that involve molecules synthesized by other genes. A variety of gene control mechanisms have been discovered since that time, in bacteria and other microorganisms. These two elements are typically present: feedback loops and short DNA sequences acting as switches. The feedback loops ensure that the presence of a substance in the cell induces the synthesis of the enzyme required to digest it, and that an excess of the enzyme in the cell represses its own synthesis. (For example, the sugar-digesting enzyme in *E. coli* is turned on or off as a consequence of the presence or absence of the sugar to be digested.)

The investigation of gene control mechanisms in mammals (and other complex organisms) became possible in the mid-1970s with the development of recombinant DNA techniques. This technology made it feasible to isolate single genes (and other DNA sequences) and to multiply them, or clone them, to obtain the quantities necessary for ascertaining their nucleotide sequence. One unanticipated discovery was that most genes come in pieces: the coding sequence of a gene is divided into several fragments separated one from the next by noncoding DNA segments. In addition to the alternating succession of coding and noncoding segments, mammalian genes, like those in bacteria, contain short control sequences that act as switches and signal where the coding sequence begins.

Much remains to be discovered about the control mechanisms of mammalian genes. The daunting speed at which molecular biology is advancing makes it reasonable to anticipate that the main prototypes of mammalian gene control systems will be unraveled within a decade or two. But understanding the control mechanisms of individual genes is but the first major step toward solving the mystery of ontogenetic decoding. The second major step will be solving the puzzle of differentiation.

A human being consists of one trillion cells of some two hundred different kinds, all derived by sequential division from the fertilized egg, a single cell 0.1 millimeters in diameter. The first few cell divisions yield a spherical mass of amorphous cells. Successive divisions are accompanied by the appearance of folds and ridges in the mass of cells and, later on, of the variety of tissues, organs, and limbs characteristic of a human individual. The full complement of genes duplicates with each cell division, so that two complete genomes are present in every cell. Moreover, experiments with other animals indicate that all the genes in any cell have the potential of becoming activated.[9] Yet, different sets of genes are active in different cells. This must be so in order for cells to differentiate: a nerve cell, a muscle cell, and a skin cell are vastly different in size and configuration. The differential activity of genes must continue after differentiation, because different cells fulfill different functions, which are controlled by different genes.

The information that controls cell and organ differentiation is, of course, contained in the DNA sequence, but only in very short segments of it. What sort of sequences are these controlling elements, where are they located, and how are they decoded? In mammals, insects, and other complex organisms, there are control circuits that operate at higher levels than the control mechanisms that activate and deactivate individual genes. These higher-level circuits act on sets rather than individual genes. The details of how these sets are controlled, how many control systems there are, and how they interact, as well as many other related questions, are what needs to be resolved to elucidate the egg-to-adult transformation. The DNA sequence of the controlling elements will have to be ascertained, but this is a minor effort that will be helped very little by plowing our way through the entire three billion nucleotide pairs that constitute the human genome.

The benefits that the elucidation of ontogenetic decoding will bring to humankind are enormous. This knowledge will make possible the understanding of the modes of action of complex genetic diseases, including cancer, and therefore their cure. It will also bring an understanding of the process of aging, the unforgiving disease that kills all those who have won the battle against other infirmities.

Cancer is an anomaly of ontogenetic decoding: cells proliferate although the welfare of the organism demands otherwise. Individual genes (oncogenes) have been identified that are involved in the causation of particular forms of cancer. But whether or not a cell will turn out cancerous depends on the interaction of the oncogenes with other genes and with the internal and external environment of the cell. Aging is also a failure of the process of ontogenetic decoding: cells fail to carry out the functions imprinted in their genetic codescript or are no longer able to proliferate and replace dead cells.

In 1985, health care expenditures in the United States were $425 billion; in 1997 they reached approximately $1 trillion. Most of these expenditures go for supportive therapy and technological fixes that seek to compensate for the debilitating effects of diseases that we do not know how to prevent or truly cure. By contrast, those diseases whose causation is understood—tuberculosis, syphilis, smallpox, and viral childhood diseases, for example—can now be treated with relatively little cost and the best of results.[10] A mere 3 percent of the nation's total health care expenditures is devoted to basic research. Doubling or tripling this percentage would result in only a modest rise in total expenditures, but would yield large savings in the near future, as cancer, degenerative diseases, and other debilitating infirmities become preventable or curable, and thus no longer require the expensive and ultimately ineffectual therapy now in practice.

The Brain-Mind Puzzle

The brain is the most complex and most distinctive human organ. It consists of thirty billion nerve cells, or neurons, each connected to many others through the axon and the dendrites. From the evolutionary point of view, the animal brain is a powerful biological adaptation; it allows the organism to obtain and process information about environmental conditions and then to adapt to them. This ability has been carried to the limit in humans, in which the extravagant hypertrophy of the brain makes possible abstract thinking, language, and technology. By these means, humankind has ushered in a new mode of adaptation far more powerful than the biological mode: adaptation by culture.

The most rudimentary ability to gather and process information about the environment is found in certain single-celled microorganisms. The protozoan *Paramecium* swims apparently at random, ingesting the bacteria it encounters, but when it meets unsuitable acidity or salinity, it checks its advance and starts in a new direction. The alga *Euglena* not only avoids unsuitable environments but seeks suitable ones by orienting itself according to the direction of light, which it perceives through a light-sensitive spot in the cell. Plants have not progressed much further. Except for those with tendrils that twist around any solid object and the few carnivorous plants that react to touch, they react only to gradients of light, gravity, and moisture.

In animals the ability to secure and process environmental information is mediated by the nervous system. The simplest nervous systems are found in corals and jellyfishes; they lack coordination between different parts of their bodies, so any one part is able to react only when it is directly stimulated. Sea urchins and starfish possess a nerve ring and radial nerve cords that coordinate stimuli coming from different parts; hence, they respond with direct and unified actions of the whole body. They have no brain, however, and seem unable to learn from experience. Planarian flatworms have about the most rudimentary brain known; their central nervous system and brain process and coordinate information gathered by the sensory cells. These animals are capable of simple learning and hence of variable responses to repeatedly encountered stimuli. Insects and their relatives have much more advanced brains; they obtain precise chemical, acoustic, visual, and tactile signals from the environment and process them, making possible complex behaviors, particularly in their search for food and their selection of mates.

Vertebrates—animals with backbones—are able to obtain and process much more complicated signals and to respond more variably than insects or any other invertebrates. The vertebrate brain contains an enormous number of associative neurons arranged in complex patterns. In vertebrates the ability to react to environmental information is correlated with an increase in the relative size of the cerebral hemispheres and of the neopallium, an organ involved in associating and coordinating signals from all receptors and brain centers. In mammals, the neopallium has expanded and become the cerebral cortex. Humans have a very large brain relative to their body size, and a cerebral cortex that is disproportionately large and complex even for their brain size. Abstract thinking, symbolic language, complex social organization, values, and ethics are manifestations of the wondrous capacity of the human brain to gather information about the external world and to integrate that information and react flexibly to what is perceived.

With the advanced development of the human brain, biological evolution has transcended itself, opening up a new mode of evolution: adaptation by technological manipulation of the environment. Organisms adapt to the environment by means of natural selection, by changing their genetic constitution over the generations to suit the demands of the environment. Humans, and humans alone, have developed the capacity to adapt to hostile environments by modifying the environments according to the needs of their genes. The discovery of fire and the fabrication of clothing and shelter have allowed humans to spread from the warm tropical and subtropical regions of the Old World, to which they are biologically adapted, to almost the whole earth; it was not necessary for the wandering humans to wait until the evolution of genes providing anatomical protection by means of fur or hair. Nor are humans biding their time in expectation of wings or gills; they have conquered the air and seas with artfully designed contrivances. It is our brain (the human mind) that has made us the most successful living species.

There are not enough bits of information in the complete DNA sequence of a human genome to specify the trillions of connections among the thirty billion neurons of the human brain. Accordingly, the genetic instructions must be organized in control circuits operating at different hierarchical levels, as described earlier, so that an instruction at one level is carried through many channels at a lower level in the hierarchy of control circuits. The development of the human brain is indeed one particularly intriguing component of the egg-to-adult transformation. But we must focus now on the issue at hand, namely, how this awesome organ, the human brain, works.

Within the past two decades, neurobiology has developed into one of the most exciting biological disciplines. An increased commitment of financial and human resources has brought an unprecedented rate of discovery. Much has been learned about how light, sound, temperature, resistance, and chemical impressions received in our sense organs trigger the release of chemical transmitters and electric potential differences that carry the signals through the nerves to the brain and elsewhere in the body. Much has also been learned about how neural channels for information transmission become reinforced by use or may be replaced after damage, about which neurons or groups of neurons are committed to processing information derived from a particular organ or environmental location, and about many other matters. But, for all this progress, neurobiology remains an infant discipline, at a stage of theoretical development comparable perhaps to that of genetics at the beginning of the century. Those things that count most remain shrouded in mystery: how physical phenomena become mental experiences, and how out of the diversity of these experiences emerges the mind, a reality with unitary properties, such as free will and the awareness of self, that persist through an individual's life.

I do not believe that these mysteries are unfathomable; rather, they are puzzles that the human mind can solve with the methods of science. And I will place my bets that, over the next half-century or so, many of these puzzles will be solved. We shall then be well on our way toward answering the injunction "Know thyself."

Limits and Power

It seems unlikely that knowing the complete sequence of the human genome will contribute in any significant way to the resolution of ontogenetic decoding or the brain-mind puzzle. Science does not make big strides by inductive inference, by accumulating descriptive information, from which important discoveries somehow emerge. On the contrary, the great leaps of science are impelled by bold hypotheses, daring conjectures about what the solution might be to a particularly significant problem. Critical testing must follow in short course, but only hypotheses can guide meaningful observation and experiment, because only they suggest what is worth observing. Newton's mechanics, Einstein's relativity, Mendel's discrete inheritance, and Darwin's natural selection, like many other great scientific discoveries, are imaginative exploits about how the natural world might function or be structured.

The complete nucleotide sequence of the human genome might be helpful to biologists and health scientists as a database for experiments. But I do not believe that it would contribute any more toward solving major biological or health problems than a computer printout of all the roads in the United States and of all the cars traveling over them in a particular year would help to ascertain the significant causes of highway accidents. The expenditures and human resources required for sequencing the human genome amount to a large fraction of those committed to all biological research. Ultimately, the question confronting policy makers was whether the returns (in terms of scientific advance and health delivery) would not be greater if the resources required for obtaining the human DNA sequence were invested instead in investigator-initiated or other models of basic research. The relevant policy-making bodies of the United States decided in 1989 to undertake the Human Genome Project, and they have continuously supported it since that time. Advances in scientific know-how and data gathering have been enormous.

The Genes and the Person

The two conundrums that I have set forth have not, however, been resolved, nor do I or anybody else expect that they will be resolved within the next decade. The time line that I suggest is fifty years. The advances have been dramatic and the rate of scientific discovery continues to accelerate in both subjects, so that a half-century time horizon is not unreasonable. Many scientists would agree that developmental biology and neurobiology are now the predominant biological disciplines—in number of researchers, prolixity of discoveries, and commitment of resources.

The progress of the Human Genome Project has also been remarkable. It is proceeding at a faster rate than had been anticipated. Shortcut approaches are being explored that might achieve much of the sequence well ahead of schedule, although completing the details may still require the fifteen years originally proposed. There have been, as anticipated, many payoffs, particularly in the identification of specific gene defects causing diseases such as Huntington's chorea, colon cancer, and cystic fibrosis. These and many other discoveries to come very well justify the investment of financial and human resources on the Human Genome Project. But the discoveries made have, I submit, contributed little, if anything, to fulfill the rhetorical promises. We have not come any closer to knowing ourselves or to deciphering our fate. Indeed, some of the promises made can never be fulfilled by biological science, let alone the Genome Project.

Knowing the human DNA sequence will be just a first step toward understanding the genetic makeup of a human being. Think of the three thousand Bible-sized volumes. At the end of the Genome Project we will know the orderly sequence of the three billion letters, but we will not have understood the full text, any more than we would understand the contents of three thousand Bible-sized volumes written in an extraterrestrial language, of which we only know the alphabet, just because we have deciphered their letter sequence. Gradually, we will come to understand more and more "sentences" of the human genome sequence, even full paragraphs, and perhaps an occasional chapter. It will be an arduous task, calling for sustained scientific research much beyond the next decade.

Human beings are not gene machines. The expression of genes in mammals takes place in interaction with the environment, in patterns that are complex and all but impossible to predict in the details—and it is in the details that the self resides. In humans, the "environment" takes a new dimension, which becomes the dominant one. A distinctive human feature is "culture," which may be understood as the set of non-strictly-biological human activities and creations. Culture includes social and political institutions, ways of doing things, religious and ethical traditions, language, common sense and scientific knowledge, art and literature, technology, and in general all the creations of the human mind. The advent of culture has brought with it cultural evolution, a superorganic mode of evolution superimposed on the organic mode, which has in the past few millennia become the dominant mode of human evolution. Cultural evolution has come about because of cultural inheritance, a distinctively human mode of achieving adaptations to the environment and transmitting the adaptations through the generations.

There are in humankind two kinds of heredity—the biological and the cultural, which have also been called organic and superorganic, or *endosomatic* and *exosomatic,* systems of heredity. Biological inheritance in humans is very much like that in any other sexually reproducing organism, as I noted above. Cultural inheritance, on the other hand, is based on transmission of information by a teaching-learning process, which is in principle independent of biological parentage. Culture is transmitted by instruction and learning, by example and imitation, through books, newspapers, radio, television, and motion pictures, through works of art, and by any other means of communication. Culture is acquired by every person from parents, relatives, and neighbors, and from the whole human environment.

Cultural inheritance makes possible for people what no other organism can accomplish—the cumulative transmission of experience from generation to generation. Animals can learn from experience, but they do not transmit their experiences, their "discoveries" (at least not to any large extent) to the following generations. Animals have individual memory, but they do not have a "social memory" (a phrase coined by the Spanish philosopher José Ortega y Gasset). Humans, on the other hand, have developed a culture because they can transmit cumulatively their experiences from generation to generation.[11]

Cultural inheritance makes possible cultural evolution, that is, the evolution of knowledge, social structures, ethics, and all other components that make up human culture. Cultural inheritance makes possible a mode of adaptation to the environment that is not available to nonhuman organisms—adaptation by means of culture. The cultural mode of adaptation prevails in humankind over the biological mode because it is a more rapid mode of adaptation and because it can be directed. A new scientific discovery or technical achievement can be transmitted to the whole of humankind, potentially at least, in less than one generation. Moreover, whenever a need arises, culture can directly pursue the appropriate changes to meet the challenge. On the contrary, a biological adaptation depends on the accidental availability of a favorable mutation, or of a combination of several mutations, at the time and place where the need arises. The expansion of a favorable mutation to the whole species typically requires hundreds of generations.

Geneticists have long recognized the phenomenon of "pleiotropy," the expression of a gene in different organs or anatomical traits. A gene that becomes changed owing to its effects on a certain trait will result in the modification of other traits as well. The cascade of consequences often is, in humans, very long and far from obvious in many cases. There is little that the genes can specifically tell us about literature, art, science, technology, ethics, and political institutions. It is not very much, either, that the genes will tell us about an individual's character. It is naively arrogant to promise that knowing the DNA letter sequence of an individual will amount to knowing the person.

The Underused Brain

We know an infinitesimal part of what there is to know, less than "a millionth of one percent about anything," in Edison's phrase. Knowledge is not easily quantifiable and we have little idea about how much there is to know, since we don't know it. But Edison's phrase is just one way of stating the limits of our ignorance. We can approach the matter differently, starting from Sir John Templeton's statement that we now know one hundred times more than we did two hundred years ago and his reasonable surmise that the acquisition of knowledge is increasing at an accelerated rate. If the rate of acquisition of significant knowledge increases by a factor of 10 every century, the amount of knowledge would have increased by a factor of 10 between the years 1800 and 1900, but 10 times faster between the years 1900 and 2000, and it will increase 100 times faster between the years 2000 and 2100, and 1,000 times faster between the years 2100 and 2200 than between 1800 and 1900. Knowledge between the years 1800 and 2200 will have increased by 10 x 10 x 100 x 1,000 or 10 millionfold. And, by the year 2300, it will have increased by one hundred billionfold, compared to the knowledge humankind had two centuries ago. These amazing numbers seem ridiculously inflated, but they follow from the reasonable assumption that the rate of acquisition of knowledge increases tenfold every century. These numbers manifest, in any case, how little we presently know, a reason for humility; but how much we may get to know in the future, a reason for hope.

Will humans be able to handle so much additional knowledge? Computers and other yet unimagined devices will be critical for storing, retrieving, and processing the immense mass of information. But what about the capacity of the human brain to deal with it in some manner and, perhaps, to benefit from it?

I wrote earlier in this chapter that the human brain consists of thirty billion neurons.[12] Neurons consist of a central main body and two ends, called axon and dendrites, with which each neuron connects to other neurons, to about one thousand other neurons on the average. The network of neurons and their interconnections is unimaginably complex and with unlimited possibilities. We may gain some idea of the complexity with the following analogy.[13] Imagine you live in a metropolitan area, like that encompassing New York City, with ten million people. Take a large spool of thread and connect yourself to one thousand people so that there is one thread running between you and each of the one thousand persons. If the average distance between you and each person is one mile, you'll need one thousand miles of thread.[14] Imagine now that every person in the city is connected to one thousand other people in the same way that you are. The total number of interconnections is given by a simple equation, which yields a "hyperastronomic" number, namely, 1 followed by several thousand zeros. This number is immensely larger than the number of atoms in the universe, which is about 1 followed by seventy-five zeros. There is not enough thread in the universe to make all the connections if each requires one mile of thread. Remember now that the number of neurons is thirty billion, rather than just the ten million people used in the calculation. Try to imagine (you cannot!) the network of connections of each neuron with one thousand other neurons, and you will get a pale approximation of the incredible complexity of the brain.

The next step is thinking about the pathways of communication between neurons that are not contiguous to each other. Imagine two neurons that have a minimum distance between them of five steps, as between A and F: A-B-C-D-E-F. There are one thousand neurons that are one step removed from A, and each one of these is connected to one thousand other neurons, each two steps removed from A, for a total of one million possible pathways to go from A to C. There are one thousand million million pathways to go from A to F (where F is any neuron five steps removed from A) by the most direct route, and untold millions more pathways to reach F through more than four intermediate neurons.

The point of these somewhat dizzying numerical exercises is simple: the number of communication channels used in the lifetime of an individual is a ridiculously tiny fraction of the realm of possibilities.[15] I will refer again to Edison's statement, but use it for a different purpose: less than a millionth of 1 percent of the capacity of a human brain is ever used in the lifetime of an individual. Indeed, less than a millionth of a millionth of a millionth. We do not now know how to make use of that unrealized potential, but I see no reason to think that we will not discover the means, as human knowledge expands thousands or millions of times over the next century or two. One way to think about how we could much more effectively use our brain potential is the model of distributive computing, which immensely increases the computing capacity of a network of connected computers.

The next step in the expansion of humankind's assimilation of future knowledge would be to find ways of effectively connecting (with communication signals, not physically) the brains of different individuals, thousands or millions of human brains.[16] The analogy with distributive computing comes again to mind. But, by now, I may have crossed the border between speculation about the future, however flimsily connected with current knowledge, and science fiction.

We know very little about the natural world, virtually nothing compared to what is there to know, and very little about questions of the meaning and value of life and the universe. That is a reason for awe and humility. The grounds for optimism and hope are that there is so much to know and that we and our descendants have, I believe, unlimited means to expand knowledge—forever.[17]

Notes

1. The *Pensées* were originally published in 1670. This is number 347.
2. *Pensées*, number 72.

3. Quoted in *Uncle John's Third Bathroom Reader* (New York: St. Martin's Press, 1990), 161.

4. Cited by D. Nelkin and M. S. Lindee, *The DNA Mystique: The Gene as a Cultural Icon* (New York: Freeman, 1995), 7.

5. Quoted in Leon Jaroff, "The Gene Hunt," *Time,* March, 20, 1989, 62–67.

6. D. Koshland, "Elephants, Monstrosities and the Law," *Science* 25 (February 4, 1992): 777.

7. The following several pages are modified from a paper that I wrote in 1987, at the request of the U.S. National Academy of Sciences. The advice of the academy had been sought by NIH and other government agencies as to whether the Human Genome Project should be undertaken. The academy asked four scientists to prepare statements that would evaluate the scientific merits of sequencing the human genome. I, in particular, was asked to look into my own crystal ball to identify the major issues facing current biology and to determine whether the human DNA sequence might be one of them or, otherwise, whether it would significantly advance those issues. The four papers were published in *Issues in Science and Technology*, the academy's science policy journal, mine under the title "Two Frontiers of Human Biology: What the Sequence Won't Tell Us"(3.3 [1987]: 51–56).

8. I am not challenging here that the Human Genome Project will have many public health applications and, indirectly, through the deciphering of the genomes of other species, in agriculture, animal husbandry, and industry. The question is how much it will contribute to solving the two most fundamental problems faced in human biology that I am expounding.

9. The sheep "Dolly" was conceived using genes extracted from a cell in an adult sheep.

10. This statement is overoptimistic, and it may be outright erroneous if the phrase "understood causation" is not precisely construed. Malaria and AIDS are two diseases whose causation is understood at a number of levels, yet we fail to treat them "with relatively little cost and the best results." In any case, one can anticipate that increased knowledge of the etiology of these diseases may lead to successful development of effective vaccines or drugs.

11. Ortega y Gasset saw the ability to transmit learned information from one generation to the next as the most distinctive human attribute, more so than high intelligence per se.

12. More numerous than the neurons are "glial" cells, generally smaller than neurons, but of which there may be one hundred billion in a human brain. Numerous books have been published, particularly in recent years, about the organization and function of the brain. An excellent overview is the Spring 1998 issue of *Daedalus* (a journal of the American Academy of Arts and Sciences, Cambridge, Mass.), titled "The Brain," with eleven articles written by eminent experts.

13. This analogy is modified from James Trefill, *Are We Unique?* (New York: John Wiley, 1997), 64.

14. Axons are long, so that connections occur not only between adjacent neurons.

15. Each time a particular pathway is used, it "widens." It becomes more likely that it will again be used next time, rather than some alternative pathway in the network.

16. The brains of different individuals communicate through the senses, most notably through spoken and written speech, but also through chemical, tactile, and all sorts of visual and auditory signals. I am suggesting here that there might be other ways of communication, or connection, between brains that would bypass the common senses. The Jesuit priest and visionary anthropologist Pierre Teilhard de Chardin saw that three successive stages of evolution had occurred on Earth until now: the geosphere, the biosphere, and the noosphere, which is the realm of human evolution. Following what he calls the "law of complexity consciousness," evolution, according to Teilhard, will progress along a "privileged axis" toward a culmination at the "Point Omega," which he describes as "a harmonized collectivity of consciousness equivalent to a sort of superconsciousness. The idea is that of the earth not only being covered by myriads of grains of thought but becoming enclosed in a single thinking envelope so as to form, functionally, no more than a single vast grain of thought on the sidereal scale, the plurality of individual reflections grouping themselves together and reinforcing one another in the act of a single unanimous reflection. This is the general form in which, by analogy and in symmetry with the past, we are led scientifically to envisage the future of mankind.

"... In the direction of thought, could the universe terminate with anything less than the measureless?" (*The Phenomenon of Man* [New York: Harper Torchbooks, 1961], 251–52.) I am not endorsing Teilhard's vision, but this quotation points in the direction of unexplored possibilities that might include intellectual cooperation between individuals, beyond the mediation of the common senses, which are now our only means of communication.

17. We need to keep in mind, however, that accumulation of information is not the same as increased wisdom. Knowing more, of itself, does not make us wiser, more virtuous or, necessarily, better human beings.

6

The Psychology of Humility

DAVID G. MYERS

Humility, like darkness, reveals the heavenly lights.

—HENRY DAVID THOREAU

Viewing the seeming contest between natural and supernatural explanation—between skeptical-seeming scientists and naive-seeming fundamentalists—it sometimes seems as if science and religion sit on opposite ends of an explanatory teeter-totter. As one rises, the other falls.

Actually, there is considerable common ground between science and religion. Part of that common ground lies in their shared emphasis on *humility.*

At the heart of theology: humility before God. "Lord I have given up my pride and turned away from my arrogance," wrote the Psalmist (131:1). Reformed theology understands the Psalmist's humility. It views human reason as fallen and limited. In the Reformation tradition, theology itself must be "ever-reforming" its always imperfect understandings.

As God's creatures we have dignity, but not deity. We are finite creatures of the one who said "I am God, and there is none like me" (Isaiah 46:9). We peer at reality in a mirror dimly. Our most confident belief can therefore be the conviction that some of our beliefs contain error. People of faith can therefore appreciate Oliver Cromwell's 1650 plea to the Church of Scotland: "I beseech ye in the bowels of Christ, consider that ye may be mistaken."

At the heart of science: humility before nature. Historians of science have reminded us that many of the pioneers of modern science were people whose faith made them humble before nature and skeptical of human authority. As Christians, Blaise Pascal, Francis Bacon, Isaac Newton, and Galileo were wary of human intuition, preferring to explore God's creation freely and to submit contesting ideas to the test. They viewed

153

themselves in God's service, whether searching God's word or God's works. To illustrate this spirit, Francis Collins, director of the Human Genome Project, likes to quote Copernicus: "To know the mighty works of God; to comprehend His wisdom and majesty and power; to appreciate, in degree, the wonderful working of His Laws, surely all this must be a pleasing and acceptable mode of worship to the most High, to whom ignorance cannot be more grateful than knowledge."

If, as previously had been supposed, nature was sacred—if nature were alive with river goddesses and sun gods—then we ought not tamper with it. But if these early scientists were right instead to view nature as an intelligible creation, a work to be enjoyed and managed, then we are set free to seek its truths through observation and experiment. Our ultimate allegiance is not to current opinion but to God alone. So, mindful of the frailty of human reason, let us humbly test our ideas. If nature does not conform to our presumptions, so much the worse for them. Disciplined inquiry—checking our theories against reality—is part of what it means to love God with our *minds*.

This attitude of humility before the created world also underlies psychological science. Christian psychologists, Donald MacKay argued, are "to 'tell it like it is,' knowing that the Author is at our elbow, a silent judge of the accuracy with which we claim to describe the world He has created."[1] If God is the ultimate author of whatever truth psychological science glimpses, then I can accept that truth, however surprising. Rigorous inquiry is not just my right, but my religious calling. What matters, then, is not my opinion or yours, but whatever truths nature reveals in response to our questioning. If animals or people don't behave as our ideas predict, then so much the worse for our ideas. As Agatha Christie's Miss Marple explained, "It wasn't what I expected. But facts are facts, and if one is proved to be wrong, one must just be humble about it and start again." This is the humble attitude expressed in one of psychology's early mottos: "The rat is always right."

Consider now how recent psychological science beckons us to humility—to an awareness of our vulnerability to error and pride, and thus to the ever-reforming spirit of faith and the inquisitive spirit of science that, brought together, help define humility theology.

Intuition: The Powers and Limits of Our Inner Knowing

What are our powers of intuition—of immediately knowing something without reasoning or analysis? Advocates of "intuitive management" believe we should tune into our hunches. When judging others, we should plug into the nonlogical smarts of our "right brain." When hiring, firing, and investing, we should listen to our premonitions. In making judgments, we should follow the example of *Star Wars*'s Luke Skywalker by switching off our computer guidance systems and trusting the force within.

Are the intuitionists correct that important information is immediately available apart from our conscious analysis? Or are the skeptics right in counseling humility and in jesting that intuition is "our knowing we are right, whether we are or not"?

The Powers of Our Inner Knowing

"The heart has its reasons which reason does not know," observed Blaise Pascal. Three centuries later, scientists have proved Pascal correct. We know more than we know we know.

Studies of our unconscious information processing confirm our limited access to what's going on in our minds. Our thinking is partly controlled (deliberate and conscious) and—more than most of us once supposed—partly *automatic* (effortless and without our awareness). Automatic thinking occurs not "on-screen" but off-screen, out of sight, where reason does not know. Consider:

- *Schemata*—mental templates—automatically, intuitively, guide our perceptions and interpretations of our experience. Whether we hear someone speaking of religious *sects* or *sex* depends not only on the word spoken but on how we automatically interpret the sound. As an old Chinese proverb says, "Two-thirds of what we see is behind our eyes."
- Some *emotional reactions* are nearly instantaneous, before there is time for deliberate thinking. Simple likes, dislikes, and fears typically involve little reasoned analysis. Although our intuitive reactions sometimes defy logic, they may still be adaptive. Our ancestors who intuitively feared a sound in the bushes were usually fearing nothing, but they were more likely to survive to pass their genes down to us than their more deliberative cousins.
- Given sufficient *expertise*, people may intuitively know the answer to a problem. The situation cues information stored in their memory. Without knowing quite how we do it, we recognize our friend's voice after the first spoken word of a phone conversation. Master chess players intuitively recognize meaningful patterns that novices miss.

- Some things—facts, names, and past experiences—we remember explicitly (consciously). But other things—skills and conditioned dispositions—we remember *implicitly*, without consciously knowing and declaring that we know. It's true of us all, but most strikingly evident in brain-damaged persons who cannot form new explicit memories. Thus, having learned how to solve a block-stacking puzzle or play golf, they will deny ever having experienced the task. Yet (surprisingly to themselves) they perform like practiced experts. If repeatedly shown the word *perfume* they won't recall having seen it. But if asked to guess a word you have in mind beginning with *per-*, they surprise themselves by intuitively knowing the answer.
- Equally dramatic are the cases of *blindsight*. Having lost a portion of the visual cortex to surgery or stroke, people may be functionally blind in part of their field of vision. Shown a series of sticks in the blind field, the patients report seeing nothing. After correctly guessing whether the sticks are vertical or horizontal, the patients are astounded when told, "You got them all right." Again, the patients know more than they know they know. There are, it seems, little minds—parallel processing units—operating unseen.
- *Prosopagnosia* patients suffer damage to a brain area involved in face recognition. They can see familiar people but are unable to recognize them as their spouses or children. Yet, shown pictures of such people, their heart knows them; its rate increases as their body shows signs of unconscious recognition.
- For that matter, consider your own taken-for-granted capacity to intuitively recognize a face. As you look at a photo, your brain breaks the visual information into subdimensions such as color, depth, movement, and form, and works on each aspect simultaneously before reassembling the components. Finally, somehow, your brain compares the perceived image with previously stored images. Voilà! Instantly and effortlessly, you recognize your grandmother. If intuition is immediately knowing something without reasoned analysis, perceiving is intuition par excellence.
- Although below our threshold for conscious awareness, *subliminal* stimuli may nevertheless have intriguing effects. Shown certain geometric figures for less than 0.01 second each, people will deny having seen anything more than a flash of light. Yet they will later express a preference for the forms they saw. Sometimes we intuitively feel what we cannot explain. Likewise, invisible flashed

words can *prime* or predispose our responses to later questions. If the word *bread* is flashed too briefly to recognize, we may then detect a flashed, related word such as *butter* more easily than an unrelated word such as *bottle*.

To repeat, many routine cognitive functions occur automatically, unintentionally, without awareness. Our minds function rather like big corporations. Our CEO—our controlled consciousness—attends to the most important or novel issues and assigns routine affairs to subordinates. This delegation of attentional resources enables us to react to many situations quickly, efficiently, *intuitively*, without taking limited time to reason and analyze.

The Limits of Our Inner Knowing: To Err Is Human

Although researchers affirm that unconscious information processing can produce flashes of intuition, they also detect grounds for humility. Elizabeth Loftus and Mark Klinger speak for today's cognitive scientists in reporting "a general consensus that the unconscious may not be as smart as previously believed."[2] For example, although subliminal stimuli can trigger a weak, fleeting response—enough to evoke a feeling, if not conscious awareness—there is no evidence that commercial subliminal tapes can powerfully "reprogram your unconscious mind" for success.

Moreover, our intuitive judgments err often enough to understand why poet T. S. Eliot would describe "The hollow man . . . Headpiece filled with straw." Social psychologists have explored our error-prone hindsight (our intuitive sense, after the fact, that we knew it all along). Other domains of psychology have explored our capacity for illusion—perceptual misinterpretations, fantasies, and constructed beliefs. Brain researchers have discovered that patients whose brain hemispheres have been surgically separated will instantly fabricate—and believe—explanations of puzzling behaviors. If the patient gets up and takes a few steps after the experimenter flashes the instruction "walk" to the patient's nonverbal right hemisphere, the verbal left hemisphere will instantly invent a plausible explanation ("I felt like getting a drink").

Illusory thinking also appears in the vast new literature on how we take in, store, and retrieve social information. As perception researchers study visual illusions for what they reveal about our normal perceptual mechanisms, social psychologists study illusory thinking for what it reveals about normal information processing, and about our human limits. So let's explore how efficient information processing can go awry, beginning with our self-knowledge.

The Fallibility of Our Self-Understanding

"There is one thing, and only one in the whole universe which we know more about than we could learn from external observation," noted C. S. Lewis. "That one thing is [ourselves]. We have, so to speak, inside information; we are in the know."[3]

Indeed. Yet sometimes we *think* we know, but our inside information is wrong. This is the unavoidable conclusion of some fascinating recent research.

Explaining our behavior. Asked why we have felt or acted as we have, we produce plausible answers. Yet our self-explanations often err. Factors that have big effects we sometimes report as innocuous. Factors that have little effect we sometimes perceive as influential.

Richard Nisbett and Stanley Schachter demonstrated this by asking Columbia University students to take a series of electric shocks of steadily increasing intensity. Beforehand, some took a fake pill which, they were told, would produce heart palpitations, breathing irregularities, and butterflies in the stomach—the very symptoms that usually accompany being shocked. Nisbett and Schachter anticipated that people would attribute the symptoms of shock to the pill rather than to the shock. Thus they (more than people not given the pill) should tolerate shock. Indeed, the effect was enormous: people given the fake pill took four times as much shock.

When informed that they had taken more shock than average and asked why, their answers did not mention the pill. When pressed (even after the experimenter explained the experiment's hypotheses in detail), they denied the pill's influence. They would usually say that the pill probably did affect some people, but not them. A typical reply was "I didn't even think about the pill."

Sometimes people think they *have* been affected by something that has had no effect. Nisbett and Timothy Wilson had University of Michigan students rate a documentary film. While some of them watched, a power saw roared outside the room. Most people felt that this distracting noise affected their ratings. But it didn't; their ratings were similar to those of control subjects who viewed the film without distraction.

Predicting our behavior. We also frequently err in predicting our own behavior. Asked whether they would obey demands to deliver severe electric shocks or would hesitate to help a victim if several other people were present, people overwhelmingly deny their vulnerability to such influences. But experiments have shown that many of us are vulnerable. Moreover, consider what Sidney Shrauger discovered when he had college students predict the likelihood of their experiencing dozens of different events during the ensuing two months (becoming romantically involved, being sick, and so forth): their self-predictions were hardly more accurate than predictions based on the average person's experience. Similarly, Robert Vallone and his colleagues had college students predict in September whether they would drop a course, declare a major, elect to live off campus next year, and so forth. Although, on average, the students felt 84 percent sure of these self-predictions, they erred nearly twice as often (29 percent of the time) as they expected. Even when feeling 100 percent sure of their predictions, they erred 15 percent of the time. Ergo, the surest thing we can say about your individual future is that it's hard for even you to predict. (The best advice is to look at your past behavior in similar situations—and be humble.)

Constructing memories. Do you agree or disagree that "memory can be likened to a storage chest in the brain into which we deposit material and from which we can withdraw it later if needed. Occasionally, something is lost from the 'chest,' and then we say we have forgotten."

In one survey, about 85 percent of college students agreed. Actually, memories are not copies of experiences that remain on deposit in a memory bank. Rather, we construct our memories at the time of withdrawal. Memory involves backward reasoning. It infers what must have been, given what we now believe or know. Like a paleontologist inferring the appearance of a dinosaur from bone fragments, we reconstruct our distant past by combining fragments of information using our current expectations. Thus, we may unconsciously revise our memories to suit our current knowledge. When one of my sons complained, "The June issue of *Cricket* never came," and was shown where it was, he delightedly responded, "Oh good, I knew I'd gotten it."

Reconstructing past attitudes. Five years ago, how did you feel about nuclear power? about Bill Clinton? about your parents? If your attitudes have changed, do you know how much?

Experimenters have tried to answer such questions. The results have been unnerving: People whose attitudes have changed often insist that they have always felt much as they now feel. Daryl Bem and Keith McConnell took a survey among Carnegie-Mellon University students. Buried in it was a question concerning student control over the university curriculum. A week later the students agreed to write an essay opposing student control. After doing so, their attitudes shifted toward greater opposition to student control. When asked to recall how they had answered the question before writing the essay, they "remembered" holding the opinion that they *now* held and denied that the experiment had affected them. After observing Clark University students similarly denying their former attitudes, researchers D. R. Wixon and James Laird commented: "The speed, magnitude, and certainty" with which the students revised their own histories "was striking."

Cathy McFarland and Michael Ross found that we also revise our recalled views of other people as our relationships with them change. They had university students rate their steady dating partners. Two months later, they rated them again. Those who had broken up were more likely to recall having recognized the partner as somewhat selfish and ill-tempered. Those who were more in love than ever had a tendency to recall love at first sight. Passions exaggerate.

It's not that we are totally unaware of how we used to feel; it's just that when memories are hazy, current feelings guide our recall. Parents of every generation bemoan the values of the next generation, partly because they misrecall their youthful values as being closer to their current values.

Reconstructing past behavior. Memory construction enables us to revise our own histories. Michael Ross, Cathy McFarland, and Garth Fletcher exposed some University of Waterloo students to a message convincing them of the desirability of toothbrushing. Later, in a supposedly different experiment, these students recalled brushing their teeth more often during the preceding two weeks than did students who had not heard the message. Likewise, when representative samples of Americans are asked about their cigarette smoking and their reports are projected to the nation as a whole, at least a third of the 600 billion cigarettes sold annually are unaccounted for. Noting the similarity of such findings to happenings in George Orwell's *1984*—where it was "necessary to remember that events happened in the desired manner"—social psychologist Anthony Greenwald surmised that we all have "totalitarian egos" that revise the past to suit our present views.

Conclusions. "Know thyself," urged the ancient Greek philosopher Thales. We try. But to a striking extent, we are often wrong about what has influenced us and what we will feel and do. Our intuitive self-knowledge errs.

This fact of life has two practical implications. The first is for psychological inquiry. Although the intuitions of clients or research subjects may provide useful clues to their psychological processes, *self-reports are often untrustworthy*. Errors in self-understanding limit the scientific usefulness of subjective personal reports.

The second implication is for our everyday lives. The sincerity with which people report and interpret their experiences is no guarantee of the validity of these reports. Personal testimonies are powerfully persuasive, but they may also convey unwitting error. Keeping this potential for error in mind can help us feel less intimidated by others and less gullible. It beckons us to humility about our own self-knowledge, and a healthy skepticism about the self-knowledge of others.

Reasons for Unreason

The mixed picture of our intuitive self-knowledge is paralleled by the mixed picture of our rationality. On the one hand, what species better deserves the name *Homo sapiens*—wise humans? Our cognitive powers outstrip the smartest computers in recognizing patterns, handling language, and processing abstract information. Our information processing is also wonderfully efficient. With such precious little time to process so much information, we specialize in mental shortcuts. Scientists marvel at the speed and ease with which we form impressions, judgments, and explanations. In many situations, our snap generalizations—"That's dangerous!"—are adaptive. They promote our survival.

But our adaptive efficiency has a trade-off; snap generalizations sometimes err. Our helpful strategies for simplifying complex information can lead us astray. To enhance our own powers of critical thinking, consider four reasons for unreason—common ways in which people form or sustain false beliefs.

1. Our preconceptions control our interpretations. A mountain of research shows that there is more to perception than meets the eye. An illustrative experiment by Robert Vallone, Lee Ross, and Mark Lepper revealed how powerful preconceptions can be. They showed pro-Israeli and pro-Arab students six network news segments describing the 1982 killing of civilian refugees at two camps in Lebanon. Each group perceived the networks as hostile to its side. The phenomenon is commonplace: presidential candidates and their supporters nearly always view the news media as unsympathetic to their cause; sports fans perceive referees as partial to the other side; people in conflict (married couples, labor and management, opposing racial groups) see impartial mediators as biased against them.

Our assumptions can also make ambiguous evidence seem support-ive. For example, Ross and Lepper assisted Charles Lord in showing Stan-ford University students the results of two supposed new research stud-ies. Half the students favored capital punishment, and half opposed it. One study confirmed and the other disconfirmed the students' beliefs about the deterrence effect of the death penalty. Both proponents and op-ponents of capital punishment readily accepted evidence that confirmed their belief but were sharply critical of disconfirming evidence. Showing the two groups an *identical* body of mixed evidence had therefore not nar-rowed their disagreement but *increased* it. Each side perceived the evi-dence as supporting its belief and now believed even more strongly.

Is this why, in politics, religion, and science, ambiguous informa-tion often fuels conflict? Presidential TV debates in the United States have mostly reinforced predebate opinions. By nearly a 10 to 1 mar-gin, those who already favored one candidate or the other in the 1960, 1976, and 1980 debates perceived their candidate as having won.

2. We overestimate the accuracy of our judgments. The intellectual con-ceit evident in our judgments of our past knowledge ("I knew it all along") extends to estimates of our current knowledge. Daniel Kahne-man and Amos Tversky gave people factual questions and asked them to fill in the blanks, as in: "I feel 98 percent certain that the air distance between New Delhi and Beijing is more than ____ miles but less than ____ miles."

Most subjects were overconfident: about 30 percent of the time, the correct answers lay outside the range they felt 98 percent confident about. Baruch Fischhoff and his colleagues discovered the same "over-confidence phenomenon" when people rated their certainty about their answers to multiple-choice questions, such as: "Which is longer: (a) the Panama Canal or (b) the Suez Canal?" If people 60 percent of the time answer such a question correctly, they will typically *feel* about 75 percent sure. (Answers: New Delhi is 2500 miles from Beijing. The Suez Canal is twice as long as the Panama Canal.)

Overconfidence also permeates everyday decision making. Invest-ment experts market their services with the confident presumption that they can beat the stock market average, forgetting that for every stockbroker or buyer saying, "Sell!" at a given price there is another saying, "Buy!" A stock's price is the balance point between these mu-tually confident judgments. Thus, incredible as it may seem, economist Burton Malkiel reports that mutual fund portfolios selected by invest-ment analysts do *not* outperform randomly selected stocks.

3. We often are swayed more by anecdotes than statistical facts. Anecdotal information is persuasive. Researchers Richard Nisbett and Eugene Borgida explored the tendency to overuse anecdotal information by showing University of Michigan students videotaped interviews of people who supposedly had participated in an experiment in which most subjects failed to assist a seizure victim. Learning how *most* subjects acted had little effect upon people's predictions of how the individual they observed acted. The apparent niceness of this individual was more vivid and compelling than the general truth about how most subjects really acted: "Ted seems so pleasant that I can't imagine him being unresponsive to another's plight." This illustrates the "base-rate fallacy": focusing upon the specific individual can push into the background useful information about the population the person came from.

There is, of course, a positive side to viewing people as individuals and not merely as statistical units. The problem arises when we formulate our beliefs about people in general from our observations of particular persons. Focusing on individuals distorts our perception of what is generally true. Our impressions of a group, for example, tend to be overinfluenced by its extreme members. One man's attempt to assassinate President Reagan caused people to bemoan, "It's not safe to walk the streets anymore," and to conclude, "There's a sickness in the American soul." As the psychologist Gordon Allport put it, "Given a thimbleful of facts we rush to make generalizations as large as a tub."

Because vivid anecdotes are more compelling than base-rate statistical information, perceived risk is often badly out of joint with the real risks of things. News footage of airplane crashes are vivid memories for most of us. This misleads people to suppose that they are more at risk traveling in a commercial airplane than in a car. Actually, U.S. travelers during the 1980s were twenty-six times more likely to die in a car crash than on a commercial flight covering the same distance.

Or consider this: three jumbo jets full of passengers crashing every day would not equal tobacco's deadly effects. If the deaths caused by tobacco occurred in horrible accidents, the resulting uproar would long ago have eliminated cigarettes. Because, instead, the deaths are disguised as "cancer" and "heart disease" and diffused on obituary pages, we hardly notice. Thus, rather than eliminating the hazard, the U.S. government continues to subsidize the tobacco industry's program for quietly killing its customers. The point: dramatic events stick in our minds, and we use ease of recall when predicting the likelihood of something happening.

4. We misperceive correlation and control. Another influence on everyday thinking is our search for order in random events, a tendency that can lead us down all sorts of wrong paths. It's easy to see a correlation—an "illusory correlation"—where none exists. As part of their research with the Bell Telephone Laboratories, William Ward and Herbert Jenkins showed people the results of a hypothetical fifty-day cloud-seeding experiment. They told their subjects which of the fifty days the clouds had been seeded and which days it rained. This information was nothing more than a random mix of results: sometimes it rained after seeding; sometimes it didn't. People nevertheless became convinced—in conformity with their supposition about the effects of cloud seeding—that they really had observed a relationship between cloud seeding and rain.

If we believe a correlation exists, we are more likely to notice and recall confirming instances. If we believe that premonitions correlate with events, we notice and remember the joint occurrence of the premonition and the later occurrence of that event. We seldom notice or remember all the times unusual events do not coincide. If, after we think about a friend, the friend calls us, we notice and remember this coincidence more than all the times we think of a friend without any ensuing call, or receive a call from a friend about whom we have *not* been thinking. Thus, we easily overestimate the frequency with which these strange things happen.

Infertile couples who adopt, it is popularly theorized, finally relax—and conceive. But no such theory is necessary, because it isn't so. Although researchers have found no correlation between adoption and conception, our attention is drawn to couples who have conceived after adopting (rather than to those who conceive before adopting or who don't conceive after adopting). Thus we easily misperceive random events as confirming our hunches.

Our tendency to perceive random events as related feeds an "illusion of control"—the idea that chance events are subject to our influence. This is what keeps gamblers going, and what makes the rest of us do all sorts of silly things. During the 1988 summer drought, for example, retired farmer Elmer Carlson arranged a rain dance by sixteen Hopi in Audubon, Iowa. The next day it rained one inch. "The miracles are still here, we just have to ask for them," explained Carlson (Associated Press, 1988).

Ellen Langer demonstrated the illusion of control with experiments on gambling. People readily believed they could beat chance.

Compared to those given an assigned lottery number, people who chose their own lottery number demanded four times as much money when asked for how much they would sell their ticket. When playing a game of chance against an awkward and nervous person, they bet significantly more than when playing against a dapper, confident opponent. Given some unusual early successes in a chance situation, they often discounted later failures. In these and other ways, Langer consistently found people acting as if they could control chance events.

Real-life gamblers also exhibit an illusion of control. Dice players may throw softly for low numbers and hard for high numbers. The gambling industry thrives on gamblers' illusions. Gamblers' hopes that they can beat the laws of chance sustain their gambling. Gamblers attribute wins to their skill and foresight. Losses become "near misses" or "flukes"—perhaps (for the sports gambler) a bad call by the referee or a freakish bounce of the ball.

Conclusions

We could extend our list of reasons for unreason, but surely this has been a sufficient glimpse at how people come to believe what may be untrue. We can't easily dismiss these experiments: most of the participants were intelligent people, mostly students at leading universities. Moreover, these distortions and biases occurred even when payment for right answers motivated people to think optimally. As one researcher concluded, the illusions "have a persistent quality not unlike that of perceptual illusions."

Research in cognitive social psychology thus mirrors the mixed review given humanity in literature, philosophy, and religion. Many research psychologists have spent lifetimes exploring the awesome capacities of the human mind. We are smart enough to have cracked our own genetic code, to have invented talking computers, to have sent people to the moon. Moreover, our intuitive hunches—our efficient mental shortcuts—generally are adaptive. "The mind works in the overwhelmingly large part to do or die, not to reason or to know why," notes Robert Ornstein. "There has never been, nor will there ever be, enough time to be truly rational."[4] Three cheers for intuition.

Well, two cheers—because the mind's priority on efficiency makes our intuition more vulnerable to error than we suspect. With remarkable ease, we form and sustain false beliefs. Led by our preconceptions, overconfident of our judgments, persuaded by vivid anecdotes, perceiving correlations and control where none exists, we construct our idea of the social world around us. "The naked intellect," observed the novelist Madeleine L'Engle, "is an extraordinarily inaccurate instrument." And that is why, rather than trusting our unaided intuition, we do science. Science always involves an interplay between intuition and rigorous test, between creative hunch and skepticism. To sift reality from illusion requires both open-minded curiosity and hardheaded rigor. This perspective disposes a healthy attitude for approaching all of life: to be critical but not cynical, curious but not gullible, open, but not exploitable—in a word, to be humble.

The New Psychology of Pride

> We are all so blinded and upset by self-love that everyone imagines he has a just right to exalt himself, and to undervalue all others in comparison to self.
>
> If God has bestowed on us any excellent gift, we imagine it to be our own achievement, and we swell and even burst with pride.
>
> —JOHN CALVIN
> *Golden Booklet of the True Christian Life*

Is it nevertheless true, what the pop psychology of our age tells us: that in an important sense most of us suffer from *excessive* humility—a condition commonly called *low* self-esteem? A generation ago, the humanistic psychologist Carl Rogers concluded that most people he knew "despise themselves, regard themselves as worthless and unlovable."[5] Many proponents of humanistic psychology have concurred. "All of us have inferiority complexes," contended John Powell.[6] "Those who seem not to have such a complex are only pretending." As Groucho Marx jested, "I don't want to belong to any club that would accept me as a member."[7]

Actually, most of us have a good reputation with ourselves. In studies of self-esteem, even low-scoring people respond in the midrange of possible scores. (A "low"-self-esteem person responds to such statements as "I have good ideas" with a qualifier such as "somewhat" or "sometimes.") Moreover, one of social psychology's most provocative yet firmly established conclusions concerns the potency of *self-serving bias*. Pride prevails.

Explanations for Positive and Negative Events

Time and again, experimenters have found that people readily accept credit when told they have succeeded (attributing the success to their ability and effort), yet attribute failure to such external factors as bad luck or the problem's inherent "impossibility." Similarly, in explaining their victories, athletes commonly credit themselves, but attribute losses to something else: bad breaks, bad referee calls, or the other team's supereffort or dirty play. And how much responsibility do you suppose car drivers tend to accept for their accidents? On insurance forms, drivers have described their accidents in words such as these: "An invisible car came out of nowhere, struck my car and vanished"; "As we reached an intersection, a hedge sprang up, obscuring my vision and I did not see the other car"; "A pedestrian hit me and went under my car." Situations that combine skill and chance (games, exams, job applications) are especially prone to the phenomenon: winners can easily attribute their successes to their skill, while losers can attribute their losses to chance. When I win at Scrabble, it's because of my verbal dexterity; when I lose, it's because, "Who could get anywhere with a *Q* but no *U*?"

Michael Ross and Fiore Sicoly observed a marital version of self-serving bias. They found that young married Canadians usually felt they took more responsibility for such activities as cleaning the house and caring for the children than their spouses credited them for. In a survey of Americans, 91 percent of wives but only 76 percent of husbands credited the wife with doing most of the food shopping. In another study, husbands estimated they did slightly more of the housework than their wives did; the wives, however, estimated their efforts were more than double their husbands'. Small wonder that divorced people usually blame their partner for the breakup, or that managers usually blame poor performance on workers' lack of ability or effort. (Workers are more likely to blame something external—inadequate supplies, excessive workload, difficult coworkers, ambiguous assignments.) Such findings bring to mind Adam's excuse: "The woman whom you gave to be with me, she gave me fruit from the tree, and I ate."

Can We All Be Better Than Average?

Self-serving bias also appears when people compare themselves to others. If the sixth-century B.C.E. Chinese philosopher Lao-tzu was right that "at no time in the world will a man who is sane over-reach himself, over-spend himself, over-rate himself," then most of us are a little insane. For on nearly any dimension that is both *subjective* and *socially desirable*, most people see themselves as better than average. Consider:

- Most businesspeople see themselves as more ethical than the average businessperson. Ninety percent of business managers rate their performance as superior to their average peer.
- In Australia, 86 percent of people rate their job performance as above average, 1 percent as below average.
- Most drivers—even most drivers who have been hospitalized for accidents—believe themselves to be safer and more skilled than the average driver.
- Most people perceive themselves as more intelligent than their average peer, as better looking, and as less prejudiced than others in their communities.
- Most adults believe they support their aging parents more than do their siblings.
- Los Angeles residents view themselves as healthier than most of their neighbors, and most college students believe they will outlive their actuarially predicted age of death by about ten years.

Every community, it seems, is like Garrison Keillor's fictional Lake Wobegon, where "all the women are strong, all the men are good-looking, and all the children are above average." Although 12 percent of people feel old for their age, many more—66 percent—think they are young for their age. All of which calls to mind Freud's joke about the man who told his wife, "If one of us should die, I think I would go live in Paris."

Subjective dimensions (such as "disciplined") trigger greater self-serving bias than objective behavioral dimensions (such as "punctual"). Students are more likely to rate themselves superior in "moral goodness" than in "intelligence." This is partly because subjective qualities give us so much leeway in constructing our own definitions of success. Rating my "athletic ability," I ponder my basketball play, not the agonizing weeks I spent as a Little League baseball player hiding in right field. Assessing my "leadership ability," I conjure up an image of a great leader whose style is similar to mine. By defining ambiguous criteria in our own terms, each of us can see ourselves as relatively successful. In one College Entrance Examination Board survey of 829,000 high school seniors, *zero* percent rated themselves below average in "ability to get along with others" (a subjective, desirable trait), 60 percent rated themselves in the top 10 percent, and 25 percent saw themselves among the top 1 percent!

We also support our self-image by assigning importance to the things we're good at. Over a semester, those who ace an introductory computer science course come to place a higher value on their identity as a computer-literate person in today's world. Those who do poorly are more likely to scorn computer geeks and to exclude computer skills as pertinent to their self-image.

Unrealistic Optimism

What is more, many of us have what researcher Neil Weinstein terms "an unrealistic optimism about future life events."[8] At Rutgers University, for example, students perceive themselves as far more likely than their classmates to get a good job, draw a good salary, and own a home, and as far less likely to experience negative events, such as developing a drinking problem, having a heart attack before age forty, or being fired. In Scotland, most late adolescents think they are much less likely than their peers to become infected by the AIDS virus. After experiencing the 1989 earthquake, San Francisco Bay-area students did lose their optimism about being less vulnerable than their classmates to injury in a natural disaster, but within three months their illusory optimism had rebounded. "Views of the future are so rosy," notes the social psychologist Shelley Taylor, "that they would make Pollyanna blush."[9]

Illusory optimism increases our vulnerability. Believing ourselves immune to misfortune, we do not take sensible precautions. Most young Americans know that half of U.S. marriages end in divorce but persist in believing that *theirs* will not. Sexually active undergraduate women who don't consistently use contraceptives perceive themselves, compared to other women at their university, as much *less* vulnerable to unwanted pregnancy. Those who cheerfully shun seat belts, deny the effects of smoking, and stumble into ill-fated relationships remind us that blind optimism, like pride, may go before a fall.

Optimism beats pessimism in promoting self-efficacy and persistence when facing initial failure. Nevertheless, a dash of pessimism can save us from the perils of unrealistic optimism. Self-doubt can energize students, most of whom exhibit excess optimism about upcoming exams. Students who are overconfident tend to under prepare. Their equally able but more anxious peers, fearing that they are going to bomb the upcoming exam, study furiously and get higher grades. The moral: success in school and beyond requires enough optimism to sustain hope and enough pessimism to motivate concern.

False Consensus and False Uniqueness

We have a curious tendency to further enhance our self-image by overestimating or underestimating the extent to which others think and act as we do—a phenomenon called the *false consensus effect*. On matters of *opinion*, we find support for our positions by overestimating the extent to which others agree. If we favor a Canadian referendum or support New Zealand's National Party, we wishfully overestimate the extent to which others agree. When we behave badly or fail in a task, we reassure ourselves by thinking that such lapses are common. We guess that others think and act as we do: "I do it, but so does everyone else." If we cheat on our income taxes or smoke, we are likely to overestimate the number of other people who do likewise.

One might argue that false consensus occurs because we generalize from a limited sample, which prominently includes ourselves. But on matters of *ability* or when we behave well or successfully, a *false uniqueness effect* more often occurs. We serve our self-image by seeing our talents and moral behaviors as relatively unusual. Thus, those who drink heavily but use seat belts will *over*estimate (false consensus) the number of other heavy drinkers and *under*estimate (false uniqueness) the commonality of seat belt use. Simply put, people see their failings as normal, their virtues as rare.

Other Self-Serving Tendencies

These tendencies toward self-serving attributions, self-congratulatory comparisons, and illusory optimism are not the only signs of favorably biased self-perceptions. Consider more:

- Most of us overestimate how desirably we would act in a given situation.
- We also display a "cognitive conceit" by overestimating the accuracy of our beliefs and judgments, and by misremembering our own past in self-enhancing ways.
- If an undesirable act cannot be misremembered or undone, then we often justify it.
- The more favorably we perceive ourselves on some dimension (intelligence, persistence, sense of humor), the more we use that dimension as a basis for judging others.

- If a test or some other source of information—even a horoscope—flatters us, then we believe it, and we evaluate positively both the test and any evidence suggesting that the test is valid.
- Most university students think the SAT (Scholastic Assessment Test) underestimated their ability. (In fact, however, the higher scores they *think* they deserved would *less* accurately predict their obtained grades.)
- Judging from photos, we not only guess that attractive people have desirable personalities, we also guess that they have personalities more like our own than do unattractive people.
- We like to associate ourselves with the glory of others' success. If we find ourselves linked with (say, born on the same day as) some reprehensible person, we boost ourselves by softening our view of the rascal.

So, is pop psychology right that most people suffer from excessive humility and insufficient self-love? *Many* streams of evidence suggest otherwise. To paraphrase Elizabeth Barrett Browning, "How do I love me? Let me count the ways!"

Reflections on Self-Serving Pride

No doubt many readers are finding all this either depressing or contrary to their own occasional feelings of inadequacy. To be sure, most of us who exhibit the self-serving bias may still feel inferior to specific individuals, especially those who are a step or two higher on the ladder of success, attractiveness, or skill. And not everyone operates with a self-serving bias. Some people *do* suffer from low self-esteem. Do such people hunger for esteem and therefore often exhibit self-serving bias? Is self-serving bias just a cover-up?

It's true: when feeling good about ourselves and unthreatened, we are less defensive and judgmental—less likely to inflate those who like us and berate those who don't. In experiments, people whose self-esteem is temporarily bruised—say, by being told they did miserably on an intelligence test—are more likely to disparage others. More generally, people who are down on themselves tend also to be down on others. Mockery says as much about the mocker as the one mocked.

Nevertheless, high self-esteem goes hand in hand with self-serving perceptions. Those who score highest on self-esteem tests (who say nice things about themselves) also say nice things about themselves when explaining their successes and failures, when evaluating their group, and when comparing themselves to others.

Although self-serving pride helps protect us from depression, it can at times be maladaptive. When challenged or insulted, people with inflated egos are at greatest risk for violence. Moreover, people who blame others for their social difficulties are often unhappier than people who can acknowledge their mistakes. Research by Barry Schlenker has also shown how self-serving perceptions can poison a group. In nine experiments at the University of Florida Schlenker had people work together on some task. He then falsely informed them that their group had done either well or poorly. In every one of these studies, the members of successful groups claimed more responsibility for their group's performance than did members of groups that supposedly failed at the task. Most presented themselves as contributing more than the others in their group when the group did well; few said they contributed less.

Such self-deception can lead individual group members to expect greater-than-average rewards when their organization does well and less-than-average blame when it does not. If most individuals in a group believe they are underpaid and underappreciated relative to their contributions, disharmony and envy are likely. College presidents and academic deans will readily recognize the phenomenon. Ninety percent or more of college faculty members rate themselves as superior to their average colleague (no excessive humility on campus!). It is therefore inevitable that when merit salary raises are announced and half receive an average raise or less, many will feel themselves victims of injustice.

Biased self-assessments also distort managerial judgment. When groups are comparable, most people consider their own group superior. Thus, most corporation presidents predict more growth for their own firms than for their competition. And most production managers overpredict their production. Such overoptimism can produce disastrous consequences. If those who deal in the stock market or in real estate perceive their business intuition to be superior to that of their competitors, they may be in for severe disappointment. Even the seventeenth-century economist Adam Smith, a defender of human economic rationality, foresaw that people would overestimate their chances of gain. This "absurd presumption in their own good fortune," he said, arises from "the overweening conceit which the greater part of men have of their own abilities."[10]

That people see themselves with a favorable bias is hardly new. The tragic flaw portrayed in ancient Greek drama was *hubris*, or pride. Like the subjects of our experiments, the Greek tragic figures were not self-consciously evil; they merely thought too highly of themselves. In literature, the pitfalls of pride are portrayed again and again. In religion, pride has long been first among the "seven deadly sins." Much as social psychologists observe self-serving, self-justifying biases clouding our self-understanding, biblical writers suggest that becoming aware of our sin is like trying to see our own eyeballs. "Who can detect their errors?" the Psalmist (19:12) wondered. Thus the Pharisee could thank God "that I am not like other men" (and we can thank God that we are not like the Pharisee). The apostle Paul must have had this self-righteous tendency in mind when he admonished the Philippians (2:3) to "in humility count others better than yourselves."

Paul assumed that our natural tendency is to count ourselves better than others, just as he assumed self-love when he argued that husbands should love their wives as their own bodies, and just as Jesus assumed self-love when commanding us to love our neighbors as we love ourselves. The Bible neither teaches nor opposes self-love; it takes it for granted.

The Bible does, however, warn us against self-righteous pride—pride that alienates us from God and leads us to disdain one another. Such pride is at the core of racism, sexism, nationalism, and all the chauvinisms that lead one group of people to see themselves as more moral, deserving, or able than another. The flip side of being proud of our individual and group achievements, and taking credit for them, is blaming the poor for their poverty and the oppressed for their oppression.

Samuel Johnson recognized this in one of his eighteenth-century *Sermons:* "He that overvalues himself will undervalue others, and he that undervalues others will oppress them." The Nazi atrocities were rooted not in self-conscious feelings of German inferiority but in Aryan pride. The arms race was fed by a national pride that enabled each nation to perceive its own motives as righteously defensive, the other's as hostile. The apostle of positive thinking, Dale Carnegie, foresaw the danger in 1936: "Each nation feels superior to other nations. That breeds patriotism—and wars."[11]

For centuries, pride has therefore been considered the fundamental sin, the original sin. Vain self-love corrodes human community and erodes our sense of dependence on one another and on God. If I seem confident about the pervasiveness and potency of pride, it is not because we have invented a new idea, but rather because the new findings reaffirm a very old idea.

All this, to be sure, is not the whole story. As Pascal taught, no single truth is ever sufficient, because the world is not simple. Any truth separated from its complementary truth is a half-truth. Although it is true that self-serving pride is prevalent and at times socially perilous, it also is true that healthy self-esteem, feelings of control, and a positive optimism pay dividends. There is a power to possibility-filled positive thinking. But that story is for another bedtime.

Finally, if pride is akin to the self-serving bias, then what is humility? Is it self-contempt? Or can we be self-affirming and self-accepting without a self-serving bias? To paraphrase C. S. Lewis, humility is not handsome people trying to believe they are ugly and clever people trying to believe they are fools. (False modesty can actually be a cover for pride in one's better-than-average humility.) True humility is more like self-forgetfulness than false modesty. As Dennis Voskuil has written, the refreshing gospel promise is "not that we have been freed by Christ to love ourselves, but that we are free from self-ession. Not that the cross frees us *for* the ego trip but that the cross frees us *from* the ego trip."[12] This leaves people free to rejoice in their special talents and, with the same honesty, to recognize others.

Obviously, true humility is a state not easily attained. "If anyone would like to acquire humility," offered C. S. Lewis, "I can, I think, tell him the first step. The first step is to realize that one is proud. And a biggish step, too." The way to take this first step, continued Lewis, is to glimpse the greatness of God and see oneself in light of it. "He and you are two things of such a kind that if you really get into any kind of touch with Him you will, in fact be humble, feeling the infinite relief of having for once got rid of the pretensions which [have] made you restless and unhappy all your life."[13]

To be self-affirming yet self-forgetful, positive yet realistic, grace-filled and unpretentious—that is the Christian vision of abundant life, a life epitomized by my friend John Marks Templeton.

Notes

This chapter draws from D. G. Myers, *Social Psychology*, 6th ed. (New York: McGraw-Hill, 1999), which documents the research described here, and from D. G. Myers, "Humility: Theology Meets Psychology," *Reformed Review* 48 (1995): 195–206.

1. Donald MacKay, Letters, *Journal of the American Scientific Affiliation* (December 1984): 237.
2. Elizabeth Loftus and Mark Klinger, "Is the Unconscious Smart or Dumb?" *American Psychologist* 47 (1992): 761–65.
3. C. S. Lewis, *Mere Christianity* (New York: Macmillan, 1960), 18–19.
4. Robert Ornstein, *The Evolution of Consciousness* (New York: Prentice-Hall, 1991).
5. Carl R. Rogers, "Reinhold Niebuhr's *The Self and the Dramas of History:* A Criticism," *Pastoral Psychology* 9 (1958): 15–17.
6. John Powell, *Happiness Is an Inside Job* (Valenia, Calif.: Tabor, 1989).
7. Groucho Marx, *Groucho and Me* (New York: Dell, 1960).
8. Neil Weinstein, "Unrealistic Optimism about Future Life Events," *Journal of Personality and Social Psychology* 39 (1980): 806–20.
9. Shelley Taylor, *Positive Illusions: Creative Self-Deception and the Healthy Mind* (New York: Basic Books, 1989).
10. Adam Smith, quoted by H. W. Spiegel, *The Growth of Economic Thought* (Durham, N. C.: Duke University Press, 1971).
11. Dale Carnegie, *How to Win Friends and Influence People* (New York: Pocket Books, 1936, 1964), 102.
12. Dennis Voskuil, *Mountains into Goldmines: Robert Schuller and the Gospel of Success* (Grand Rapids, Mich.: Eerdmans, 1983), 147–48.
13. Lewis, *Mere Christianity,* 99.

7

The Case of Chemistry

GIUSEPPE DEL RE

Open-Mindedness in the Study of Matter

If men followed ancient wisdom and kept in mind that *historia magistra vitae* (history is the teacher of life), many errors and ills would have been avoided in all fields. The general lesson of history, taught by concrete and often terrible examples, is that humility is the foundation of all lasting success, of all real progress. We have before our eyes the failure of political ideologies whose founders and supporters not only were convinced that their own ideas were the truth, the whole truth, and nothing but the truth, but also treated as enemies those who did not accept them. Those ideologies ended in disasters.

The same applies to the progress of science. Science owes whatever contribution it has given to knowledge practical and theoretical to a built-in rule of the game, faithfulness to reality.[1] Nevertheless, pride is always at work. In the seventeenth century, the mental scheme behind astronomy and mechanical design proved to be an extremely useful approach for understanding the facts of nature, and so modern physics was born; in the nineteenth century that mental scheme was transformed into a dogma, according to which whatever does not fit into a mechanical model of pieces acting one on the other as in a clockwork, albeit at the level of particles and with the inclusion of fields, is a mere delusion.[2] Thus, the view called "mechanistic reductionism" or "physicalism," according to which the models and methods of physics would in due course allow human beings to know all there is to know in the sensible world, became the creed of most scientists and philosophers of

176

science; eventually it became the assertion that reality is "nothing but atoms and quanta." Warnings against this were issued by eminent scientists, as the solid-state physicist Alan Cottrell and the neurophysiologist Donald MacKay.[3] But those warnings went unheeded, for the recovery of openness, prudence, allowance for the possibility of error, willingness to examine other views, awareness of possible ethical implications—in a word, intellectual humility—is hindered in many ways by the scientists' ego.[4]

History also tells us that in the long run, if human folly has not gone so far as to destroy its heritage of knowledge, ideas, moral principles entirely (or to destroy humanity itself), what the path of humility would have led to is reached by the force of things, often at a high cost. In the case of physicalism, a slow drift toward its abandonment has been taking place since the rise of modern biology; in the last few decades, even the claim that chemistry is a chapter of physics has been challenged with serious arguments. Intellectual humility requires that this point should be explored, the more so as chemistry is a pillar of our civilization both as a body of pure knowledge and as an applied science; as we shall see, an open-minded approach to such an apparently irrelevant question as the relation between physics and chemistry can throw light on the nature of sensible reality as apprehended by science as well as on man's place in the universe.

The various faces of intellectual humility are illustrated by chemistry in several ways. Four are perhaps most significant. First, the already mentioned question whether or not chemistry is actually an approach to features of reality which physics somehow ignores; the first part of this article is devoted to this question. Second, the existence of molecules and their structure is both the subject of an internal dispute of science and a point on whose elucidation hinges a decision about a notion which certain philosophers and theologians have often used to avoid problems with science: that of *ens rationis* (entity of reason), applied to submicroscopic particles. Third, disputes about the ethical implications of chemistry as an applied science have shown a perplexing tendency to shift the responsibility for the misuses of science from man to the very discipline involved. Fourth comes the famous question of the spontaneous emergence of life from nonliving matter; an unsettled question, to be sure, but one in which prejudices suggesting a measure of arrogance are at work on all sides, the physicists, the biologists, the chemists, the theologians.

Let us explore these fascinating subjects and the lessons they teach.

The Specificity of Chemistry

Chemistry and Physics

The claim that chemistry is a chapter of physics is a truism if *physics* is taken to mean *science;* it is in need of proof otherwise, considering what chemistry and physics are about. The philosopher of science Mario Bunge pointed out several decades ago that chemistry has a "field of inquiry" different from that of physics;[5] one may well go as far as to claim that the four main ingredients of physics and chemistry as scientific disciplines—specific field of inquiry, characteristic concepts, program, method—have in common only the fact that both are concerned with the nature of matter, and that chemistry accepts, as do all other natural sciences, the general principles discovered and studied by physics.

That physics and chemistry are answers to problems of different classes can be proved by their historical separation: suffice it to mention that Isaac Newton, the founder of mathematical physics, was deeply interested in alchemical work, but it seems that he never thought that it would be possible to do for it what was being done for physics.[6] It was with statistical mechanics and later with quantum mechanics that the physicists, possibly thinking of physical chemistry rather than of organic chemistry, became convinced that chemistry had been reduced to a chapter of physics. A less radical attitude was taken by Werner Heisenberg, one of the founding fathers of quantum mechanics, for he suggested that physics and chemistry had merged together to give quantum mechanics, the original contribution of chemistry being the atom.[7] That is certainly true as far as quantum mechanics is concerned, but it seems to ignore that chemistry is not the science of atoms, it is the science of molecules.

On Differences in Disciplines

Physics used to be called the "queen of the sciences." It still deserves that title, not because of nuclear energy and other applications, but because, by searching for the most fundamental and general laws of nature, physics has made it possible to give the other sciences a firm base; for one thing, it has provided the theoretical material on which astrophysics has been built.

At the other extreme there is biology, whose method and object are completely different. Biology studies living organisms as such, in their immense variety and incredibly complicated patterns of behavior; it also studies the parts of which they are made, but stops at the great molecules of life, whose chemical nature is not of direct interest to it.

Chemistry has provided the connection between biology and physics, with the discoveries showing that not only is life a coordinated, organized, finalized network of chemical reactions, but the very hereditary characters of a living organism are inscribed in special molecules (DNA). Since molecules are closer to atoms and quanta than cells, the way in which the laws of physics apply to living matter is thus easier to grasp; even so, it has taken a chemist—the Nobel laureate Ilya Prigogine—to discover that the puzzling difference between living beings and nonliving systems is not the presence of a special force field or principle, as the "vitalists" would claim, but rather the fact that they are organized systems out of equilibrium, preserving their individuality, in virtue of a network of interdependent chemical reactions, by a continuous exchange of matter, energy, and information with their environment.

Thus, chemistry appears to situate itself somehow midway between biology and physics. Let us examine its peculiarities in more detail.

The Language of Chemistry

Every scientific discipline has a language of its own. To be sure, a person not proficient in an ordinary language is unlikely to do better science in any field than mere experiments which somebody else will utilize, for language is an essential tool already for correctly describing a scientific observation. However, each particular discipline requires in addition its own system of "words" and "sentences." The case of physics is well known: physics uses as sentences mathematical equations involving "symbols" that represent, directly or indirectly, measurable quantities. For example, Newton's fundamental equation, $F = ma$, can be expressed in ordinary language provided certain terms (force F acting on body, the mass m of that body, the resulting acceleration a) have been defined, but, at variance with ordinary sentences, it can be transformed and combined with other equations of the same kind according to the rules of mathematics, and the resulting equations still represent aspects of reality that are observable and measurable— as is demonstrated by the magnificent edifice of analytical mechanics built in the nineteenth century by Joseph-Louis Lagrange, William R. Hamilton, and others.

If chemistry were just a chapter of physics, it would certainly be susceptible to "formalization" in a mathematical language. The great Russian chemist, philologist, and poet M. V. Lomonosov expressed this belief, and the founder of positivism, Auguste Comte, strongly denied it.[8]

Lomonosov was a precursor of the kinetic theory of gases, a great achievement of mechanics, and lived long before the rise of organic chemistry; it is therefore not surprising that he should think of chemistry as amenable to a mathematical formulation. Even today, there is no doubt that quantum chemistry, a branch of theoretical chemistry, relies on the equations of quantum mechanics; but quantum chemistry is a chapter of physical chemistry, which also relies on equations precisely because it is a part of chemistry that overlaps physics, and vice versa. But what about genuine chemistry? By way of an answer, suffice it to mention an eminent theoretical chemist, C. K. Ingold, whose analysis of organic reaction mechanisms is the foundation of many great advances in organic chemistry of the past forty years. In his classic book *Structure and Mechanism in Organic Chemistry*, Ingold briefly reviewed the quantum mechanical treatment of molecules, and there he relied on the mathematical equations of physics; but then he moved on to chemical reactions, and his formalism changed completely.[9] Instead of symbols representing the measured values of certain quantities (and therefore susceptible to treatment as numbers or arrays of numbers), Ingold used the structural formulas of the molecules involved, thus employing the formalism created by the organic chemists as an extension of what was originally mere stoichiometric equations such as $2H_2 + O_2 = 2H_2O$. The elegant symbolism thus arising is illustrated in Figure 1 on cyclooctatetraene, a ring molecule formed by eight carbon atoms each carrying a hydrogen atom.

Chemistry as Art

Today, we call art any activity aimed at realizing something people like independent of its possible usefulness. This has not always been so, as is suggested by the word *artisan*: art was the name for craftsmanship in a particular field in which design and know-how, developed in years of training and experience, were fundamental. A surviving example is the art of pottery, which in the hands of certain artisans produced veritable masterpieces, but whose purpose was primarily the making of vessels, jars, mugs, jugs, and so on for the everyday use of nobility and commoners alike. This technical dimension, the need for special know-

FIGURE 1.   Isomerism of cyclooctatetraene in the symbolic language of chemistry. (From Eugen Müller: *Neuere Anschauungen der organischen Chemie* [Berlin-Heidelberg: Springer Verlag, 1957], 355.)

how, remains in art today too, albeit as a subordinate aspect, and art requires something like a scientific framework: the rules received from tradition, causal relations detected by the accurate examination of facts, "if . . . then" arguments are indispensable for good results. In other words, art is the result of traditional know-how and rational understanding of facts in terms of causes and effects applied to making something beautiful, interesting, and possibly useful. In the frame of this definition, an experimental science whose program includes as a major feature the making of different objects from the same "material," thus actualizing the potentialities of the latter according to an idea in the mind of a scientist, is an art much in the way modeling clay into beautiful artifacts is an art. This is particularly the case with chemistry, which makes millions of molecular species out of a handful of atomic species. In this sense, chemistry is the art of constructing edifices of atoms by a wise (and often extremely difficult) combination of procedures.

Physics has mastered and reproduced the transformations of matter that nature uses in stars; chemistry does something different, because it produces uncountable new forms of matter, or forms of matter that so far only nature could produce, and makes them part of our ordinary environment. Just think of artificial monocrystals. Made with the strangest elements—rhenium, palladium, titanium, vanadium, and so on—they equal or surpass in beauty (although not in value because they can be made on order) many of the most exquisite stones—topazes, rubies, amethysts, emeralds—that nature produces directly.

There is more: working in an ordinary laboratory, chemists apply the rules of valency and their mysterious recipes to put atoms together so as to produce the most incredible molecules.[10] For example, they make from molecules of four to eight atoms each a molecule having forty-eight carbon atoms arranged in eight hexagons linked to one another to form a ring of sixteen carbon atoms; the protruding hexagons also carry four hydrogen atoms each. One such ring has an inner diameter of about 0.7 nm (nm stands for nanometer, a billionth of a meter) and an outer one of about 3.1 nm. The inner hole can accommodate a particle the size of a sodium ion. From achievements of this kind the art of making strange molecules has moved to greater and greater heights, equaling in many respects the molecules nature uses in living beings. A new branch of chemistry has arisen, supramolecular chemistry, that is concerned with very large molecules made of ordinary molecules held together, as it were, by mechanical tricks, as in the *catenanes*, made by ring molecules fitted one into the other as the rings of a chain.[11] The wonder of this is that, in order to make those supermolecules, it is necessary to open and close them, which have outer diameters on the order of a few nanometers; chemists apply procedures at the scale of our ordinary world, which bear on thousands of billions of billions of molecules. The technique for making their operations work as if they had the molecules clamped in their workshop vices to be sawn and welded relies on selection from billions of billions molecules according to the laws and rules of chemistry; if the chemical bond did not exist, the whole field of supramolecular chemistry would be mere fiction.

This feature of chemistry—emulation of nature at its atomic level by scientific methods—is probably unique among the natural sciences, whose fields of inquiry concern marvels of quite other sorts. It shows why physicalistic reductionism, if extended beyond its proper scope, could be dangerous, as all forms of integralisms are: in the case of chemistry, by treating it as a merely technical activity it would, for one thing, discourage many bright young people from becoming chemists.

Unfortunately, the creativity of chemistry has also made possible some of the most novel and disquieting trends of biological manipulations. Chemical operations can alter the genetic code or the conditions of its expression, and help to create monsters in the name of science. Another type of humility is needed there, and we will consider it in the section on alchemy.

New Perspectives

Chemistry deals with molecules, which are objects of a peculiar nature, and because of this it has rediscovered a forgotten dimension of sensible reality, complexity. We shall pause on this general theme in a subsequent section; here we want just to see why molecules are peculiar objects worth a special discipline.

Molecules were originally defined as the ultimate result of repeated subdivision by "physical" operations of pure chemical substances—physical operations being those which involve energies at most on the order of those needed to make water boil, and pure substances being homogeneous materials such that no physical operations can separate them into two different homogeneous materials. In the course of history, molecules turned out to be so small that they cannot be seen even if magnified by the most powerful microscope using ordinary light. The requirement that they should withstand physical operations was replaced by the requirement that they should be stable under ordinary conditions, but the definition has remained essentially the original one. What has emerged is that those ultimate ultratiny pieces of a chemical substance have a characteristic feature, their "structure."

In principle, the possible existence and properties of molecules can be quantitatively predicted from the properties of the constituent particles (atoms, or nuclei and electrons in the appropriate number). This consideration led to the belief that molecules are no more than collections of nuclei and electrons, and therefore physicalism is right. But things are not so simple.

The idea that molecules are clusters of atoms was introduced, as is well known, by John Dalton (1766–1844) in 1808, and for fifty years it was found sufficient to require that those clusters should obey the laws known as laws of proportion, despite the discovery in 1811 by Amedeo Avogadro (1776–1856) that in many cases they were unitary particles capable of persisting alone in the vacuum. For example, due to poor experimental data, it was believed that water should contain oxygen and hydrogen in a one-to-one proportion, and Dalton's symbol for its molecule (called atom) was: $\odot\bigcirc$ (HO instead of H_2O). A similar symbol, with three circle symbols in contact with a central $\oplus$ (standing for sulphur S), represented the "atom" of sulphur trioxide SO_3.[12] In his proposal, Dalton was not particularly interested in the possibility that the atoms of the elements should be arranged in a particular order or geometrical configuration. Fifty years later, the rise of organic chemistry imposed a further step. F. A. von Kekulé (1829–1896) discovered molecular structure: a molecule is analogous to a collection of small spheres (the atoms) connected in a characteristic way by sticks (the bonds) in a number specific of each atom (its valence) and of lengths characteristic of the pair of atoms involved. The analogy with the stick-and-ball model, naturally, is not strict: its main implication is that a molecule of a given species has some characteristic matching the structure of the model, and other ways of connecting the same atoms and possibly of arranging them in space correspond to different molecules and different substances (isomers). A simple and famous example is the two molecules CH_3CH_2OH (ethyl alcohol, a well-known liquid) and CH_3OCH_3 (dimethyl ether, a gas with anesthetic properties). Another example is provided by the isomers of benzene. (See Figure 2.) Given six carbon atoms and six hydrogen atoms, the rules of valency, discovered a long time before quantum mechanics and never derived from it, predict 217 isomers (and hence 217 different chemical substances). Although a much greater number of aggregates of the same number and species of atoms can be imagined, no chemist has any doubt that those 217 and only those 217 can be synthesized, the reserves being that some of the possible molecules can be relatively unstable because of steric hindrance or bond bending, and therefore they might have to be isolated under special conditions, say, very low temperatures; some isomers may be equivalent forms of the same molecule.

In conclusion, it seems evident that chemistry offers to us a completely new view of matter—new facts, new rules, new concepts. By its unique ability to design and make molecules (objects having a variety of properties resulting in properties of the ordinary matter around us, but so tiny that millions of them in a line cover a few millimeters), it has opened to us that aspect of the physical universe which the alchemists had vainly tried to grasp since the dawn of civilization. Such an achievement should be cause of wonder and of thankfulness for the Divine Artificer who has allowed us to know his secrets. Of course, the physicists are right when they say that the theories of physics are so general that chemistry must be contained in them; but, as we have tried to show, it is so in much the same way as a beautiful Greek vase was contained in the clay with which it was made. The potter adds to clay an idea; chemistry follows the guidance of nature to find and apply the concepts and rules that the general equation for a cluster of atoms contains only as a potentiality. Thus a humble approach suggests, without diminishing the glory of physics, that chemistry is a novel scientific approach to reality, one in which attention is shifted from the parts to the wholes they form, and the way in which the parts are connected so as to make any particular whole.

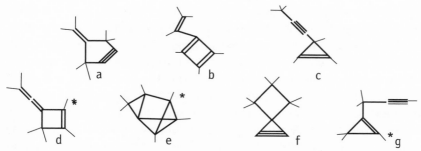

FIGURE 2. Graphs showing seven isomers of benzene allowed by the rules of valency; d, e, and g have been prepared; a and f are unlikely to be stable because of Baeyer strains.

The Relevance of Chemistry

Around 1960, the Benedictine monk Stanley Jaki wrote *The Relevance of Physics*, a book praised by none less than Werner Heitler, one of the founders of modern physics, from whom many other great physicists learned how to do research. Jaki meant that physics was important not only as the part of science dealing with the ultimate structure of the universe but also in connection with existential issues. What about chemistry? After what we have seen, can one speak of the "relevance of chemistry"? Let us try to answer this question step by step.

The word *relevance* means "being relevant," "standing out as being of special import." Import to what or for what? In the case of chemistry, as in general for any body of knowledge, one might consider for an answer at least three fields: people's living conditions, philosophical and scientific thought, the ordinary person's *Weltanschauung*, that is, the personal, often merely intuitive manner in which that person recognizes trends and patterns in the world. These three fields are all affected or receive contributions from the intellectual and practical activities of man, and the question of the relevance of chemistry amounts to asking how great and how important its part is. Let us briefly examine the answers.

Chemistry and Technology

Humility and respect for facts might have avoided a paradoxical situation in which our society has placed itself during the past few decades with regard to chemistry. On the one hand, the irresponsible use or abuse of certain chemicals, starting with DDT, has brought about a campaign against chemical factories, cynically amplified by the mass media, so that "chemical" ended up denoting something unnatural, dangerous for the health and the environment; on the other hand, the use of chemical products in all fields of technology is so extensive and all-pervading that any serious reduction in the availability of those products would mean the collapse of most economies, epidemics, famine. Many examples have been given, albeit without explicit reference to chemistry, in Sir John Templeton's *Is Progress Speeding Up?* an optimistic book about our material progress.[13] Let us mention just a few. If there were no artificial fertilizers and no pesticides, the yield of wheat seeds would fall back to the levels of a century ago: and since the population of granivores has increased, regions depending on wheat for their subsistence would have great difficulties. Moreover, if chemical plants were eliminated or greatly reduced, tires, diesel oil, lubricants, paints, and many other products needed for farming would no longer be available, and a vicious circle would be entered. Even the replacement of tractors in agriculture by animals would be hindered by the reduced productivity of farming. In an ideal world, there might be ways out resulting from increased solidarity and abnegation, but the failure of all attempts to found societies based on those virtues, including the first Christian communities (Acts 4:32–5:11), does not encourage hopes in that direction. Also communications and energy distribution would be seriously impaired if chemical plants were stopped, for electrical cables, magnetic materials, solid-state devices cannot be made without chemical operations and substances. In fact, all modern materials depend on sophisticated chemical procedures.

Chemistry is also essential for repairing or preventing damage to the environment resulting from modern cultivation practices, for the restoration of paintings, sculptures, monuments. And, of course, it is necessary for cosmetics.

Last but not least, chemistry is indispensable for identifying, purifying, and conditioning drugs found in nature; indeed, many drugs have to be prepared from simple chemicals either because of difficulties in their extraction (e.g., vitamin B_{12}) or because they are entirely new products, such as drugs against stomach ulcers, psychoactive drugs, and anesthetics.

With this record of contributions to the welfare of humanity, how is it possible that the man in the street should consider chemistry an invention of Lucifer? This comes from the undeniable fact that, besides such side effects as pollution, chemistry has made possible the deliberate production of explosives, poison gases, and addictive drugs.

There is, therefore, an "aporia," a seemingly insoluble conflict of two contradictory truths: chemistry is good and bad at the same time. But why is it an aporia? Only because our permissive society wants to indict chemistry, in order to avoid having to deal with issues of personal responsibility toward nature and other human beings, not to say toward God. Apparently, for some reason closed to our understanding, three centuries ago the Creator, as it were, decided that he would allow us to discover the way in which he performed the transformations of matter that take place by invisible processes all around us, and to imitate him. Because of that permission, chemists have succeeded in discovering and making use of what the ancients (perhaps rightly) considered the secret recipes and procedures of the Divine Artificer. But—in utter respect, as the Christians believe, for our freedom of choice—the Creator did not set limits to the use we could make of the new power at our disposal. And we used it for good and evil: to fight hunger and diseases, as well as to produce terrible tools of death.

The Ontology of Molecules

Are Molecules and Their Structures Real?
The second aspect of the relevance of chemistry is the answer to the question, Do atoms and molecules exist? This question may well sound idle to nonspecialists, but then they should consider that their ordinary source of information about what exists and what does not is often just the mass media. I should not go as far as saying that they believe that Saddam Hussein exists only because the mass media tell them so, for there they have, as a criterion of truth, the indirect evidence of a variety of pieces of information from different sources not likely to have organized a colossal fraud. But when it comes to particles belonging to a level of reality not even accessible to the microscope, they must rely on the experts' statements as relayed by the mass media, and there they have no way to check; this is why a large number of mere hypotheses or conjectures of current science are believed to be facts, only to be replaced by different "facts" as soon as an influential scientist offers a different view.

One might doubt that such invisible and intangible objects as atoms and molecules really exist, on the grounds that after all we have nothing but theories which simply assume that they exist.[14] In fact, Ernst Mach (1836–1916), a great Austrian physicist, refused for a long time to believe in the existence of atoms, and Wilhelm Ostwald (1853–1932), a great German physical chemist, did the same for molecules. They agreed that everything worked *as if* atoms and molecules existed; but that, they claimed, is not a proof of existence. Nowadays, few scientists would accept their doubts, for more and more information has been obtained: we can tell a lot of things about the properties of a molecule, including its shape, its weight, and its possible deformations. Yet, after all, we cannot show it and say, Go and feel for yourself that it is not an optical illusion. This difficulty has been a significant temptation for certain theologians, who find it particularly pleasing (especially in connection with the difference between living and nonliving entities) to be able to claim that, when it comes to submicroscopic processes causing the transformations of materials, science is a mere intellectual construction. One could answer that, if so, then an intellectual construction can spread destruction and desolation—as proved on Flanders fields in World War I and by Hiroshima and Nagasaki in World War II. But that is not an acceptable answer. The right one is perhaps a question: are you claiming that atoms and molecules do not exist, that they are *entia rationis* mainly because otherwise you would have to revise your personal approach to the interpretation of sensible reality, or can you offer serious arguments against the existence of objects having a size such that they cannot be reached directly by our five senses?

Among scientists (with the exception of many mathematicians) the consensus is now practically universal: it would make no sense to retain the safety clause "as if," if the circumstantial evidence is overwhelming, far greater than that on whose grounds people were hanged. And since in scientific matters it is scientists who have the last word, then one should accept their judgment even if doing so requires revision of a theological or philosophical standpoint.

But there are facts in the world of atoms and molecules whose reality is still refused by certain scientists: one of them is molecular structure, and we shall dwell a little on it, because it contains a general point about the conception of the physical universe which an open-minded science offers to us, now that radicalisms of all kinds have lost their former attraction.

Foundations

Let us start from the beginning. Intellectual humility requires that we admit that there is no logical way to prove that there is a reality other than the thinking subject; we must start from an axiom, that is, a declaration worthy of acceptance because of its ability to ensure simplicity and coherence in our understanding of the world. For the vast majority of thinkers the simplest and most satisfactory choice is the strong-realism axiom, according to which there are things, events and processes independent of our own existence and will, and they can be individually known by us, within limits imposed by our senses and brains, as existing and distinct from other objects. It is convenient to add to this axiom the classical view that ordinary intuitive existence judgments should be considered the proper referents of a critical analysis, needed anyway to determine, as the case may be, either what precisely the existence judgment applies to, or why it is mistaken.[15]

A double classification of real entities is essential for an assessment of molecular reality. The first one is that between *first-class entities*,[16] that is, objects existing per se (say, a tree or a molecule), and *second-class entities* (say, the psyche of a dog or a man), which presuppose a "carrier," even though they can be treated, within certain limits, as if they were first-class entities.

A familiar example of second-class entities is provided by a computer program. It exists beyond any reasonable doubt: yet, if the ideas of most scientists applied, it should not be so, for a program cannot be separated from its support and subjected to experiment as such. Its independent existence is demonstrated by the fact that it can be transferred from one computer to another, written on paper or on magnetic material, and so forth. There are second-class entities that cannot be copied from one support to another, but they are so similar in nature to computer programs that there can to be no doubt that they have the same sort of existence. All of them are cases of "information"—which is, as we have already seen, what a clay vase has with respect to shapeless clay, or what a molecule has with respect to its atoms.

The second distinction is between entities directly and indirectly accessible to sensible experience—which, following Rom Harré, we shall call R1 and R2 entities, respectively.[17] More precisely, we use R1 for entities that can be perceived as such and R2 for entities believed to exist because of analogical and logical evidence similar in nature to that by which a judge will condemn a person as the author of a crime even in the absence of flagrant evidence.

The Discovery of Molecular Structure
In the seventeenth century Robert Boyle pointed out that, having accepted the Democritean hypothesis that matter consists of atoms, it would still be convenient to recognize in the world a sort of architectural

principle that had operated since the beginning of the universe.[18] Since Boyle was referring to chemistry, it is clear that he felt that atoms should be arranged into edifices; but it was only after 1858, amidst heated disputes, that molecular structure became a central concept of chemistry —when Kekulé realized that the properties of hydrocarbons could be explained by assuming that their molecules were analogous to chains of carbon atoms.[19] After long years of debate, in recent times a clear-cut line of thought has been emerging, centered on the following two points.

Reality of molecular structure. It has been admitted since the dawn of philosophy that, even if what we know of a thing is at least part of what the thing really is, our knowledge of it involves representations made by our minds. Even now that science and technology have taken our knowledge beyond the limits of the world directly accessible to our sense, analogies with objects in that world still play a fundamental role.

It seems, therefore, that within the frame of realism one should accept this conclusion: what we call the "structure" of a molecule is a principle (a second-class entity) inherent to molecular reality, and hence real. It can be known by analogy through the mediation of a macroscopic model, to which the notion of structure properly applies, certain features not present in the model being added by an operation of logic and imagination.

The geometrical face of molecular structure. This face is at first sight distinct from the chemical one, an impression somehow perpetuated by classical textbooks, despite the unavoidable acceptance of geometrical considerations when considering such topics as Baeyer's strain theory, or the mechanism of alkene hydrogenation. Actually, as appears from Kekulé's passage quoted above, arrangement in space was included in the very idea of structure since its first appearance; the view that there were the bonds and the bonds were like joining sticks with a precise orientation in space had been expressed even before 1874, when Jacobus Van't Hoff and Joseph-Achille Le Bel made the spatial configuration of molecules a direct subject for reflection. Since then, it was found that the topology described by a written formula or the corresponding graph was a representation of reality rather than a mere thinking aid, indeed it was not helpful enough in the latter capacity.

One might insist that actually all we have is a macroscopic model, the stick-and-ball or the spring-and-ball model, but then one should also answer with scientific rigor and experimental evidence the following question: why do all experiments give results in agreement with the claim that molecules have a structure corresponding to that model in the analogical sense discussed above?

Philosophical Implications

Thomas F. Torrance pointed out that today's science provides examples of things neither visible nor tangible, first of all the space-time continuum discovered by Einstein.[20] Chemistry provides another rich source of examples of this class of entities. Influences, sympathies, and correspondences have been replaced by experimentally observable objects, atoms and molecules. But how do we know that they exist? Only by a chain of inferences. Moreover, molecules have a structure, and not only is molecular structure invisible and intangible because of the extreme smallness of molecules, but it cannot be subjected to experiment as a separate entity. This raises several doubts regarding the tenets of the scientistic outlook on reality. As already mentioned, some theologians have felt (perhaps correctly) that certain points of religious views needed protection against attacks in the name of the new science, and (perhaps mistakenly) they have tried to counter such attacks by the hardly humble method of dismissing as useful fiction whatever in science did not fit their interpretation of religion. The trial of Galileo is a famous example, but there are examples closer to us, specifically, Samuel Wilberforce and a number of contemporary theologians. Admitting this is not the same, however, as admitting that science is the only way to knowledge of reality. The statement, "Scientists do not think, they observe," made on NBC radio around 1980 by the American educator Robert Hutchins, in a subtle parody of modern scientific philosophy, summarizes a myth still followed by naive worshipers of science. What we have seen with regard to the existence of molecules and their structure is invaluable material for a cautious and honest revision of such myths: it would benefit science and religion.

With special reference to molecular structure, the fact that it exists and characterizes a molecule with respect to a generic collection of atoms is of the greatest philosophical import, because, *mutatis mutandis*, it gives a hint of what distinguishes living beings from other objects in the universe: a second-class entity, a principle that characterizes them as integrated unitary systems. Let us briefly see how this consideration can be used to build a view of the physical world that does away with "nothingbutteries" such as physicalistic reductionism and the refusal to grant atoms and molecules citizenship in the real world.

The traditional expression "physical world" covers all that can be detected directly or indirectly by our five senses. As we have seen, chemistry shows at the simplest possible level that the claim that the whole physical world is nothing but "atoms and quanta" is as untenable as the claim that airplanes, tractors, cars, trains, bridges, and so on, are but the materials of which they are made.

Generalizing this consideration, one gets the following picture of the world around us. There are objects of all sizes, from elementary particles to nebulae. In general, these objects are collections of parts, each of which is also a collection of parts, down to elementary particles and beyond, to a shapeless and timeless principle, which is a mere potentiality, for it can become anything material; it is the stuff of which all material things, living and nonliving, are made. It used to be called "prime matter"; now it might be identified with Einstein's space-time continuum. Now consider an object. If it is just an extremely loose collection of certain parts, and has no property that is not the sum of the properties of its constituents, then one could say that it is nothing but the given collection of those parts; a typical case is known in science as a perfect gas. On the other hand, if it has novel properties with respect to its parts, and a sufficient "lifetime," then the interaction and ordering of the parts have made actual something which was only potential in the parts as such: we shall say that the reality of the given object includes a new second-class entity—precisely the interaction and ordering of the parts. An example is given by chemistry with molecules and their structure. They are a simple example of the general fact *that information about possible wholes is partly either latent or not uniquely specified* in the constituents, meaning by "latent" that the problem remains of knowing which global properties are possible that are not sums of the properties of the parts, and by "not uniquely specified" the fact that a specific system of n given particles is formed by selection out of many possibilities.

Let us now consider two aspects of the objects making up the universe: complexity and size.

Complexity Levels

Objects that are highly integrated and persistent collections of parts have a unitary character, and they can be treated as "elementary" (indivisible) with respect to more complex objects. Chemistry offers the simplest example: for the chemist, an atom is essentially an elementary building block of molecules. Other examples are the cells of a tissue and the organs of a body. One could thus build a scale of "complexity levels" each of which corresponds to a given type of elementary objects. A given object endowed with a sufficient degree of unitariness can be analyzed in general at a variety of levels of complexity. For example, a molecule can be studied as a collection of atoms, a collection of electrons and nuclei, a collection of electrons and nucleons, and so on, down to quarks. Is it right to say that its reality is what it appears to be at any of the complexity levels thus defined? It is not: its reality covers all the pertinent complexity levels, from that at which it is seen itself as an elementary object to that at which it is seen as a collection of fundamental particles.

As you go down the complexity scale the numbers of parts into which a given object can be divided increases, and the number of properties to be considered decreases. Again, an example is a molecule, which at the atomic level is a collection of several atoms chosen out of about a hundred possibilities, and at the elementary particle level is a collection of many electrons, neutrons and protons, and so on. As to the number of properties, the question is more complicated. In principle, it decreases: for example, since different molecules can be made with the same atoms, there must be a number of properties that will become mere potentialities when it is divided into its atoms; and, since the same neutrons and protons can make different nuclei, some of the remaining properties will disappear when the molecule is considered as just a cluster of protons, neutrons, and electrons. What do we mean when we say that certain properties disappear? We mean that they become a mere potentiality, a possibility that becomes actual (in modern terms, "emerges") when the elementary objects are put together in a specific way. But this is not the whole story. When you move up the scale, certain properties of the parts become irrelevant or at least negligible in a first approximation—like most nuclear properties for molecules, or many details of the molecular structure of enzymes for the biochemical processes studied by molecular biology. But precisely these simple examples can be used to show that complete knowledge cannot be reached by analysis in terms of a single complexity level; which means, once again, that no reductionism can be accepted. Science is a unitary whole; the various disciplines work at different complexity levels, but the others should not be ignored; indeed, there are reasons to believe that even the whole spectrum of science is not sufficient to exhaust the enormous richness of reality.[21]

Size Levels

Size is related to complexity because there is a rough parallelism between size and degree of complexity of a physical system, whether non-living or living. However, the epistemological import of size is quite different, because it operates a threefold partition among objects of the world in which any given living being capable of knowledge, albeit rudimentary, is immersed. There are objects whose sizes lie within the range of the bodily senses, and which, therefore, can be entirely touched and seen (or detected by smelling, hearing, or possibly tasting) without the help of instruments. In the case of a human "perceiver," those objects have sizes ranging approximately from not more than that of, say, a car or a big animal, to those of tiny things that are barely visible. They belong to a "size level" we shall call the "direct-access level." The direct-access level is the size level of our ordinary experience, on which immediate, normally reliable reality judgments are based.

Then there are objects—like the earth, or even just a mountain—that we think we know directly but actually we do not, because what we perceive of them at the direct-access level is either a remote, intangible image, or parts of them, from which we reconstruct the whole. Similarly, but the other way around, we think we know directly that a powder is made of extremely tiny grains, but as a matter of fact we only see the powder. These are simple examples of a procedure modern science has systematically applied since the time of Galileo: with the help of the telescope and the microscope, it has extended the range of the direct-access level by entrusting reality judgments to indirect sight and inference by analogy, as already mentioned on the example of a microscopic mite. Whenever the analogy is immediate (the earth with a sphere, the mite with other *acari*, the reality judgment is assumed to have the same validity as one made within the direct-access level. We can therefore speak of an extended direct-access level.

A mountain and a mite are first-class entities, for they need no support to exist, and their existence is considered evident by the vast majority of scientists and philosophers. The case of second-class entities is different, because, in the direction of decreasing sizes the development of modern science was accompanied by their identification with microscopic or submicroscopic first-class entities acting as causes; for example, diseases were traced back to the action of specific microorganisms. The enthusiasm for the applications of this discovery made people forget logical rigor, for example, that those microorganisms are not the disease, but its cause. Properly speaking, a disease is today what it was in ancient Greece: an alteration of the normal operation of the body, that is, a modification of the relations among the parts of the body. And those relations, like it or not, exist, and they are second-class entities.

If, as it seems, our inner representations are faithful to external reality only at the direct-access level, our knowledge of things, events, and processes at a size level of Harré's R2 type can only be the result of inferential arguments based on analogies with the direct-access level that include both first-class and second-class entities. This is clearly shown by chemistry, because the discovery of molecular structure has been the discovery of an analogy indispensable to make the reality of molecules, which lie outside the extended direct-access level, detectable and treatable in terms of concepts and images our mind can handle. Coherent sets of relations among the parts of an object that can be thought of independently of their material support (in particular a structure) can be expected to exist in the submicroscopic world by analogy. This consideration, which also applies to other invisible and intangible realities, for example, the "souls" of human beings, is the ontological foundation on which what is often called "molecular reality," particularly molecular structure, can be understood.

The Nature of Life

Chemistry has revealed that, at the complexity level of atoms and molecules, life appears as a network of extremely complicated chemical reactions. This has led many scientists to infer that life is a set of physicochemical processes. That would be a fact admitted by everybody, if it were not taken to mean (as is often the case) that there is nothing more to tell about a living being. As a matter of fact, it would be easy to show countless sets of physicochemical processes that are not living beings. The point is, it seems, that those who think that the above definition is exhaustive stop at the chemical complexity level, and ignore the higher ones.[22]

Yet, it was precisely a physical chemist, Ilya Prigogine, who introduced the two concepts that have helped science get an insight into the riddle of life. He pointed out, first of all, that life is not amenable to the standard tenet of physics, that whatever lasts is at equilibrium; that is to say, its energy is at a minimum, albeit a relative one. That is true of molecules, but it cannot be true of what grows and changes and yet retains its identity. He next proceeded to show that there is another class of systems that last and yet are "out of equilibrium": he called them "dissipative structures" or "stationary systems out of equilibrium." They survive because of a ceaseless exchange of matter and energy with their environment. Some of them arise as a result of self-amplification of spontaneous statistical fluctuations under the action of external regularities (for example, Bénard's structures); others arise by more complicated mechanisms, but they have the same fundamental characteristic: they are the seats of *coherent* (organized) processes that feed on a chaotic environment in order to replace losses of energy and matter, and yield to that environment degraded energy as heat or as chemicals with a lower energy content.[23]

After this description it seems clear that living beings are in fact stationary systems out of equilibrium: they are nothing really new in science, if chemistry is taken in due account, but they are at the same time coherent wholes with a clear-cut identity, and environment-dependent systems, because they retain their specific characteristics by chemical processing of energy and matter extracted from their environment. The question "What is life?" is thus answered satisfactorily, without falling into the trap of naive reductionism, and yet without resorting to "vital fluids" and the like.

The complexity viewpoint also helps to explain another riddle: how can properties such as sight be just the result of the constitution and operation of collections of molecules? The answer lies in the emergence of new properties as the complexity of a system increases; the "principle" to which these new properties can be traced back is organization, or, better, organized dynamic activity, by virtue of which each chemical process in a living being is dependent on all others and participates, as it were, in a huge joint venture, aimed at ensuring persistence and functioning of a being that has a role to play in its environment.

As mentioned, the simplest dissipative structures can arise spontaneously, indeed by chance, by amplification of a fluctuation. What about living beings? There are two points here. On the one hand, one should clearly understand what is meant by the word *spontaneously*. The simple structures of Bénard arise spontaneously by chance, but in the presence of a constant heat flow, which acts as an organizing factor. Living beings, if they arose spontaneously, did so following the rules of chemistry, which would act as organizing factors. Thus, the notion that performances such as intelligent behavior are the result of chance would anyway be misleading: they are inscribed in the laws that govern matter, and at most their actual manifestation might be a matter of chance. Moreover, it is unreasonable for everybody to think that a higher organism could arise spontaneously by chance. At most, random events leading to the spontaneous emergence of life should be looked for in the origin of life. Chemistry can throw light on this point, too.

The Origin of Life

The origin of life has aroused disputes within science and between scientists and thinkers interested in the spiritual dimension of reality; among the former, many physicists and a number of biologists sided against chemists and other biologists. The hypothesis of the spontaneous emergence of life from nonliving matter involves chemistry, because, if life appeared spontaneously at a certain moment of the history of the earth (say, 4.5 billion years ago), then the initial processes must have been the formation from simple molecules (CO_2, H_2O, NH_3, etc.) of the molecules that are the bricks with which all living beings are made, amino acids and purine, essentially. Then, perhaps in appropriate receptacles in the rocks, molecules capable of self-replication should have formed, and one or a few types should have survived a first Darwinian selection. These types might have formed systems in which each molecule influenced the formation of the others, something like a unitary system would emerge, as it were, out of a system capable of metabolizing smaller molecules, growing by replication, and eventually dying.

Chemistry is (or should be) called to pronounce on this scenario. But a subtle point should be clear to everybody, a point that unfortunately is usually ignored. Life is so complicated, even from the point of view of chemistry, that the hope of reproducing in the laboratory what really happened (if it happened) is next to nil. The importance of reflections in this direction is rather one of *plausibility*; that is to say, of finding arguments showing that the sort of process which could have led to the emergence of life from a "primordial soup" of nonliving molecules is perfectly compatible, in its general features, with what chemistry knows about molecules and their reactions.

Much has been found in such a plausibility study. For example, molecules are known that assemble spontaneously to form much larger, ordered units; artificial micelles have been prepared which simulate cells in that they selectively absorb certain substances from the solvent in which they are suspended and grow, until they generate on their surface a smaller micelle, which then breaks loose and begins a new "life"; and so on. However, the experimental evidence and the theoretical arguments are not (and cannot be expected to be) decisive; what they belong to, we repeat, is an exploration intended to answer a number of general objections, such as the difficulty of explaining why, as far as is known, there is only one basic chemical structure for DNA, while one would expect that at least a few different molecules could perform the same task.[24]

By its very nature, a plausibility study should be accepted by everybody as the right way to collect information on which further discussion could be based. But it is not so, and one has the feeling that the main reason is the tendency to judge this kind of research on the basis of beliefs and fear that certain basic tenets could be shaken. For example, it would seem that much of the physicists' resistance to the whole chemical scenario arises from their professional habit of thinking that systems which remain the same for a relatively long time are systems at equilibrium (i.e., in a minimum-energy state) and those systems do not interact with their environment. Systems in a stationary state but not at equilibrium are only found in physics under the influence of external perturbations, (e.g., fields). Now, living beings can be looked at as stationary systems out of equilibrium, and it seems there are still biophysicists who are looking for a force field that would act as the external perturbation keeping a living being in a stationary state. This might make chemists smile, because they know, for example, that a protein will take a particular structure in a certain environment at a certain temperature, and no external "field" is needed for that. But it would be a lack of humility on the part of the chemists to think that those biophysicists have no point at all. Their quest for some external force holding a living being in a stationary state serves at least to emphasize a point that is often ignored: the survival of a living being depends on the existence of appropriate physical and chemical conditions in its environment—an appropriate temperature range (for an unprotected man roughly 18–30 degrees centigrade), an appropriate concentration of oxygen and carbon dioxide in the atmosphere, and so on. These conditions do not force the being to stay alive, but they must be there, and they may determine some of its characteristics.

Humility in Chemical Research

We have seen that chemistry is not a detached meditation on the laws governing matter; it is the art of producing transformations in the stuff of which nature is made, in the materials which the Divine Artificer used and uses to realize the marvels that surround us. It so difficult an art, and one so rich in new problems, that traditional recipes are but a minor part of it. A framework of scientific concepts and rules as well as a scientific approach are necessary. They may be (and are) interesting in themselves, but their source and their end, the problems from which they arose and the use for which they were developed are practical ones—performing transformations of the inner, submicroscopic nature of materials. The aim, as in all genuine arts, is not money or power, although those motives are always present, as in all human enterprises; it is the pleasure of seeing the dream come true of transforming matter as the Creator does in minutes or hours in volcanoes, in centuries or millennia in hidden caves, in a few months or years in the living world.

Chemistry and the Spirit of Alchemy

As is well known, long before modern chemistry, the practical chemistry of metal processing, of fabric dyeing, cosmetic and drug preparation had given rise to a science called alchemy. It is purported by popular books to be either magic or the attempt (often resulting in frauds) to systematize the craftsmen's traditional knowledge in order to make it possible to obtain gold from less noble metals; but that is only part of the story. The great alchemists (like St. Albert the Great, teacher of Thomas Aquinas) were moved by the nobler desire to unveil the mysteries of matter. The Galilean "revolution"—the adoption by the natural sciences of the rule that principles should be accepted on observational grounds and the requirement of internal consistency rather than on the authority of tradition—which originally concerned the mechanics of celestial bodies and was soon extended to all of physics, also took place in chemistry, starting with the contributions of Robert Boyle. However, the change was far less deep than in astronomy and physics.

First, just as alchemy, chemistry still deals with the secret processes that change the materials making up the world in which human beings have been living since the dawn of civilization, and this gives it a continuity with ancient Western and Eastern cultures unknown to other sciences. Second, whereas physics actually introduced new principles and even changed its "program," alchemy accepted the spirit of Galileo's doctrine without changing either its most general principles or its program. For example, the concepts of atom and of element remained fundamental, albeit redefined in terms of observational criteria. The program of chemistry—to understand, reproduce, and in-novate on the basis of those transformations of which our senses only perceive the result, sometimes a catastrophic one—was the same as that of the better part of alchemy.

Nevertheless, it is also true that something was lost in the process by which alchemy became chemistry. The most significant loss was perhaps the abandonment of the analogy between the soul's progress toward wisdom (in both a philosophical and a theological sense) and transformations of matter induced by human agents.

Many modern thinkers might well claim that science has removed nonsensible realities altogether from statements susceptible of a true-false alternative; but, as we have seen, the complexity viewpoint strongly affirms the reality of intangible and invisible objects such as molecular structure, which is technically the equivalent of what the soul is for us.[25] Although a detailed discussion would be required for our purpose here we can take the term *soul* to be the equivalent of what current usage calls "personality." By this convention, the notion of a parallel between the progress of the soul toward wisdom and the conquest of the secrets of matter can be made palatable to the modern mind.

Mysticism in Science

The soul enters the *Weltanschauung* of alchemy in two ways: (1) through the attribution of a sort of life to inorganic matter; (2) through the assumption that the success of transformations of matter induced by a human being would closely match the latter's spiritual progress.

These views, of course, cannot be accepted as they stand; but it may well be claimed (as Carl Jung did) that they are expressions of in-variants in our relation to reality, invariants which society, in its un-ceasing swaying between extremes, has now temporarily forced out of the stage, possibly to rediscover them and give them too important a role in the near future. Hints of such an inversion in the average per-son's "credibility space" can be found in the popularity of esoterism.

In connection with the first point, suffice it to recall that not only have chemistry and physical chemistry confirmed the existence of the "affinities" postulated by alchemy, but, as mentioned above, they have shown theoretically that under appropriate conditions even nonliving matter tends to form structures of a greater and greater degree of order, possibly of organization.[26] Taken in this sense and within the proper limits, the presence in nonliving matter of behavior patterns having some analogy with the activity of living beings is thus confirmed by experimental work.

As to the second point, alchemy took very seriously the involvement of the operator at the "spiritual" level; that is to say, a psychological involvement that calls into play the whole personality of the operator. As Maurice Blondel (1861–1949) pointed out a century ago, conscious, deliberate action is a commitment of the whole person, and even its success may depend on the frame of mind within which it is carried out.[27]

An example will clarify this point. Thomas Alva Edison, the inventor of the incandescent electric lamp, invested $40,000 to meet the challenge of making electric lamps cheap enough for everybody to afford them. He thus gave an example of how genuine interest in the product and consideration of others' welfare may be conditions for great technological realizations.

In the alchemical frame of mind, this was precisely the point: the idea that as long as personal interest, especially that of gaining power and profit, were the motives of alchemical activity, the results would be poor. In fact, the principle that all parallel processes are faces of a single process in the true underlying reality applies to the experimenter with the only novelty that he, inasmuch as he is a human being, is free not to change in the proper way; then also his operations will follow a path different from the expected one. In the "white" Christian branch of alchemy, this side always appears with reference to God: the alchemist is trying to emulate the operations by which the Supreme Technologist causes transformations in matter; therefore, he should be a worthy apprentice. Nicolas Flamel (1330–1418) wrote a prayer that illustrates this spirit.

> Almighty, eternal God, Father of celestial light, from whom also come as a gift all things good and perfect, we pray to your infinite mercy that you suffer that we recognize correctly your eternal Wisdom, by which all things were created and made and in this very moment are ruled and held in being. Let it accompany us step by step in all our operations, so that by means of its spirit we can find the true knowledge and the sure procedure of this very noble Art, that is, the miraculous stone of the wise, which you concealed from the world, and sometimes reveal to your elected. Grant to us that we begin rightly and well in the first place, that we [then] progress with constancy in our work, and that we at last complete it in a blessed way, and that we may enjoy it with eternal joy, by that celestial and miraculous cornerstone founded before the beginning of time.[28]

This prayer suggests a mystical path to personal elevation parallel to experimental work. It is a path at least partially open independently of adhesion to a specific religion, for the term *God* may be taken to represent nonsubjective values we ought to respect and cultivate if we are to pursue the fundamental values of truth, justice, and beauty.

Alchemy thus suggests that the practical operations of science and technology require a total personal involvement of the operator, indeed are parallel to the progress of the operator in his renunciation to his ego in favor of noble ideals. There is a measure of literal truth in this. Consider specifically the operations of chemistry. It would be too much to claim that the end products of a reaction depend on the virtues of the chemist performing them. However, there may be a psychological component at least in the yield, which is often sensitive to small changes in the reaction conditions: a patient person, deeply interested in what he or she is doing, will obtain better results and possibly detect unexpected byproducts, if for no other reason than because of the loving care applied to the least detail.

In general, all practical operations have this dependence on the experimenter's psychological attitude. If we consider technology developed in view of applications, then the role of the virtues of the operator—particularly humility—is even more evident.

Conclusion: About Spiritual Standards

Thus, humility toward history discovers another lesson of chemistry. Those who have developed chemistry and in general technology without even a trace of the spirit of alchemy (i.e., without a parallel upgrading of their spiritual standards, particularly their sense of responsibility) are contributing not only to the material ills of humanity but, especially by their example, to more devastating ills—ignorance and neuroses—which no vaccine can prevent. Even those who believe that religion should be replaced by merely human ideals should have grounds for lamenting its loss, since ideals seem to have vanished altogether. Edison invested his own money in the dream that even low-income families should be able to afford the joy of electric light; contemporary technological geniuses, if there are any, may be expected to use their minds to make money or gain fame by experiments like the cloning of human beings.

The "white" alchemists believed in the necessity of high spiritual standards because they thought that the Divine Master would not allow the unworthy to learn his secrets, and that, if with Satan's help they could do so without permission, that would be cause of ills without end. Those who "do science" today belong to three different categories: people who just have a job in science, people who consider that science offers promises of career and success, and people who are sincerely interested in know-why and know-how. The spirit of alchemy implies that only the latter are worthy of participating in the technological enterprise, because they are humble, because, as Einstein wrote, "The true value of a man is first of all determined by the extent and the sense in which he has succeeded in freeing himself of his ego."[29]

In conclusion, in an approach to chemistry as an independent way of questioning nature, interpreting its answers, and using the knowledge thus gained, humility—openness, willingness to listen, awareness of the responsibility of scientists—appears to be the basic prescientific condition for real progress in three different modes: inner humility, mutual humility with other disciplines, openness to God who has allowed man to master some of the deepest and subtlest mechanisms by which nature realizes its wonders.

Chemistry is perhaps also the discipline where the need is most evident for a greater open-mindedness by those theologians who dismiss certain aspects of science by classifying them as "entities of reason," mere descriptions, and so on. On the side of science, especially because of the essential role of chemistry in genetic engineering, it seems unquestionable that humility is needed to resist the temptation of many scientists to think that what they do is above ethical limitations. The man of science is a person, and as such is involved in science. This fact is now widely admitted, and yet that temptation still lurks in the hearts of the scientists, as in the hearts of all of us. To resist it is not easy; but, after all, "for us, there is only the trying. The rest is not our business."[30]

Notes

1. Cf. Michael Polanyi, *Personal Knowledge: Towards a Post-Critical Philosophy* (Chicago: University of Chicago Press, 1958; rpt. New York: Harper 1964).
2. A famous example of difficulties caused by the mechanistic dogma goes back to Clerk-Maxwell's theory of the electromagnetic fields. See Thomas F. Torrance, *Transformation and Convergence in the Frame of Knowledge* (Belfast: Christian Journal Ltd. 1984), chapter 6.

3. Alan Cottrell, "The Natural Philosophy of Engines," *Contemporary Physics* 20 (1979): 1–10; Donald M. MacKay, *The Clockwork Image* (London: Inter-Varsity Press, 1974).

4. Cf. John M. Templeton, *The Humble Approach* (New York: Continuum, 1995).

5. Mario Bunge, "Is Chemistry a Branch of Physics?" *Zeitschrift für allgemeine Wissenschaftstheorie* 13.2 (1982): 210ff.

6. Cf. Cherry Gilchrist, *Alchemy* (Longmead, Shaftesbury, Dorset, UK: Element Books, 1991).

7. Werner Heisenberg, *Physics and Philosophy* (New York: Harper and Bros., 1958).

8. Mikhail V. Lomonosov, *Elementa chymiae mathematicae* (1741) in *Sobraniie Socinienii* (St. Petersburg, 1891–1902); A. Comte, *Cours de philosophie positive* (1830–1842), lecture 35.

9. C. K. Ingold, *Structure and Mechanism in Organic Chemistry* (London: Bell, 1962).

10. This side of chemistry has been presented by the Nobel laureate Roald Hoffmann in "Molecular Beauty," *Journal of Aesthetics and Art Criticism* 48:3 (Summer 1990): 191–204.

11. V. Balzani and F. Scandola, *Supramolecular Photochemistry* (New York-London: Ellis-Horwood, 1991).

12. Sir Thomas Edward Thorpe, *Essays in Historical Chemistry.*

13. John Marks Templeton, *Is Progress Speeding Up? Our Multiplying Multitudes of Blessings* (Philadelphia and London: Templeton Foundation Press, 1997).

14. The literature on this point is next to infinite; suffice it to recall two books that are representative of ontology today: W. V. O. Quine, *From a Logical Point of View* (Cambridge, Mass.: Harvard University Press, 1961); Hilary Putnam, *The Many Faces of Realism* (La Salle, Ill.: Open Court, 1987). A critical study of realism in science with an emphasis on chemistry has been given by Joachim Schummer, *Realismus und Chemie* (Würzburg: Königshausen und Neumann, 1996).

15. Martin Heidegger presents this point very clearly in *Was heißt Denken?* Vorlesungen des Wintersemesters 1951–52 (Stuttgart: Reclam, 1992), 26–28.

16. Called *substances* in the Aristotelian tradition.

17. R. Harré, *Varieties of Realism* (Oxford, 1986); cf. Schummer, *Realismus und Chemie*, 63.

18. Robert Boyle, *The Sceptical Chymist* (1661), chapter 6.

19. Cf. F. A. v. Kekulé, *Berichte der Deutschen Chemischen Gesellschaft* 23 (1890): 1302. Translated into English by O. Theodor Benfey in the *Journal of Chemical Education* 35 (1958): 21–23.

20. T. F. Torrance, *Transformation and Convergence,* chapter 7.

21. John M. Templeton, ed., *How Large Is God? Essays of Scientists and Theologians* (Philadelphia and London: Templeton Foundation Press, 1997).

22. A brief comment on this question was given, with particular reference to Francis Crick, one of the discoverers of the genetic code, by R. Olby, *The Path to the Double Helix* (Seattle: University of Washington Press, 1974).

23. See Ilya Prigogine, *From Being to Becoming* (San Francisco: Freeman, 1980), and other books by the same author.

24. For a broader spectrum of reasons of perplexity see J. M. Templeton and R. L. Herrmann, *Is God the Only Reality? Science Points to a Deeper Meaning of the Universe* (New York: Continuum, 1994), chapter 5.

25. Cf. G. Del Re, "Technology and the Spirit of Alchemy," *Hyle* (Karlsruhe) 3 (1997): 51–63, and "The Question of the Soul," *La Nuova Critica* (Rome), n.s., no. 30 (1997): 75–98.

26. I. Prigogine, *From Being to Becoming* (San Francisco: Freeman, 1980); for experimental evidence at the molecular level cf. e.g., V. Balzani, F. Scandola, *Supramolecular Photochemistry* (New York-London: Ellis-Horwood, 1991).

27. Maurice Blondel, *L'Action* (1893; Paris: Quadrige/Presses Universitaires de France, 1993).

28. Nicolas Flamel, *Le livre des figures hiéroglyphiques* (Paris: Planète, 1971); our translation.

29. Albert Einstein, *Mein Weltbild* (1934; Frankfurt: Ullstein Materialien, 1979), 10.

30. T. S. Eliot, *Four Quartets: East Coker,* line 191.

8

Mind/Body Medicine and Spirituality

HERBERT BENSON
AND PATRICIA MYERS

As far back as the legend of Gilgamesh in the third millennium B.C.E., the earliest surviving writings, people have believed in something more than mortal existence. We have believed in powers, forces, energies beyond us, God if you will. Without such beliefs, the knowledge of death would be "counter-evolutionary." Why should we go on if we have only death to look forward to? Why have children and subject them to pain and suffering? A belief in something more allows us to hope, and that hope helps us to go on. Certainly from an evolutionary point of view such convictions are to our benefit. And as it turns out they are good for our health as well. This chapter discusses how beliefs are an important yet often neglected factor contributing to our health and well-being and how such beliefs can help promote healing.

The Three-Legged Stool

Self-care is important to health, yet it has been largely disregarded by modern medicine. Relaxation procedures, nutrition, exercise, and stress management, as well as beliefs and faith, are all aspects of self-care. For more than a hundred years, Western medicine has relied almost exclusively on prescribing surgery and procedures and medications in treating disease. The ideal health-care model would incorporate self-care and might best be viewed as a three-legged stool: one leg representing surgery and procedures; a second leg, pharmaceuticals; and the third, self-care. Optimal health care is achieved when the stool is balanced by the appropriate application of self-care, medications, and surgical procedures.

Beliefs can enhance the effectiveness of surgical, pharmaceutical, and self-care treatments. If doctors and other caregivers who prescribe drugs or perform procedures and if those who engage in self-care approaches believe in their efficacy, the effectiveness of these interventions can be enhanced by engendering the "placebo effect."

The Placebo Effect

A profound example of the powerful influence of beliefs on healing is the placebo effect. Throughout history, medicine and healing have relied heavily on such nonspecific factors.[1] Well into the late nineteenth century, physicians used placebos and were aware of their effect. Richard Cabot, of the Harvard Medical School, noted, "I was brought up, as I suppose every physician is, to use placebos, bread pills, water subcutaneously, and other devices acting upon a patient's symptoms through his mind."[2] And Charles Rosenberg wrote, "No mid-century physician doubted the efficacy of placebos (as little as he doubted that the effectiveness of a drug could depend on his manner and attitude)."[3] Physicians knew that what patients believed could have profound effects on the outcome of an illness. Positive beliefs could have healthful effects, negative beliefs injurious effects. Yet, modern medicine has largely relegated these mind/body interactions to a placebo response. Such pejorative statements as "It's all in your head," "It's just the placebo effect," and terms like "dummy pill" became common.

Since the time of Louis Pasteur and Robert Koch 150 years ago, the Western tradition of incorporating these nonspecific, placebo-inducing factors into treatment has been progressively replaced by an almost total reliance on specific remedies for specific illnesses. Because such specific therapies have proved to be so dramatically effective, they have become the sole form of acceptable treatment. Mind/body approaches clearly cannot be substituted for insulin or antibiotics in patients with diabetes or infections. But rather than using a combination of specific and nonspecific therapies to promote healing, modern practitioners value and have come to rely on the specific effects of pharmacological and surgical or procedural interventions and devalue or ignore the healing power of beliefs.

In the 1950s the placebo effect was revisited in the work of Beecher. He established that in patients suffering from headaches, cough, seasickness, pain, and the common cold, the placebo effect ameliorated symptoms in about 35 percent of cases. Since these early findings, approaches that result in the placebo effect have been documented to be effective in 50 to 90 percent of patients with conditions such as duodenal ulcer, bronchial asthma, angina pectoris, and herpes simplex.[4]

Turner and her colleagues evaluated the placebo effect in relieving pain in a review of three books and seventy-five articles.[5] They found that the effect of placebos was "strikingly high on average" and concluded that clinicians must no longer assume that placebos work only one-third of the time. And in a review by Roberts and colleagues of medical and surgical treatment of bronchial asthma, cold sores, and duodenal ulcers, the placebo effect led to relief 70 percent of the time.[6] These researchers concluded that "under conditions of heightened expectations" the power of the placebo effect "far exceeds that commonly reported in literature."

In a study of Japanese students who were allergic to the wax of a lacquer tree, the students were first blindfolded and then told that one of their arms would be stroked with leaves from the lacquer tree and the other arm would be stroked with leaves from a chestnut tree to which they were not allergic.[7] Although the subjects of this experiment were told which arm would receive which leaves, the researchers actually switched the leaves. In many instances, the arm the subjects believed to have been brushed with the poisonous leaves, but which actually had been stroked with chestnut tree leaves, developed a rash, whereas the arm that had contact with the poison often did not react.

In England, an ultrasonic "generating wand" was used to reduce swelling in dental patients who had had their wisdom teeth removed. In standard practice, dentists used such a handheld device called a transducer to massage the patient's face with ultrasonic waves after surgery. There is no physiologic explanation for why this technique could work. In London, in 1988, Hashish and colleagues compared the experiences of postoperative patients who received no ultrasound treatment to those who received ultrasound massage as well as to those who received mock treatments, in which the ultrasound machine was turned off. All three groups were told that this technique would reduce postoperative pain and swelling. Results showed that patients treated with the mock ultrasound had 35 percent less swelling than did those who received no treatment at all. Patients treated with the mock circular treatment and those treated with the actual ultrasound massage had 30 percent less swelling compared to the control group.[8]

In a study conducted at Cook County Hospital in Chicago in 1957, patients with rheumatoid arthritis benefited from placebos.[9] Patients experienced improvements in their symptoms that lasted for three months or more.

An investigation by Horwitz and colleagues reported in the *Lancet* in 1990 compared the effects of beta blockers, drugs that prevent adrenergic hormones from causing the heart to beat too rapidly or forcefully, to the effects of placebos. The study revealed that the men who did not comply with the treatment regimen (i.e., who took the pills less than 75 percent of the prescribed amount)—whether they received the active medication or the inert placebo—were 2.6 times more likely to die within a year of follow-up than were those who complied. Remarkably, the death rate among the men who did not take the placebo pills was much higher than among those who took them regularly.[10]

A similar result was reported in an investigation of men who received either a cholesterol-lowering drug or a placebo after having a heart attack. This study, conducted by the Coronary Drug Project Research Group and published in the *New England Journal of Medicine*, revealed that after five years of follow-up, only 15 percent of those who complied with treatment (i.e., took 80 percent or more of their placebo treatment) died compared with 28 percent of less compliant placebo-treated men. Again, not taking a placebo led to an increased rate of death.[11]

The Power of Beliefs

The placebo effect is dependent on one or more of three sets of beliefs: (1) the belief of the patient; (2) the belief of the health-care provider (or healer); and (3) the belief that ensues from the relationship between the provider and the patient. The following are some examples of the power of these beliefs.

Wolf studied women who experienced persistent nausea and vomiting during pregnancy.[12] These patients swallowed balloon-tipped tubes that, once positioned in their stomachs, allowed researchers to record the contractions associated with waves of nausea and vomiting. The women were then given a drug that they believed would cure the problem. But instead, researchers gave the women a drug (ipecac) that would do the opposite, that would cause vomiting. But the vomiting ceased, and, in one, the stomach contractions returned to normal as measured by the balloons. The women believed that they were receiving an antinausea medicine. With beliefs alone they cured themselves and reversed the pharmacological action of a drug.

One example of how beliefs of the health-care practitioner can affect disease outcome was shown through an examination of therapies for angina pectoris.[13] A number of therapies have been used throughout the years that are now known to have no therapeutic value for angina pectoris. These include xanthines, aminophylline, vitamin E, and rather bizarre internal mammary artery surgeries. When they were used and believed in by physicians, they had a dramatic effect. They were found to be 70–90 percent effective in relieving the chest pain of angina pectoris. Not only would the pain disappear, but the electrocardiograms and exercise tolerance would improve. However, when these therapies were later invalidated and no longer believed in by physicians, their effectiveness dropped to 30 percent or lower.

The beliefs that ensue from the relationship between physicians and patients is the third component of the placebo effect. A study by Egbert and colleagues at the Massachusetts General Hospital compared two matched groups of patients who were to undergo similar operations. The doctor responsible for their anesthesia visited both groups of patients the night before the surgery, but interacted with them quite differently. He or she made only cursory remarks to patients in one group, but treated the other group with warm and sympathetic attention, detailing the steps of the operation, and discussing the pain they might expect during recovery. The patients who received the friendlier, more supportive visits were discharged from the hospital an average of 2.7 days earlier than those patients in the other group and required only half the amount of pain-alleviating medication.[14]

The Nature of Personal Beliefs and Belief Systems

The medical profession achieves some of its success not from the medications it prescribes or the surgeries it performs. Rather, the success of a number of medical treatments should be attributed to the inherent healing power with the patient. In a study by Kroenke and Mangels-dorff, 74 percent of the complaints patients brought to medical clinics were found to be of unknown origin and likely caused by psychosocial factors.[15] Other studies indicate that between 60 and 90 percent of all visits to doctors' offices are stress-related and the problem probably cannot be diagnosed, much less treated effectively, with the medications and surgery and procedures on which the medical profession relies almost exclusively. In other words, in the vast majority of cases the medical concerns brought to the attention of a health-care provider could not be helped by means of external tools or devices. A patient's self-care mechanisms must be relied on.

Recognition of factors that influence the placebo effect could aid physicians and in many cases strengthen the effect of their prescriptions and recommendations. All patients are susceptible to the effects of the placebo effect. Situations and conditions such as the timing and environmental stimuli may increase the effectiveness of the placebo effect.

A patient's positive frame of mind can be very therapeutic. Butler and Steptoe used two competing powers of suggestion in their study of asthmatics. After inhaling what they believed to be a bronchial tube-constricting chemical, the asthmatics' breathing ability deteriorated significantly. But if these patients had been treated beforehand with what they were told was a powerful new bronchial tube–expanding drug, they showed no such deterioration. In both instances, the "new drug" was inert; it was distilled water. Thus, bronchial constriction was both caused and prevented by belief alone.[16]

Neither biology nor belief can be completely isolated, so it is often difficult to demonstrate the strength of belief. A study conducted in 1988 by Riley et al. determined that patients diagnosed with symptoms of chronic pain were more likely to be impaired, despite the severity of pain they reported, if they believed that the pain implied impairment. The investigators surveyed fifty-six patients who experienced pain in various parts of their bodies for an average of 35.1 months. They were questioned about their attitudes toward pain and disability and were asked to keep pain diaries. Patients' physical strength and mobility were tested and in the end, independent of the pain levels reported, those who believed pain should inhibit their movement were the most inhibited. In other words, the belief that pain implies disability has more to do with disability than the pain itself.[17]

Just as it is a physician's responsibility to encourage good nutrition and exercise, to discourage smoking and its devastating effects, to oversee medications, and to advise patients on healthy lifestyle decisions, it is just as important for physicians to encourage an appetite for positive, hopeful expectations and to steer patients away from beliefs that can be destructive. This is a role most physicians and other health-care practitioners instinctively understand and sometimes even value. An individual's beliefs can affect his or her health, and a physician's reassurance can make a measurable, physiologic difference.

The Brain and Beliefs

The brain comprises approximately one hundred billion nerve cells (neurons). These cells have extensions called axons and dendrites. The axon sends messages to other nerve cells, while the dendrite receives messages from the neighboring axons. There are nerve endings for each axon and dendrite that total between five thousand and five hundred thousand per nerve cell. Nerve cells "fire" or transmit messages to other nerve cells through neurotransmitters. At any given millisecond, there are possibly up to ten raised to the hundredth trillionth power possible communications.

A good example of how the message-routing system works is what happens when a person burns a finger on a stove. The pain-attuned nerve cells in the finger react. Multitudes of axons send signals to deliver the message from the finger to the spinal cord to the brain and the brain sends messages back to the muscles of the arm and finger to remove the finger from the stove. Distinct regions of the brain are responsible for certain actions—one interprets pain messages and orders pain relief. Yet another gauges the emotional importance of the event and triggers emotional reactions. After the event, the brain retains a memory of the nerve-cell activations and interactions associated with this type of injury.

The body responds in the same way when a person recalls a vivid memory or imagines some event. For example, if someone had a previous accident while driving a car, recollection of the experience can trigger a nerve-cell response that makes the event seem real. The brain reconstructs the image stored in memory by re-creating the pattern of nerve cell activity that occurred when the accident really happened. The heart rate increases, and the mind orders the same fight-or-flight response it would have for the real threat of an accident. Whether a person recalls an event or imagines a scene, the experience is real to the brain.

Remembered Wellness

Kosslyn and colleagues examined how the brain processes information both real and imagined. Subjects were asked to look at a grid of inter-connecting vertical and horizontal lines upon which a letter, for example, an *A* was present. As they did so, the investigators used a PET scan (positron-emission tomography) to determine which areas of the brain showed the nerve cell activity. PET scans allow researchers to view the brain in action by giving patients a small dose of a radioactive substance that zeros in on the increased blood flow indicative of increased nerve cell firing. Then the letter upon the grid was taken away, and the participants were asked to look at the grid and visualize the letter upon it. As they did, another set of PET scans was obtained. The second scans revealed that the same areas of the brain were activated by simply visualizing—but not actually seeing—the letter. Thus, either actually seeing an object or visualizing it brings the same brain cells into activity.[18]

To revive a memory (in this case, a remembered letter), the brain reconstructs the activity that occurred when the letter was viewed initially and activates the same nerve cells, synapses, and circuits. This pattern of brain activity is called a "neurosignature." All life events and emotions create neurosignatures, but because people's lives are different, each person's neurosignatures are unique. The brain and nervous system entertain a constant dialogue that cultivates and maintains life memories, emotions, personalities, ethics, and morals.

We have neurosignatures for pain, for skin rashes, and for asthma, and thus we can, through the mind, turn on these symptoms. We also have neurosignatures to turn off pain, skin rashes, and asthma. It is necessary for us to remember the wellness of being without the pain or rash. To do so, we must be able to firmly believe in the caring agent. Thus we can explain the actions of the placebo effect. With adequate belief in a pill, a surgery, a physician, the placebo effect can be evoked. The term *placebo effect* might therefore be redefined as "remembered wellness"—not only because this expression more accurately describes the probable brain mechanics involved, but because *placebo effect* has become a pejorative term in its medical usage.[19] Many in the medical community refer to successes attributed to the placebo effect in much the same way as one might dismiss ailments as being "all in your head." Yet, "all in your head" actually reflects rather impressive results.

The Relaxation Response

Benson and coworkers examined the cultural, religious, philosophical, and scientific underpinnings of meditation and found that many different religions and cultures had similar practices.[20] Early religious practices often included the repetition of a word or phrase and disregard of distracting thoughts. For example, the anonymous author of *The Cloud of Unknowing*, a fourteenth-century Christian treatise, discusses how to reach a union with God through an altered state of consciousness. To attain the appropriate level, one needed to reduce distractions and repeat a one-syllable word:

> Choose whichever one you prefer, or, if you like, choose another that suits your taste, provided that it is of one syllable. And clasp this word tightly in your heart so that it never leaves it no matter what may happen. This word shall be your shield and your spear . . . with this word you shall strike down thoughts of every kind and drive them beneath the cloud of forgetting. After that, if any thoughts should press upon you—answer him with this word only and with no other words.[21]

Also in the fourteenth century, Gregory of Sinai, at Mount Athos in Greece, described a method of repetitive prayer using "The Prayer of the Heart" or "The Prayer of Jesus."[22] In the early days of Christianity, young monks were taught in the use of prayer by skilled instructors:

> Sit down alone and in silence. Lower your head, shut your eyes, breathe out gently, and imagine yourself looking into your own heart. Carry your mind, i.e., your thoughts, from your head to your heart. As you breathe out, say "Lord Jesus Christ, have mercy on me." Say it moving your lips gently, or simply say it in your mind. Try to put all other thoughts aside. Be calm, be patient and repeat the process very frequently.[23]

In Merkabalism, one of the earliest forms of Jewish mysticism, similar practices date back to the time of the second temple from the fourth century B.C.E. to the first century C.E. Descriptions include subjects repeating the name of a magic seal while sitting with their heads between their knees. Hymns and songs would also be incorporated.[24]

In Shintoism and Taoism, two traditional religions in Japan and China, meditative practices, such as repetition of words and concentration on nothingness, are important features.[25] Similar practices can be found in other cultures throughout the world. Tribal practices in

Africa, Indonesia, North and South America, and Siberia have included shamanism. Shamans use songs or chants, usually with a drum, to elicit trances. Generally these techniques are practiced in solitude.[26]

Based on their review, Benson and his colleagues concluded that the essential components of these meditative practices were two specific steps: (1) focusing one's attention on a repetitive word, sound, prayer, phrase, image, or physical activity; and (2) passively returning to this focus when distracted. These two steps lead to a set of measurable, predictable, and reproducible physiological events within and outside the central nervous system that are associated with a sense of calm. Benson labeled this set of physiological events "the relaxation response."

To appreciate the effects of eliciting the relaxation response it is necessary to understand the physiology of stress. At the Harvard Medical School in the early part of the twentieth century, Walter B. Cannon observed that cats react to life-threatening situations with internal secretion of adrenalin and noradrenlin, so-called sympathetic nervous system arousal, that prepares them to either face a threat or run away from it.[27] He labeled this reaction the "fight-or-flight response." This response stimulates physiological changes to facilitate vigorous skeletal muscle activity. Mediated by the release of these hormones, metabolism, heart rate, rate of breathing, and blood pressure increase, which in turn increases blood circulation to the muscles to react to the threat. Platelet activity also increases to enhance coagulation in the event of potential injury and loss of blood.

The perception of stress or danger automatically elicits the fight-or-flight response. For primitive people who were faced with wild beasts and other dangers, this response was necessary for survival. Today, most of the stresses we face are not physical, but rather are often threats to our egos—everyday stresses, such as annoying coworkers, financial demands, being kept waiting in lines or traffic. Yet, even though we are not in physical danger, we experience the same fight-or-flight response.

The behavioral and physiological opposite of the fight-or-flight response is the relaxation response. Hess described this effect as the "trophotropic" response. In experiments with cats he found that he could reduce sympathetic nervous system activity by stimulating a portion of the brain. His procedures resulted in decreases in blood pressure, muscle tension, and respiration.[28]

The early experimental work of Cannon and Hess, combined with the more recent observations of Benson and his colleagues, suggests that these two responses are actually symmetrical.[29] Although both involve brain and peripheral nervous system changes, the fight-or-flight response arouses the organism for action while the relaxation response prepares the organism for rest and calmness and restorative physiologic changes. Whereas repeated or prolonged elicitation of the fight-or-flight response has been implicated in illness related to the arousal of stress, repeated elicitation of the relaxation response appears to reduce stress-related symptoms.

Relaxation response–based approaches have been demonstrated to be effective in the treatment of many medical conditions. They are frequently used in combination with exercise, nutritional, and other stress management interventions. In other words, they are components of the third leg of the three-legged stool. Specifically, they have been found to be effective in treating cardiac arrhythmias, anxiety, hostility, depression, hypertension, premenstrual syndrome, infertility, chronic pain, and insomnia.[30]

With repeated practice, patients can experience benefits of the relaxation response not only during actual practice periods, but throughout the day.[31] There is decreased responsivity to plasma norepinephrine.

Benson and his colleagues developed the following instructions as one technique for eliciting the relaxation response:

Step 1. Pick a focus word or short phrase or prayer that is firmly rooted in your belief system.
(E.g., Secular words—ocean, one, love, peace, calm, relax; Religious words—"Shalom," "Insha'allah," "The Lord is my shepherd," "Our Father who art in heaven," "Hail Mary, full of grace," "Lord Jesus Christ, have mercy on me," "Sh'ma Yisroel," "Echod," "Om.")

Step 2. Sit quietly in a comfortable position.

Step 3. Close your eyes.

Step 4. Relax your muscles.

Step 5. Breathe slowly and naturally, and as you do, repeat your focus word, phrase, or prayer silently to yourself as you exhale.

Step 6. Assume a passive attitude. Don't worry about how well you're doing. When other thoughts come to mind, as they inevitably will, simply say to yourself, "Oh, well," and gently return to the repetition.

Step 7. Continue for ten to twenty minutes.

Step 8. Do not stand up immediately. Continue sitting quietly for a minute or so, allowing other thoughts to return. Then open your eyes and sit for another minute before rising.

Step 9. Practice this technique once or twice daily.[32]

A variety of techniques can be used to elicit the relaxation response, including meditation, repetitive prayer, progressive muscle relaxation, yoga, Tai Chi, Qi Gong, and exercise. All these strategies incorporate the two essential components (mental focusing and adopting a passive attitude toward distracting thoughts) and thus result in the same physiological response.

The Faith Factor

Spiritual feelings often accompany the elicitation of the relaxation response. Kass and colleagues developed a questionnaire to measure the frequency of such feelings and to examine their association with health benefits. Because the majority of respondents indicated that they believed in God it was not possible to distinguish the effects of this belief on health.[33]

However, when the data from the study were compiled, people's descriptions of the spiritual experience they felt while eliciting the relaxation response focused on some common themes. Those who reported an increase in spirituality (25 percent of subjects), described two aspects of their experience: (1) the presence of an energy, a force, God, if you will, that was beyond themselves, and (2) a feeling that this presence was close to them. Furthermore, those subjects who experienced the feeling of this "presence" reported the most health benefits. It did not matter whether the subject used a religious or secular focus; both resulted in feelings of spirituality.

The relaxation response and remembered wellness can interact in influential and meaningful ways. These mechanisms complement each other well. It is important to emphasize, however, that beliefs and remembered wellness are not necessary to generate the relaxation response. It will occur with the use of any word (e.g., ocean, one, love, calm, relax), sound, prayer (e.g., "Hail Mary, full of grace," "Echod," "Om") or phrase, when the instructions are followed. However, when a focus is chosen that is believed in, then the powers of belief are added to those of the relaxation response.

The combined force of remembered wellness (placebo effect) and the elicitation of the relaxation response is called the "faith factor." Many patients naturally combine the relaxation response with remembered wellness. Often they use religious terms (e.g.,"Insha'allah," "The Lord is my shepherd,") as their focus while eliciting the relaxation response.

Religious convictions or life philosophy can enhance the basic effects of the relaxation response in three ways:

1. People who choose an appropriate focus, one that draws upon their deepest philosophic or religious convictions, are more apt to adhere to the elicitation routine; they look forward to it and enjoy it;
2. Affirmative beliefs of any kind bring forth remembered wellness, reviving patterns in the brain that are associated with good health;
3. When present, faith in an eternal or life-transcending force seems to make the fullest use of remembered wellness because it is a soothing belief that disconnects one from unhealthy logic and worries.

The relaxation response can disconnect everyday thoughts and worries, calming people's bodies and minds more quickly and to a degree otherwise unattainable. It appears that beliefs can add to the response, transporting the mind/body even more dramatically, quieting worries and doubts better than the relaxation response alone.

Religious Faith

Religious faith is likely more influential than other affirmative beliefs. But religious faith also has a mystical component. Karen Armstrong, in her popular book *A History of God: The 4,000-Year Quest of Judaism, Christianity and Islam,* traces the spiritual experience brought on by "silent contemplation," a method used by diverse religious communities for millennia.[34] Armstrong characterizes the experience of God that silent contemplation engenders as "mystical" because unlike the reading of scripture and other reason-based forms of worship, this experience is intuitive and nonverbal. The presence of God one might feel during silent contemplation is much less distinct or identifiable and more mystical because "words" and theologies are not imposed upon this experience. She writes:

The mystical experience of God has certain characteristics [that] are common to all faiths. It is a subjective experience that involves an interior journey, not a perception of an objective fact outside the self; it is undertaken through the image-making part of the mind—often called imagination—rather than through the more cerebral, logical faculty. Finally, it is something that the mystic creates in himself or herself deliberately: certain physical or mental exercises yield the final vision; it does not always come upon them unawares.

The "physical or mental exercises" Armstrong refers to have already been documented. They are the steps that elicit the physiologic relaxation response combined with a person's spiritual beliefs. This mystical experience that is common to different faiths is most likely the same feeling that patients express as "the presence of an energy or force that seemed close to them."

It is likely that the expectancy of God's help works in the same way as does the expectancy of help from a medication, procedure, or caregiver, according to Levin:

The mere belief that religion or God is health enhancing may be enough to produce salutary effects. That is, significant associations between measures of religion and health . . . may in part present evidence akin to the placebo effect. Various scriptures promise health and healing to the faithful, and the physiological effects of expectant beliefs such as this are now being documented by mind/body researchers.[35]

The scriptures do promise healing through faith. In Luke 18:42, Jesus says, "Receive thy sight; thy faith hath saved thee." And in Acts 14:9, one of Jesus' disciples, Paul, hears the pleas of a man in Lystra who has been crippled from birth and has never walked. "Perceiving that he had faith to be healed," Paul told the man to stand upright, and the man leapt up and walked. On the side of the road into Jericho, a blind man begs for mercy, a cry that falls on the deaf ears of passersby except for Jesus, who commands the man to come near. What the Gospel authors imply is clear: faith heals and makes the body whole.

Evidence That Religious Belief and Faith Heal

According to a 1990 Gallup poll, 95 percent of Americans say they believe in God and 76 percent say they pray on a regular basis. And in a comprehensive and impressive review of the scientific literature on the medical effects of spiritual experiences, religious factors were involved with increased survival; reduced alcohol, cigarette, and substance use; reduced anxiety, depression, and anger; reduced blood pressure; and improved quality of life for patients with cancer or heart disease.[36]

One of the most significant studies to date was conducted by Oxman at Dartmouth Medical School. He studied patients who had undergone open-heart surgery for either coronary artery or aortic valve disease. He found that those who found comfort in their religious beliefs were three times more likely to survive than those who did not.[37] Pressman and colleagues studied thirty elderly women recovering from hip surgery and looked at the relationship between their religious beliefs and their medical and psychiatric symptoms. Those with strong religious beliefs were able to walk significantly farther and were less likely to be depressed.[38] Even if their function improved because these women were less depressed, the outcome is still impressive. Religious commitment has been associated with lower blood pressure and fewer psychological symptoms, as well as better overall health and longevity. This association has been found in patients with varying conditions, among different age groups, religions, and races.[39]

Religion usually promotes healthy lifestyles and behaviors. For example, Mormons and Seventh-Day Adventists discourage their members from drinking, smoking, or having extramarital sex and encourage exercise and healthful diets. When compared with the general population, Seventh-Day Adventists have substantially lower rates of cancer (particularly colon, lung, and bladder cancer). Their rates of cancer are even lower than those who completely refrain from alcohol use.[40] These religious practitioners, as well as clergy members of all faiths, are mentally and physically healthier than the average American.

Religious people consistently report greater well-being, life satisfaction, altruism, marital satisfaction, and self-esteem than do nonreligious people. Given what we know both about remembered wellness and about the impact of stress on our health, the happiness and contentment engendered by faith can prove to be an extraordinary contributor to health.

Evidence of God's Existence?

It appears that Western medicine has neglected certain aspects of living that patients would identify as the essence or meaning of their lives. This is frustrating because research has shown that the "essence of life" is also a wellspring of health. But does the evidence from mind/body approaches tell us anything about the existence of God?

Studies of those who elicit the relaxation response have documented that stress can be reduced by mental processes designed to generate physiologic changes in the body. Furthermore, as previously noted, people from most religions and cultures throughout the world rely on similar practices when they pray. In fact, there seems to be a tendency for humans to worship and believe. Perhaps this tendency is rooted in our physiology in some way. Perhaps people have known that worshiping a higher power was good for them.

In this chapter, we have demonstrated that beliefs can have physical repercussions. We've discussed how the brain stores our life experiences and that nerve cell activation is constantly shifting the cellular pathways that determine all our thoughts, movements, feelings, and functions. Our brains develop strategies for survival and the continuation of the species. We also unconsciously react to all the things that happen to us and to all our ideas with emotional markers.

Humans are the only species that recognizes its own mortality. The inevitability of death can be such a torment, so depressing and anxiety-producing, that it impairs our survival. To counter this angst, it helps to believe in a higher power. Whether or not God exists, our genes may guarantee that we will bear faith and that our bodies will be soothed by believing in some antithesis to mortality and human frailty. In order not to be incapacitated by the acknowledgment and dread of death, our brains harbor the belief in a better, nobler meaning to life.

As long as humankind has existed, people have worshiped. In the words of Karen Armstrong, "Jews, Christians, and Muslims have developed remarkably similar ideas of God, which also resemble other contemplations of the Absolute. When people try to find an ultimate meaning and value in human life, their minds seem to go in a certain direction. They have not been coerced to do this; it is something that seems natural to humanity." Indeed, a belief in God is as natural to humankind as our instincts to fight or flee. These predetermined instincts often lead to common archetypes, people with common fears and tendencies becoming legends in every culture. Similarly, we develop ideas of the Almighty because we seem to be programmed "to go in a certain direction."

Whether or not one believes in God, people attach purpose and significance to their lives. They derive the most enduring strength and solace from the transcendent. Some look to children for their inspiration because children are untainted and ripe with possibilities. For others, a garden may be deeply soothing. Still others find contentment in music and art. Faith in God, however, seems to be particularly influential in healing. "God" by definition is limitless, and it is natural for us to believe in and rely on an almighty power to prevent having our health undermined by knowing the fact that all of us must die.

Kathryn Harrison makes the point that "the modern world's replacement of faith with science means that, for most of us, there is no Mystery, only mysteries, and that . . . we are about to solve [them]."[41] Society seems to subject everything to empirical analysis, in an attempt to limit the number of unknowns and reduce our understanding of the universe to statistics and formulas. Perhaps in this way we can tame the wildest variables—destiny, human choices, interpersonal relationships— and all other mysteries and make them succinct and predictable.

Yet even when we acquire new information and feel we have solved all the mysteries, we feel vaguely empty and unfulfilled. Faith then provides solace. In part, this occurs because faith in an Infinite Absolute is an adequate counterforce to the inevitability of disease and death. In addition, faith allows us to appreciate the unseen and unproved, generating a kind of hope that cannot be achieved with reason alone. Armstrong writes that primitive men and women worshiped gods "not simply because they wanted to propitiate powerful forces; these early faiths expressed the wonder and mystery that seem always to have been an essential part of the human experience of this beautiful yet terrifying world."

Spiritual beliefs quiet the mind, short-circuiting the nonproductive reasoning that so often consumes our thoughts. Although the body is very effective at healing itself, all too often this process is hindered by negative thoughts and doubts. Worries elicit the fight-or-flight response and the stress-related symptoms and disease that can blunt the healing capacities honed through evolution. Moreover, perpetual fretting makes an impression on our nerve cells, so the body tends to "remember" illness.

Because faith seems to transcend experience, it succeeds beyond expectation in relieving distress and generating hope and expectancy. With such positive feelings comes "remembered wellness"—the cerebral call for healing that mobilizes our body's resources and reactions. Such beliefs are effective in relieving 50–90 percent of common medical problems.

Faith in an invincible, infallible force exerts a remarkable healing power. Believing in an Infinite Absolute appears to be part of our nature. By the process of natural selection, mutating genes seem to have deemed faith important to the survival of our forebears. Ironically, it might be argued that evolution favors religion, causing our brains to generate the impulses we need to carry on. Faith, hope, and love have been incorporated in our approach to living.

Belief in God offers us a will to live that we would not have without belief in a supreme being, which may explain why religion becomes more important to us as we grow older. The inevitable onset of declining health and death increases our torment, and our need to venerate current experience expands proportionately. This may be why people in the midst of life-threatening disease find solace in religion, and why congregations pray for those who are hospitalized.

Some contend that humans invented the idea of God over time as a crutch or balm to stave off an otherwise cruel reality of pointlessness. Others maintain that the capacity for faith and for conjuring up God— what many would call the "soul"—was genetically implanted by a Divine Maker who wanted to be known to us. Do we have faith because God intended us to worship, pray, yearn, and be fulfilled by believing in an Infinite Absolute?

Science cannot possibly determine which came first: human beings or God. But, from the very narrow perspective of healing and medicine, it does not matter which came first. Believing that God exists, or simply believing in God, allows us to reap rewards both in terms of improved health and greater personal fulfillment. Faith is good for us, whether you believe that God planted these genes within us or that humans created the idea of God to nourish a body yearning to survive. And it is important to bear in mind that affirmative beliefs unrelated to God have been demonstrated to be therapeutic as in our earlier discussion of remembered wellness.

Atheists and agnostics can experience the health benefits from their own positive beliefs; a belief in God may not be necessary for them. Affirmative beliefs and hopes can be therapeutic, and faith in God in particular can have many positive effects on health. There are, of course, many other benefits to believing in God far beyond those of medicine and healing, but such effects are beyond the scope of this discussion.

Notes

1. H. Benson and R. Friedman, "Harnessing the Power of the Placebo Effect and Renaming It 'Remembered Wellness,' " *Annual Review of Medicine* 47 (1996): 193–99.
2. R. Cabot, "Truth and Falsehoods in Medicine," *American Medicine* 5 (1903): 344–49.

3. C. Rosenberg, "The Therapeutic Revolution," in *Sickness and Health in America*, 2d ed., ed. J. Leavitt and R. Numbers (Madison: University of Wisconsin Press, 1985).

4. H. Beecher, "The Powerful Placebo," *Journal of the American Medical Association* 159 (1955): 1602–6; Benson and Friedman, "Harnessing the Power of the Placebo Effect"; H. Benson, *Timeless Healing: The Power and Biology of Belief* (New York: Scribner, 1996).

5. J. A. Turner, R. A. Deyo, J. D. Loeser, M. Von Korff, and W. E. Fordyce, "The Importance of Placebo Effects in Pain Treatment and Research," *Journal of the American Medical Association* 271 (1994): 1609–14.

6. A. H. Roberts, D. G. Kewman, L. Mercier, and M. Hovell, "The Power of Nonspecific Effects in Healing: Implications for Psychosocial and Biological Treatments," *Clinical Psychology Review* 13 (1993): 375–91.

7. Y. Ikemi and S. Nakagawa, "A Psychosomatic Study of Contagious Dermatitis," *Kyoshu Journal of Medical Science* 13 (1962): 335–50.

8. I. Hashish, H. K. Hai, W. Harvey, C. Feinmann, and M. Harris, "Reduction of Postoperative Pain and Swelling by Ultrasound Treatment: A Placebo Effect," *Pain* 33 (1988): 303–11.

9. E. F. Traut and E. W. Passarelli, "Placebos in the Treatment of Rheumatoid Arthritis and Other Conditions," Annals of the Rheumatic Diseases 16 (1957): 18–22.

10. R. I. Horwitz, C. M. Viscoli, L. Berkman, R. M. Donaldson, S. M. Horwitz, D. J. Murray, D. F. Ransohoff, and J. Sindelar, "Treatment Adherence and Risk of Death after a Myocardial Infarction," *Lancet* 336 (1990): 542–45.

11. Coronary Drug Project Research Group, "Influence of Adherence to Treatment and Response of Cholesterol on Mortality in the Coronary Drug Project," *New England Journal of Medicine* 303 (1980): 1038–41.

12. W. Wolf, "Effects of Suggestion and Conditioning on the Action of Chemical Agents in Human Subjects: The Pharmacology of Placebos," *Journal of Clinical Investigation* 29 (1950): 100–109.

13. H. Benson and D. P. McCallie, Jr., M. D., "Angina Pectoris and the Placebo Effect," *New England Journal of Medicine* 300 (1979): 1424–29.

14. L. D. Egbert, G. E. Battit, C. E. Welch, and M. K. Bartlett, "Reduction of Postoperative Pain by Encouragement and Instruction of Patients," *New England Journal of Medicine* 270 (1964): 824–27.

15. K. Kroenke and A. D. Mangelsdorff, "Common Symptoms in Ambulatory Care: Incidence, Evaluation, Therapy and Outcome," *American Journal of Medicine* (1989): 262–66.

16. C. Butler and A. Steptoe, "Placebo Responses: An Experimental Study of Psychophysiological Processes in Asthmatic Volunteers," *British Journal of Clinical Psychology* 25 (1986): 173–83.

17. J. F. Riley, D. K. Ahern, and M. J. Follick, "Chronic Pain and Functional Impairment: Assessing Beliefs about Their Relationship," *Archives of Physical Medicine and Rehabilitation* 69 (1988): 579–82.

18. S. Kosslyn, N. M. Alper, W. L. Thompson, V. Maljkovic, S. B. Weise, C. F. Chabris, S. E. Hamilton, S. L. Rauch, and F. S. Buonanno, "Visual Mental Imagery Activates Topographically Organized Visual Cortex: PET Investigation," *Journal of Cognitive Neuroscience* 5 (1993): 263–67.

19. Benson, *Timeless Healing;* Benson and Friedman, "Harnessing the Power of the Placebo Effect."

20. H. Benson, J. F. Beary, and M. P. Carol, "The Relaxation Response," *Psychiatry* 37 (1974): 37–46.

21. I. Progoff, ed. and trans., *The Cloud of Unknowing* (New York: Julian Press, 1969).

22. J. J. Norwich and R. Sitwell, *Mount Athos* (New York: Harper & Row, 1966).

23. R. M. French, trans., *The Way of a Pilgrim* (New York: Seabury Press, 1968).

24. G. G. Scholem, *Jewish Mysticism* (New York: Schocken, 1967).

25. J. Herbert, *Shinto: At the Fountain-Head of Japan* (London: Allen & Unwin, 1967); C. Chang, *Creativity and Taoism* (New York: Julian Press, 1963).

26. R. C. Johnson, *Watcher on the Hills* (New York: Harper, 1959); J. Segal, ed., *Mental Health Program Reports–5* (Washington, D.C.: National Institutes of Mental Health, 1971).

27. W. B. Cannon, "The Emergency Function of the Adrenal Medulla in Pain and the Major Emotions," *American Journal of Physiology* 33 (1941): 356.

28. W. R. Hess, *The Functional Organization of the Diencephalon* (New York: Grune & Stratton, 1957).

29. H. Benson and E. M. Stuart, *The Wellness Book* (New York: Simon & Schuster, 1992).

30. H. Benson, S. Alexander, and C. L. Feldman, "Decreased Premature Ventricular Contractions through Use of the Relaxation Response in Patients with Stable Ischemic Heart-Disease," *Lancet* 2 (1975): 380–82; H. Benson, F. H. Frankel, R. Apfel, M. D. Daniels, H. E. Schniewind, J. C. Nemiah, P. E. Sifneos, K. D. Crassweller, M. M. Greenwood, J. B. Kotch, P. A. Arns, and B. Rosner, "Treatment of Anxiety: A Comparison of the Usefulness of Self-Hypnosis and a Meditational Relaxation Technique," *Psychotherapy and Psychosomatics* 30 (1978): 229–42; E. Stuart, M. Caudill, J. Lesserman, C. Dorrington, R. Friedman, and H. Benson, "Nonpharmacologic Treatment of Hypertension: A Multiple-Risk-Factor Approach," *Journal of Cardiovascular Nursing* 1 (1987): 1–14; I. L. Goodale, A. D. Domar, and H. Benson, "Alleviation of Premenstrual Syndrome Symptoms with the Relaxation Response," *Obstetrics and Gynecology* 75 (1990): 649–55; A. D. Domar, M. M. Seibel, and H. Benson, "The Mind/Body Program for Infertility: A New Behavioral Treatment Approach for Women with Infertility," *Fertility and Sterility* 53 (1990): 246–49; M. Caudill, R. Schnable, P. Zuttermeister, H. Benson, and R. Friedman, "Decreased Clinic Use by Chronic Pain Patients: Response to Behavioral Medicine Interventions," *Clinical Journal of Pain* 7 (1991): 305–10; G. D. Jacobs, H. Benson, and R. Friedman, "Home-Based Central Nervous System Assessment of a Multifactor Behavioral Intervention for Chronic Sleep-Onset Insomnia," *Behavior Therapy* 24 (1993): 159–174; G. D. Jacobs, P. A. Rosenberg, R. Friedman, J. Matheson, G. M. Peavy, A. D. Domar, and H. Benson, "Multifactor Behavioral Treatment of Chronic Sleep-Onset Insomnia Using Stimulus Control and the Relaxation Response: A Preliminary Study," *Behavior Modification* 17 (1993): 498–509.

31. J. Hoffman, H. Benson, P. Arns, G. L. Stainbrock, L. Landsberb, J. B. Young, and A. Gill, "Reduction in Sympathetic Nervous System Responsivity Associated with the Relaxation Response," *Science* 215 (1982): 190–92.

32. Benson, *Timeless Healing*, 136.

33. J. D. Kass, R. Friedman, J. Lesserman, P. C. Zuttermeister, "Health Outcomes and a New Index of Spiritual Experience," *Journal for the Scientific Study of Religion* 30 (1991): 203–11.

34. K. Armstrong, *A History of God: The 4,000-Year Quest of Judaism, Christianity and Islam* (New York: Knopf, 1993).

35. J. S. Levin, "Religion and Health: Is There an Association, Is It Valid, and Is It Causal?" *Social Science and Medicine* 38 (1994): 1475–82.

36. D. A. Matthews, C. B. Larson, and C. P. Barry, *The Faith Factor: An Annotated Bibliography of Clinical Research on Spiritual Subjects,* vol. 1 (Philadelphia: John Templeton Foundation, 1993).
37. T. E. Oxman, D. H. Freeman, Jr., E. D. Manheimer, "Lack of Social Participation or Religious Strength and Comfort as Risk Factors for Death after Cardiac Surgery in the Elderly," *Psychosomatic Medicine* 57 (1995): 5–15.
38. P. Pressman, J. S. Lyons, D. B. Larson, and J. J. Strain, "Religious Belief, Depression, and Ambulation Status in Elderly Women with Broken Hips," *American Journal of Psychiatry* 147 (1990): 758–60.
39. Matthews, Larson, and Barry, *The Faith Factor.*
40. O. M. Jensen, "Cancer Risk among Danish Male Seventh-Adventists and Other Temperance Society Members," *Journal of the National Cancer Institute* 70 (1983): 1011–14.
41. K. Harrison, "In His Brother's Shadow," *New York Times Book Review,* May 29, 1994, 3, 12.

9

Health's Forgotten Factor

Medical Research Uncovers
Religion's Clinical Relevance

DAVID B. LARSON
AND SUSAN S. LARSON

Medicine remains entrusted with the momentous opportunity to uncover means to alleviate physical and emotional suffering by employing objective scientific methods. In leaving no stone unturned to improve clinical outcomes, we as medical scientists have the potential to humbly explore new areas previously left outside the realm of scientific investigation to find promising ways to engender healthier lives.

In the field of epidemiology, identifying what factors foster health and what puts people at risk for illness and earlier death stands as a central focus. Epidemiologists observe factors that prevent illness often before discovery of underlying mechanisms of why an intervention might prove effective. Willingness to undertake these investigations to ascertain what works, and then further investigate why, requires a certain professional humility that refuses to disregard potential clinical factors not yet esteemed significant within current theories. New findings that are clinically relevant and practical in enhancing health then may open new vistas to launch new theories on a stream of new empirical data. Previously overlooked factors await discovery.

As Sir John Templeton writes in *The Humble Approach*, "The more we learn about the universe the more humble we should be, realizing how ignorant we have been in the past and how much more there is still to discover."[1]

In epidemiology, a surprising link that protects against disease may serve as the touchstone for further scientific inquiry. Epidemiology is rooted in phenomenology—objective, scientific observations that lead to further research "to see if these things are so." For instance, when

John Snow, one of the historical founders of epidemiology, mapped the London cholera outbreaks in the mid-1800s, he traced one localized epidemic to the now infamous Broad Street pump. He convinced the city leaders to remove the pump handle to halt the spread. The only theoretical knowledge at work at the time was Snow's conviction of the disease's association with the water system. We now know bacteria from sewage were contaminating the water. But at that point the cholera bacillus had not been discovered, nor was its mechanism of action in the gastrointestinal tract understood. Preventing cholera's spread in London started with shutting down the Broad Street pump. Incorporation of subsequent knowledge of disease mechanisms and the discovery of antibiotics allowed for more effective treatment strategies in later years, but the observed association of the pump and the disease was the initial step toward enhancing health.[2]

Such epidemiologic observations may run counter to current clinical views or theory, which then calls for humility to examine the observations and not disregard or disparage them until they have been evaluated objectively. In another historic example in medicine, in a Vienna hospital in 1847, Hungarian physician Ignaz Semmelweis noticed as much as a ten times difference in death rates among new mothers apparently based on their respective wards. In one ward, served by midwives who carefully washed their hands, the patient death rate was 3.3 percent. But in the ward where new mothers were cared for by medical students who had just finished autopsies but had failed to wash their hands, the death rate of new mothers ranged from 9.9 percent to 29.3 percent. Semmelweis, years in advance of Louis Pasteur's germ theory of disease, hypothesized that the medical students were carrying "putrid particles" that were causing fatal fevers in their patients. After medical students were ordered to wash their hands in lime chloride, the death rates in that ward plummeted to 3 percent in the first year and to 1.27 percent in the second. Despite these striking results, however, Semmelweis's medical superior vigorously objected as a result of his own conflicting theoretical perspective, forcing Semmelweis to leave Vienna.[3] More humility on the part of the medical superior would have improved care and reduced deaths among new mothers.

Relevant clinical factors that may be linked with improving physical and mental health deserve scientific focus and potential incorporation into care, and should not be dismissed out of hand if current views or theories overlook them. Currently, published medical research is revealing such a relevant, beneficial factor for preventing illness, coping with disease, and enhancing recovery.[4] This factor is linked with longer lives in studies that track thousands of people over decades, as well as with lower blood pressure, greater ability to handle stress, less depression, and diminished drug and alcohol abuse.[5] Yet this factor has yet to be included in the vast majority of clinical studies. What is this often-overlooked factor? It is the strength of a person's spirituality or religious commitment.

The link between spirituality and health is currently mounting in clinical and medical recognition based on studies published in peer-reviewed medical journals. In 1998, a Consensus Report culminated the collaborations of more than seventy top researchers in the fields of physical and mental health, addictions, and neuroscience to review current research findings and to map out future research directions as well as barriers to overcome. The Consensus Report stated that "the data from many of the studies conducted to date are both sufficiently robust and tantalizing to warrant continued and expanded clinical investigations."[6]

Spiritual vitality and its potential salutary links with physical and emotional health stand as emerging relevant clinical factors, meriting expanded scientific study. Yet delving into this new area of research requires humility to see if this factor—so long overlooked if not disregarded in the medical academic community—is indeed effectual.

Humbling Research

What are some of these "robust and tantalizing" findings?

Three recent studies will provide an initial illustrative sampler of the growing scientific literature of hundreds of peer-reviewed published studies further referred to below. They focus on three critical medical areas: recovering from heart surgery, longevity, and immune system functioning.

Heart Surgery

When is religious commitment clinically relevant? Can it make a difference in surviving surgery? Many researchers and clinicians might dismiss religious commitment as irrelevant. Yet a recent study at Dartmouth Medical School showed that a consistent predictor of who survived heart surgery was the strength of a patient's religious commitment. In this study of 232 patients, those who said they derived no strength or comfort from their religious faith had almost three times the risk of death at the six-month follow-up as patients who found at least some strength. None of those who saw themselves as deeply religious prior to surgery had died six months later, compared to 12 percent of those who rarely or never went to church. If the study had omitted these religious commitment variables, as many studies continue to do, this finding would have remained undiscovered, and a potential means for enhancing recovery for a critical, costly medical procedure left unknown.

As a result of the significance of these findings, the primary investigator, Dr. Thomas Oxman, suggested that inquiring about a patient's religious commitment can be as important to his or her prognosis as inquiring about other lifestyle habits such as smoking. "Cigarette smoking and hypertension are risk factors for coronary artery disease through still unknown mechanisms, yet physicians recommend reduction," they stated. "Physicians may eventually be advised to make relatively simple inquiries about and reinforcement of group participation and religious involvement as routinely as they inquire and advise about cigarette smoking and hypertension."

The researchers added that a physician "probably cannot convince a patient to participate privately in religion . . . any more than he or she can successfully convince a patient to stop smoking." Yet, encouraging these behaviors when appropriate "may improve quality of life and . . . alter survival behaviors."[7]

Longevity

A rather striking clinical outcome that remains difficult to dispute is death. Since 1965, a long-term study of health and mortality has followed more than 5,280 people in Alameda County, California, to examine what health practices and lifestyle factors might reveal links with living longer. For the study's 28-year follow-up period, W. J. Strawbridge and colleagues found that persons who usually attended religious services weekly or more were 25 percent less likely to die during that time than infrequent or nonattenders.[8]

Immune Functioning

A study of more than 1,700 older adults from North Carolina conducted by researchers at Duke University Medical Center found that persons who attended church to any degree were only half as likely as nonattenders to have elevated levels of a blood protein that can reveal problems in immune system functioning. High levels of interleukin-6 (IL-6) can be linked to ineffectiveness in the immune system, making the body more susceptible to a variety of diseases.

The researchers noted that high levels of stress are associated with the release of hormones, such as cortisol and IL-6, which may reflect an impaired immune system. The researchers hypothesized that if religious commitment improved stress control, as indicated in other study findings, then religious commitment might also reduce the production of IL-6 and the release of cortisol and other substances that adversely affect the immune system.

"By helping to improve stress control, greater religious involvement may help keep down the production of biological substances that impair the body's capacity to fend off disease," noted lead researcher Dr. Harold Koenig.

The study found a relationship between low religious attendance and high levels of IL-6 that could not be explained by other controlled-for variables, including depression or negative life events, which might also increase these levels.

"This finding provides some support for the hypothesis that older adults who frequently attend religious services have healthier immune systems," the researchers concluded.[9] It is important that future studies investigate the link between religious commitment and immune functioning, and also neurochemical functioning as well in humbly pioneering new frontiers of medical research.

A Paradigm Shift in Medical Care

In light of these findings, and significantly more that will be discussed later, medical research, education, and care stand poised on the brink of a potential paradigm shift in which the possible role of spiritual factors are recognized in health. The earlier, more traditional medical paradigm overlooked religious commitment as a clinical factor, viewing it as either insignificant or irrelevant. A few clinical fields even previously presumed religious commitment was consistently associated with harm.[10] Furthermore, spirituality was assumed to be either too controversial or too difficult to measure, or based on transcendent values beyond the reach of empiricism. However, the effect of religious and spiritual commitment can be studied empirically. Indications of people's religious commitment can be measured by asking questions about participation in religious activities, such as how often they attend religious services, pray, or read sacred writings. Spiritual commitment can be asked about by inquiring what factors provide ultimate meaning and purpose in a person's life. How a person rates the personal importance of his or her religious faith can be inquired about, as well as asking to what degree, if any, God is a source of strength or comfort. The religious commitment measures can then be compared to various indexes of physical or emotional health or personal well-being. The best approach to studying the links between religious commitment and health is multidimensional. Yet one need not feel overwhelmed by the assessment of spiritual or religious factors, but proceed step-by-step, as in any area of scientific investigation. Surprisingly, even simplistic measures (e.g., frequency of church attendance) reveal noteworthy health findings. But the more reliable and relevant dimensions that are measured, the more instructive the outcomes.

Thomas S. Kuhn's groundbreaking work *The Structure of Scientific Revolutions* describes how the acceptance of new paradigms comes only after the old paradigm appears incomplete. The way of perceiving a particular scientific domain can remain stable as long as the established paradigm is thought to be capable of solving the significant challenges or problems in the field. Only when the limitations of the older model are revealed—often through new research—do groups of scientists begin to challenge the theory and develop a more complete paradigm, which can help to take into account the newer findings. Consequently, with the new and growing amount of research discovering links between religious commitment and physical and mental health in preventing illness, coping with disease and stress, and enhancing recovery, as well as living longer lives, medicine is beginning to develop a health-care model that includes a spiritual dimension. Why should a factor so prevalent among patients and important for so many remain overlooked? Humility invites and encourages us to expand our knowledge and to reexamine our views.

Kuhn warns that accepting a new paradigm remains challenging and complex. Often scientists will want to explain new findings in terms of the old paradigm until they recognize that the old paradigm is too limited. Kuhn highlighted an experiment that elucidated this resistance to acknowledging new findings. Study participants were asked to identify playing cards after a brief exposure to them. Some cards had been altered so that the hearts were black and the spades were red. Those in the study identified the normal cards correctly, but they also identified the altered cards as normal without hesitation. For example, a black four of hearts was identified either as a four of hearts or a four of spades. The card was perceived as belonging to one of the already known paradigms. Only after a prolonged process of many exposures to the new cards did the study participants sense something was new or different and then, often quite suddenly, announce the manner in which some cards had been altered. In recognizing the new cards, they finally underwent a paradigm shift.[11]

This struggle over paradigms continues in the arena of spiritual or religious commitment and health. Some researchers still try to explain findings based on old paradigms. Blocking religious commitment from becoming a part of clinical research and care, the findings regarding the relative and frequently positive health links with religious commitment are reductionistically interpreted as another previously recognized factor. They attribute the effects of religious commitment to "nothing but" religion as social support, or "nothing but" religion's enhancing the practicing of healthier lifestyles. Yet when these factors are controlled for in studies, religious commitment still stands out as a statistically significant beneficial clinical factor. Some investigators and clinicians have yet to recognize this new card in the deck. But now increasing numbers of medical researchers and practitioners are acknowledging the relevance of religious and spiritual commitment in preventing, coping with, and recovering from illness.

Questioning Unexamined Premises—A Personal Story

Theory based on unexamined premises that dismissed, belittled, or rejected religious commitment as a relevant clinical factor created initial roadblocks to a paradigm shift that recognizes religious commitment's potential positive links to health. Yet conducting objective, quantified research for publication in peer-reviewed journals helps open the door to further inquiry. Employing the best scientific methods can bring us back to where we see with new eyes and recognize the importance of what we once forgot. As Russell Stannard so aptly states in chapter 1, one's "pet theory" must give way to the practical evidence.

In my own field of psychiatry, during my residency training in the mid-1970s, I heard that religion was generally harmful to one's mental health. I wondered if that were true. In my work with patients as a psychiatrist, I observed that patients' religious commitment often appeared to help them cope and sometimes gave them added motivation in working in therapy. However, no forum existed in which to address the issue. If one proposed that religion might not always be harmful—in fact, might be neutral or at times even beneficial—one was laughed at as a relic of the Dark Ages or condemned as unprofessional, having yet to "work through" personal religious issues. Yet in my opinion, the unquestioned tenet that religion was harmful deserved some further investigation. I wanted to see what the research showed.

The founder of modern psychiatry, Sigmund Freud, who brilliantly elucidated the concept of the unconscious, wrote strong statements about his perception of religion. An avowed atheist himself, he proclaimed religion "a universal obsessional neurosis . . . infantile helplessness . . . a regression to primary narcissism."[12] Other mental health professionals seemed to rally to his assertions. Religion had been labeled a "borderline psychosis . . . a regression, an escape, a projection on the world of a primitive infantile state," in the mid-1970s by the Group for the Advancement of Psychiatry.[13] The contemporary psychologist Albert Ellis, best known for his work on rational emotive therapy, wrote:

> Religiosity is in many respects equivalent to irrational thinking and emotional disturbance. . . . The elegant solution to emotional problems is to be quite unreligious . . . the less religious they are, the more emotionally healthy they will be.[14]

However, another eminent psychoanalyst, Carl Jung, made the following observation:

> Among all my patients in the second half of my life . . . there has not been one whose problem in the last resort was not that of finding a religious outlook on life. It is safe to say that every one of them fell ill because he had lost that which the living religions of every age have given their followers and none of them has been really healed who did not regain his religious outlook.[15]

Research versus Unexamined Assumptions

To what degree are any of these suppositions supported by objective research? As clinical professionals, do we have the humility to examine these historically conflicting professional presumptions by researching them? As Proverbs 18:2 states, "A person deficient in wisdom takes no pleasure in learning, but only in expressing their opinion." We need more than opinion. We need a more objective standard such as research to review the available evidence and move forward. When we humbly and honestly apply the scientific method, what do do we find in the published data? Science can take precedence over name-calling, and research can replace potential "bigotry" of unexamined personal opinion by instead becoming "big on investigating" new factors relevant to patients.

Commenting on the importance of conducting empirical studies on religious variable, John Foglio, D.Min., and Howard Brody, M.D., Ph.D., state in the *Journal of Family Practice:*

> Research into religious issues and variables in family medicine might be rejected or undervalued because it seems wedded to the realm of anecdote or opinion. Ironically, the absence of a solid literature on religion and family medicine will assure that our knowledge remains in the realm of anecdote and opinion, instead of progressing to the empirical assessment of beneficial, neutral, and harmful roles of religion among patients and providers.[16]

If religious commitment proved primarily harmful, as Freud and later mental health professionals assumed, then the research in psychiatry's journals should demonstrate this. I turned to the research to see if the data supported what was taught in psychiatry at that time. I decided to comprehensively survey the research to see how frequently psychiatry investigated religious commitment and then also to summarize the valence of the findings. I hypothesized that the findings would follow a normal distribution, in other words, a bell curve with a small portion negative, another small portion positive, with the large central portion of the bell curve neutral or nonsignificant. I was committed to remaining scientifically objective to avoid bias.

To eliminate selection bias in what articles I surveyed, I developed a scientifically objective process called the "systematic review." Our research team looked at every single published in psychiatry's four leading journals over a five-year period (1978–1982) to see how many contained a quantified religious variable. Examining every article made the review replicable and ensured objectivity, more so than subjectively deciding what articles I might choose to survey or ignore. This method also gave a comprehensive "state of the art" summary by looking at the corpus of studies in the specified journals during the review time frame.

The Method of the Systematic Review

To provide background on this review approach that we have now used in a number of fields, I would like to explain more about how this clinical systematic method can be such an important step in the objective consideration of controversial factors.

Traditional Reviews

An often unrecognized aspect of the development of a research field is the influence of research reviews. Especially in underdeveloped research areas, growth can be spurred by summarizing the research published to date and making recommendations for future research. Traditionally, the review process has relied on the individual reviewer's subjective expertise. The process allowed him or her to make individual judgments on which articles to include, to decide which portions of those articles were most significant, and to determine how best to interpret the findings. On the positive side, this strategy offers flexibility and allows for individual expression of expert opinion within a given field. Yet the process could be described as more art than science, since the traditional review process is for the most part determined by the expertise of the particular reviewer. Consequently, a disadvantage of this approach is its potential for introducing personal review biases. In addition, since this review process is relatively unstructured, even if biases are suspected, it may be difficult if not impossible to replicate the review to assess it objectively. Also, even if the review accurately reflects a field of research, it is vulnerable to criticism by others who may hold differing perspectives.

These disadvantages can be particularly key when the topic under review is often overlooked or controversial, such as the study of religious commitment and health. These traditional reviews are susceptible to insertion of bias as well as to criticism of subjectivity in both the selection and interpretation of the data in the reviewed publications.[17]

Meta-Analysis Reviews

A different strategy from the more traditional, potentially subjective art form of review is the meta-analysis, in which statistical findings can be combined across studies to provide literature-wide estimates of particular clinical results or effects. With its clear statistical methodology, it is useful for minimizing bias in investigating controversial topics.

However, meta-analysis is highly restrictive in its inclusion criteria. It is intended for a series of studies with (1) homogeneous study populations, (2) similar interventions, and (3) variables measured along similar dimensions. Thus the more objective meta-analysis method remains inapplicable to reviewing a wide topic with diverse study populations, diverse study methodologies, or diverse measurement assessments, as is often the case in various studies of the link between religious commitment and health.

The Systematic Review

Consequently, my research colleague John Lyons, Ph.D., and I evolved a new review strategy—the systematic review. A cousin of meta-analysis, it also owes its conceptualization to Richard Light and David Pillemer, whose book *Summing Up* laid the groundwork for developing the systematic review.[18] By using an objective and replicable review method, the systematic review minimizes the opportunity for reviewer bias found in the more traditional review approach, but is more inclusive than meta-analysis in terms of the kinds of studies and study populations that may be reviewed or assessed. All aspects of the review design are quantified, including inclusion and exclusion criteria of studies.

The sampling frame for the systematic review most frequently comprises all quantified articles in certain leading journals published during a specified number of years, usually a recent time period. A quantified study contains data that is collected and analyzed. The systematic review does not include case reports, commentaries and editorials in its review. Variables of interest to be reviewed are identified, such as various quantified measures of religious commitment. The review team then searches by hand through every article within the specified sampling frame to identify articles containing any of the variables under review. Running totals are kept on the number of articles scanned and the number of articles and types of measures contained on the topic of interest.

Also specified are the method for analyzing the quality of the studies, determining and specifying interrater reliability (generally above 0.80), and summing the results across all reviewed studies. Results can be simply presented and understood as numeric items, thus making both the review findings and results, as in any good research protocol, replicable.

A computerized search has remained an inadequate substitute for hand searching to find all pertinent articles. When it comes to the variables of interest they are often buried in tables or text and frequently represent such a minor part of the article that they are not denoted as key words for computer searching. We demonstrated that the systematic review appears to be more sensitive than literature searches by computer. We compared systematic review tabulations with librarian-assisted computer database literature searches and found that the computer searches located only 65 percent of relevant articles in a specific set of journals.[19] Although time-consuming and tedious, to remain thorough, reviewing by hand is critical. Once the articles within the sampling frame are reliably obtained, the final step is one of abstracting the data regarding the variables of interest.

The systematic review, by including all quantitative articles, keeps selection bias at a minimum, thus objectively assessing the quantity and quality of studies in a potentially sensitive or controversial area. One such area is the study of religion and health. We had developed the new review method to remain as objective as possible, which humility and researcher openness demands in the quest for new knowledge.

A Systematic Review of Four Psychiatry Journals

Given psychiatry's historical lack of objectivity in assessing and interpreting a patient's religious beliefs and practices, we first focused on psychiatry's research findings as published in the *American Journal of Psychiatry,* the *British Journal of Psychiatry,* the *Canadian Journal of Psychiatry,* and the *Archives of General Psychiatry* from 1978 through 1982. All studies in those journals were first examined to see if they contained quantified data. As noted above, case studies and opinion pieces were thus omitted from the review. We then sought to discover how often and how well the quantified research studies contained a quantified religious variable, defined as a religious variable about which data were collected for a group of subjects. For instance, a religious commitment variable might be a response to a question asking how frequently a person attended religious services.

During that five-year period in those four journals, 3,777 articles were published with 2,348 including quantitative data. Among the quantitative studies, 59, or 2.5 percent included one or more religious measures. In only 3 of the 2,348 studies was a religious variable a central focus of the study.[20] With such a minimal focus in the research literature, sweeping statements about the negative impact of religion could ostensibly appear questionable, unless this five-year time period was unrepresentative of psychiatric research in general. Our view, not yet countered, was that these five years were representative. With so little data, were these negative assertions a result of personal opinion or objective research?

Multidimensional Measures of Religious Commitment

We then looked at the religious measures employed in the studies. Religious commitment is a complex, multidimensional factor, and multiple reliable clusters of questions more accurately address it. Measures that ask about frequency of various religious practices, such as attending religious services, praying, reading scripture, or giving of time or financial resources, help quantify religious activity and involvement. Measures that focus on how important one's religion is personally, such as to what degree God is a source of comfort or strength, or whether one consults a higher power when making personal or health-care decisions, helps to assess another aspect. Other measurement scales help define whether a person's religious commitment might be more "intrinsic" or "extrinsic" to address the complexity of religious dimensions. Intrinsic and extrinsic forms of religious commitment can make a difference in study outcomes. Gordon Allport at Harvard distinguished these concepts:[21]

Extrinsic
The extrinsically religious person uses religion as a means of obtaining status or personal security, for self-justification and for sociability, thus making religion more utilitarian and self-oriented.

Instrinsic
The intrinsically religious person internalizes beliefs and lives by them regardless of outside extrinsic social pressure or other possible personal consequences.

By 1982, nearly three hundred religious commitment questions covering a range of dimensions were available for measuring religious status, including intrinsic and extrinsic religious commitment. In contrast, a far less definitive measure is denomination or affiliation, or even broader population groupings such as "Protestant, Catholic, Jewish, and Other/None." These denominational categories ignore the diverse range of religious devotion and practices within them, much less the personal degree of importance and actual practice an individual may engage in. Employing such measures presumes that each denomination has particular attributes that distinguish it as unique. But, when assumed denominational attributes are not more definitively described by using measures of religious practices, findings concerning denomination are left to the realm of individual impression and inter-pretation. What is truly being measured? Depending on the context, denomination or affiliation may reflect social or ethnic background rather than one's actual beliefs or practices. In fact, when denomina-tion is employed as a measure in clinical studies, most findings indicate a nonsignificant or "neutral" effect, demonstrating its not surprising in-effectiveness as a distinguishing or clarifying measure of religious com-mitment. Consequently, we assessed what types of measures the quan-titative studies containing a religious variable employed.

Our data hunt discovered only a tiny oasis of attention to religious commitment. We found that less than 1 percent of all quantitative studies published in four major psychiatric journals over a five-year period included a religious commitment variable. Of the fifty-nine studies that included a religious variable, thirty-seven measured reli-gious commitment with denomination as the quantified variable, sev-enteen used a religious commitment measure, and five used both types. As for the number of religious items or questions used, most or 83 percent of these fifty-nine studies used a single question, 14 percent used two, and 3 percent used three or more.

Furthermore, only one of the 2,348 quantitative studies identified during this five-year period included a multidimensional religious commitment questionnaire employing measurements that earlier had been statistically tested to assess, for example, the measure's reliability. Only ten studies employed more than one religious question, and sur-prisingly only eight studies that assessed religion cited available, rele-vant research, indicating a lack of familiarity or inquiry into other re-search findings in this or other fields. And again, although a small proportion used more than one measure of religious commit-ment, most used only a single, less preferred measurement—denomination.[22]

This systematic review revealed how infrequently psychiatry actu-ally studied religious commitment. Consequently, the basis of psychia-try's primarily negative views on the impact of religious commitment remained at best highly questionable. Given our initial results, we wondered whether, in the few studies that did include acceptable reli-gious commitment measures, the association with mental health was found to be beneficial, negative, or neutral. As previously noted, we hypothesized the bell-shaped curve with preponderant neutral find-ings, and a few harmful and a few positive findings as well.

To provide the field of psychiatry with a comprehensive review of the findings we conducted a systematic review of the two leading

American psychiatry journals from 1978 to 1989.[23] The study investigated whether positive, negative, or neutral mental health associations were either found, hypothesized, or reported. First, all quantified religious measures were located in the studies published in the *American Journal of Psychiatry* and the *Archives of General Psychiatry* during those years. Measures of denomination were excluded since they were not actually assessments of religious commitment. Remaining measures were categorized into six dimensions.

The review of articles for the twelve years found 139 religious commitment assessments employed in the quantitative studies. Somewhat surprisingly, for only 36 percent (50) of the 139 measures did the studies actually report an association between religious commitment and mental health. No findings were presented for the other eighty-nine, which means that for the majority of the data, they either remained unanalyzed or they were analyzed and not reported. For the fifty measures whose findings were presented, 72 percent were positive associations with mental health, 16 percent were negative, and 12 percent were nonsignificant. This differed widely from the bell-shaped curve we had hypothesized of finding primarily neutral associations. In fact, more than 90 percent of the findings for four out of the six dimensions were found to be beneficial to mental health: participating in religious ceremony, social support, prayer, and relationship with God. Furthermore, these results were substantially more positive than what was concurrently taught in psychiatry residency programs regarding religion and mental health.

The remaining two categories, religious meaning and the indeterminate, which contained ambiguous measures such as "religion" with no further specification, accounted for seven of the eight negative findings and five of the six nonsignificant findings. The fact that the indeterminate, or ambiguous measures, accounted for most of the nonsignificant findings was not surprising. Inadequate measurement is generally associated with unreliability and increased probability of lowering a demonstrated statistical relationship.

"Meaning" appeared to have a greater potential for more negative associations. To clarify this, future studies would need to precisely define and accurately measure aspects of meaning to better evaluate negative as well as positive relationships. For example, one approach would be to compare the clinical associations of persons with high levels of religious meaning and low levels of religious practice. It could be hypothesized that persons who attest to the high meaningfulness of religion or spirituality but do not attend religious services could experience this incongruity as personal conflict, thus resulting in a potentially negative mental health relationship.

Most surprisingly in this review, among most studies where a religious commitment variable was specified, no hypothesis was given. For only 30 (22 percent) of the 139 potential religious-mental health assessments was a hypothesis presented. This deficiency quite probably reflected that a theoretical framework in approaching religious commitment and mental health was still lacking. It demonstrated the need for future researchers to become more intentional about studying religion and spirituality.

Room for Progress

Through these objective, replicable, systematic reviews, findings on the relationship between religious commitment and mental health emerged to be strikingly positive. However, the numbers of research studies remained surprisingly few. This lack of research attention raises questions as to whether scientists are open to objectively investigating the relationship of religious factors to mental health. Our systematic review established that the field of psychiatry, if it hoped to seek scientific objectivity, had a great opportunity before it—to increase the number of quantitative studies that would include religious commitment variables and make new scientific discoveries about what was apparently a somewhat surprisingly generally beneficial clinical factor.

A humble approach would encourage further investigation and objective inquiry. Groundbreaking researchers in this area, psychologists Allen Bergin and Reed Payne termed this situation of minimal attention a "conspiracy of silence":

> It is paradoxical that traditional psychology and psychotherapy, which foster individualism, free expression and tolerance of dissent, would be so reluctant to address one of the most fundamental concerns of humankind—morality and spirituality. In fact, therapeutic efforts have studiously avoided controversy, concerns and needs associated with religion. Regarding this conspiracy of silence, one could accusingly reflect that:
>
> > We speak of wholeness but insist on parts;
> > We value openness but stay partly closed;
> > We like to be accepting but only of some things;
> > It is good to be tolerant, but not of things we don't understand.[24]

Psychiatry seldom addressed spiritual and religious variables in the field's leading journals, reflecting a lack of understanding of the importance of these factors in many patients' lives. Yet the field has since made changes as discussed below.

Reversing a Negative Portrayal of Religious Commitment

A rarely researched topic would provide little grounds for comment, one might assume. However, psychiatry's overlooking the field's published findings became evident in a review of its definitive diagnostic guidebook, *The Diagnostic and Statistical Manual*. The DSM was developed through the consensus of prominent mental health researchers, clinicians, and academicians, and was subjected to numerous field evaluations and reviews before publication. Consequently, the manual is designed to reflect the latest understandings of the mental health field in general and psychiatry in particular, and is used not only by psychiatrists but also by psychologists, social workers, and other mental health professionals. The third edition, revised, of *The Diagnostic and Statistical Manual* (DSM-III-R) contained a glossary that provided definitions and sometimes case examples for the one hundred most widely used technical terms in the manual. This particular edition included forty-five illustrative cases to define terms.

Since psychiatry included religion in empirical research only 2.5 percent of the time, one might presume the field would draw upon religion as an example to the rather infrequent same degree. However, a striking contrast appeared. Of the forty-five examples developed to illustrate technical terms in the glossary, 22 percent had religious content—almost a tenfold increase over the amount of research that included at least a single religious measure. Furthermore, although the published research showed religious commitment as primarily beneficial to mental health, these examples used religion all too frequently to illustrate psychopathology. In addition, in contrast to the numerous examples with religious content, merely two of the forty-five had occupational content, only one had family content and none had ethnic, racial, age, gender, educational, or cultural content. Surprisingly, none of the forty-five included sexual content either, despite psychiatry's substantial sexual Freudian roots.[25]

Psychiatrists responsible for the glossary showed a marked insensitivity to religion, both by disproportionately using it to illustrate psychopathology and by potentially misinterpreting religious language. For instance, the glossary stated the following for the term *delusion:* "If someone claims he or she is the worst sinner in the world, this would generally be considered a delusional conviction" (DSM-III-R, 395). Evidently, the glossary writers were unaware of the expression, the "worst of all sinners" appears in some religious liturgies, as well as in St. Paul's writings in the New Testament. The terms would have been recognized by someone more familiar with religious culture. The expression could also reflect hyperbole, portraying a depth of feeling rather than an exact, concrete rating scale. St. Paul writes in 1 Timothy 1: 15, 16:

> Christ Jesus came into the world to save sinners—of whom I am the worst. But for that very reason I was shown mercy so that in me, the worst of sinners, Christ Jesus might display his unlimited patience as an example for those who would believe on him and receive eternal life.

A person using the expression "worst of sinners" could simply be echoing the words of St. Paul, a highly revered apostle in Christian religious culture.

Lack of familiarity with a culture could cause misunderstanding of any number of expressions or idioms, such as "It's raining cats and dogs." Someone from a non-English-speaking culture hearing the expression for the first time might think it is delusional. How could cats and dogs rain down? However, those who know the expression could recognize that the person might be declaring it's storming outside with intensity—like a raging cat-and-dog fight—rather than claiming to see poodles, Dobermans, collies, Persians, and tomcats falling from the sky. The uninformed would need to clarify what the person means: is it a metaphor or a concrete statement? Sensitivity to the cultural context of the language is key or else a religious expression may be labeled psychopathologic.

To psychiatry's credit, the *American Journal of Psychiatry* published our research team's review of the deficiencies of the DSM-III-R glossary. Furthermore, the next edition, the DSM-IV, removed the many illustrations of psychopathology that were insensitive to religious beliefs and language. By objectively quantifying the degree to which psychiatry had cast religion in a psychopathological light in the glossary on the one hand, and pointing out how rarely the field researched it on the other, this peer-review published article helped promote important and needed change. The field exercised humility in acknowledging its mistake and modifying the next edition of *The Diagnostic and Statistical Manual.*

Divergence in Worldviews

That many psychiatrists lack awareness of religious language could stem from diminished personal interest in religion compared to the general population. For example, according to Gallup poll data, while 6 percent of the U.S. population are atheist or agnostic, 21 percent of psychiatrists and 28 percent of clinical psychologists are atheist or agnostic. Also, while among the U.S. population 72 percent agreed with the statement "My whole approach to life is based on my religion," only 39 percent of psychiatrists and 33 percent of clinical psychologists agreed with a similar statement: "My religious faith is the most important influence in my life."[26]

Consequently, the majority of mental health professionals are dealing with patients whose frequently strong religious views differ from their own. Education can thus play a crucial role in helping these professionals begin to understand the religious culture of the persons they care for.

Addressing this divergence, the American Psychiatric Association Board of Trustees called for greater mental health provider sensitivity in handling patient religious issues in the "Guidelines Regarding Possible Conflicts Between Psychiatrists' Religious Commitments and Psychiatric Practice" in 1990. For example, the guidelines gave an illustration of a devoutly religious man treated by a psychiatrist with a differing view. The psychiatrist denigrated his patient's long-standing religious commitment, calling it "foolishly neurotic." The guidelines noted: "Because of the intensity of the therapeutic relationship, the interpretations caused great distress and appeared related to a subsequent suicide attempt." In contrast, the guidelines underscored that "psychiatrists should maintain respect for their patients' beliefs."[27]

Recognizing the potential divergence in provider-patient worldviews can lead to greater sensitivity in dealing with a patient's religious culture by mental health professionals. This then leads to addressing whether patients receiving medical treatment desire to discuss spiritual or religious concerns in their care.

Religion's Prominence in the General U.S. Public

For more than a half century the Gallup Organization has conducted polling among Americans. During this time, the proportion of Americans who believe in God has remained remarkably constant: 96 percent in 1944 and 95 percent in 1993. Furthermore, 85 percent of Americans consider religion "very important" or "fairly important" in their lives, and 95 percent profess a belief in God.[28] More than 90 percent of Americans want some form of religious education for their children.[29]About 40 percent weekly attend one of the 500,000 places of worship in the United States, including churches, synagogues, and mosques. Another 20 percent attend at least monthly for a total of 60 percent attending monthly or more.[30]

These trends are likely to continue in the next generation, based on a 1992 national Gallup survey of teenagers. Large numbers of American teens believe in God (95 percent), pray alone frequently (42 percent), read scriptures weekly (36 percent), belong to a religion-sponsored youth group, and attend services weekly (45 percent). Somewhat surprisingly, 27 percent of teens consider religious faith more important to them than to their parents.[31]

Are these substantial national figures at all relevant to the medical or health-care arena, or are they merely interesting demographics?

Religious Coping Prevalent among Patients

Since according to this survey data, religion plays a central role in many Americans' lives, do patients want spiritual issues addressed by their physicians? A study published in the *Journal of Family Practice* surveying more than two hundred inpatients found that 77 percent said physicians should consider patients' spiritual needs. Furthermore, 37 percent wanted their physicians to discuss religious beliefs with them more frequently, and nearly one in two, or 48 percent, wanted their physicians to pray with them. However, only 32 percent stated their physician had ever discussed their religious beliefs with them.[32] Similarly, a national survey conducted by *USA Weekend* found that 63 percent of those sampled felt that physicians should talk to patients about their spiritual faith, but only 10 percent of their doctors had done so.[33]

Why might so many physicians be reluctant to ask questions such as "What helps you cope?" or "Does your religious faith or spirituality play a role in your illness?" Why might they hesitate to inquire how the patient might want any spiritual support incorporated into his or her care?

Illness and Spiritual Crisis

Perhaps many physicians remain unaware of the importance of spiritual issues for many patients as they struggle with chronic or serious illness. One study from Duke University Medical Center found that 44 percent of patients believed that religious beliefs are the most important factor in coping with illness, compared to only 9 percent of physicians.[34] Some physicians may feel that a discussion of patients' religious and spiritual beliefs is inappropriate based on a perceived lack of clinical relevance, resulting from their lack of familiarity with the growing clinical research on the impact of religious commitment on health.

In addition to a lack of awareness of its importance, physicians may feel personally uncomfortable with the subject matter or have an understandable reluctance or fear of projecting their own beliefs on patients. Yet, as noted by physicians Timothy Daaleman and Donald Nease in the *Journal of Family Practice*, "Spiritual and religious issues have a place in the physician-patient encounter since they are a component of patient health and well-being."[35] These researchers also found that by taking a spiritual history along with a social and physical history a physician could identify patients most interested and eager to discuss spiritual concerns with their doctors—patients who frequently attended religious worship services. Some 90 percent of patients who attended religious services monthly or more felt doctors should refer to chaplains or clergy, and 68 percent felt a religious evaluation or history should be part of the medical record.

Why do patients so strongly perceive the potential relevance of spirituality to their medical care? A decline in physical health often precipitates a spiritual crisis, notes researcher Harold Koenig of Duke University Medical Center. When serious illness strikes, patients often start to question their purpose in life, the importance or meaning of their work, their personal relationships, and their personal identity, as well as the meaning and purpose of life, or their ultimate destiny. Furthermore, patients hospitalized with severe medical illness face high stress as well, including anxiety about their diagnosis, pain and discomfort from their illness and therapeutic procedures, a sense of isolation, and a potential loss of control over personal activities like eating and sleeping.

Consequently, almost one-half of hospitalized patients experience some degree of clinical depression, found Dr. Koenig. How do some patients handle such stress? In a study funded by the National Institute of Mental Health, nearly 40 percent of seriously ill patients said that religious beliefs or practices were their most important means of handling stress, and over half said they used religious coping such as prayer and scripture reading to a large extent. Other studies discussed below have shown that this religious coping can help prevent depression among the seriously ill, and those who do become depressed recover faster.

How does religious coping help? Dr. Koenig in his study of severely physically ill patients found religious coping helped provide the following:

1. Hope—for a cure, hope they will be able to cope, hope for their families and loved ones, hope for life after death.
2. Control—over their condition because they could pray to God who they believe is ultimately in control.
3. Strength—to cope with their condition.
4. Meaning—to help make sense of their suffering.
5. Purpose, usefulness, and a sense of mission—which help preserve self-esteem in the midst of a stressful, painful, or debilitating illness.[36]

As Foglio and Brody point out, "The family physician who would heal cannot choose whether to confront religious variables in practice; they are operating whether recognized or not."[37] Often when doctors ask patients about these deeper spiritual issues, their patients may tend to trust them more and consequently more openly discuss their symptoms and problems. Medical students have noted that once they started talking with patients about spiritual beliefs and what gives meaning to their lives they established a rapport with them that previously was missing.

Medical Schools Address Clinical Relevance of Spirituality

A further reason physicians have avoided discussing spiritual concerns with patients is lack of clinical training about how to address and manage patients' spiritual issues. In the past, religion was rarely mentioned in medical schools. It was deemed too personal, too nebulous, and of little clinical relevance. However, this lack of attention in medical education has substantially shifted based on the impact of the growing wealth of research findings showing significant clinical relevance, as well as from the support of the John Templeton Foundation's Spirituality and Medicine Curricular Awards. In 1992, only two or three medical schools offered courses on spirituality. By 1999, some sixty-two medical schools now incorporate teaching how to address patients' spiritual concerns, with twenty-seven, including Johns Hopkins, Harvard, Georgetown, Brown, Emory, Vanderbilt, and George Washington having received Templeton Curricular Awards. The research findings, along with discovering sensitive ways to facilitate patients' coping and recovery, have opened up course after course.

Medical Curriculum Components

Key components in the medical school courses have been elucidated by Dr. Christina Puchalski, director of education at the National Institute for Healthcare Research, which oversees the Templeton Curricular Awards. She also serves as director of clinical research and education in the Center to Improve Care of the Dying at the George Washington School of Medicine. These course components include:[38]

1. Teaching students to include a spiritual assessment as part of routine history in a respectful, non-judgmental, and non-imposing fashion.
2. Presenting published research on the role of spirituality and health.
3. Incorporating chaplains and other spiritual counselors as integral members of the health-care team.
4. Assessing problem-based learning cases in which patients' spiritual beliefs are integrated and discussed in addition to the pathophysiological, social, and psychological aspects of cases. Both potential positive and/or negative links and ways to respond are discussed.
5. Communicating effectively and compassionately with chronically ill and dying patients about their suffering, beliefs, and choices for therapy and care. The students learn to continue to care for dying patients even when disease-specific treatment is no longer available.

6. Learning necessary skills to break bad news caringly and compassionately and to use patient beliefs as a clinical resource when appropriate.

7. Encouraging exploration of the students' own belief system and how it might help or hinder the ability to cope with the stress of medicine as well as how it might affect how they care for their patients.

8. Reviewing major religious traditions and specific aspects of religious or cultural traditions that may affect health-care choices and coping.

These components are woven into various medical schools' courses with students becoming more skilled in addressing spiritual concerns and more open to collaborating with hospital chaplains and other members of the health-care team to better address and meet patients' spiritual needs. To assess potential spiritual resources, students learn to take a spiritual history.

Taking a Spiritual History

What might taking a spiritual history entail? In a 1998 seminar for medical students at the national meeting of the American Association of Medical Colleges, Dr. Christina Puchalski suggested using the acronym FICA to structure questions. FICA assesses a potential wealth of a patient's spiritual resources:

Faith and belief: "Do you consider yourself spiritual or religious?" If the patient says yes, the physician can continue with the other questions. If the patient says no, the physician might ask, "What gives your life meaning?" Sometimes patients respond with answers like their family, careers, or nature.

Importance and influence: What importance does your spiritual or religious commitment have in your daily life? Do you like to pray or read scripture? Has your involvement in religious practices changed at all recently? Has it been helpful? Harmful? Does your faith have an influence on how you care for yourself?

Community involvement: Do you belong to a church or synagogue or other religious or spiritual group? How often do you attend? Has there been a recent increase or decrease in attendance?

Address in care: How do you want me to address spiritual issues in your clinical treatment or care? Are there any aspects of your beliefs that might affect your choices of treatment? Is there anything else you would like to tell me about the importance of spirituality in your life?

If patients answer yes to the question of whether they consider themselves spiritual or religious and it is important to them, they often elaborate without further questions. People enjoy talking about themselves, especially aspects of their lives they find important. Asking questions about what gives a person's life meaning can bring compassion back into medical care, providing "touch" to what has become a "high-tech" medical world. Taking a spiritual history can be conducted in a time-efficient manner, and can save time in the long run by discovering potential treatment resources like religious social support on the one hand, or potential clinical problems or roadblocks, such as perhaps a patient's reluctance to take a certain medication.

Dr. John Tarpley, coordinator of the general surgery residency at Vanderbilt Medical School and a 1998 Templeton Curricular Award winner, described why he values taking a spiritual history. He noted that in dealing with oncology patients, he undertakes a nutritional assessment. If his patient is nutritionally depleted in any way, he refers to a nutritional consultant for help. When patients face a crisis such as cancer or surgery, they may not have the spiritual reserves to deal with it, and it would be appropriate to enlist the help of a hospital chaplain. "It's not only acceptable, but better medicine to address the spiritual needs of patients," Tarpley stated at the 1998 Templeton Curricular Awards in Washington, D.C.

In taking a spiritual history, Dr. Puchalski recommends keeping the discussion centered on the patient and working within the patient's frame of reference or religious tradition. It's crucial that physicians not impose their own beliefs—or lack of them—on their patients, she cautions.

In further education efforts, the John Templeton Foundation began in 1997 to award psychiatry residencies for incorporating curriculum in religion and health, with Harvard among those receiving the first awards. A model curriculum guide for addressing spiritual issues based in part on the data from systematic reviews of the mental health research literature has also been developed by a group of psychiatrists from differing faith traditions—Hindu, Buddhist, Jewish, Protestant, Catholic, and Muslim. Now employed in a number of psychiatric residencies, this curriculum effort was also supported by the John Templeton Foundation. A curriculum guide for primary care residencies is under way and should be available in 2000.

This expanded focus in medical school and now residency training education to modify an earlier paradigm by incorporating this previously often forgotten factor in medical care manifests a profound and laudable humility on the part of the medical community to respond to new published research findings. Since it is to be hoped that what is taught in medical school is supported by scientific research, the question of adding a potentially controversial factor such as spirituality must also be investigated, if not supported, scientifically. These research studies are relevant not only in training the next generation of physicians, particularly those revealing high patient need for including spiritual issues in clinical care, but more important, for improving the care and clinical outcomes for those we care for—our patients. What are more of these findings that are leading to a more comprehensive paradigm and new focus in medical care?

Research Findings Published in Medical Journals

Publication in medical journals differs substantially from data highlighted in newspaper or magazine articles. Expert scientists scrutinize research studies before they are accepted for publication. This peer review helps weed out suspect studies that fall short of scientific standards; it helps ensure high-quality, credible research with acceptable research methods. Consequently, when a medical or clinical journal publishes a study, peers or fellow scientists have ascertained that it meets acceptable scientific standards and the findings merit consideration by the medical community.

Peer-reviewed studies published in clinical areas such as recovering from surgery, coping with severe medical illness and major depression, reducing hospital stays, lowering blood pressure, living longer, preventing suicide, and preventing and treating substance abuse are reviewed below. These studies point to spirituality and health as a fertile field for significant new research. Humility provides the impetus for inquiring further into this clinically relevant factor.

Recovery from Surgery
Religious commitment can play a significant role among patients facing surgery. As a Dartmouth Medical School study cited earlier found,

a consistent predictor of who survived heart surgery was the strength of a patient's religious commitment. In this study of 232 patients, those who said they derived no strength or comfort from their religious faith had almost three times the risk of death at the six-month follow-up as patients who found at least some strength. None of the deeply religious had died, compared to 12 percent of those who rarely or never went to church.

But are these enhanced survival rates among those with a stronger religious commitment merely the result of increased social support that might stem from belonging to any social organization, whether a church or other group? This study looked at both religious commitment and participation in organized groups and found both have a role to play, but have differing effects. Of the thirty-seven patients who described themselves as deeply religious, none had died at the six-month follow-up. Only 4 percent of the patients who engaged in organized groups such as "local government, a church supper group, a senior center, or historical society," had died compared to 14 percent of the uninvolved. Patients active in both areas had the best clinical outcomes. Those who found strength and comfort in their faith and were also socially involved in their communities were fourteen times more likely to remain alive at least six months after surgery. When appropriate, encouraging both types of activities promotes health with religious commitment the stronger predictive factor of survival in this study.[39]

Similarly, a study of heart transplant patients at the University of Pittsburgh found that those with strong beliefs and who participated in religious activities showed more improved physical functioning at the twelve-month follow-up. Furthermore, the more religiously active complied better with their medical regimen, had higher self-esteem, and experienced diminished anxiety and fewer health worries.[40]

Another study of elderly women recovering from hip fractures by our research team at Northwestern University Medical School also found patients' religious commitment enhanced recovery. Women with the best surgical outcomes were those to whom God was a strong source of strength and comfort and who frequently attended religious services. Testing showed they were less depressed and could walk down the hall farther at discharge then patients who lacked a strong religious commitment. In essence, the significance of their faith lowered their risk of depressive symptoms and aided them in better handling a very stressful medical event.[41]

Reduced Medical Costs

Enhanced recovery not only diminishes personal suffering, but can lead to potential lower costs for Medicare and Medicaid. Elderly men hospitalized for heart surgery had 20 percent shorter postoperative stays if they had a strong religious commitment.[42]

Similarly, a study of older medical patients admitted to Duke University Medical Center for a variety of serious physical illnesses found that patients with some religious link reduced hospital stays by more than half. Those with no religious affiliation spent an average of twenty-five days in the hospital compared to eleven days for patients who did have a religious affiliation. Controlling for other clinical predictors that could prolong the hospital stay, patients who attended religious services weekly or more were also 43 percent less likely to have been hospitalized in the previous year. Those admitted had briefer stays than patients who attended religious meetings less often, when controlling for factors like age, physical functioning, and severity of illness.[43]

Finding a factor like religious commitment that can cut both frequency and length of hospital stays among the elderly has potentially substantial cost-saving benefits, the study noted. Nationally, people age sixty and over enter the hospital twice as often as do younger adults. These elderly already account for almost 50 percent of all short hospital stays, even a decade before the seventy-six million baby boomers start reaching age sixty-five. In addition, Medicare costs have skyrocketed from $38 billion in 1980 to $170 billion in 1995, according to the American Hospital Association. The future will also see another wave of elderly needing care. Generation Y, today's American young people born since 1979, number 77.6 million, outstripping the 76.8 million baby boomers born from 1946 to 1964.

"It is clearly premature to suggest that high utilizers of health services be encouraged to join and participate in a religious community or suggest that those who attend church more frequently be granted special health insurance rates," the study's authors commented. Yet, they concluded:

> Nevertheless, given the demographic and economic trends that are facing this nation, the apparent relationship between religious involvement and use of hospital services, and the widespread availability of and low cost of religious community participation, it behooves . . . healthcare organizations to take a closer look at the relationship between religious activity and use of health services.

Why might a patient's religious link help slash stays? Religion may help people cope more effectively and thus hasten recovery from medical illness. In addition, the more religious seem to experience less depression than those who are less religious, which may also help cut stays. "Studies indicate that persons who are depressed or anxious use more health services," the researchers stated. In one study, older depressed medical inpatients had double the length of stay compared to those without depression. A growing number of studies are revealing that religiously active persons are less likely to become depressed and recover faster from depression if it occurs. Enhanced coping by drawing from spiritual resources could help shrink stays.

Coping with Serious Illness

Coping with Cancer

A diagnosis of a life-threatening illness like cancer thrusts patients into a maelstrom of concerns and fears. To discover how to better meet the needs of cancer patients, a University of Michigan research team surveyed 108 women undergoing treatment for various stages of gynecological cancer. What helps these women cope and what do they expect from their doctors? Some 93 percent of these cancer patients said their religious lives helped them sustain their hopes. Another 75 percent said religion had a significant place in their lives, and 41 percent noted that their religious lives supported their sense of worth. Almost half—49 percent—felt they had become more religious after having cancer.

"Somewhat surprisingly, not one patient noted becoming less religious since being diagnosed with cancer," the researchers commented.

Regarding their relationship with doctors, 96 percent of the patients wanted "straight talk" about their illness. Fear of pain seized most, so they wanted information on potential pain management as soon as receiving the diagnosis. As for their need for physician caring, some 64 percent evaluated their doctors by the compassion they showed. Based on these findings, the researchers concluded that responsive care for cancer patients would include compassionately providing frank information about the illness, educating the patients on pain relief, maximizing patient comfort and dignity, and supporting the patients in their religious coping.[44]

Coping with AIDS

Hearing the diagnosis of HIV infection can also plummet patients into a trajectory of despair. Yale University School of Medicine surveyed ninety HIV-positive patients about their fear of death, end-of-life decisions, religious status, and guilt about HIV infection. They found that those who were religiously active had less fear of death and may have better coping skills than nonreligious patients. Fear of death was more likely among the 26 percent of patients who felt their disease was some form of punishment (17 percent felt it was punishment from God). Fear of death diminished among patients who read the Bible frequently, attended church regularly, or stated that God was a central part of their purpose in life. Those patients who believed in God's forgiveness were more likely to engage in discussions about resuscitation status, indicating that their religious beliefs played at least some role in helping them face how they wanted to handle their death.

"HIV infection challenges the deepest belief that HIV-positive patients have," the researchers noted. As their data revealed, "Belief in a God who forgives and comforts may signify an ability to accept HIV infection or premature death."[45]

Coping with a Chronically Ill Child

One of parents' greatest worries is having illness strike their child. When illness lingers and becomes chronic, the anxiety easily grows and can stress all family members. Such long-term stress can lead to changes in family roles and patterns of intimacy, social isolation, and marital stress as well. How parents cope with a child's chronic illness can influence not only their own levels of distress, but also the social and personal adjustment of their child and his or her siblings.

A study of 102 parents with chronically ill children looked at how parents used various coping resources—religious, familial, personal, financial, social, and health care—both before the child became ill and then to meet the needs of caring for their chronically ill child.

The researchers found that "if religion is not serving patients' coping needs, then other areas may suffer." Among families without satisfactory religious resources, other resources such as extended family and financial reserves paid a higher toll. The authors added: "In other words, parents whose current religious practices met their needs in coping with their child's illness were more likely to require little or no change in familial, financial, and social coping resources." They concluded: "Religion and coping are meaningfully interconnected."[46]

Coping with Medical Concerns—Prayer as an Indicator

If prayer is believed by patients to have potential coping effects, then likely it will increase in times of need. This indicates again the clinical importance of taking a spiritual and religious history to learn how patients cope and to what extent they are using these coping mechanisms currently. A rise in how often patients pray may indicate a heightened concern relevant to medical care.

A study of more than 250 pregnant African American and Hispanic mothers in Galveston, Texas, found that although 48 percent of the mothers prayed daily for their developing babies, the mothers who prayed the most for their babies experienced poorer health either just prior to becoming pregnant or during their pregnancy. Healthier mothers prayed less often for their babies. These findings persisted after controlling for self-rated religious commitment, age, marital status, and years of education.

Consequently, inquiring not only about frequency of religious practices in general, but about whether these practices have increased or declined in recent months or during a particular time of treatment, may serve as another clinical indicator of potential medical concerns that could be further addressed by physicians.

Unfortunately, some clinicians, especially in mental health fields in the past, may have misinterpreted frequent prayer by suggesting that since the patient has a problem and he or she is praying often, the prayer must be the problem. Rather the more frequent prayer could also indicate an attempt to draw upon spiritual resources in an attempt to better handle a physical or emotional health problem the patient is concerned about. Humility urges us to look beneath the surface to uncover patient beliefs and concerns.

Recovery

In addition to prevention of disease, religious commitment in some instances enhances recovery from illness.

Faster Recovery from Depression among the Medically Seriously Ill

Depression often strikes older patients hospitalized for medical illness. While major depression afflicts only 1 percent of older adults living in the community, the figure rises to a much larger 10 percent among medically ill hospitalized elderly and to 35 percent or more among those suffering with less severe types of depression. Often these depressions persist long after treatment of the medical illness. Most of these depressions probably result from the suffering, physical disability, and loss of control the hospitalized elderly encounter as a result of their physical illness. Besides impairing quality of life, depression appears to delay recovery from physical illness, lengthen hospital stays, and potentially increase the occurrence of other clinical problems and even increase risk of death.

Researchers from Duke University Medical Center investigated whether coping resources such as religious commitment might help patients recover faster from their depression. They used multidimensional measures, including questions about frequency of religious attendance, private religious activities like prayer or Bible study, as well as Hoge's ten-item validated scale to measure intrinsic religious commitment. As noted previously, intrinsic religiousness pertains to the extent to which patients take their religious beliefs to heart as one of the major motivating factors in their decisions and behavior.

The study sample included eighty-seven depressed older adults hospitalized with medical illness. The course of their depression was tracked for almost a year. To the greater extent a patient's religious commitment was a central motivating force in their lives, the faster they recovered from depression, the study found.

"For every 10-point increase in intrinsic religiosity score, there was a 70 percent increase in speed of remission," the researchers noted. This effect remained after controlling for multiple demographic, psychosocial, physical health, and treatment factors.

Curiously, unlike in a number of other studies on religious commitment and health, frequency of church attendance or personal devotional activities did not significantly show a link with the health outcome—in this case, more rapid recovery from depression. This was true despite the fact that both church attendance and private religious activities were strongly related to intrinsic religious commitment. But, as demonstrated here, they are not the same. Consequently, had the researchers used only those two frequency-of-participation questions, no effect on a recovery from depression would have been found. This underscores the importance of using appropriate, multi-item measures, not merely single items such as religious attendance, and thus, for example, including an intrinsic-extrinsic measure to more fully and accurately assess links between religion and health.

"Religious beliefs and behaviors are commonly used by depressed older adults to cope with medical problems and may lead to faster resolution of some types of depression," the researchers stated. "Psychiatrists should feel free to inquire about and support the healthy religious beliefs and activities of older patients with disabling physical health problems, realizing that these beliefs may bring comfort and facilitate coping."[47]

Faster Recovery from Depression by Adding Religious Content in Therapy for Religious Patients

In another study of religion and depression, an intervention drawing upon personal spiritual resources also hastened recovery. Among religiously committed patients suffering from depression, those receiving religiously oriented cognitive behavioral therapy had better scores on measures of both post-treatment depression and clinical adjustment than those whose therapy omitted religious content.

This study utilized a highly creative research design, since patients cannot be randomized to becoming religious or not. Instead, this design randomized religious patients to receiving two different types of therapy—religious or nonreligious—from two different types of therapists—religious or nonreligious. Patients were thus assigned to four different treatment groups. Patients in one group received cognitive therapy without religious content from a religious therapist. Patients in the second received cognitive therapy without religious content from a nonreligious therapist. The other two groups gave cognitive therapy with religious components, one with therapy provided by a religious therapist, the other treated by a nonreligious therapist. The two groups using the religious components had the most effective treatment outcomes—whether the therapist was religious or not.[48]

These findings supported an earlier observation by researchers Bergin and Jensen that for the more than 70 percent of the population for whom religious commitment is a central life factor, "secular approaches to psychotherapy may provide an alien values framework": "A majority of the population probably prefers an orientation . . . that is sympathetic, or at least sensitive, to a spiritual perspective. We need to better perceive and respond to this public need."[49] Drawing upon a patient's spiritual resources within the patient's religious framework thus can help enhance recovery.

Prevention

Besides serving as a strong factor in coping and recovery, studies also show that religious commitment plays an imposing role in the prevention of physical disease. It may help improve immune functioning, as cited earlier, reduce the risk of high blood pressure, and overall enhance chances of living longer. Furthermore, religious commitment can protect against emotional disorders involving self-destructive behaviors like suicide and substance abuse. Part of the reason for disease reduction and potentially longer life may be the healthier lifestyle choices persons with a strong religious commitment might make, such as avoiding smoking or alcohol. Choosing healthier behaviors in itself stands as an important contribution religious commitment can make in enhancing health. But healthy choices alone fail to fully account for religious commitment's links with health. In a number of studies, even when these healthy behaviors are controlled for, the health links with a strong religious commitment remain.

Preventing High Blood Pressure

Cardiovascular disease remains the number one killer in the United States. Nearly one-third of all Americans suffer from some form of high blood pressure. Even a relatively small decrease in an individual's diastolic blood pressure by two millimeters to four millimeters if generalized to a national basis could significantly reduce cardiovascular disease by 10–20 percent.

A recent community survey undertaken by researchers at Duke University of nearly four thousand people aged sixty-five years and older found that people who both attended religious services at least once a week and prayed or studied the Bible at least daily had consistently lower blood pressure than those who did so less frequently. Regular participants in these religious activities were 40 percent less likely to have diastolic hypertension, which is the type of blood pressure placing one at higher risk of heart attacks and strokes. These findings remained after taking into account age, gender, race, education, and other variables that could affect outcomes. The study also found that the associations between religious involvement and measures of blood pressure were stronger in blacks than in whites and in the "younger older" people—those aged sixty-five to seventy-five—than in those over seventy-five.[50]

These findings confirm the findings of previous studies investigating the relationship between religious commitment and blood pressure, even when taking into account lifestyle factors. In the old paradigm, researchers hypothesized that the religious effects may be "nothing but" a healthy lifestyle. Does religious commitment remain as a significant health factor once unhealthy habits are controlled for?

In a study of white men who smoked—a risky lifestyle behavior—our research team discovered that smokers who both attended religious services weekly and rated their religion as important to them were seven times less likely to have abnormal pressures than the smokers who had no interest in religion. This difference could not be explained by simply avoiding risky lifestyles such as the unhealthy behavior of smoking. Furthermore, those smokers who attended religious services weekly or more but did not rank their faith as highly important were still four times less likely to have abnormal diastolic pressure. These results indicated that the two factors—attendance and personal importance of one's religion—showed the greatest protection against abnormal blood pressure, also underscoring the need for multidimensional measures to identify what aspects of religious commitment might contribute the most to healthier lives.[51]

Previously, Levin and Vanderpool surveyed epidemiological research and found nearly twenty studies published over thirty years examining religious factors and blood pressure. In those studies examining religious commitment—measures of frequency of attendance or religious attitudes—all but one found an association with lower blood pressure or lower rates of hypertension. The authors concluded: "Hypertension is a common and serious problem which appears to be mitigated by religion."[52]

Longevity

Factors predicting greater survival have become an important focus in epidemiologic research. When investigating what psychosocial factors contribute to living longer and when studying large numbers of people through community surveys over time, religious commitment stands out as a potentially important factor. As cited earlier, at the twenty-eight-year follow-up in a study of 5,286 people in Alameda County, California, persons who attended religious services weekly or more were 25 percent less likely to die than infrequent attenders.[53] Not only were frequent attenders likely to live longer, once they began to attend church they also made healthier choices, becoming more apt to quit smoking, increase exercising, expand social contacts, and stay married over time. Thus, these health-enhancing behaviors of the religiously committed helped to contribute to their lower death rates. The researchers noted that, in addition to attending religious services, "improved health practices, increased social contacts, and more stable marriages occurring in conjunction with attendance" contributed to the lower mortality rates.

Could these findings be explained by the interpretation that those in better health are more likely to attend church? On the contrary, the study found that persons "with significant impairment in mobility were in fact more likely to be frequent attenders."

Recently our research team undertook a meta-analysis to examine the association of religious commitment and death by any cause. After an extensive literature search, we found more than forty studies that together represented nearly 126,000 people. Most of these studies used only a single-item measure of religious commitment, usually one of the following : (1) religious attendance, (2) self-rated personal importance of religion, or (3) strength and comfort derived from religion. If the studies had employed more than one measure, the findings in these studies may have showed even stronger outcomes in the link between lower death rates and religious commitment. Consequently, the odds ratios found were probably conservative estimates.

The statistical meta-analysis that rigorously summed the results in these studies found that the odds of dying for people who scored higher on measures of religious commitment was about 29 percent lower compared to the odds of dying for people who scored low during a specified multiyear follow-up period.[54] Based on these findings, the lack of religious involvement stands out as a potential health risk for earlier death to the same degree as heavy alcohol consumption, exposure to organic solvents in the workplace, and hostility.

Furthermore, studies in this analysis that followed peoples' lives for the longest periods of time and had the oldest participants at follow-up found the strongest links between religious commitment and longevity. Controlling for other relevant variables that might contribute to earlier death failed to eliminate the link of religious commitment and longer life. Our research team concluded:

> Religious involvement has a non-trivial favorable association with all-cause mortality. The magnitude of this association appears to be on the same order of other behavioral and psychological variables such as hostility and alchohol use. . . . The preponderance of the associa-

tion appears to be substantive, perhaps mediated by factors such as social support, marital longevity, and sustained physical health.

Other studies have similarly shown the protective effect of religious commitment, especially among the elderly. For instance, a well-designed study of an elderly population living in the vicinity of New Haven, Connecticut, found that those with a strong religious commitment were twice as likely to remain alive two years later.

In this study, age, marital status, education, income, race, gender, the person's health, and previous hospitalizations were all controlled for. After two years of follow-up, the less religious had mortality levels twice those of the more religious.[55]

With consistent strong findings like these, a humble approach would seek to launch further research, focusing perhaps on at-risk populations and adding religious items or even better, religious measures such as intrinsic and extrinsic items to uncover how developing spiritual beliefs, practices, and resources might help protect people from earlier death.

Suicide Prevention

Surging suicide rates plague adolescents. In the United States, one in seven deaths among those fifteen to nineteen years of age results from suicide. Suicide rates in this age group have soared 400 percent from 1950 to 1990, according to the National Center for Health Statistics (NCHS). One study of 525 adolescents found that religious commitment significantly reduced risk of suicide.[56] Adolescent suicide has also been linked to depression. Another study of adolescents found that frequent church attenders with high spiritual support had the lowest scores on a depression screening instrument, the Beck Depression Inventory. Those high school students of either gender who infrequently attended church and had low spiritual support had the highest rates of depression, often at clinically significant levels.[57]

How significantly might religious commitment prevent suicide? One large-scale study found that persons who did not attend church were four times more likely to kill themselves than were frequent church attenders.[58] Stephen Stack found that the rate of church attendance predicted suicide rates more effectively than any other evaluated factor, including unemployment.[59] He proposed several ways in which religion might help prevent suicide, including enhanced self-esteem and moral accountability or responsibility to God. Religious commitment can provide a unique source of self-esteem through a belief that one is loved and created by God. Given that low self-esteem may contribute to suicidal thoughts, the self-esteem derived from one's religious commitment could play an important role in deterring suicide.

In addition, many religions believe in a holy God who responds caringly to human needs. The beliefs in justice, an afterlife, and the possibility of accountability for taking one's own life may play a relevant role in reducing the appeal of potentially self-destructive behavior.

In the face of these compelling findings, researchers who continue to omit the significance of religious commitment may miss an important factor, necessitating a more humble approach to enlarging one's clinical paradigm. Reseachers evaluating suicide assessment instruments recently observed that, "although religion is noted as a highly relevant factor in suicide literature, the number of religious items included on assessment scales approaches zero."[60] These researchers noted the need to begin to recognize and include religion in suicide prevention, treatment, and care. Delving into this research with a humble, open mind in order to develop new measurement tools that include an assessment for lack of spiritual commitment, linked with a greater risk for suicide, would better serve both patients and mental health professionals in potentially improving mental health care.

Prevention and Improved Treatment of Drug Abuse

The lack of religious commitment also arises as a potential risk factor for drug abuse, according to published studies. Benson reviewed nearly forty studies documenting that people with stronger religious commitment are less likely to become involved in substance abuse.[61] This confirmed a review by Gorsuch and Butler who found that lack of religious commitment stood out as a predictor of those who abuse drugs:

> Whenever religion is used in analysis, it predicts those who have not used an illicit drug regardless of whether the religious variable is defined in terms of membership, active participation, religious upbringing or the meaningfulness of religion as viewed by the person himself.[62]

Loch and Hughes surveyed almost 14,000 youths and found that an analysis of six measures of religious commitment and eight measures of substance abuse showed that religious commitment was linked with less drug abuse. In this study, the measure of "importance of religion" to the person was the best predictor in indicating not substance abusing. The authors believed the results implied "that the controls operating here are deeply internalized values and norms rather than . . . fear . . . or peer pressure."[63]

Not only can religion help prevent drug abuse, but developing and drawing upon spiritual resources can also make an important difference in enhancing drug treatment. For instance, 45 percent of participants in a religious treatment program for opium addiction were still drug free one year later compared to only 5 percent of participants in a nonreligious public health service hospital treatment program.[64] More drug treatment studies are needed.

Given the continually escalating substance abuse rates in the United States, taking a second look at the research on religious commitment and drug use and better integrating it into prevention and treatment programs might help mitigate this challenging and quite costly societal and medical problem.

Prevention and Improved Treatment of Alcohol Abuse

As well as reducing use of illicit drugs, religious involvement similarly predicts fewer problems with alcohol.[65] Studies reveal that persons lacking a strong religious commitment are more at risk of abusing alcohol. Also, religious involvement tends to be low among people diagnosed for treatment for alcohol abuse.[66] In an earlier study of the religious lives of alcoholics, our research team found that 89 percent of alcoholics had lost interest in religion during their teenage years, whereas among the community control group, 48 percent had increased interest in religion and 32 percent had remained unchanged.[67] Alcoholics often report having had negative experiences with religion and seem to hold concepts of God that are punitive, rather than loving and forgiving.[68]

Furthermore, a relationship between religious commitment and the nonuse or moderate use of alcohol has been documented. Amoateng and Bahr state that whether or not a religious tradition specifically teaches against alcohol use, those who were active in a religious group consumed substantially less alcohol than those who were not active.[69]

Even after alcoholism has taken hold, religion may be an important force in achieving abstinence. Alcoholics Anonymous invokes a higher power to help alcoholics recover from addiction. Those who participate in AA are more likely to remain abstinent after inpatient or outpatient treatment.[70]

Smoking Prevention

Currently, more than one-quarter of all Americans smoke regularly. Most begin as teenagers or young adults, and about a third of smokers quit by the time they reach sixty-five. What might help smokers kick the habit or, better yet, help prevent people from lighting up in the first place?

An important community-based study of smoking and religious activity in older Americans found that the lifelong, strongly religious are much more likely never to have smoked at all. Furthermore, the elderly who actively participate in their religious faith were nine times less likely to smoke, discovered researchers at Duke University Medical Center. Among those older adults who did smoke, the number of cigarettes smoked per day sank significantly among the more religiously active.

Frequently attending religious services stood out as the most important religious factor linked with less smoking in this study. Private study of scripture and prayer didn't show nearly as strong a link. Watching religious TV or listening to religious radio had no connection to smoking reduction.[71]

Not only potentially effective in prevention, religious involvement has also been found to be associated with higher success rates in smoking cessation treatment, findings in other studies indicate.[72]

Potential Harmful Effects Linked with Religious Commitment

A comprehensive scientific examination of the instances in which religion may have deleterious effects on physical and mental health is needed. How might abusive, manipulative, punitive, and condemning religion adversely affect health? The tragic events in Waco, Texas, and Jonestown stand out as prime examples of certain religious sects becoming not only harmful but also fatal to their adherents. What characterizes these sects, and how can people avoid their death-giving rather than life-giving messages?

Also, medical ethics come into play regarding some religious denominations' teachings. For instance, Jehovah's Witnesses refuse blood transfusions. Do physicians allow Jehovah's Witnesses to refuse blood transfusions for their children—who are minors and therefore not making decisions for themselves—or do physicians seek a court order when they feel a child's life is at stake?

Even within conventional religious traditions, what aspects of religious commitment tend to be more health-producing than others? Some studies on anxiety and fear of death show that persons who are extrinsically religious, but not intrinsically, have higher rates of anxiety than persons who have either internalized their faith or rejected religion completely.[73] This contrasts with persons with a strong religious commitment who have lowered death anxiety, an important factor to explore for those with serious or life-threatening illness.

When God is seen as condemning and punitive, rather than forgiving, what are mental health outcomes? How can hospital chaplains or clergy become better involved to help in instances of spiritual distress that may arise if a person's religious commitment appears to be hindering rather than helping treatment and recovery? Further investigation remains warranted.

Systematic Reviews Reveal Opportunity to Expand Research

Medical research stands poised on the brink of further humble investigation of the impact of what research has demonstrated can be a highly beneficial factor in preventing, coping, and enhancing recovery from illness—a strong religious or spiritual commitment.

Finally, to map out where to focus future research attention, research teams have begun conducting systematic reviews in various medical fields to assess how frequently and how well religious commitment has been addressed to date. Findings of systematic reviews of quantitative research published in leading journals will be discussed for family medicine, adolescence, mental health nursing, and psychology, similar to the method of the systematic review of psychiatry research discussed earlier.

Family Medicine

The field of family medicine often considers health and illness within physical, social, emotional, and even spiritual contexts. Has the field more adequately addressed the role of religious commitment and health in the research literature? In order to see how often and how well religious variables were considered and what type of measurement was used, our research team undertook a systematic review of all articles published in the *Journal of Family Practice* from 1976 to 1986.

In family medicine, only 3.5 percent of the articles that analyzed any data contained a quantified religious variable—only 1 percent higher than psychiatry. A total of 1,086 studies were reviewed. Some 603 (55 percent) measured at least one quantified variable, and 468 of those measured at least one psychosocial variable. Of the 468 studies, only 21 measured at least one religious variable. However, in contrast to psychiatry, family medicine did employ religious commitment measures most of the time, about 60 percent, rather than merely including measures of denomination. Yet, as with psychiatry, in only one case did it use state-of-the-art, pretested, multidimensional measures of religion.[74]

We then analyzed these studies to see if religious commitment was harmful, neutral, or beneficial to health. Results implying a beneficial link between spiritual commitment and health were almost three times as frequent as evaluations implying a harmful relationship in the sixty-four religious variables. The dimensions of social support, ceremony and relationship with God were positive in twenty-one cases and neutral in three with no negative relationships found. Denomination's sixteen results were all neutral, which is not surprising since denomination describes religious demographics and not levels of religious commitment. Meaning references had the most negative associations with five out of nine associations found. Similarly, for the category "unclear," four out of six associations were also negative. As in the psychiatry systematic review, the results for "unclear" were also not surprising since one is uncertain exactly what the study variable is measuring.[75]

This systematic review, the second we performed after undertaking one in psychiatry, also found that the field had a long way to go in improving methodology with the need to include reliable religious or spiritual commitment measures. Nevertheless, as in psychiatry, when religious commitment measures were even simply defined and assessed, the studies found generally preponderantly positive links with health.

Adolescence

At what level stands the field of adolescent research in recognizing the clinical relevance of religious commitment? Are there certain at-risk behaviors for which greater research attention to religious commitment could reduce risk or enhance care?

A systematic review of quantitative studies published in five leading adolescent journals between 1992 and 1996 revealed that 109 out of 922 articles (nearly 12 percent) included a measure of religious commitment. This more than fivefold increase compared to psychiatry journals suggests that adolescent researchers are more sensitive to the role of religious factors in physical and mental health. Furthermore, regarding quality, in almost half the studies investigating religion, two or more measures of religious commitment were used as opposed to only a single measure. These findings indicate that adolescent studies also tend to have improved methodologies in the assessment of spiritual and religious commitment.[76]

Research further indicates that religious commitment can help teens reduce risky behaviors like alcohol and drug use, delinquency, premature sexual involvement, unsafe sexual behaviors, and suicide. Thus, it is important for this field to continue in its study of this quite relevant factor.

Mental Health Nursing

Similar to adolescence journals, a systematic review of quantitative studies in three mental health nursing journals from 1991 to 1995 found that 31 of 311 studies (roughly 10 percent) included a measure of religious commitment, substantially higher than in psychiatry journals. Also, almost 40 percent of these used two or more questions to assess religious commitment, also a step ahead in measurement compared to psychiatry.[77]

Nursing has a history of recognizing and affirming the importance of religion and spirituality that stands in marked contrast to the negative attitudes toward religion previously promulgated by psychiatry and psychology. Florence Nightingale taught that spirituality was intrinsic to human experience and compatible with scientific inquiry.[78] Furthermore, since 1988 "spiritual distress" has been an official nursing diagnosis.

In addition, nurses have been much more likely to receive training in spiritual-religious issues than other mental health professionals. In a 1990 national sample, 60 percent of registered nurses said spiritual care issues had been addressed to some degree in their training. Two other 1990 surveys had found only 5 percent of psychologists had spiritual issues addressed in training while only 18 percent in psychiatry residencies received such training. With the recent changes in medical school curriculum and psychiatry residencies that percentage should grow.

Psychology

The lack of research in psychology to date on the relationship between mental health and religion provides an opportunity to humbly launch further investigation in a very important field. A systematic review of seven major American Psychological Association journals from 1991 to 1994 found that only 2.7 percent—or 62 out of 2,302 quantitative studies—contained a religious variable. In most cases—about 80 percent—measures consisted of only a single religious question. These findings suggest that psychology lacks an empirical literature foundation that can enable a scientific evaluation of the beneficial, neutral, or harmful effects of religion.[79]

In the 1992 Centennial Address before the American Psychological Association the distinguished Yale University psychologist Seymour B. Sarason lamented the absence of "transcendence" in modern psychology. He presented what he observed as a negative prejudgment of religion among many of his peers:

> I think I am safe in assuming that the bulk of the membership of the American Psychological Association would, if asked, describe themselves as agnostic or atheistic. I am also safe in assuming that any one or all of the ingredients of the religious world view are of neither personal nor professional interest to most psychologists. And there are more than a few psychologists who not only have difficulty identifying with any of those ingredients but who also regard adherence to any of them as a reflection of irrationality, of superstition, of immaturity, of neurosis. Indeed, if we learn that someone is devoutly religious, or even tends in that direction, we look upon that person with puzzlement, often concluding that that psychologist obviously had or has personal problems.[80]

Further empirical research could better inform psychology's premises. Humbly acknowledging and expanding the peer-reviewed research findings could widen understanding to recognize potential religious commitment benefits as well as potential harm. The very low rate of original research that considers a religious variable, usually measured with a single question, within mainstream psychology remains inconsistent with the historical leadership psychology researchers have offered to the social sciences in sensitivity to important, salient, personal, or social influences. As a result, substantial, exciting opportunities remain for the field to humbly expand the paradigm and investigate the link between spirituality and mental health.

Conclusion

In the midst of medicine's quest to discover more effective ways to enhance health, spiritual and religious commitment stands out as a clinically relevant factor. An active religious commitment can help prevent illness, enhance recovery, and assist patients in coping with the suffering and disability that illness inflicts. Empirical research scrutinized through the scientific peer-review process in the medical and clinical literatures has provided rather substantial and consistent findings that a strong religious commitment can generally reap beneficial health results.

Expansion of the medical paradigm already spans more than half of U.S. medical schools that incorporate curriculum on taking a patient's spiritual history alongside a psychosocial history and physical exam. Young physicians trained in this new approach will begin to recognize this important factor—both when it helps and when it harms—and will learn how better to incorporate it in the care of their patients.

Furthermore, the research findings in medicine can kindle curiosity and encourage previously resistant fields to better scientifically examine this factor in academic honesty. As Sir John Templeton writes in *The Humble Approach*, "Without humility we will not be wide-eyed and open-minded enough to discover new areas for research." Findings like these can spark clinical fields to enlarge their empirical knowledge and improve clinical care by investigating links between religious and spiritual commitment and physical and mental health, as well as aid in facing social challenges like drug and alcohol abuse. For a field to remain open and objective, opportunities await for further researching this promising, but nearly forgotten, health factor.

Notes

1. Sir John Marks Templeton, *The Humble Approach: Scientists Discover God* (New York: Continuum,1995), 10.
2. Kimberly A. Sherrill and David B. Larson, "The Anti-Tenure Factor in Religious Research in Clinical Epidemiology and Aging," in *Religion in Aging and Health*, ed. Jeffrey S. Levin (London: Sage,1993), 155.
3. Dale A. Matthews and David B. Larson, "Faith and Medicine: Reconciling the Twin Traditions of Healing," *Mind/Body Medicine*, 2.1 (1997): 2–3.

4. Dale A. Matthews, Michael E. McCullough, David B. Larson, Harold G. Koenig, James P. Swyers, and Mary G. Milano, "Religious Commitment and Health Status: A Review of the Research and Implications for Family Medicine," *Archives of Family Medicine* 7 (1998): 118–24.

5. David B. Larson and Susan S. Larson, *The Forgotten Factor in Health: What Does the Research Show?* (Rockville, Md.: National Institute for Healthcare Research, 1994).

6. David B. Larson, James P. Swyers, and Michael E. McCullough, eds., *Scientific Research on Spirituality and Health: A Consensus Report* (Rockville, Md.: National Institute for Healthcare Research, 1998).

7. Thomas E. Oxman, D. H. Freeman, and E. D. Manheimer, "Lack of Social Participation or Religious Strength and Comfort as Risk Factors for Death after Cardiac Surgery in the Elderly," *Psychosomatic Medicine* 57.1 (1995): 5–15.

8. W. J. Strawbridge, R. D. Cohen, S.J. Shema, et al., "Frequent Attendance at Religious Services and Mortality over 28 Years," *American Journal of Public Health* 87.6 (1997): 957–61.

9. Harold K. Koenig, H. J. Cohen, et al., "Attendance at Religious Services, Interleukin-6, and Other Biological Parameters of Immune Function in Older Adults," *International Journal of Psychiatry in Medicine* 27.3 (1997): 233–50.

10. David B. Larson and Mary G. Milano, "Making the Case for Spiritual Interventions in Clinical Practice," *Mind/Body Medicine* 2.1 (1997): 20–30.

11. Thomas S. Kuhn, "The Structure of Scientific Revolutions," *International Encyclopedia of Unified Science*, ed. Otto Neurath, vol. 2 (Chicago: University of Chicago Press, 1970), 1–210.

12. Sigmund Freud, "Obsessive Actions and Religious Practices," in *The Standard Edition of the Complete Works of Sigmund Freud*, vol. 9 (London: Hogarth Press, 1959), 126–27.

13. Group for the Advancement of Psychiatry, "Mysticism: Spiritual Quest or Mental Disorder," in D. Lukoff, F. Lu, and R. Turner, "Toward a More Culturally Sensitive DSM-IV: Psychoreligious and Psychospiritual Problems," *Journal of Nervous and Mental Disease* 180 (1992): 673–82.

14. Albert Ellis, "Psychotherapy and Atheistic Values," *Journal of Consulting and Clinical Psychology* 48 (1980): 635–39.

15. Carl J. Jung, "Psychotherapies on the Clergy," in *Collected Works*, vol. 2, 2d ed. (1969), 327–47.

16. J. R. Foglio and H. Brody, "Religion, Faith, and Medicine," *Journal of Family Practice* 27.5 (1988): 473–74.

17. David B. Larson, Kimberly A. Sherrill, and John S. Lyons, "Neglect and Misuse of the R Word: Systematic Reviews of Religious Measures in Health, Mental Health, and Aging," in *Religion in Aging and Health,* ed. Jeffrey S. Levin (London: Sage, 1993), 178–95.

18. Richard J. Light and David B. Pillemer, *Summing Up: The Science of Reviewing Research* (Cambridge, Mass.: Harvard University Press, 1984).

19. J. C. Bareta, D. B. Larson, J. J. Zorc, and John S. Lyons, "A Comparison of the MEDLARS and Systematic Review of the Consultation-Liaison Psychiatry Literature," *American Journal of Psychiatry* 147 (1990): 1040–42.

20. D. B. Larson, E. M. Pattison, D. G. Blazer, A. R. Omran, and B. H. Kaplan, "Systematic Analysis of Research on Religious Variables in Four Major Psychiatric Journals, 1978–1982," *American Journal of Psychiatry* 149 (1986): 329–34.

21. G. W. Allport and J. M. Ross, "Personal Religious Orientation and Prejudice," *Journal of Personality and Social Psychology* 5 (1967): 432–43.

22. Larson et al., "Systematic Analysis of Research."

23. D. B. Larson, K. A. Sherrill, J. S. Lyons, F. C. Craigie, S. B. Thielman, M. A. Greenwold, and S. S. Larson, "Dimensions and Valences of Measures of Religious Commitment Found in the *American Journal of Psychiatry* and the *Archives of General Psychiatry*: 1978 through 1989," *American Journal of Psychiatry* 149 (1992): 557–59.

24. A. E. Bergin and I. R. Payne, "Proposed Agenda for a Spiritual Strategy in Personality and Psychotherapy," *Journal of Psychology and Christianity* 10.3 (1991): 197–210.

25. D. B. Larson, S. B. Thielman, et al., "Religious Content in the Diagnostic and Statistical Manual, Third Edition-Revised, Appendix C: The Glossary of Technical Terms," *American Journal of Psychiatry* 150 (1993): 1884–85.

26. A. E. Bergin and J. P. Jensen, "Religiosity of Psychotherapists: A National Survey," *Psychotherapy* 27 (1990): 3–7.

27. American Psychiatric Association Board of Trustees, "Guidelines Regarding Possible Conflict between Psychiatrists' Religious Commitment and Psychiatric Practice," *American Journal of Psychiatry* 147.4 (1990): 542.

28. G. H. Gallup, *Religion in America: 1992–1993* (Princeton, N.J.: Gallup Organization, 1993).

29. D. R. Hoge, "Religion in America: The Demographics of Belief and Affiliation," in *Religion and the Clinical Practice of Psychology* (Washington, D.C.: American Psychological Association, 1996), 21–41.

30. G. H. Gallup, *Religion in America: 1996* (Princeton, N.J.: Gallup Organization, 1996).

31. G. H. Gallup and R. Bezilla, *The Religious Life of Young Americans* (Princeton, N.J.: George Gallup International Institute, 1992).

32. D. E. King and B. Bushwick, "Beliefs and Attitudes of Hospital Inpatients about Faith, Healing, and Prayer," *Journal of Family Practice* 39 (1994): 349–52.

33. Tom McNichol, "The New Faith in Medicine," *USA Weekend,* April 5–7, 1997, 4–5.

34. H. G. Koenig, L. B. Bearon, M. Hover, et al., "Religious Perspectives of Doctors, Nurses, Patients and Families," *Journal of Pastoral Care* 45 (1991): 254–67.

35. Timothy P. Daaleman and Donald E. Nease, "Patient Attitudes Regarding Physician Inquiry into Spiritual and Religious Issues," *Journal of Family Practice* 39.6 (1994): 564–68.

36. Harold G. Koenig, "Use of Religion by Patients with Severe Medical Illness," *Mind/Body Medicine* 2.1 (1997): 31–43.

37. Foglio and Brody, "Religion, Faith, and Medicine," 473.

38. Christina M. Puchalski and David B. Larson, "Developing Curricula in Spirituality and Medicine," *Academic Medicine* 73.9 (1998): 970–74.

39. Oxman, Freeman, and Manheimer, "Lack of Social Participation."

40. R. C. Harris, M. A. Dew, A. Lee, et al., "The Role of Religion in Heart Transplant Recipients' Long-Term Health and Well-Being," *Journal of Religion and Health* 34.1 (1995): 17–32.

41. P. Pressman, J. S. Lyons, D. B. Larson, and J. J. Strain, "Religious Belief, Depression, and Ambulation Status in Elderly Women with Broken Hips," *American Journal of Psychiatry* 147.6 (1990): 758–60.

42. E. McSherry, M. Ciulla, S. Salisbury, and D. Tsuang, "Spiritual Resources in Older Hospitalized Men," *Social Compass* 35.4 (1987): 515–37.

43. Harold G. Koenig and David B. Larson, "Use of Hospital Services, Religious Attendance, and Religious Affiliation," *Southern Medical Journal* 91.10 (1998): 925–32.

44. J. A. Roberts, D. Brown, T. Elkins, and D. B. Larson, "Factors Influencing Views of Patients with Gynecological Cancer about End-of-Life Decisions," *American Journal of Obstetrics and Gynecology* 176.1 (1997): 166–72.

45. L. C. Kaldijian et al., "End-of-Life Decisions in HIV-Positive Patients: The Role of Spiritual Beliefs," *AIDS* 12.1 (1998): 103–7.

46. Carolyn M. Rutledge, Jeffrey S. Levin, David B. Larson, and John S. Lyons, "The Importance of Religion for Parents Coping with a Chronically Ill Child," *Psychology and Christianity* 14 (1995): 50–57.

47. H. G. Koenig, L. K. George, and B. L. Peterson, "Religiosity and Remission of Depression in Medically Ill Older Patients," *American Journal of Psychiatry* 155.4 (1998): 536–42.

48. L. R. Propst, R. Ostrom, P. Watkins, T. Dean, and D. Mashburn, "Religious Values in Psychotherapy and Mental Health: Empirical Findings and Issues," *Journal of Consulting and Clinical Psychology* 60 (1992): 94–103.

49. Bergin and Jenson, "Religiosity of Psychotherapists."

50. H. G. Koenig et al., "The Relationship between Religious Activities and Blood Pressure in Older Adults," *International Journal of Psychology in Medicine* 28.2 (1998): 189–213.

51. D. B. Larson, H. G. Koenig, B. H. Kaplan, R. S. Greenberg, E. Logue, and H. A. Tyroler, "The Impact of Religion on Men's Blood Pressure," *Journal of Religion and Health* 28.4 (1989): 265–78.

52. J. S. Levin and H. Y. Vanderpool, "Is Religion Therapeutically Significant for Hypertension?" *Social Science Medicine* 29.1 (1989): 69–78.

53. Strawbridge et al., "Frequent Attendance at Religious Services and Mortality over 28 Years."

54. Michael E. McCollough, David B. Larson, William T. Hoyt, Harold G. Koenig, and Carl Thoresen, "Religious Involvement and Mortality: A Meta-Analytic Review," *Health Psychology* 19.3 (2000): (in press).

55. D. M. Zuckerman, S. V. Kasl, and A. M. Ostfeld, "Psychosocial Predictors of Mortality among the Elderly Poor," *American Journal of Epidemiology* 119 (1984): 410–23.

56. D. Stein, E. Witztum, D. Brom, A. K. DeNour, and A. Elizur, "The Association between Adolescents' Attitudes toward Suicide and Their Psychosocial Background and Suicidal Tendencies," *Adolescence* 27.108 (1992): 949–59.

57. L. S. Wright, C. J. Frost, and S. J. Wisecarver, "Church Attendance, Meaningfulness of Religion, and Depression Symptomatology among Adolescents," *Journal of Youth and Adolescence* 22.5 (1993): 559–68.

58. G. W. Comstock and K. B. Partridge, "Church Attendance and Health," *Journal of Chronic Disease* 25 (1972): 665–72.

59. S. Stack, "The Effect of Religious Commitment on Suicide: A Cross-National Analysis," *Journal of Health and Social Behavior* 24 (1983): 362–74.

60. N. C. Koehoe and T. G. Gutheil, "Neglect of Religious Issues in Scale-Based Assessment of Suicidal Patients," *Hospital and Community Psychiatry* 45.4 (1994): 366–69.

61. P. Benson, "Religion and Substance Use," in *Religion and Mental Health*, ed. J. F. Schumaker (New York: Oxford University Press, 1992), 211–20.

62. R. L. Gorsuch and M. C. Butler, "Initial Drug Abuse: A View of Predisposing Social Psychological Factors," *Psychological Bulletin* 3 (1976): 120–37.

63. B. R. Loch and R. H. Hughes, "Religion and Youth Substance Use," *Journal of Religion and Health* 24.3 (1985): 197–208.

64. D. P. Desmond and J. F. Maddox, "Religious Programs and Careers of Chronic Heroin Users," *American Journal of Drug and Alcohol Abuse* 8.1 (1981): 71–83.

65. P. H. Hardesty and K. M. Kirby, "Relation between Family Religiousness and Drug Use within Adolescent Peer Groups," *Journal of Social Behavior and Personality* 10.2 (1995): 137–42.

66. D. A. Brizer, "Religiosity and Drug Abuse among Psychiatric Inpatients," *American Journal of Drug and Alcohol Abuse* 19.3 (1993): 337–45.

67. David B. Larson and William P. Wilson, "Religious Life of Alcoholics," *Southern Medical Journal* 73.6 (1980): 723–27.

68. R. L. Gorsuch, "Assessing Spiritual Values in Alcoholics Anonymous," in *Research on Alcoholics Anonymous: Opportunities and Alternatives*, ed. B. S. McCrady and W. R. Miller (New Brunswick, N.J.: Rutgers Center for Alcoholic Studies, 1993), 301–18.

69. A. Y. Amoateng and S. J. Bahr, "Religion, Family, and Adolescent Drug Use," *Psychological Perspectives* 29 (1986): 53–73.

70. H. A. Montgomery, W. R. Miller, and J. S. Tonigan, "Does Alcoholics Anonymous Involvement Predict Treatment Outcome?" *Journal of Substance Abuse Treatment* 12.4 (1995): 241–46.

71. H. G. Koenig et al., "The Relationship between Religious Activities and Cigarette Smoking in Older Adults," *Journal of Gerontology: Medical Sciences* 53A.6 (1998): M1–M9.

72. C. C. Voorhees, F. A. Stillman, R. T. Swank, et al., "Heart, Body, and Soul: Impact of Church-Based Smoking Cessation Interventions on Readiness to Quit," *Preventive Medicine* 25.3 (1996): 277-85.

73. M. Baker and R. Gorsuch, "Trait Anxiety and Intrinsic-Extrinsic Religiousness," *Journal for the Scientific Study of Religion* 21.2 (1982): 119–22.

74. F. C. Craigie, I. Y. Liu, D. B. Larson, and J. S. Lyons, "A Systematic Analysis of Religious Variables in the *Journal of Family Practice, 1976–1986*," *Journal of Family Practice* 27.5 (1988): 509–13.

75. F. C. Craigie, Jr., D. B. Larson, and I. Y. Liu, "References to Religion in the *Journal of Family Practice:* Dimensions and Valence of Spirituality," *Journal of Family Practice* 30.4 (1990): 477–80.

76. Andrew J. Weaver, Judith A. Samford, Virginia J. Morgan, Alex Licton, David B. Larson, and James Garbarino, "An Analysis of Research on Religious Variables in Five Major Adolescent Research Journals: 1992–1996" (accepted for publication, *Journal of Nervous and Mental Disease*).

77. Andrew J. Weaver, Laura T. Flannely, Kevin J. Flannely, Harold G. Koenig, and David B. Larson, "An Analysis of Research on Religious and Spiritual Variables in Three Mental Health Nursing Journals, 1991–1995," *Issues in Mental Health Nursing* 19 (1998): 263–76.

78. J. Macrae, "Nightingale's Spiritual Philosophy and Its Significance for Modern Nursing," *Image: Journal of Nursing Scholarship* 27.1 (1995): 8–10.

79. Andrew J. Weaver, Amy E. Kline, Judith A. Samford, Lea Ann Lucas, David B. Larson, and R. L. Gorsuch, "Is Religion Taboo in Psychology? A Systematic Analysis of Research on Religious Variables in Seven Major American Psychological Association Journals: 1991–1994," *Journal of Psychology and Christianity* 17.3 (1998): 220–32.

80. S. B. Sarason, "American Psychology and the Need for Transcendence and Community," *American Journal of Community Psychology* 21 (1993): 185–202.

10
Artificial Intelligence

FRASER WATTS

Few scientific topics raise such fundamental religious issues as artificial intelligence (AI). Perhaps only cosmology has such far-reaching implications, but the issues raised by cosmology have been extensively discussed, whereas those relating to artificial intelligence have been relatively neglected. Whereas cosmology bears on doctrines about creation, AI bears mainly on doctrines of human nature. It is an interesting matter why some areas of science raise large religious issues, while others (chemistry, for example) seem not to do so. I will suggest that it is those areas of science in which worldviews or ideologies are prominent that have most contact with religion.

In considering scientific work on AI, it will be important to distinguish the scientific work itself from the rather grandiose claims with which it is often, though not necessarily, associated. It is these grandiose claims that sometimes bring AI into conflict with religious insights; if AI is pursued in a more humble spirit, the sense of conflict disappears. Because of the grandiosity that often surrounds AI, religious thinkers have often seemed to be threatened by it; the question posed about AI is the negative one of how far it constitutes a threat to religious insights. I will suggest that, although that question needs to be discussed, it is important to move beyond the rather negative approach that it represents. I would like to see theology approaching AI in a humble spirit, not asking whether AI is a threat, but asking how theology can enter into constructive dialogue with AI and what it can learn from it.

The Aims of AI

Before considering the religious issues raised by artificial intelligence, it would be wise to see what scientists working in this area are trying to achieve. Recent decades have seen enormous strides in the development of AI, and its implication can be divided into the practical and the theoretical. At the practical level, computers are revolutionizing industrial production, and most writers these days use a word processor. Much computer technology is developed for strictly practical purposes, and any theoretical significance it may have is incidental.

Alongside this there has been a more basic scientific enterprise of using the computer as an aid to understanding the human mind. Much work has been done on programming computers to simulate various mental functions. Computer programs provide a precise mode of theorizing. For example, to program a computer to perform the same kind of logical reasoning as people do forces scientists to put their ideas about human reasoning in a clear form. The computer simulation of human thinking has thus, at the very least, been a stimulus to a more precise form of theorizing in the scientific study of human cognition.

AI also produces cognitive theories that are testable in a new kind of way. When you have programmed a particular mental function on a computer you can run the program and see how the results match up against human performance. At this point there needs to be a to-and-fro between careful observation of the performance of people and computers, and this is a feature of the best scientific work in the field. Unfortunately, many scientists working on AI know more about computers than they do about people, and when that happens work on the computer simulation of human thinking gets derailed. The "tail starts to wag the dog"; or rather the computer, which was supposed in this context to be an aid to the scientific study of human intelligence, sets the agenda and takes over the enterprise.

Testing how well computer and human mental functions match each other is actually a rather subtle business. In doing logical reasoning, for example, people make mistakes. There is a lot to be learned about how people think from watching to see exactly what kind of mistakes are made. If the programming has been done well, and the computer really is doing things in the same way as people, it will make exactly the same kind of mistakes, and for the same reasons. That is quite a stringent scientific test to apply.

There is no need, so far, to make any particularly strong assumptions about how close the overall similarity may be between a computer and the human mind. You just need to assume that it is possible to simulate at least some mental functions on a computer. The basic assumption is that the analogy between minds and computers is close enough to be able to get started on this business of the computer simulation of intelligence, but you don't need to make any strong assumptions at the outset about how close the analogy will turn out to be. You can take a "try it and see" approach. Even if the analogy turns out to be less close at some points than you originally hoped, you will probably have learned quite a lot about human minds by pressing the analogy to the limits and finding out what the dissimilarities are.

What I have described so far might be called the "humble" approach to artificial intelligence. Up to this point, there is nothing that raises any particular philosophical problems, and nothing that should worry people who have a religious view of the human person. I have deliberately started in this uncontroversial way because I want to set my face firmly against the idea that what goes on in AI is at best worthless, and at worst the work of the devil. Most scientists concerned with AI work in the kind of modest, exploratory way that I have indicated so far. What they do is not controversial, from either a philosophical or a religious point of view.

The AI Creed

However, there are people working in AI who *do* make very strong claims for the scope and potential of what they are doing, claims that often go under the name of "strong AI." The creed of strong AI is essentially twofold: (1) that it will eventually be possible to capture *all* aspects of human intelligence in computer form, and (2) that the human mind is, to all intents and purposes, just a computer program.

The first claim is about the future, and it consists of a strong prediction about what computers of the future will be able to do; that is, they will be able to perform all intelligent activities. As the part of theology that deals with beliefs about the future is called eschatology, we can call this part of the AI creed "eschatological." The other claim is about what the human mind really is; namely, it is like a computer. Note that this is not a straightforward descriptive statement about the human mind, certainly not something that you could check out by making the necessary scientific observations. It is a more basic assumption about the nature of mind, what philosophers would call a "metaphysical" assumption.

In the creed of strong AI, the belief that the human mind is essentially a computer (the metaphysical claim) supports the vision of the future in which computer intelligence will match or exceed human intelligence (a kind of AI eschatology). Generally these two claims go together, though there is probably no necessary connection between them. Theologians, of course, understand a lot about how metaphysics and eschatology support each other in religious thinking. In Christian thinking, the metaphysical belief that the world is essentially God's supports the eschatological belief that his kingdom will eventually be established. It is intriguing to find metaphysics and eschatology supporting each other in similar ways in the quasi-religious AI creed.

The first general comment to make on the strong AI creed is that it floats some way above the actual day-to-day scientific work done in the field. Some scientists working on AI would hold this creed; others would not. I submit that it makes very little difference to their actual scientific work whether or not they are adherents of this grand vision of AI. Indeed, in many cases you probably could not tell from their actual scientific work whether or not they subscribe to it. Equally, the strong AI creed is in no sense a conclusion from scientific research. There is sometimes a tendency to assume that all the claims made by scientists are the result of their research, but in fact many of them are basic preresearch assumptions. The strong AI creed is that kind of basic assumption, rather than a scientifically justified conclusion from research. So far as I can see, the creed of strong AI is neither a necessary assumption of AI research, nor a conclusion from it.

There is something instructive here. I know of no scientific research that raises any theological problems, though there are many views that are commonly held by scientists that raise such problems. Note that it is not the actual research, but the more general worldviews that clash with religious beliefs. This is not surprising as scientific worldviews are often quasi-religious themselves; they are ideological rather than straightforwardly scientific. It seems to me enormously important in trying to maintain clear lines of communication between science and religion to keep a careful watch on this distinction between empirical research and scientific worldviews.

The Scope of AI: Where Are the Limits?

Let us look first at predictions about the future of AI. Given the track record of AI so far, does it seem likely that computers will eventually be able to simulate all intelligent activities? Bold predictions about the potential of computer intelligence have been around since the beginning of modern AI in the 1960s. Partly there have been specific predictions, such as that within so many years a computer would be able to do some particular thing, for example, play chess so well that it would have the status of a grand master. Partly there have been more general claims that *any* intelligent activity could eventually be programmed.

One of the key issues here is what one means by an "intelligent" activity. What is clear is that any rule-based intelligent activity can be programmed into a computer. Once the rules that underpin some particular intelligent activity are understood, it is a mere technical task to write the program. The problem arises over how far human intelligence is rule-based. It may be, but the rules are often not easy to discern. For example, it is now clear from empirical research that when people do reasoning tasks, they are not following the rules of formal logic.

One very obvious point about the track record of delivering on these predictions is that progress has always been slower and more difficult than was expected.[1] It was a long time, for example, before chess programs became really successful. Now they are. Real progress is being made, and it is no part of my purpose here to deny it, but there has been a consistent tendency to underestimate the problems. Computers are now, of course, enormously more powerful than in the early days, and a great deal cheaper. There is an impressive technological success story here, but the scientific success story of capturing human intelligence in computer form has not been quite so good.

Indeed, it is tempting to say that there are certain *kinds* of intelligent activity that computers will never be able to simulate. I am a little wary of that view, because there are signs that at least some progress is being made, even with the more difficult things. It has been tempting, for example, to say that computers can't learn, that they can only do what they have been programmed to do. But that would no longer be quite correct. Computers can, in effect, be programmed to reprogram themselves on the basis of experience. Again, it is tempting to say that they could never be creative, but there are some forms of musical composition that computers can be programmed to do, and it is not yet clear what the limits are to computer creativity. So, we need to be very careful about pontifications of the form "computers could never . . ." We could well be proved wrong.

Nevertheless, there are some things that seem such major challenges for computers that we simply don't know how to tackle them, and perhaps never will. We don't know how to give a computer the kind of fluid intelligence that would enable it to work out from scratch how to solve a problem quite unlike anything it had ever encountered before. We also don't know how to program it to recognize when the boundaries of a particular rule-governed activity have been transgressed. For example, if a computer is giving someone nondirective counseling, which it can do reasonably convincingly, it simply cannot recognize when its interlocutor breaks off the counseling and switches to some other kind of conversation.

Also, we don't know how to give computers feelings. We can program some aspects of emotion. Computers can recognize when a particular kind of emotional reaction, such as anger, would be appropriate. They could even be programmed to utter angry sentences through their voice box, and perhaps even to do angry things, like scrambling your data. However, we have no idea how to get them to *feel* anger.

At this point, some people are inclined to redefine emotions in such a way that computers *could* have them. However, I am not impressed by people who say that there is nothing more to anger than the components computers *can* replicate. Angry feelings, on any commonsense view, are an essential part of what we mean by anger. Neither am I impressed by the argument that you can never know what another person is feeling, and that, for all we know, computers may be feeling angry. It is true that there is never absolute certainty about other people's feelings, but there are reasonable grounds for assuming that people have feelings and that present-day computers don't.

In correspondence that followed an article I once published in the *Tablet,* the computer scientist Edmund Furse claimed that prayer was an intelligent activity, and so computers could be programmed to pray. It is a problem rather like programming emotions. They could perhaps be programmed to recognize when a particular kind of prayer is appropriate, thanksgiving, confession or whatever. They could no doubt be programmed to compose prayers. Prayers are, after all, a fairly predictable, rule-governed "art form." They could also utter prayers using a voice box. It seems to me, however, that they do not have the kind of inner life that would allow us to say that they really were praying. There is much more to praying than simply formulating and uttering prayers.

Minds and Persons

This brings us to the metaphysical part of the strong AI creed, that the human mind is essentially a computer program. The idea is that minds can be defined in terms of the "functions" they perform, and that the ways in which those functions are carried out in minds and computers are essentially the same. In one case the program runs on the brain; in the other it runs on silicon, but the programs are essentially the same in each case.[2]

However, there are some key differences between people and computers. One is that, when we think and talk, we know what we are referring to; our concepts relate to things in the world. Even when computers are successfully manipulating symbols in a way that is passably similar to human thought, they don't know how their symbols relate to the world. This shows up in translation, for example. In a sentence such as "The box was in the pen," it is very difficult to decide which of the two meanings of "pen" applies in this context without knowing what in the real world the sentence refers to.

One famous way of making the point that computers lack knowledge of what their symbols refer to is due to the philosopher John Searle.[3] Imagine a room in which you are alone. You are being asked questions in Chinese, which are passed in to you, and you have to pass answers in Chinese out again. The problem is that you know no Chinese. However, it is not an impossible situation. You could be supplied with a massive and complex set of rules that enabled you to get from a question to an appropriate answer without understanding anything about what the Chinese symbols meant.

Searle's point is that this is essentially how computers work. The rule books correspond to the programming of the computer. The fact that correct answers can be arrived at in no way implies that you understand them. In fact, a computer is in the same situation as you would be in if you understood no Chinese. Neither you nor the computer would know what in the world the symbols related to, what they actually meant. This is not what ordinary human thought is like. We *do* know what our words refer to. Sometimes it seems to be suggested that the Chinese room parable shows that computers do not understand, but all it really shows is that successful performance does not necessarily presuppose understanding. There have been many attempts to refute this argument,[4] though none of them seems wholly convincing. The fact that there are many different refutations in circulation perhaps makes the point that none of them really works.

A central problem with seeing states of mind as equivalent to computational states is that doing so involves looking at them in such an abstract way, removed from the actual context in which they occur. No two human beings have the same history, and even when they hold what appear to be the same beliefs, their different histories can't be entirely ignored. To take the ultimate religious example, the statement "I believe in God" could never be defined in a completely abstract way that left out the different resonance that a statement of belief had for each person of a different background. Yet that is what is assumed by the equation of mental and computational states.

Many of the problems with AI seem to rest on a mistaken and simplistic idea of how human intelligence works, and I suggest that radical advances in AI now depend on understanding better how people think. That, in turn, could lead to consideration of how computers might emulate such thinking. One of the clearest statements I know of this radical approach to AI is by William Clocksin, a computer scientist at the University of Cambridge who also happens to be an ordained minister in the Church of England. Clocksin calls for a "social constructionist" approach to AI that recognizes that "an individual's intelligent behaviour is shaped by the meaning ascribed to experience, by its situation in the social matrix, and by the practices of self and relationship into which its life is recruited."[5]

Central to Clocksin's understanding of human intelligence is the role of narrative. We understand ourselves and all our experience in relation to narratives. Indeed, human action is itself a kind of narrative. In our actions, we are telling a story about ourselves. An approach to AI that was based on this understanding of the key role of narrative in human intelligence would no longer see intelligence as the manipulation of symbols relating to arbitrary and externally defined problems. Clocksin's vision of an AI of the future that saw intelligence as narrative would be very much more congenial from a religious point of view, partly because in recent years theologians have also come to realize how much theology is a narrative process. The Bible is essentially telling a narrative about the actions of God. Indeed, to understand anything in religious terms involves placing it in the context of a religious narrative.

There are thus serious problems with the view that human minds and (present-day) computers are essentially the same. In saying this I am not doubting that the analogy between minds and computers has been scientifically fruitful. It has sharpened our thinking about human minds

and has helped to make technological advances in computer programming. It is a big step, however, to go from the idea that there is a useful analogy between minds and computers to saying that they are essentially the same. Whether computers of the future become more like the human mind depends on how far it is possible to make progress with the view of narrative intelligence that Clocksin has outlined.

Computers and Consciousness

Perhaps the key issue about the analogy between computers and the human mind is whether computers could be conscious, as we are. In considering this, it will be helpful at the outset to try to clarify what we mean by "consciousness." Like many terms that become the focus of fierce debate, it has a range of different meanings, and there is a danger of arguments arising from using the same word to mean different things. I will follow here a helpful classification of the meanings of consciousness set out by Copeland.[6]

First, there is a baseline meaning in which an organism is said to be conscious if it has sensory experience of the world and can perform some kinds of mental activity. It is an important property of human beings that we are conscious in this minimal sense, but it does not raise any particularly controversial issues. There is also no particular problem about claiming an equivalent to this kind of sensory consciousness for computers, especially robotic computers,

Next, more interestingly, there is consciousness in the sense of monitoring our experience, or knowing that we know something. Car drivers who find that they have been driving on "autopilot" know that you can register information and respond to it appropriately without being "consciously" aware of doing so. Recently, there have been some intriguing scientific demonstrations of this kind of thing as in the phenomenon of "blindsight." Sometimes, after a brain operation, people have a particular part of their visual field in which they have no awareness of seeing. What is remarkable is that, even without any conscious experience of seeing, they can "guess" the location of a point of light with such accuracy that they clearly are registering it at some level. They might be said to be conscious of it in the first, minimal sense, but not in this second sense of knowing what they know.

Computers can go some way toward simulating this reflective consciousness about what they know. It is perfectly feasible in principle to construct a self-describing computer—a hierarchical computer that monitors what it "knows." However, as Philip Johnson-Laird points out, this falls short of human self-reflection. The crucial additional step is that the self-description be used as a model in guiding its interaction with the world; this is also possible in principle for a robotic computer. However, even such a computer would lack conscious *experience*, which brings us to Copeland's last sense of consciousness.

There is, third, consciousness in the sense of having the subjective "feel" of something. We know what it is like to be us, to have our experience of color and pain and so on. We don't know for sure what it is like to have other people's experiences, though we assume they are something like ours. We certainly don't know, as Thomas Nagel famously argued what it would be like to be a bat.[7] Philosophers often talk about these "feely" properties of experience as *qualia*. As I have already argued, it is an aspect of consciousness that seems especially important in emotion. Indeed, without it, we would be reluctant to say that someone actually had an emotion. Also, much of psychotherapy is concerned with expanding the range of potentially threatening things that people experience in a "feely" way rather than simply know about. Nevertheless, this last "feely" meaning of consciousness is the most controversial theoretically. There are many, such as Dan Dennett, who think this aspect of consciousness is something of a mirage, and that the problems associated with explaining *qualia* scientifically are pseudoproblems.[8]

Although there is currently enormous scientific interest in consciousness, this conceals a serious disagreement about how important it actually is. For a long time, behaviorist psychology ignored all mental activity completely. Even when behaviorism gave way to cognitive psychology, however, there remained a wariness about consciousness. Sometimes this took a strategic form, along the lines of "We are not ready yet for big questions like consciousness; let's work on some more basic questions about mental life for now, and see where we get to Other people took a more dogmatic stand that consciousness was ply not important; they said that it was relatively inciden human beings were conscious and that consciousness, a nomenon," served no essential function. This provid theoretical defense for approaches to the study of human cognition that left consciousness to one side. The modeling of the human mind in computer form cannot easily simulate consciousness, and the popularity of computational modeling in recent years is probably one practical reason cognitive scientists have been attracted to the argument that consciousness is not fundamentally important.

This is one of the few points in philosophical debates about consciousness at which scientific evidence becomes relevant. The indications are that it actually does make a difference whether we become conscious of something. There are many ways of making this argument.[9] In the therapeutic field, accessing a previously repressed memory is often decisive in leading to personal change. It is also clear, in various forms of cognitive therapy, that carefully controlled exercises involving thinking about or imagining the subject of particular preoccupations can bring about significant, measurable change. Becoming conscious of something in our environment probably allows us to adapt our behavior more rapidly and effectively than if we were not aware of it. Sometimes being conscious of something is more hindrance than help. For example, consciously worrying about something when we go to bed is likely to delay the onset of sleep. Most generally of all, those who think that consciousness makes no difference have to respond to the argument that it is unlikely that consciousness would have evolved at all if it had no function.

Powerful as these kinds of argument are, they are not decisive. It is still possible to accept that there is a distinct functional value in states of consciousness, but to resist the conclusion that it is the consciousness itself that gives them that value. Perhaps states of consciousness correspond to a particular kind of brain state, and it is the brain state rather than its correlate in conscious experience that has functional value for us. I do not see how this argument can be finally refuted, but it is manifestly a highly speculative position that currently has no direct scientific support.

These different kinds of "conscious shyness" are still around, though I believe that the tide is going out on them. Certainly, there is a growing body of experimental research that takes consciousness seriously.[10] There are many strands to the current scientific interest in consciousness. In psychoanalysis, the exploration of the borderline between the conscious and the unconscious has been a key focus of theoretical and practical interest. Within cognitive psychology, now that it has extricated itself from behaviorism, there is considerable interest in the paradoxes of consciousness, such as how it is possible to be conscious of something by one criterion but not by another. Brain scientists have become intensely interested in how consciousness arises within the physical structure of the brain. Within evolutionary thinking, attention is being given to how and why consciousness evolved.

In AI, the computational modeling of consciousness represents one of the greatest challenges. Johnson-Laird, for example, recognizes that conscious cognitive processes probably proceed rather differently from nonconscious ones.[11] Conscious thought, as we all know from introspection, is couched in symbols, usually words or pictures. However, it seems that nonconscious cognition proceeds in a different kind of code. If this is right, one of the big challenges for any computational theory of mind is how to capture these two kinds of code, and the transformations between them. There is overwhelming evidence that remembering something involves reconstructing it, not just bringing it within the spotlight of consciousness, and in this human memory is quite unlike computer memory. Modeling the transformations that take place when material is accessed in consciousness is perhaps one of the key challenges that now face computational theories of mind. There is no reason in principle that scientific progress should not be made with this enterprise, though it is not likely to be quick. Even if it were successful, it would be an entirely different question whether a computer in which these cognitive processes had been successfully modeled would actually be conscious. I think that is highly unlikely.

Some people may feel frustrated with the approach to the question of whether computers could achieve consciousness on the basis if what is likely in the future, given what current computers can do. It may be tempting instead to look for an argument of principle that will settle the matter. The most interesting argument of this kind comes from an application of Kurt Gödel's theorem, and claims that computers could never achieve consciousness.

Gödel's theorem is basically a theorem about mathematics, and it states that there could never be a sound system of mathematics that enabled us to prove all the propositions of ordinary arithmetic. About that, there is no dispute. The question is whether it has implications for human beings and AI. The most enthusiastic current advocate of the relevance to AI of Gödel's theorem is Roger Penrose, who believes that it shows that consciousness could not be computable, just as arithmetic is not mathematically provable.[12] Other people, and I am inclined to agree with them, think that this is just too big an extrapolation from mathematics to people to be convincing.[13] However, the arguments are complex and rigorous, and not easily dismissed.

Brains and Bodies

The philosophical argument about whether the mind is essentially a computer continues to run in the way that philosophical arguments do tend to run and run. Meanwhile, on the ground, or at least back in the

labs, things have been moving on. The hard-line view that mind is essentially a computer program and that it makes no difference whether it runs on the biological stuff of the human brain or in a silicon computer is definitely on the way out.

Recent years have seen an upsurge of interest in how the physical structure of the human brain affects the way we think. This has led in turn to a great deal of interest in finding ways of programming computers so that they are more like the human brain in how they do things. Considerable progress has been made in developing this new generation of more biologically realistic computers, and this has brought about advances in what computers can do. In particular, we now have computers that are much better able to learn than the computers of ten years ago. On the one hand, this has probably fueled the fantasy that computers will eventually be able to do everything. However, the metaphysical support for this confidence, based on the assumption that it was irrelevant that the human mind ran on a biological brain, is being cut away.

The key technical change in programming computers in a more biologically realistic way has been the move from a sequential approach in which one operation is carried out at a time, to a parallel approach (parallel distributed processing, PDP) in which multiple operations are carried out simultaneously in a massively interconnected network that in some way resembles a network of neurons, an approach to programming known as "connectionism."

However, there is disagreement about how biologically realistic this connectionist approach to programming is. There are some, such as Gerald Edelman, who has been at the forefront of asserting the importance of the physical human brain in human cognition, who have been rather dismissive of it, saying that a connectionist computer is really nothing like the brain.[14] He has a point. This approach to programming is just a first pass at getting something biologically realistic. No doubt, having set out down this road, we will gradually get better at it. The important thing is perhaps the great change in intellectual climate involved in taking the physical brain seriously. As someone who thinks it is important, both philosophically and theologically, to treat people as integrated wholes, rather than as minds that can just as well be realized in computers as in bodies, I think this change of climate is of enormous importance.

Of course, there are dangers in this new emphasis in the brain. History gets forgotten quickly, and it is worth remembering one of the reasons the idea that the mind is essentially a computer was so attractive in the first place. We had been through a period in which it had been fashionable to say that the state of your mind and the state of your brain are really identical. When you described what was on your mind, you were really just describing the state of your brain, albeit describing it in a useful kind of shorthand. To talk about minds as being like a computer program helped to get us out of the dead-end idea that the mind was nothing more than the physical brain. Having extricated ourselves from that view, I don't want us to go back there.

There are also arguments about whether computers, made of silicon, and with nothing resembling a human body, could possibly simulate human intelligence. This leads on to the question of whether it would further the AI project if computers were given bodies.

The way humans think is profoundly influenced by our bodies. Many of our concepts, even apparently abstract ones, come from metaphors that originate in our physical experience. We would not think as we do if we had no bodies, and a computer that had no body, or had a nonbiological body, could not think in exactly the same way as we do. The idea that minds can be abstracted from bodies is part of the inheritance from philosophical "dualism"—the separation of human persons into quite distinct minds and bodies. Although most philosophers have now abandoned dualism as an untenable view of the human person, it is strange to find it surviving in AI. The basic mistake is to say that it is our "minds" that think. No! It is people that think, and people have bodies as well as minds.

These arguments have been accepted by some scientists working on AI, and a new movement of "Embodied AI" has grown up as a result. It began with the development of artificial insects, but at MIT there is now a humanoid computer called Cog that has many of the elements of a human body.[15] Moreover, it interacts with the world through its body, and it learns from that interaction, having been programmed to develop through its interaction with the world.

Such a computer is not open to many objections that have been raised against classical AI. Cog has a body, it interacts, it learns, and thus it potentially has individuality. The weakness of Cog at present seems to be that it cannot actually do very much. Even its insectlike computer forebears don't seem to have had the intelligence of insects, and Cog so far clearly is nowhere near human intelligence. Some may hope that Cog's successors will get closer to that goal. It is equally likely, however, that the long-term impact of computers such as Cog will be to remind us of the huge gulf between human and computer intelligence.

One of the limitations might be the material that computers are made out of: silicon. Searle has claimed that consciousness could only arise out of the biological stuff of the brain, not out of silicon.[16] Although that might turn out to be the correct conclusion, it is not clear that there is any convincing argument to support it. Even if he is right, it is not clear that computers will always be made out of silicon. There might be a new generation of computers made of biological stuff to which Searle's argument would not apply.

The AI Vision of the Future

I have tried to give a balanced indication of the current boundaries of computer competence. Compared to this, some of the confident predictions about what computers will be able to do are quite extraordinary. Take, for example, the book *Mind Children* by Hans Moravec of Carnegie-Mellon University.[17] He has a grand vision that the computers of the next century will be "entities as complex as ourselves," but "transcending everything we know." Whereas we are limited by the constraints of our bodies, we will create successors in computer form that will take us into a new phase of "postbiological" or "supernatural" existence. These computer-successors will be able to exist in hostile climates in space that would be impossible for us, and in this sense will be superior to us. They will, Moravec says, be entities "in whom we can take pride when they refer to themselves as our descendants."

One of the puzzles about this kind of vision of the future is to see what it is based on. It is not, apparently, based on a particularly rosy view of our present computers. Moravec comments that "the best of today's machines have minds more like those of insects than humans." A lot of Moravec's optimism seems to be based on the expected continuing improvement in computer power, though it is not clear that all problems in AI require only additional power for their solution. Moravec is relying on a marriage between robotics, in which he is highly expert, and AI, in which he is less expert. I suspect that what AI can deliver in the marriage he envisages will turn out to be a disappointment to him.

Moreover, it is doubtful whether Moravec's vision is really a scientific one at all. It is more an article of faith than a secure extrapolation from how computers are currently developing. His vision of the future seems to be a quasi-religious one, and he is unusually explicit about it. The frank borrowing of theological terms like *immortality* and the *supernatural* to characterize the world of his envisaged new entities makes this pretty clear.

Frank Tipler also has made use of AI for his scientifically based form of immortality.[18] The essence of his idea is that the unique personality of each of us could be preserved in computer form, not subject to the vagaries of the human body. Then, through some rather suspect cosmology about the Omega point, these preserved intelligences become fully immortal. However, we are so far from being able to simulate individual differences in computer form that this project is, at best, massively speculative. It is also very doubtful whether human personalities could be captured at all in the disembodied form of a computer program.

It is very strange that AI is perpetuating the dream of immortality as some kind of disembodied existence, and that this should be fashionable at the same time as neuroscience is emphasizing the closeness of the link between brain and mind. Many of the same scientists are interested in both neuroscience and AI, and sometimes seem scarcely aware of their discrepant assumptions.

There is thus something rather naive and unbalanced about strong AI as a quasi-religious vision. It is also, to my mind, rather distasteful in its assumptions about what kind of immortal life will be desirable. There has, of course, long been a strand in Western thought that has postulated a sharp dichotomy between minds and bodies and has seen the indefinite existence of the disembodied mind as something to be hoped for. The Christian tradition has generally taken a much more positive view of the physical side of our existence than this, rightly so in my view. I don't believe that the mind can be disentangled from the body and given an independent life of its own, and I would not want it to be so disentangled. The Judeo-Christian tradition values the bodily existence of human beings.

Unfortunately, like many of the secular eschatologies of the last century or so, AI eschatology is not good eschatology. It represents a naive application of some half-understood concepts in a new context in which they don't work properly. Christian eschatology has worked hard to hold different strands together. There needs to be a place both for what God will do and what we can do; Moravec dispenses with this. There is also, in classical eschatology, a balance between whether the vision is of a distant goal, or something that can be expected imminently. Moravec's AI eschatology is rather like that of a fringe religious sect confidently predicting the second coming during the next century.

It is hard to know quite how to place some of the wilder predictions coming out of strong AI, such as those of Moravec and Tipler. It is the sort of vision you can find in much science fiction, though Moravec is not claiming to be writing fiction. Stephen Clark has argued persuasively that the central theme of science fiction is in fact how to achieve immortality, and various schools of science fiction approach it in different ways.[19] Among them, there is a prominent stream of science fiction, such as William Gibson's cyberpunk novels, that speculates about immortality achieved through overcoming dependence on the human body. There is probably no area of contemporary science in which the boundary between science and science fiction becomes as blurred as it does in AI.

Theology and AI

There is a tendency among religious people to be suspicious of AI. I want to suggest, however, that this instinctive suspicion is misplaced and that the dialogue between theology and AI needs to move on to a new and more constructive level.

As an example of concern in religious circles about AI, I can propose the report of the Church of England Doctrine Commission, *We Believe in God*.[20] The report suggests that there is a debate about human personality going on between those who "claim that the model of artificial intelligence explains the physical and mental phenomenon so fully that it can be regarded as having scientific warrant" and those who "know that there is more to people than this model allows." This strikes me as a polarized way of framing the issues. Most detailed scientific work on artificial intelligence does not make any strong or controversial assumptions about human personality. Actually, most work in AI is not about *personality* at all, but about more specific mental functions, often relatively low-level ones, such as vision.

Another question a religious person might want to raise is whether the analogy between computers and human beings implies that humans do not have souls. This depends on what you mean by *soul*. As I have argued elsewhere, soul is best thought of, not as some kind of "thing," but in terms of certain human capacities.[21] The soul is no more an entity than the mind is. We need rather to say that we have *powers* of mind that arise from our bodies and brains and that interact with them. In the same way, I don't want to say that we have a third kind of thing, called a soul, that is separate from and additional to, our bodies and minds, but instead that we have soul capacities. Keith Ward has made a similar point in his book *Defending the Soul*.[22]

But if souls are not separate from our bodies and minds, how do they relate to them? If we were trying to capture a complete human personality in computer terms, I would not want to include a module called the soul, along with modules dealing with various other faculties. Neither would I want to have it as a kind of homunculus in the middle, monitoring and controlling everything that was going on. Rather, I would see soul as an emergent property of the whole system. The recent trend toward "connectionist" modeling of the mind as a distributed system may eventually be helpful here. That way of modeling is leading us to see various mental and emotional properties as emergent properties of a distributed system, and I believe this is the direction in which we should eventually look for thinking about how properties of soul arise within people and affect them. AI might thus help religious people to think more clearly about what they mean by *soul*.

Many of the fears of the humanoid creatures that might arise from AI seem to involve a confusion about whether or not they would really be like us. Although I do not think it at all likely that such creatures will be constructed, I do not see that they would represent any threat to religious beliefs. When asked about this in a radio interview with Russell Stannard, Keith Ward replied, "I don't see any reason why, in principle, it shouldn't be open to us to create intelligent and rational—and spiritual—beings. I would be prepared to baptise them."[23] That seems a reasonable reply, given the assumption that the computers of the future would be like us in every way.

It would be a quite different matter if they were under the control of the computer scientists who created them. The issue here is whether they would have the capacity to make their own decisions or not. If they did not, then they clearly would not be equivalent to human beings. On the other hand, if they did have a capacity to make autonomous decisions, they would clearly not be under the control of scientists. There are similar points to make about their moral qualities. If they were like us, they would generally have good moral intentions, but be unreliable about carrying them out. Computers that were wholly evil, or wholly good, would not be like humans.

A central religious suspicion of AI comes from the idea that creating computers that are like human beings would be "playing God." To create something that is effectively like a human being seems to place us in the role of God, and to challenge the unique role of God as creator. However, I think this is a mistake. Talk of God as "creator" is, like all talk about God, an analogy, but the analogy can't be pressed too far. God's creative work is not like ours. One of the traditional ways in which this point has been made is to say that God creates "out of nothing," that he is not dependent on any prior existence for his creative work. Clearly, when humans make something they are not creating out of nothing; they are making use of pre-existing materials. As Donald MacKay has put it in his Gifford Lectures, making a computer is more like an act of procreation than the creative work of God, and it no more challenges the doctrine of God as creator than does the more usual biological form of procreation.[24]

John Puddefoot has developed an interesting comparison of the work of God in creating human beings with the task of scientists in AI, in a way that illuminates the nature of both.[25] He suggests that the three problems faced by God in creating human life and of AI scientists in creating humanoid computers are essentially the same: (1) how to create the kind of free life God wished to see, (2) how to prevent it from becoming monstrous, and (3) how to hide himself from it sufficiently that it will relate to him for the right reasons. Puddefoot suggests that God's solution to this was essentially to "grow" life rather then to make it according to some prespecified plan. He suggests that whether the attempt to create humanoid computers will succeed depends largely on whether the resulting computers are able to surprise us. If so, they may be accepted by God as part of his humanlike creation. As Anne Foerst has put it, they may, like humans, become part of the "imago dei."[26]

One of the most fruitful of recent theological uses of AI of which I am aware concerns the nature of sin. The question of whether a computer could sin forces us to clarify the concept of sin in a helpful way. It is clear that computers can do bad things, in the sense of doing things with harmful consequences. Whether or not these ought to be called "sin" is another matter. Tim Bull has used this question to proceed, though a series of iterations, to a more adequate definition of sin as "freely willing a state of affairs that is known to be contrary to the will of God."[27] The question of whether or not a computer could sin thus turns out to depend on how far computers could have free will, and how far they could know the will of God.

This leads back to distinctions rather like those we have already discussed. Whether a computer could know the will of God is rather like whether it could pray. There seems no difficulty, in principle, with a computer having, on the basis of scripture and tradition, at least some knowledge of what the will of God was. However, discerning and experiencing the will of God in particular situations might not be possible. If sin is taken to involve not just a lack of knowledge of the will of God but a deliberate turning away from such knowledge, then it seems unlikely that a computer could sin.

Foerst has offered a rather different reflection on the relationship between AI and sin, drawing on Tillich's concept of sin as involving the sense of estrangement that comes from unresolved polarities, such as the wish both to be an individual and to be in community, and the wish to be free while acknowledging the necessity of working within causal laws.[28] Foerst suggests that AI resolves some of these polarities by treating them in mechanistic terms, though it is surely debatable how effectively this resolution is carried through. However, she acknowledges that AI introduces its own polarities, for example, the hope that computers will come to have subjectivity, while simultaneously taking an objectifying view of human beings.

I see no reason why the rigorous way of thinking about mind introduced by AI, shorn of the more bizarre metaphysics and eschatology of the strong AI creed, should not help Christian thinkers to make *their* points about human personality. Although most AI scientists hold that there need be no essential difference between humans and computers, I do not see that AI as a discipline need be committed to that view. On the contrary, AI may eventually help to locate and define the essential differences between computers and humans much more precisely.

Here, I would like to cite a farsighted churchman, H. C. N. Williams, the first provost of the rebuilt cathedral in Coventry.[29] Back in 1967, in a lecture on the Christian faith from the standpoint of cybernetics (one of the sources of modern AI) he said:

> I have come in recent years to welcome cybernetics as a discipline which defines more clearly than any other I know the limits of a mechanistic approach to life and values, and makes more definable the area of existence which is broadly the concern of religious belief.

It is my hope, too, that the language of computer simulation will increasingly be seen as a philosophically neutral way of framing a broad range of issues about human nature, including religious ones, in a rigorous and helpful way.

Notes

This chapter is a revised and expanded version of a Templeton Lecture given at the Edinburgh Science Festival.

1. See H. L. Dreyfus and S. E. Dreyfus, *Mind over Machine* (New York: Macmillan, 1986).
2. See, for example, Hilary Putnam, *Mind, Language and Reality* (Cambridge: Cambridge University Press, 1975). Recently, Putnam has been vocal in arguing that his earlier view was wrong; see Putnam, *Representation and Reality* (Cambridge, Mass.: MIT Press, 1998).
3. John Searle, *Minds, Brains and Science* (London: Penguin, 1989).
4. J. Copeland, *Artificial Intelligence: A Philosophical Introduction* (Oxford: Basil Blackwell, 1993).
5. William F. Clocksin, "Artificial Intelligence and Human Identity," in *Consciousness and Human Identity*, ed. J. Cornwell (Oxford: Oxford University Press, 1998).
6. Copeland, *Artificial Intelligence*.
7. Thomas Nagel, "What Is It Like to Be a Bat?" *Philosophical Review* 83 (1974): 435–50. (Reprinted in his *Mortal Questions*.)
8. D. Dennett, *Consciousness Explained* (Boston: Little, Brown, 1991).
9. B. J. Baars, *A Cognitive Theory of Consciousness* (Cambridge: Cambridge University Press, 1988).
10. See, for example, M. Davies and G. W. Humpreys, *Consciousness: Psychological and Philosophical Essays* (Oxford: Basil Blackwell, 1993); A. J. Marcel and E. Bisiach, eds., *Consciousness in Contemporary Science* (Oxford: Clarendon Press, 1988).
11. P. N. Johnson-Laird, *The Computer and the Mind* (London: Fontana, 1988).
12. Roger Penrose, *Shadows of the Mind* (Oxford: Oxford University Press, 1994).
13. See, for example, M. A. Arbib and M. B. Hesse, *The Construction of Reality* (Cambridge: Cambridge University Press, 1986).
14. Gerald Edelman, *Bright Air, Brilliant Fire: On the Matter of the Mind* (London: Allen Lane, 1992).

15. Anne Foerst, "Cog, a Humanoid Robot, and the Question of the Image of God," *Zygon* 33 (1998): 91–111. See also K. H. Reich, "Cog and God: A Response to Anne Foerst," *Zygon* 33 (1998): 255–62; M. Gerhard and A. M. Russell, "Cog Is to Us as We Are to God: A Response to Anne Foerst," *Zygon* 33 (1998): 263–69; A. Foerst, "Embodied AI, Creation and Cog," *Zygon* 33(1998): 455–61.
16. Searle, *Minds, Brains, and Science*.
17. Hans Moravec, *Mind Children* (Cambridge, Mass.: MIT Press, 1988).
18. Frank J. Tipler, *The Physics of Immortality* (Basingstoke: Macmillan, 1994).
19. Stephen R. L. Clark, *How to Live For Ever: Science Fiction and Philosophy* (London: Routledge, 1995).
20. *We Believe in God: Report of the Doctrine Commission of the Church of England*. See also F. Watts and M. Williams, "The Doctrine Commission and Artificial Intelligence," *Theology* 91 (1988): 216–17.
21. Fraser Watts, "Brain, Mind and Soul," in *Science Meets Faith*, ed. Fraser Watts (London: SPCK, 1998); also Fraser Watts, "Towards a Theology of Consciousness," in *Consciousness and Human Identity*, ed. J. Cornwell (Oxford: Oxford University Press, 1998).
22. Keith Ward, *Defending the Soul* (Oxford: Oneworld, 1992).
23. Quoted in Russell Stannard, *Science and Wonders: Conversations about Science and Beliefs* (London: Faber & Faber, 1996), 118.
24. Donald M. MacKay, *Behind the Eye* (Oxford: Basil Blackwell, 1991).
25. John Puddefoot, *Artificial Intelligence and the Mind Machine* (London: SPCK, 1996).
26. Anne Foerst, "Artificial Intelligence: Walking the Boundary," *Zygon* 31 (1996).
27. Tim M. Bull, "Artificial Intelligence and the Doctrine of Sin" (Undergraduate dissertation, Faculty of Divinity, University of Cambridge, 1988).
28. Foerst, "Artificial Intelligence."
29. H. C. N. Williams, *Nothing to Fear* (London: Hodder & Stoughton, 1967).

Epilogue

Because of the power of the humble approach in bringing scientists and theologians together, Sir John Templeton is committed to a research program to multiply spiritual information one hundredfold. What follows is a consideration of the scientific possibilities for interdisciplinary research and for collaboration with theologians as suggested by the authors of the chapters of this book and by others working in these fields.

Astronomy

Robert Russell suggests in chapter 2 that space exploration with a view to a search for evidence of life could bring rich theological rewards. This research could involve further examination of neighboring planets and moons for primitive living forms, and the expansion of efforts to discover planets of nearby stars that have climates suitable for life. Perhaps even more theologically significant is the ongoing search for intelligent life by such efforts as the SETI project, scanning space for signals possibly transmitted from other inhabited worlds. But Owen Gingerich, in chapter 4, points out that the occurrence of intelligent, self-conscious life elsewhere in the universe is far from inevitable. Stephen Jay Gould says we are a wonderful accident of evolution, never to be repeated. And Ernst Mayr says that if any such living beings do occur elsewhere in the universe, they would be drastically different from us. Yet, the urge to explore the unknown is a powerful motivation.

Timothy Ferris, near the end of his book The *Mind's Sky,* says:

When speculating about interstellar communication one gets the odd feeling that there is something natural and intuitive about it—that we are *meant* to do it, as we are meant to write poetry, love our children, fret about the future and cherish the past. Perhaps this inchoate connotation of appropriateness, sustaining as it does so many SETI researchers through their long and daunting quest to make contact with life elsewhere among the stars, derives from this: that by participating in interstellar communication we would not just be exchanging facts and opinions and art and entertainment, but would be adding to the total of cosmic understanding.[1]

The potential benefits, from the viewpoint of better understanding God and his vast creation, are for some of us irresistible. Perhaps of equal potential is the recent discovery that supernovae in distant galaxies appear to be receding from us at an accelerating speed, suggesting that a hitherto unknown large-scale repulsive force permeates the universe. Further observations, especially of even more distant supernovas may support the intriguing conclusion that the bulk of the universe consists not of matter but of pure energy.

The Neurosciences

Francisco Ayala, in chapter 5, points us to the enormous potential of the human brain: less than one millionth of 1 percent of its capacity is ever used in the lifetime of an individual. He suggests that research might be directed to discovering how to recover this unrealized potential, perhaps using the model of distributive computing, which is capable of greatly increasing the computing capacity of a network of connected computers.

Fraser Watts also looks to the computer, focusing on artificial intelligence research, to enlarge our understanding of how the human brain works. Sharpening the distinctions between states of mind and computational states brings out the importance of the unique history that each human being possesses. Understanding human intelligence seems to require more attention to the role of narratives, the stories we tell about ourselves. The future of artificial intelligence seems bound up with progress with this kind of view of narrative intelligence. It is interesting that in recent years, theologians have come to realize the degree to which theology is a narrative process.

One thing on which all researchers seem to agree is that the brain remains a mystery, and that its study is full of surprises. V. S. Ramachandran, a neurologist and researcher at the University of California in San Diego, has described some of those surprises in his book with Sandra Blakeslee titled *Phantoms in the Brain*.[2] Of special interest from a theological standpoint is his experience with patients suffering from temporal lobe epilepsy. It is well known that patients with epileptic seizures originating in the left temporal lobe of the brain can have "intense, spiritual experiences during the seizures and sometimes become preoccupied with religious and moral issues even during the seizure-free . . . periods." "Most remarkable," the authors state, "are those patients who have deeply moving spiritual experiences, including a feeling of divine presence and the sense that they are in direct communion with God."[3] These seizures are known to be localized in the brain's limbic system, to persist usually for a very few seconds, but sometimes to permanently alter the personality. It is conjectured that in these cases the repeated passage of massive volleys of nerve impulses within the limbic system may permanently open certain pathways, and even open new channels. This process, which might be likened to water from a storm pouring downhill, opening new furrows and rivulets on the hillside, has been called "kindling."

The fact that these seizures sometimes lead to a new level of emotional experience, to what some neurologists refer to as the "temporal lobe personality," makes these patients important subjects for spiritual studies. Indeed, Ramachandran studied two such patients in terms of their response to a variety of words and images, using a galvanic skin response (GSR). He describes the experiment:

> Both were eager to participate. In what may turn out to be the very first scientific experiment ever done on religion directly, I sat them in comfortable chairs and attached harmless electrodes to their hands. Once settled in front of a computer screen, they were shown random samples of several types of words and images—for example, words for ordinary inanimate objects (a shoe, vase, table and the like), familiar faces (parents, siblings), unfamiliar faces, sexually arousing words and pictures (erotic magazine pinups), four-letter words involving sex, extreme violence and horror (an alligator eating a person alive, a man setting himself afire) and religious words and icons (such as the word "God").
>
> If you and I were to undergo this exercise, we would show huge GSR responses to the scenes of violence and to the sexually explicit words and pictures, a fairly large response to familiar faces and

usually nothing at all to other categories (unless you have a shoe fetish, in which case you'd respond to one).

What about the patient? The kindling hypothesis would predict a uniform high response to all categories. But to our amazement what we found in the two patients tested was a heightened response mainly to religious words and icons. Their responses to other categories, including the sexual words and images, which ordinarily evoke a powerful response, was strangely diminished compared to what is seen in normal individuals.

Thus the results show that there has been no general enhancement of all the connections—indeed, if anything, there has been a decrement. But rather surprisingly, there's been a selective amplification of response to religious words.[4]

The results from these and other experiments seem to suggest that there are circuits in the brain that are involved in religious experience and that these become hyperactive in some patients with temporal lobe epilepsy.

Malcolm Jeeves, a psychologist at the University of St. Andrews, writing in another very recent volume, *Whatever Happened to the Soul?* argues against a direct causal relationship between repeated seizure discharge in the temporal lobes and what he calls hyperreligiosity.[5] Clearly, more research is called for to further elucidate the nature of religious-like experience in temporal lobe epileptics. However, one might be tempted to speculate that further research of the brain process of kindling, which can lead to such dramatic changes in personality and to deeply moving spiritual experiences, could be an important source of new spiritual information.

Actually, the experience of the transcendent described by some temporal lobe epileptics has occurred in varying degree with a significant number of more normal people—philosophers, scientists, holy men and women of all religions, most of them greatly respected and rational. The physicist Paul Davies writes of some of them in his concluding chapter to *The Mind of God,* mentioning the physicist Roger Penrose's description of his experience of mathematical inspirations as a sudden "breaking through into a Platonic realm," of the mathematician Kurt Gödel's "other relation to reality" through meditation, and the cosmologist Fred Hoyle's sudden brilliant vision of a solution to a challenging mathematical puzzle.[6] Also mentioned are the Nobel laureate Richard Feynman's experiences of inspiration followed by intense feelings of euphoria on several occasions. The teacher and science writer Timothy Ferris examines this phenomenon of mystical experience in *The Mind's Sky*,[7] pointing out the breadth of its occurrence and its similarity from culture to culture:

> But if mystical ecstasy has come to different individuals in different ways, they have described its qualities in surprisingly similar terms. This, indeed, is the most striking thing about the mystical experience — that witnesses from disparate cultures and backgrounds should have recounted it so consistently. As the American philosopher William James wrote, "The everlasting and triumphant mystical tradition [is] hardly altered by differences of clime or creed. In Hinduism, in Neo-platonism, in Sufism, in Christian mysticism, in Whitmanism, we find the same recurring note, so that there is about mystical utterances an eternal unanimity which ought to make the critic stop and think."
>
> Now, I have been a professional journalist for half my life, and an amateur scientist for longer than that, and I would be among the last to argue against taking a skeptical, critical attitude toward sensational reports of extraordinary and purely personal experiences, of which none is more extraordinary and personal than the mystical experience. Nevertheless, I feel that these accounts ought to be taken seriously. The estimable character of many of the individuals who have reported experiencing enlightenment, plus the remarkable uniformity with which they have described the experience, leaves scant grounds for dismissing their testimony as involving deceit, self-deception, or fraud. On the contrary, it seems to me that once we better understand the human nervous system, mystics may come to be viewed as pioneers in its exploration, whose accounts will prove to have illuminated previously uncharted inner landscapes.[8]

Another area of opportunity for obtaining new spiritual information seems to be suggested from recent research on brain development during embryogenesis and early childhood and under certain circumstances with adults. Ayala mentions that neural channels for information transfer have been found to undergo reinforcement or maybe even be replaced after damage. The degree to which this phenomenon occurs is quite surprising and has led to the important concept of brain plasticity.[9] In the developing embryo and the early stages of child development, major changes in brain structure occur. In adults, a related phenomenon, which has been called functional plasticity, occurs where, upon injury, little or no physical reorganization of brain cortical circuitry may occur, but overlapping receptive fields of neurons may assume the function of adjacent damaged areas.[10] The foundation for these studies was laid in the 1940s and 1950s by the Canadian neurosurgeon Wilder Penfield, who found that electrical stimulation of a narrow strip of cortex running from top to bottom on both sides of the brain elicited responses in different parts of the body. For example, up at the top of the brain, in the cleft or groove between the right and left hemispheres, electrical stimulation elicited sensations in the genital area. Just below the top of the brain, electrical stimulation led to sensations in the feet. Following on down the strip, brain areas were discovered which affected the legs and trunk, then the upper arm and shoulder, then the hand, then the face, and at the bottom, the thorax and voice box. This data allowed Penfield to draw a map of the sensory area of the cerebral cortex, which has since been refined by numerous experiments by others, primarily with monkeys.

Brain plasticity comes into this picture because of some very interesting research, initially with monkeys, but most recently with a patient who had had an arm amputated and was experiencing sensations in his "phantom arm." The monkey studies, performed by Timothy Pons and his coworkers at the National Institutes of Health, demonstrated that the brain map can be altered to compensate for disrupted connections in an adult animal.[11] A monkey with a surgically denervated arm showed no response upon stimulation of the brain map area for the hand, as expected. But surprisingly, when the monkey's face was touched, brain cells corresponding to the hand responded vigorously. The sensory information from the monkey's face not only went to the face area of the cortex, it also invaded the territory of the paralyzed hand.

Ramachandran realized that this could be the explanation for the often-reported experience of patients with phantom limbs. To test this hypothesis, he enlisted the help of a seventeen-year-old amputee who had been distressed because of itching and painful sensations in his phantom fingers. The goal was to see if there was a human counterpart to the compensation seen in the monkeys. Would the patient experience a crossover of adjacent areas of the brain map?

Ramachandran describes the procedure:

> With Tom seated comfortably in my basement laboratory, I placed a blindfold over his eyes because I didn't want him to see where I was touching him. Then I took an ordinary Q-tip and started stroking various parts of body surface, asking him to tell me where he felt the sensations. (My graduate student, who was watching, thought I was crazy.)

I swabbed his cheek. "What do you feel?"

"You are touching my cheek."

"Anything else?"

"Hey, you know it's funny," said Tom, "you're touching my missing thumb, my phantom thumb."

I moved the Q-tip to his upper lip. "How about here?"

"You're touching my index finger. And my upper lip."

"Really? Are you sure"?

"Yes. I can feel it both places."

"How about here?" I stroked his lower jaw with the swab.

"That's my missing pinkie."

I soon found a complete map of Tom's phantom hand on his face! I realized that what I was seeing was perhaps a direct perceptual correlate of the remapping that Tim Pons had seen in his monkeys. For there is no other way of explaining why touching an area so far away from the stump—namely, the face—should generate sensations in the phantom hand; the secret lies in the peculiar mapping of body parts in the brain, with the face lying right beside the hand.[12]

The experiment was continued, exploring the rest of Tom's body, and a second "map" of the missing hand was found on the left arm just above the line of amputation. Stroking the skin surface of this second map evoked precisely located sensations on the individual fingers of the phantom hand. So there were two maps involved in the response, and these could be explained by their proximity in the sensory cortex, one locus on either side of the hand locus. Both had altered connections to take on some of circuitry for the hand.

These findings could be very important for our understanding of the functioning of the adult brain. It would appear that new, highly precise and functionally effective pathways can emerge in the adult brain within a few weeks of injury. This implies that the adult brain has considerable plasticity and opens up the possibility that some degenerative diseases of the brain may be treatable if the affected area can be reactivated by enlisting adjacent functional tissue. This could be of enormous value, for example, in the aging process, where the loss of abstract processes like judgment, foresight, and planning, usually associated with the frontal lobes, is so devastating.

The capacity of brain cells to respond to environmental changes as a part of embryonic development is well established. Likewise, it has been established that there is considerable responsiveness of brain tissue during learning and also upon injury during childhood development. In view of the demonstrated plasticity of adult brain, it would also seem appropriate to carry out research on conditions for enhancing learning and memory in individuals whose brains have suffered injury or have undergone degeneration during the aging process.

These experimental approaches could initially utilize studies of a number of individuals with congenital brain defects in the visual and auditory systems, where compensation by brain plasticity also appears to be involved. In the long term, it could be expected that restorative results in these systems might provide the basis for the enhancement of the deeper, more profound thought processes that make us human and spiritual beings.

Genetics

We have mentioned the keen interest shown by geneticists in the mechanism of control of embryonic development and noted that this is an area in which interdisciplinary research with the help of developmental biologists will be an essential aspect. Another area with strong interdisciplinary ties is behavioral genetics, joining psychologists, neurophysiologists and epidemiologists with geneticists in the study of the heritability of human behaviors.

The human geneticist Elving Anderson, of the University of Minnesota, in his book with Bruce Reichenbach, *On Behalf of God*, points out that the proportion of the variability in human behavior due to genetic differences is generally between 40 and 60 percent, with the balance generally attributed to the environment.[13] Seldom is heritability close to 100 percent or to zero percent.

Actually, within the term *environment* we would wish to include not just external effects—everything that surrounds and affects the individual—but also aspects of human agency: purpose, considered choice, and deliberation. Understanding the degree to which the genetic and environmental factors contribute to a given behavioral disorder can supply important insights into the concepts of human choice and freedom. Anderson has discussed the role of choice in another book, *Whatever Happened to the Soul?*:

> Discussion of the roles of genes and environment still leaves us with the need to understand human freedom. Is it possible that human behavior could, in principle, be explained fully by a combination of genes *and* circumstances (environment)? Here we confront a gap in our knowledge of ourselves. However, in our everyday experience we

act as if, in varying degrees, we are major contributors to our actions. The more we see ourselves as meaningful contributors to our behavior, the more we call ourselves free. The less we feel we contribute, whether the restrictions are genetic or environmental or both, the less we see ourselves as free. Of course, our choices must in some way set in motion the physiological mechanisms required to implement the desired actions, but the exploration of the intervening steps has just begun in the detailed investigation of the brain and central nervous system.[14]

Anderson goes on to explain that there is data from the study of monozygotic (identical) twins raised together that indicates that their behaviors never approach equality. Thus, genes and environment together cannot produce complete uniformity of behavior.

He concludes:

Several things follow from these considerations. Our actions lie on a continuum between complete freedom and complete determinism. Freedom is a matter of degree; it is an opportunity that must be seized and used. We create our freedom as we engage the world around us utilizing the resources of our genes and the environment at our disposal.

Further research into the interface between brain physiology and our minds and the choices we make should be very profitable. Ayala has said that understanding the physical-mental transformation is the greatest issue we face. Its achievement will provide us with an understanding of ourselves and our place in nature. That should be spiritual information of immense importance.

Medicine

As David Larson and Susan Larson have described in chapter 9, the new realization of the significant impact of spiritual values on human health demonstrates yet another influence that can transcend the usual nature—nurture fixation. We now have empirical evidence for the impact of emotions such as those related to religious commitment on health outcomes. The scientific basis for this influence again points to the mind/body relationship. It has been found that there exists an intricate network involving the immune system and the brain, a network that allows the two systems to signal each other continuously and rapidly. The molecular messengers, called cytokines or interleukins, are produced by immune cells and communicate not only with other parts of the immune system but also with the brain and nerves, and other messengers released by nerve cells can act as signals to immune cells. The field has brought together social scientists, neuroscientists, and immunologists, and has been called psychoneuroimmunology. Esther Sternberg, Chief of the Section on Neuroendocrinology and Behavior of the National Institute of Mental Health, one of the pioneers, writes of recent evidence that is convincing the skeptics:

> But now, taking off from a few central observations, the field has exploded and is taking on a life of its own. The initial documentation of the extensive network of neural and molecular communications between the nervous and immune systems, coupled with the finding that molecules of one system could stimulate the other, provided the necessary evidence that the two systems could communicate with each other at an anatomical and molecular level. Thus, immune organs such as the spleen and thymus are innervated by sympathetic nerves. Neuropeptides released by peripheral nerves stimulate inflammation and interleukins (IL) such as IL-1 stimulate the hypothalamus to release corticotropin releasing hormone (CHR). Furthermore, specific antagonists of these molecules block these effects. Finally, central administration of IL-1 induces a prolonged suppression of peripheral cellular immune responses in rats.[15]

The central players appear to be the hypothalamus, the pituitary and the adrenals, which together respond to stress by mediating the controlled release of cortisol from the adrenal gland. Cortisol not only arouses the body to meet the challenge but also acts upon the hypothalamus to inhibit continued release of corticotropin-releasing hormone. The cortisol formed in the stress-induced process also has a strong effect on the immune system, functioning as both regulator and anti-inflammatory agent. It plays a key role in preventing the immune system from overreacting to stress. Together cortisol and corticotropin-releasing hormone directly link the body's brain-related stress response and its immune response. These research results are very important as solid empirical evidence for the explanation of psychosocial, behavioral, and particularly religious influences on health and disease. They could provide much new information of a spiritual nature.

One additional area related to medicine which has an important potential for new spiritual information is related to the diagnosis and treatment of genetic disease. This is a field in rapid development, especially with the advent of the project to sequence the entire human genome. As data accumulate, it becomes apparent that the number and kind of possible diseases identified that are genetic in origin are much greater than first anticipated.

It has been found possible to characterize carrier states (heterozygotes) in inherited disorders such as cystic fibrosis and Duchenne muscular dystrophy. It has also been possible to forecast the later development of a condition such as Huntington's chorea (Woody Guthrie's disease) and, more commonly, genes which predict "susceptibility" or "vulnerability" to conditions like Alzheimer's disease and bipolar disease, the hereditary manic-depressive illness suffered by Winston Churchill. This last illness is one member of what appear now to be a large number of "contingent" diseases whose expression in later life is quite variable. In a recent article in the *Hastings Center Report,* Kathleen Nolan and Sara Swenson describe these contingent genetic conditions as common, and often coded for by more than a single gene.[16] Furthermore, they are strongly affected by environmental factors—biological, psychological, and social—that lead to a wide variety in the expression of the underlying illness. (The defective gene causes a severe condition in one individual but an almost unnoticeable condition in another.) Here again, there appear to exist new opportunities for the study of the impact of religious variables which could lead to much new spiritual information.

The Social Sciences

Nancey Murphy, a philosopher at Fuller Theological Seminary and George Ellis, a mathematician at the University of Cape Town, in their book, *On the Moral Nature of the Universe,* provide an important new approach to moral and ethical values through a "kenotic" (self-emptying) model.[17] In their proposal, self-sacrifice and nonviolence replace the currently accepted account of ultimate reality which includes selfishness and violent coercion as basic aspects of human nature. They point out that this kenotic concept, when applied to God, is widely accepted in discussions of the relationships between theology and the natural sciences, but that the ethical consequences are almost universally rejected as impracticable within the social sciences. They therefore propose an empirical approach to the question of workability of the concept of kenosis, choosing an examination of the possibility of a society based upon nonviolence as a research model. Murphy and Ellis suggest studies of the general quality of life for dedicated members of groups such as Quakers and Mennonites that are committed to nonviolence.

How do these subcommunities fare in psychological health and effective social institutions, compared to typical inhabitants of our Western societies? They also suggest more individualistic, "smaller scale" hypotheses such as:

> Courageous suffering changes subjects' attitudes toward the sufferer in the direction of greater respect.
> Consistent avoidance of signs of hostility reduces the opponent's level of fear.
> Reduced fear increases one's reasoning ability and susceptibility to persuasion.[18]

Murphy and Ellis then provide a list of factors that affect the outcome of such actions. These include external factors such as degree of conflict of interest, social distance (the degree to which the opponents see the sufferers as members of the moral order), personality structure of the opponents, and whether opponents and sufferers share the same belief system. Internal factors include refraining from hostility, openness of intentions, refraining from humiliation, being sacrificial, and demonstrating trust in the opponent. All of these factors, they point out, are empirically testable.

The impact of these kinds of studies can be far-reaching. As Murphy and Ellis suggest:

> . . . a radical consequence of our treatment of ethics is that the distinction between pure and applied social science disappears. Sociology was originally conceived as the science of social transformation; but in the late modern pluralist West, values and ultimate goals came to be seen as beyond the ken of science. Thus, pure social science must be value-free; applied social science could study means of achieving social ends, but determining those ends was not within its competence.
>
> Yet with an answer to the question of what is the (objective, true) end of human existence, sociology (and its fellow social sciences) can become again the scientific study of the means of social transformation, proposing hypotheses regarding subsidiary ends and effective methods of achieving them and then testing them empirically through the design of social programs.[19]

These kinds of studies, operating as they do at the level of the search for the moral principles that govern our universe, will aid significantly the search for new spiritual information.

These studies are akin to those John Templeton has proposed based upon his *Worldwide Laws of Life*[20] and extended through studies of forgiveness as described by Everett Worthington, a professor of psychology at Virginia Commonwealth University, and others in *Dimensions of Forgiveness: Psychological Research and Theological Perspectives.*[21]

In 1997, a request for proposals for forgiveness research was distributed internationally by the John Templeton Foundation. Of the large number of proposals submitted, fifty-eight were deemed of sufficient merit for funding. David Myers, one of the contributors to this book and a member of the panel of judges said, "These proposals promise to make significant scientific advances in the understanding of forgiveness and reconciliation and in interventions (based on research to promote forgiveness and reconciliation)."

The future of interdisciplinary studies of the kind anticipated here, with the humble approach as an added dimension of motivation and encouragement, promises to be an exciting one. We have touched on only a few of the numerous possibilities, and the goal of a one hundredfold increase in spiritual information does not seem unreasonable. As Sir John has said, "We are here for the future."

Notes

1. Timothy Ferris, *The Mind's Sky* (New York: Bantam Books, 1992), 221.
2. V. S. Ramachandran and Sandra Blakeslee, *Phantoms in the Brain* (New York: Morrow, 1998), 175.
3. Ibid., 179.
4. Ibid., 186.
5. Malcolm Jeeves, "Brains, Mind and Behavior," in *Whatever Happened to the Soul?*, ed. Warren Brown, Nancey Murphy, and H. Newton Malony (Minneapolis, Minn.: Fortress, 1998), 93.
6. Paul Davies, *The Mind of God* (New York: Simon & Schuster, 1992), 228–29.
7. Ferris, *The Mind's Sky,* 85–96.
8. Ibid., 86–87.
9. Michael S. Gazzinaga, Richard B. Ivry, and George R. Mangun, *Cognitive Neuroscience* (New York: Norton, 1998), 465–93.
10. Ibid., 489–92.
11. T. P. Pons, E. Preston, and A. K. Garraghty, "Massive Cortical Reorganization after Sensory Deafferentation in Adult Macaques," *Science* 252 (1991): 1857–60.
12. Ramachandran and Blakeslee, *Phantoms in the Brain,* 28–29.

13. Bruce R. Reichenbach and V. Elving Anderson, *On Behalf of God* (Grand Rapids, Mich.: Eerdmans, 1995).
14. V. Elving Anderson, "A Genetic View of Human Nature," in *Whatever Happened to the Soul?*
15. Esther M. Sternberg, "Emotions and Disease: From Balance of Humors to Balance of Molecules," *Nature Medicine* 3 (1997): 264.
16. Kathleen Nolan and Sara Swenson, "New Tools, New Dilemmas, Genetic Frontiers," *Hastings Center Report* 18.5 (October–November 1988).
17. Nancey Murphy and George F. R. Ellis, *On the Moral Nature of the Universe* (Minneapolis, Minn.: Fortress Press, 1996).
18. Ibid., 163.
19. Ibid., 142.
20. John M. Templeton, *Worldwide Laws of Life: 200 Spiritual Principles* (Philadelphia: Templeton Foundation Press, 1997).
21. Everett L. Worthington, Jr., ed., *Dimensions of Forgiveness: Psychologic Research and Theological Perspectives* (Philadelphia: Templeton Foundation Press, 1998).